SAINT MICHAEL

and the

HOLY ANGELS

SAINT MICHAEL
and the
HOLY ANGELS

Their Relations with the Visible World

By

Rev. Eugène Soyer

Translated from the French by

Ryan P. Plummer

LAMBFOUNT
St. Louis, Missouri

Published in 2022 by Lambfount · St. Louis, Missouri
www.lambfount.com

Rev. Eugène Soyer, *Saint Michael and the Holy Angels: Their Relations with the Visible World*, translated by Ryan P. Plummer.

Originally published in French in 1870 by Imprimerie de J.-J. Salettes, in Coutances, France, under the title *Saint Michel et les saints anges considérés dans leurs relations avec le monde visible, traité suivi du Manuel des pèlerins au Mont Saint-Michel*. The original French edition was approved for publication by Bishop Jean-Pierre Bravard of the Diocese of Coutances and Avranches.

ISBN 978-1-7328734-1-4

Printing and manufacturing information for this book may be found on the final page.

Cover image: Digitally modified reproduction of Guido Reni's *St. Michael the Archangel*.

CONTENTS

PART ONE: THE HOLY ANGELS

PART TWO: ST. MICHAEL THE ARCHANGEL

BOOK ONE: ST. MICHAEL'S PREROGATIVES AND GLORIOUS MINISTRIES

CHAPTER 5

CHAPTER 6

CHAPTER 7

CHAPTER 8

CHAPTER 9

CHAPTER 10

CHAPTER 11

BOOK TWO: DEVOTION TO ST. MICHAEL

CHAPTER 1

BOOK THREE:
APPARITIONS OF ST. MICHAEL, PILGRIMAGES & NORMANDY'S ST. MICHAEL OF THE MOUNT

TRANSLATOR'S PREFACE

In the Basilica of St. Gervais, in the northern French city of Avranches, is enshrined a most curious relic. It is the skull of St. Aubert, the city's early eighth-century bishop. Tradition tells us that the conspicuous hole in the skull's upper-right side, large enough to insert a human thumb, is attributed to St. Michael the Archangel, who, in order to literally impress upon the bishop's mind an unheeded command he had given him in two previous apparitions, physically poked him in his head. A seventeenth-century manuscript, written by the relic's former Benedictine custodians and preserved in the National Library of France, describes the holy artifact this way:

> The head of the same St. Aubert, on which can be seen a hole the width of a finger, which he received by divine permission the third time that the most glorious archangel St. Michael appeared to him, commanding him on behalf of God to build a church in his name on this mount of Tombe; and what is quite remarkable is that he lived another fifteen years, without this sacred wound causing him any trouble.[1]

After this third apparition had left an enduring sign on St. Aubert's very person, the holy bishop did in fact, with urgency, have a shrine to St. Michael built on Mount Tombe as commanded. Over the centuries, this island shrine's physical appearance evolved into the much grander and more glorious landmark known today, the world over, as Mont Saint-Michel.

Fr. Eugène Soyer, the author of this book you are about to read, was a native of the diocese in which Mont Saint-Michel is located.[2] He knew well the marvels St. Michael had deigned to work at this blessed pilgrimage site through the ages, even long after St. Aubert had gone to his eternal reward. As Fr. Soyer alludes in his preface, the reopening of Mont Saint-Michel to pilgrimages in the 1860s, after it had been restricted to use as a prison for seventy years following the cataclysm of the French Revolution, was a key inspiration for this work. As the Catholic social order in Christian Europe was rapidly dissipating amidst a rising tide of revolution and apostasy from the kingship of Christ, the reopening of the shrine of the great Archangel—who long ago defeated and expelled from heaven that anti-Christian rebel and apostate-in-chief we call Satan—was an invitation for all faithful Christians to rally under the banner of St. Michael, confidently imploring him for protection, grace, and the Church's glorious triumph over present evils. To incite us to this confidence in St. Michael and the holy angels, Fr. Soyer leaves us this book. In it he inspiringly instructs us on the reality and nature of the angelic world, St. Michael's preeminent place in it, and the precious bonds that exist between angels and men.

Biblical quotations in this English translation, unless otherwise noted, are taken from the Challoner version of the Douay-Rheims Bible, with names of biblical books, persons, and places revised as needed to conform to their generally accepted renderings in contemporary English. References to the Psalms are given in the Vulgate numbering, with Hebrew numbering following in brackets when different. The parenthetical scriptural citations within the running text are not present in the original French and are an enhancement to this English edition; only in cases where Fr. Soyer is quoting from another author will these parenthetical citations be enclosed in brackets if they are the translator's insertions rather than the quoted author's own citations.

Among the many venerable Christian sources Fr. Soyer draws from in his treatment of the angels are the theological writings of Pseudo-Dionysius the Areopagite. Having inherited a popular misconception from prior generations, Fr. Soyer will at times conflate the author's identity with both St. Paul's disciple St. Denis (or Dionysius) the Areopagite and St. Denis of Paris. The reader should be mindful that it is *Pseudo*-Dionysius the Areopagite, also referred to simply as "Dionysius" by scholastics like St. Thomas Aquinas, who is the author of these mystical writings on the angels.

Shortly before the initial 1870 French edition of Fr. Soyer's book, St. Aubert's successor, Bishop Jean-Pierre Bravard of the Diocese of Coutances and Avranches, wrote in a letter authorizing its publication that all those who had reviewed the manuscript found it "very suitable for instructing and edifying, and considered it one of the best works that can be published on this subject so worthy of interest."[3] More than one hundred fifty years later, with this work's debut in English, may many more readers now find Fr. Soyer's work on St. Michael and the holy angels a veritable source of instruction and edification.

– R. P. P.

AUTHOR'S DEDICATION

To His Excellency Jean-Pierre Bravard,
Bishop of Coutances and Avranches

Your Excellency,

The bishops most celebrated for their sanctity and the apostolic men most zealous for the glory of God have honored St. Michael and the Holy Angels as powerful supporters given them by God to fulfill their difficult and perilous mission. One of your illustrious predecessors on the see of Avranches, St. Aubert, understood this when he became the apostle of this precious devotion. Everyone knows what abundant blessings God lavished on his glorious episcopacy.

This devotion is also Your Excellency's own; and it will be the glory of your episcopacy to have worked, without losing courage and amidst countless obstacles, to revive it among people who are, alas, too forgetful of the past.

For you, speech does not suffice; you desire a book that recounts something of the glory and patronage of the great archangel, as well as of the heavenly spirits whose leader he is.

This work, Your Excellency, called for an experienced, scholarly, and pious pen. However, following the example of God, Who uses the weakest instruments to enact His plans, and also, certainly, due to a combination of circumstances arranged by Divine Providence, you chose from the first group of youth your episcopal hands raised to the priesthood.

I could say with the prophet and with greater reason, "Behold, I cannot speak, for I am a child" (Jer 1:6). I obeyed. May I see the fulfillment of these beautiful words from our Holy Books: "An obedient man shall speak of victory" (Prv 21:28)!

May these black and white pages meet Your Excellency's expectations and do some good! May the hopes of those to whom you have confided the examination of this work be fulfilled!

May Your Excellency deign to accept this little tribute of my submission and, at the same time, the sentiments of profound veneration with which I have the honor of being Your Excellency's humble and obedient son in Our Lord Jesus Christ.

Eugène Soyer

LETTER OF BISHOP JEAN-PIERRE BRAVARD

Coutances, 10 September 1869
Feast of St. Aubert, Bishop of
Avranches and founder of the first
religious establishment in honor
of St. Michael the Archangel on
Mount Tombe at the beginning of
the eighth century.

Dear Fr. Soyer,

Your book on St. Michael and the Holy Angels greatly interested all those who read the manuscript; they admired its wise structure, apt style, considerable research, and the spirit of piety manifested on each page; they found it very suitable for instructing and edifying, and considered it one of the best works that can be published on this subject so worthy of interest.

I therefore authorize you to have it published, and I heartily wish for it to be disseminated among the faithful.

Devotion to the Holy Angels is too neglected in our time. People, even the most pious, seem to forget the existence of these heavenly spirits, their apparitions, their nature, their qualities, their privileges, and their ministry with respect to God, with respect to ourselves, and with respect to other creatures.

As a result of this forgetfulness, people do not pray to them, do not have recourse to them, and do not render them the veneration that is due them; people thus deprive themselves of the numerous benefits the Lord has wanted to attach to our interactions of faith and confidence with these *armies of the Almighty.*

Devotion to St. Michael, prince of the heavenly militia, ought to be especially dear to us, among all others.

St. Michael had chosen, in our diocese, on the rock of Mount Tombe, a place where he drew for long centuries the populations of all Europe; he manifested there through dazzling and oft-repeated prodigies his goodness towards those who came there to invoke him, be it for their individual needs, for the needs of their homeland, or even for the needs of the Church. St. Michael is, in fact, the courageous protector of the Savior's holy spouse, who struggles amidst the dangers of the present life; he has under his watch Christian nations, especially France, which was consecrated to him by our kings; he defends our souls from their powerful enemies and presents them to the Sovereign Judge at the moment of death.

May your book revive confidence in this leader of the heavenly spirits! May it more and more bring back into his shrine, *at the peril of the sea*, the faithful who, for a few years already,[1] have been coming onto this rock and beneath its somber arches, to seek support and graces for themselves and for others!

These results, dear Father, will be for you a sweet reward, like I wish you to have already in the assurance of my full and cordial esteem.

+J.-P., Bishop of Coutances and Avranches

Author's Preface

The wondrous shrine of St. Michael had barely been restored to religion when a son of the seraphic St. Francis wrote us the following:

> The glorious Archangel St. Michael would be yet more glorified if someone once more undertook to chronicle his great deeds… Spiritualism is making rapid progress: "The devil is come down unto you, having great wrath" [(Rv 12:12)]. It is time to oppose him with that powerful vanquisher of whom it is written: "Michael and his angels fought with the dragon, and the dragon fought and his angels: And they prevailed not, neither was their place found any more in heaven" [(Rv 12:7-8)].
>
> To work then, to work! St. Michael waits and requests that those he has entrusted with the custody of his shrine relate his apparitions and miraculous deeds.

Yes, it must be admitted that spiritualism, or the worship of evil spirits, is making lamentable progress.

Implacable enemy of the Word, Satan's supreme goal is to substitute himself for Him, as King and as God. His means, in antiquity as much as in modern times, have been the three great errors that ultimately destroy the dogma of the Incarnation: pantheism, materialism, and rationalism.

If everything is God, there is no Incarnation.

If everything is material, there is no Incarnation.

If all truth is enclosed within the limits of reason, there are no mysteries, therefore no Incarnation.

Now, to dethrone the Word is to acclaim Satan, the first enemy of the Word; it is to recognize Satan as master and God; for man cannot be without a master or a God.

Jesus Christ as God and King, or Satan as God and King—if Jesus Christ is denied, Satan is the unavoidable alternative.

But interior worship calls for external worship. Satan enjoyed it in antiquity as in our own day. He asked for sacrifices, and he had them. A contemporary writer states, "The imagination recoils in horror at the incalculable multitude of animals of all species, and the amazing sum of wealth of all kinds, stolen from poor mankind by its hateful and insatiable tyrant." Drinking long drafts of animal blood did little to satisfy the great *murderer*. He demanded, through his oracles, human blood. Athens and Rome, the cities which, in antiquity, marched at the forefront of civilization, imitated the barbarians and savages of Africa and India. Multitudes of human victims were burned alive or subjected to the bloody knife of priests offering sacrifices. Satan obtained this worship by means of oracles, conjurations, apparitions, healings, and all kinds of marvels.

Today, Satan wants to reconquer what Christianity took from him. By means of the Revolution, which is his church, he wants to paganize the world by spreading the three great errors we have already mentioned: pantheism, materialism, and rationalism. As in antiquity, he comes with a suite of mysterious practices, cleverly modified according to times and persons. Turning tables, talking boards, medium writers, medium conjurers, medium healers—such are, in our time, the principal spirit phenomena and ordinary modes of communication with the spirits.[1]

These phenomena exist; no one can deny it. They are not tricks of physics or at the most the results of certain fluidic influences. These phenomena are produced by spirits.

What are these spirits? They can only be good or bad angels, holy souls or damned souls. Now, neither the good angels nor the holy souls are at the orders of men. The demons alone then are, according to universal testimony, the authors of these phenomena.

The word of St. John is thus true for our day: "The devil is come down unto you, having great wrath" (Rv 12:12).

One must admit that if the clergy and the *real* Catholics do not oppose spiritualism with a powerful alliance, and if God does not intervene in a sovereign manner in this decisive battle, then nothing will prevent the new cult from assuming unseen proportions before the end of this century.

What will be the conditions for this alliance? St. Augustine gives us an idea. This doctor states, "For as the truth counsels men to seek the fellowship of the holy angels, in like manner impiety turns men aside to the fellowship of the wicked angels."[2] Thus, the means for fighting successfully is to unite with the holy angels, who were the first, with St. Michael at their head, to overcome the Dragon.

But first, it is necessary to solidly instruct ourselves on the power of the good and bad angels. On this point, a modern writer says, we are to be educated and re-educated.

We have indicated the goal of this modest writing. May God deign to make it useful to some souls.

As for the structure, it is organized by subject.

We shall speak first of the holy angels, of their nature, their prerogatives, their power, and their ministries. We shall try to highlight everything that can contribute to a love for their veneration and to the practice of this devotion that is so beautiful, so precious, and so salutary.

The angels, we forget too often, have the closest ties with us. From the crib to the grave, man is unceasingly under their influence. From the blade of grass in the valley to the radiant star in the firmament, everything is confided to their vigilant protection.

Man's defenders in perils, they fight the *great enemy*, Satan.

We shall look to the Faith, Tradition, and Reason to make known to us this powerful adversary of God and men. This study will be of great interest to us and will naturally, at the same time, produce the most precious results.

Fr. [Frederick William] Faber says:

> The doctrine of the personality and influence of the devil is peculiarly needed just now to meet the Saduceism of the day, as has been remarked by Dr. [Orestes] Brownson. Even [Pierre] Bayle in his *Dictionnaire* (Art. Plotinus) says to Christians, ["]Prove to your adversaries the existence of evil spirits and you will soon see them forced to grant you all your dogmas.["]... Frederick Schlegel well said that history was nothing more than "an incessant struggle of nations and individuals against invisible powers."[3]

Fr. [Xavier] de Ravignan says with as much aptness as power when speaking of demons in our own time: "Their master stroke is having this age deny their existence."

The science of the angelic world is little known and little studied. Why? Because this science is generally regarded as uncertain or as largely relying on data where the Faith has no part.

However, the science of the angelic world is a science that is certain; certain because it is true; true because it is universally recognized. Revelation, Tradition, and even the reasoning of all peoples have taught it and teach it still.

The Old and New Testaments, in a multitude of places, speak to us of the angels and their functions.

St. Denis, the illustrious disciple of St. Paul who, taken to the third heaven, relayed on earth a profound knowledge of the angels, listing all the angelic orders, this St. Denis left us a scholarly and sublime treatise on the angelic world.[4]

The Church Fathers, in their turn, and especially the incomparable genius St. Thomas Aquinas, did magnificent studies on this subject.

The Roman Ritual, a most competent authority, a surest and most authorized organ of orthodox teaching, and the most authentic monument of Tradition, speaks very often of angels and demons, and makes known to us the activity of one and the other on the world and on man.

To the Roman Ritual, we can add the Roman Pontifical, another monument of the Catholic Faith.

It is from these sources that we shall draw; and we shall have the assurance that nothing is being put forward in this writing that is not based on these serious authorities.

Mary of Agreda, in her *Mystical City of God*, made revelations of the greatest interest about the angels, and particularly about St. Michael. We shall quote some of them. Bossuet, it is true, upon the publication of this writing, solicited Rome for its condemnation; but two subsequent decrees of Innocent XI and Benedict XIII authorized the reading of this work. Dom Guéranger wrote a few years ago in the newspaper *L'Univers* a great number of articles defending this book. Moreover, however predisposed one might be against revelations in general, one need only read the holy and almost miraculous life of the venerable daughter of St. Francis to be convinced that the *Mystical City of God* is not at all the product of a delirious imagination. In any case, we ask here that one not deny the quotations we make from Mary of Agreda the authority one grants an individual writer who presents such marks of truthfulness and who has been defended by such men whose names we have just mentioned.

We shall try, in a second section, to make known the one who is the head of all the heavenly spirits, St. Michael.

We shall divide it into three books.

St. Michael is the guardian of the Church of God. All of his titles and all of his functions are tied to this glorious ministry.

The Church, according to the full extent of this word, is composed of angels and men.

St. Michael has shown himself her vigilant guardian by supporting, in Heaven, the faithful angels against the apostasy of Satan. On earth, he fulfilled this important ministry by preserving, amidst universal idolatry, knowledge of the true God, first among the patriarchs, then among the chosen people. He still fulfills it by watching over the Church of Jesus Christ, of which he is the faithful minister on earth, by defending her against the incessant attacks of Satan, and by ushering the just souls into Heaven, the true Church of God.

Such will be the subject of the first book.

In the second, we shall speak of devotion to St. Michael. Is it not just that we honor him who has been placed so highly, and that we invoke him who has so much merit before God? Besides, we shall only be following the example of peoples, saints, and religious orders.

This devotion, the Archangel has obtained it by ordering the building of shrines in his honor, and by rewarding with signal benefits the confidence of those who have had recourse to his protection. We shall recount briefly, in a third book, the history of the principal apparitions and of the most frequented pilgrimage sites. We shall elaborate further on the story of the founding of Mont Saint-Michel and on the history of this great place of pilgrimage.

This second part demanded of us immense research. In the Middle Ages, it is true, much was written about St. Michael, but most of those works have either disappeared or are buried in the dust of some library; we were unable to consult a single one of them.

We then studied the commentators of Holy Scripture, the Fathers, the history of the Church and of religious orders; we looked at the liturgy to tell us what value the Church attaches to invoking the Archangel; we also looked to the arts: architecture, paintings, and sculptures on monuments erected through the devotion of peoples.

May this study revive among us a devotion that is, alas, too neglected! It is needed for our time, and God has given it to us as a powerful help to fight victoriously against Satanism. "Michael and his angels fought with the dragon, and the dragon fought and his angels. And they prevailed not" (Rv 12:7-8).

The venerable son of St. Francis who asked us for this work adds that several times he tried to write about St. Michael, but that the demon always set up obstacles. We admit in turn that he did the same for us. However, convinced by this that it was God's work, and also encouraged by our venerable bishop, we fought courageously against all obstacles.

May St. Michael deign to put under his protection this writing consecrated to his glory and that of *his Angels*!

Following this treatise, we shall have the "pilgrim's manual" for the Basilica of St. Michael "at the peril of the sea."

God, it is our conviction, has wanted to return to religion this celebrated shrine of Mont Saint-Michel, this wonder, this Jerusalem of the West as it was called in other times, in order to give to our own time a sensible sign of His protection, through the mediation of His glorious Archangel. It seems to us this venerated shrine should be a center and rallying point for those who want to join the fight. From here would shine forth works of reparation, of which St. Michael is the patron.

The "visitor's guide,"[5] which crowns this work, will make known the illustrious abbey and will call on the Holy Archangel for the blessing of his visible protection. And why should we not fully speak our mind?

We are asking for miracles! But there is one visible and great miracle among all the miracles, a permanent one: It is the preservation of this splendid monument amidst fires eleven times renewed, amidst sieges, assaults, and bloody wars which, during the fifteenth century, furiously worked for its destruction, whereas time alone has made almost all its contemporaries disappear!

Glory then to the Bishop, the worthy successor of St. Aubert, who, despite countless obstacles, has worked with untiring solicitude to return to religion and to France the incomparable shrine of St. Michael!

PART ONE: THE HOLY ANGELS

CHAPTER 1:
EXISTENCE OF THE ANGELS. – THEIR NAME. – THEIR CREATION. – THEIR NATURE. – THEIR QUALITIES.

O Lord my God… Who makest thy angels spirits.
– Psalms 103:1, 4 [104:1, 4]

The existence of the angels is a truth reason shows possible, to whose certainty mankind's faith attests, and which is confirmed by revelation.

Here, we shall say nothing of the proofs from authority; they will present themselves in great number throughout this study.

Reason demonstrates without difficulty that our visible world, by its imperfect nature, does not have nor can have within itself the reason for its existence, nor the principle of the laws which govern it. They must be sought elsewhere, for, as St. Paul says, knowledge of the visible world leads us to knowledge of the invisible.[1]

The most scholarly observation of divine laws proclaims this axiom: There is no leap in nature, nor any rupture in the chain of beings. All creatures visible to our eyes build on each other, are on a continuum, and follow one after another. Degree by degree, everything reaches its apex in man. Spirit and matter, man himself is the merging together of two worlds. By his body, he is on the highest rung of the ladder of material beings, and by his soul, he is on the lowest rung of the ladder of spiritual beings. A being's perfection, in fact, is calculated according to its more or less complete resemblance to God. Now, the purely material creature is less perfect than the creature that is simultaneously material and spiritual. In turn, the latter is less perfect than the purely

1

spiritual creature. Admirable harmony! Man, by his nature, unites two worlds: the world of matter and the world of the spirits. And these pure spirits are, with respect to man, what man is with respect to purely material creatures: they link man to God as man himself links matter to spirit.

The word "angel" signifies "messenger" and "envoy"; it is not an appellation of nature, but of office, taken from the ministry they exercise. As all the heavenly spirits are notifiers of divine thoughts, the name of angel is common to them. They are especially and par excellence honored with the name of angels, St. Denis says, for the revelation of secrets above us is made through their intervention.[2]

At what moment did God create the angels? Did He create the invisible and intelligible world inhabited by Spirits before the visible and material world? A number of Greek and Latin Church Fathers thought so: Origen, St. Basil, St. Gregory Nazianzen, St. John Chrysostom, St. Clement, St. Ambrose, St. Hilary, and St. Jerome. "Our universe," the last one said, "is not yet six thousand years old. But beforehand, how many eternities of time, from the beginnings of ages, must there have been during which the Angels, the Thrones, the Dominations, and the other Virtues would have served God and subsisted without any vicissitude or measure of time." However, theologians in general, including St. Augustine and St. Thomas, think that God, as a perfect laborer making a work worthy of Himself, created the angels on the first day. Moses says so implicitly: "In the beginning God created heaven" (Gn 1:1), meaning heaven and all those who dwell therein.

The angels, these firstborn of God, are spirits, that is to say creatures who are incorporeal, invisible, incorruptible, spiritual, and endowed with an intellect and a will.

The angels thus have no bodies, nor have they been created to be united with bodies. They are therefore incapable of exercising any act of sensitive or vegetative life, such as seeing corporally, hearing, eating, and the like.

From the air or from any other already existing matter, however, they can form bodies and give them a shape and an accidental form. The

Archangel Raphael said to Tobias, "For when I was with you, I was there by the will of God…. I seemed indeed to eat and drink with you: but I use an invisible meat and drink" (Tb 12:18-19).

One must not believe, however, that these corporeal forms are only imaginary visions. An imaginary vision is only in the imagination of the one who sees it; it eludes others. Scripture often speaks of angels who appear in sensible forms, seen equally by everyone. The angels who come to save Lot are seen not only by this just man, but also by his entire family and the inhabitants of Sodom.

It is necessary then to put aside any material or coarse ideas that our senses give us, and which the representations of painters and sculptors, and even the overly literal interpretation of Holy Scriptures would seem to confirm.

It is thus necessary to understand in a figurative sense the wings of which the Prophets speak: They signify the rapidity with which these spirits go from one place to another to fulfill God's orders. These gracious forms, these youthful bodies, and these ravishing faces are the expressions of the spiritual beauty and immortal youth which they enjoy in their beatitude.[3]

It is also necessary to understand in a mystical sense what the Holy Books tell us of the golden vessels and censers in which they offer to God our prayers, the harmonies of voices and instruments, and the melodious symphonies by which they praise *Him that liveth forever and ever.*

From the incorporeality of their nature, it follows that the angels are incorruptible. Exempt from languor and illness, they do not experience the need for food or rest, nor the weaknesses of childhood, nor the infirmities and debilitations of old age. They are endowed with beauty, intelligence, agility, and strength incomprehensible to man.

God being infinite beauty and the source of all beauty, the more a being resembles Him, the more it is beautiful. Of all material beings, the body of man is the most beautiful because it reflects to a greater degree the beauty of the Creator. The soul is more beautiful than the body because it is the more perfect image of eternal beauty. In turn, and for the same reason, the angel is more beautiful than the human soul.

Moreover, humans have an instinct for this beauty, for to indicate the most perfect degree of sensible beauty, they say, "Beautiful like an angel." When St. Stephen was brought before the council of Jews, his face became so bright and so august that it appeared, the sacred historian says, "as if it had been the face of an angel" (Acts 6:15).

"As beautifully and magnificently adorned as men might be," St. Francis de Sales says,

> they are nothing compared to the angels; their luster has no shine, and they are not worthy of comparison in their presence. Thus, one sees in Holy Scripture that whenever angels have appeared to men, that the latter fell on their faces, incapable of bearing the splendor and radiance of angelic beauty. The Most Holy Virgin herself, so highly distinguished above all pure creatures, and so specially favored above all the angels, Cherubim and Seraphim, was nevertheless amazed at the sight of the angel St. Gabriel when he came to speak to her of the most-high and sacred mystery of the Incarnation.[4]

This beauty is so radiant, in the opinion of St. Anselm, that if a single angel were to make himself visible in all his glory, his light would efface as many suns, if they existed, as there are stars in the firmament.

In some places the Savior calls the blessed spirits "angels of light," an expression clearly indicating that the knowledge of the angels is far superior to all the riches of human science. Who will speak of the scope of the angelic intellect? "It does not acquire," St. Thomas says, "intelligible truth from the variety of composite objects;... it understands the truth of intelligible objects not discursively, but by simple intuition."[5] Its intellectual power is always active,[6] in such a way that the angel currently knows all it can know naturally.[7] It knows it all entirely, as a whole and in its details, in its principle and in its final consequences. "So therefore, no falsehood, error, or deception can exist of itself in the mind of any angel."[8]

From these intellects, heaven and earth have hidden nothing hidden in the natural order; and since they are confirmed in grace, they know most truths of the supernatural order. We say "most," for the Angelic Doctor further states that until the day of Judgment, they will receive new communications concerning the governing of the world and particularly about the salvation of the predestined.

From the incorporeality of the angels comes their agility. In man, the soul's movement is hindered by the organs. For the angels, no obstacle delays them. The rapidity of their movements is such that it is almost equivalent to being omnipresent. In the blink of an eye they can be in one place, and in another blink of an eye in another place, without any lapse in time. Their subtlety is such that the opaquest bodies are less to them than a diaphanous veil is to the rays of the sun.

The holy hosts of heavenly natures receive from the divine liberality, at the moment of their creation, more than the natures that exist simply, or that have an irrational life, or even those who, like us, are endowed with reason. Today, confirmed in grace, in possession of the beatific vision, these pure spirits tend towards but one goal: "It is," St. Denis says, [as paraphrased by Church historian Fr. René François Rohrbacher,]

> continual love towards God and divine things, love inspired by God and consummated through union; it is… the absolute and irrevocable flight from what is contrary to this love; it is the knowledge of things in the reality of their being, the vision and knowledge of sacred truth; it is divine participation, as much as possible, in the unique perfection of Him Who is supremely one; it is enjoyment of the intuition, which intellectually nourishes and deifies whoever contemplates it.[9]

Their innocence has never been sullied by the least stain; the intensity of their love for God and the zeal for His glory have never suffered any alteration. Immersed night and day in the ocean of divine love and in transports of joy, they repeat the eternal canticle. Like the twenty-four elders of the Apocalypse, they throw their crowns at the foot of the throne of God, saying, "Thou art worthy, O Lord our God, to receive glory and honour and power" (Rv 4:11).

They are the adornment of the heavens. The angels, St. Anselm says,

> are the living stars of the higher heaven, the lilies of the inner
> paradise, the rose-trees planted by the silent-flowing waters of
> Siloe, with their roots immovably fixed in Thee [God]. O River
> of peace, O Breath of the garden of delights, O only Wisdom
> ranging round about the circling bourne of heaven; by Thee they
> shine, and burn, and glow in perfect wisdom, in virginal chastity,
> and in the ardours of a deathless love.[10]

On the day when it will be given us to see them in Heaven face to
face, we shall enter into a rapture inexpressible even for St. Paul, who
was a witness to it. It will be, according to St. Thomas, the recompense
due to the mortification of the senses and to the angelic life that we led
here below, in the hope of enjoying the company of the angels.

CHAPTER 2:
THE POWER OF THE ANGELS
OVER THE WORLD AND OVER MEN.

For an angel of the Lord descended from heaven, and coming, rolled back the stone.
– Matthew 28:2

And them that were without, they struck with blindness from the least to the greatest.
– Genesis 19:11

The strength and power with which the angels are endowed has its source in the essence of their being, which participates more abundantly than any other in the divine essence, which is infinite power. It is so great that a single angel suffices to set into motion all the bodies in the planetary system.

The consequence of this power is that the angels can displace the largest bodies and transport them where they want at a speed which defies calculation. A single angel, St. Thomas says, by its natural virtue, can lift the enormous weight of the earth. According to St. Augustine, the natural power of the least of the angels is such that all corporeal and material creatures obey him, regarding their local movement, and within the sphere of their activity, unless God or a superior angel should place an obstacle. If God permitted it then, a single angel could transport an entire city from one place to another, just as they did for the holy house of Mary in which the Incarnation of the Word took place. They transported it from Nazareth to Dalmatia, then from Dalmatia to Loretto, where it today receives the homage of the Catholic world.

Can the angels, by their own natural power, work miracles?

Taken in the absolute sense, this power belongs to God alone, "Who alone doth great wonders" (Ps 135:4 [136:4]). If one understands the word "miracle" as meaning "a wondrous thing," it is certain that, through the profound knowledge they have of nature's secrets, the angels can do amazing things.

Man is subject body and soul to the angelic powers. Scripture is filled with incidents which demonstrate in the most incontestable manner the truth of this assertion. The exterminating angel put to death, in a single night, the firstborn of the Egyptians (Ex 12:23, 29); one hundred eighty-five thousand men in the army of Sennacherib, King of Assyria, were cut to pieces by a single angel (2 Kgs 19:35); the inhabitants of Sodom were struck blind, from the least to the greatest, by two angels in the form of young men (Gn 19:11).

As for our soul, the angels can exercise, and in fact do exercise on it an activity, sometimes ordinary and sometimes extraordinary, whose power is difficult to measure.

They enlighten and fortify the understanding. "The revelations of divine things," St. Denis says, "come to men by means of the angels." This illumination takes place in various ways: Sometimes the angel fortifies man's understanding so that he can conceive the truth; sometimes he presents him sensible images by means of which he can know this truth.

Here would be the place to speak of visions and revelations, whether corporeal like the mission of Gabriel to the Blessed Virgin, or imaginary like the apparition of the angel to St. Joseph during his sleep. The limits we have set for ourselves, however, prevent us from going into these details.

The angels are not at all masters over man's will such that they could force him to decide contrary to his wishes. "The heart of the king is in the hand of the Lord: whithersoever he will, he shall turn it" (Prv 21:1). However, they know how to stir the very powerful passions over the will, all while leaving man the freedom to resist or consent.

By means of the exterior senses they exercise a great influence over the imagination, in which they produce more or less vivid impressions.

We shall see this power at work when we study the functions of the holy angels with respect to man and material creation. Let us only add here that they cannot know, by virtue of their natural power, the secret thoughts of man. The heart of man is "unsearchable" (Jer 17:9). God alone knows it, He Who "knoweth the secrets of the heart" (Ps 43:22 [44:21]).

Let us admire the providence of God, Who wants our interior to be thus hidden from the angels, principally from the demons. These wicked spirits would refrain from tempting virtuous men if they knew their firm resolutions, which would make these men lose the opportunity to fight, vanquish, and triumph. Other times, they would tempt man with greater boldness if they saw him vacillating in his resolutions or interiorly disposed to some sin. They would thus ruin men more surely. That is why God only willed to give the angels knowledge of our thoughts insofar as we reveal them ourselves on the exterior, or when we want them to have this knowledge.

O holy angels, we desire to make known to you the most secret thoughts of our hearts. If they are not for God, then make use of your power before us to banish them from our minds and to inspire in us good and holy thoughts instead.

CHAPTER 3:
NUMBER OF ANGELS AND THEIR VARIETIES.
– THEIR HIERARCHY AND THEIR CHOIRS.

Thousands of thousands ministered to him, and ten thousand times a hundred thousand stood before him.
– Daniel 7:10

When the inspired writers want to indicate the vast number of angels, they speak only of millions or hundreds of millions. Let us listen to what Daniel says after having had a heavenly vision:

> I beheld till thrones were placed and the Ancient of days sat. His garment was white as snow and the hair of his head like clean wool: his throne like flames of fire: the wheels of it like a burning fire. A swift stream of fire issued forth from before him: *thousands of thousands* ministered to him, and *ten thousand times a hundred thousand* stood before him. (Dn 7:9-10)

St. John, a witness to the same spectacle, makes use of similar terms. It is quite clear that neither Daniel nor John was able to count them; they intend, through their language, to indicate an infinite multitude. Job asks, with amazement, if it is possible to count them.

The blessed hosts of heavenly spirits, St. Denis says, surpass in number all the poor calculations of our earthly arithmetic. Do not suspect any exaggeration in the words of the prophets; the number of angels is incalculable.

The Angelic Doctor, St. Thomas Aquinas, gives the reason. Here is his thinking: The principal goal God has in mind in creating beings is the perfection of the universe. The perfection or beauty of the universe results from the most brilliant manifestation of God's attributes, within the limits set by His wisdom. It follows from this that the more beautiful certain creatures are, the more abundant was their creation. The material world confirms this reasoning. Two kinds of bodies are found in it:

corruptible bodies and incorruptible bodies. The first kind is limited to our globe, the habitation of corruptible beings; and our globe is almost nothing compared to the globes of the firmament. Now, as size is the measure of perfection for bodies, number is so for spirits.

What about the varieties of angels? Some theologians have taught that each of these spirits forms a species unto himself, the thought of which overwhelms our imagination with God's magnificence. Others tell us that the grace of each angel is a beauty and an excellence entirely different from the grace of those similar to him; and if we follow this line of thought, we shall find delight in considering the perfection of this amiable worship rendered to God Whom we on earth serve so poorly.

A multitude without order is confusion; such cannot be the angelic world. God has "ordered all things in measure, and number, and weight" (Wis 11:21), meaning with perfect order—this the material world reveals to us. Now, order produces harmony, and harmony presupposes mutual subordination of all parts within the whole, and this harmony presupposes an intelligent cause that has ordered everything. The world of spirits, an archetype of the world of bodies, must then present a yet more perfect harmony, if that be possible. The subordination of beings to the hierarchy of which they are a part is therefore the law of the invisible world.

A hierarchy, the Angelic Doctor says, is a sacred princedom: "*Hierarchia est sacer principatus.*"[1] A princedom signifies both the prince who governs and the multitude under his command. Now, since God is the unique sovereign of both the visible world and the invisible world, one can say that there is but a single hierarchy, of which He is the Supreme Hierarch.

However, if one considers a princedom in its relations to the multitude, one calls a hierarchy the *ensemble of beings subject to a single and same law*. Inasmuch as there are different laws, there are distinct hierarchies.

It is the same for the monarchies of the earth: inasmuch as there are peoples or cities ruled by different laws, laws specific to them, there are equally many provinces and principalities, without them ceasing however to be subject to the same sovereign.

Now, beings are only subject to the same laws because they have the same nature and the same functions. Angels and men, due to the diversity of their natures and functions, thus form two distinct hierarchies. But the angels, in turn, do not all have the same functions, and it follows that the angelic world must be divided into multiple hierarchies.

Moreover, the angels do not all possess the same perfections, that is to say, they do not equally receive divine illuminations. Thus, there are angels who have a more or less perfect, a more or less universal, knowledge of the truth. It follows that there are three hierarchies, or three degrees, among the angels, degrees which are based upon the three possible manners of seeing the truth.

Let us listen to St. Thomas's explanation of the threefold manner in which angels are enlightened:

> First as proceeding from God as the first universal principle, which mode of knowledge belongs to the first hierarchy, connected immediately with God, and, *as it were, placed in the vestibule of God*, as Dionysius says (*Coel. Hier.* vii). Secondly, forasmuch as these types depend on the universal created causes which in some way are already multiplied; which mode belongs to the second hierarchy. Thirdly, forasmuch as these types are applied to particular things as depending on their causes; which mode belongs to the lowest hierarchy.[2]

Each hierarchy must be a wisely ordered multitude. Likewise, we see, in the principalities here below, three different classes of citizens. Those of the first rank are the aristocracy; those of the last rank are the people; those who are in the middle rank are the bourgeoisie. It is the same among the angels. It follows that in each hierarchy there are three choirs or distinct orders. A "choir" or "angelic order" refers to a specific multitude of angels who are similar to each other by reason of their gifts of nature and grace.

St. Gregory the Great categorizes them as follows: In the first hierarchy, there are the *Seraphim*, the *Cherubim*, and the *Thrones*; in the second, the *Dominations*, the *Principalities*, and the *Powers*; and in the third, the *Virtues*, the *Archangels*, and the *Angels*.[3]

Composed and divided in this way, the angelic world appears to us as a magnificent army arrayed in battle. However, to have a more complete idea of this angelic world, let us look at it in action and examine each hierarchy in the exercise of its functions.

CHAPTER 4:
THE ANGELS' COMMUNICATIONS WITH EACH OTHER.
– THEIR LANGUAGE.

And they cried one to another, and said: Holy, holy, holy....
– Isaiah 6:3

The angels form, as we have already stated, a wisely ordered multitude. They have relations which unite them and put them in communication with each other.

St. Denis makes known to us the origin of this. The angels do not all equally receive the divine illuminations and do not all equally know the divine secrets. The lights they draw from within God Himself, the angels of the first hierarchy communicate them, as much as is fitting, to the angels of the second hierarchy; the second hierarchy communicates them to the third hierarchy; and the third hierarchy makes them known to men. But reciprocity does not occur; for it is an immutable law established by the divinity that what is inferior be brought to God by what is superior. Men have nothing to teach the angels, and inferior angels have nothing to teach superior angels. It is for this reason that St. Denis calls the superior angels divine doctors of the inferior ones.

This unceasing communication encompasses what the same Father calls purification, illumination, and perfection. The manifestation of a truth purifies the understanding by dissipating the darkness of ignorance; it illuminates it by shining light where obscurity reigned; and it perfects it by giving it a certain knowledge of the truth.

With what docility the inferior angels receive the illuminations which come to them from their superiors! Oh, how beautiful do they find these lights, which are desired and ardently sought! On the other hand, with what love and charity do the superior angels communicate their knowledge to the inferiors and make them participators in it! It is without envy, St. Denis states further, that they show the others the divine visions with which they were favored first. Oh, why am I not full of this zeal of the superior angels! O blessed Seraphim and Cherubim, as you purify, illuminate, and perfect the angels subject to you, deign likewise to purify, illuminate, and perfect my mind, in order to raise it towards God.

However, how are these communications made?

By word. Isaiah makes this known to us when he reports hearing the Seraphim cry "one to another," saying, "Holy, holy, holy..." (Is 6:3). St. Paul also teaches the same thing when he says, "If I speak with the *tongues* of men and *of angels*, and have not charity, I am become as sounding brass, or a tinkling cymbal" (1 Cor 13:1). And if men can manifest their thoughts and desires to one another by a language that is particular to them, will one deny this prerogative to the angels, who are more perfect and more excellent creatures? Would this not prevent their union, their society, and their familiarity?

But human language does not resemble angelic language. The internal conception of our mind is as though closed by two doors which prevent it from appearing, says St. Thomas Aquinas. First, by our will: no one, except God, can know our interior thoughts. Secondly, it is stopped by the materiality of our body; for although a man might want his thoughts to be known by another, it would be in vain; the body, like a thick wall, keeps it out of sight. There must then be a sensible sign such as gesturing or speech.

But since the angels do not have bodies, there is not this obstacle to the communication of thoughts. The will alone can oppose it. Thus, when an angel directs his thoughts towards another, and desires that he know them, then this direction of the will is like a locution or a word by which he makes known his thoughts and speaks to another.

Oh, how heavenly these conversations! And how divine these exchanges! Blessed is he who can converse with these glorious spirits and listen to their discourse! How embarrassing for us who so often speak of trifles and nothingness, and perhaps of evil things! Learn then, O Christian, learn from the conversation of the angels, to speak a new language, and to converse more frequently about heavenly and divine things.

CHAPTER 5:
ROLES OF THE ATTENDANT ANGELS AT THE THRONE OF GOD. – THEY BELONG TO THE FIRST HIERARCHY. – THE SEVEN ATTENDANT ANGELS. – THEIR ROLES. – TEMPLE BUILT IN ROME IN THEIR HONOR. – ROLES OF THE ADMINISTRATOR ANGELS. – THEY BELONG TO THE SECOND AND THIRD HIERARCHIES.

For I am the angel Raphael, one of the seven, who stand before the Lord.
– Tobit 12:15

According to their dignity and functions, the angels are divided into *attendant* angels and *executive*, or *administrator*, angels. The former consider in God Himself the reason of the things to do and manifest them to the inferior angels tasked with executing them. Such is the image with which Scripture represents to us the angels of the first hierarchy.

This appellation of *attendants at the throne of God*, applied to the angels, has multiple meanings. The angels are present before God when they take His orders, when they offer him the prayers and good works of mortals, when they plead man's cause against the demons, when they plunge their gazes into the rays of the divine face, the source of ineffable delights constituting the happiness of heaven. In this sense, all the angels, without exception, are attendants at the throne of God, for all enjoy the beatific vision.

Understood in the strict sense, this appellation belongs to the angels who have no outside ministry: They are called *Seraphim*, *Cherubim*, and *Thrones*. It is these who form the first hierarchy.

The *Seraphim*, or *Ardents*, the most sublime creatures God has drawn from nothingness, are called thus because the divine fire, of which they receive the fieriest ardors, sets ablaze in them an incomparable love. These are the familiars of the heavenly court.

16

Stationed in love's eternal hearth, they repeat unceasingly, in transports of joy, this eternal canticle heard by Isaiah: "Holy, holy, holy, the Lord God of hosts, all the earth is full of his glory" (Is 6:3).

The *Cherubim*, admitted into the secrets of the Prince, possess the fullness of knowledge, a supereminent knowledge which comes to them from contemplating, closer than others, the divine splendor.

The *Thrones*, dazzlingly beautiful, are raised above all the choirs in the inferior hierarchies, to whom they signal the orders of the great King, all while sharing with the Cherubim and Seraphim the intuiting of truth in God Himself, a privilege reserved for the first hierarchy.

Here is the place to say something about the *seven attendant angels at the throne of God*. "For I am the angel Raphael," one of these angels said to Tobit, "one of the seven, who stand before the Lord" (Tb 12:15). The apostle St. John wrote to the seven churches in Asia: "Grace be unto you and peace from him that is, and that was, and that is to come, and from *the seven spirits which are before his throne*" (Rv 1:4).

The Catholic Church venerates seven angels who are more beautiful, more powerful, and greater than the others. They surround the throne of God and are ready to execute His orders.

One tradition attributes to these seven angels the supreme government of the physical world and the moral world. Symbolized, St. Jerome says, by the seven-branch candelabra of the Mosaic tabernacle, they preside over the seven great planets, whose revolutions determine the movement of all the secondary gears in the wondrous machine called the material universe. They also preside over the moral world. One theologian says:

> There are seven angels superior to all others. Their special roles are to attend to the seven gifts of the Holy Ghost, in order to obtain them, communicate them to us, and make them fruitful; to subdue, by virtue of a special power, the seven demons who preside over the seven capital sins; to preside over the seven brightest bodies in the firmament; to have us practice the seven virtues necessary for salvation, that is to say, the three theological virtues and the four cardinal virtues.[1]

Let us also listen to Fr. Faber:

> Each of the seven angels who stand before the Throne are said
> to have one of the Sacraments committed specially to their
> custody. The Eucharist is assigned to St. Michael, Baptism to St.
> Gabriel, Confirmation to St. Uriel, Penance to St. Jehudiel,
> Extreme Unction to St. Raphael, Order to St. Sealtiel, and
> Matrimony to St. Barachiel.[2] It is of course extremely difficult
> to estimate at their proper value such pious beliefs. There is
> mostly something divine in them, but, as usual, clouded with
> uncertainty.[3]

The Church could not neglect to render them a special cult of
gratitude and veneration. Their memory is celebrated in all parts of the
Catholic world; but nowhere is it so alive as in Sicily, Naples, Venice,
Rome, etc.

Mgr. Gaume states:

> Palermo, the capital of Sicily, has a beautiful church dedicated
> to the seven angels, princes of the heavenly militia. In 1516, their
> images, of great antiquity, were discovered by the archpriest of
> this church, the venerable Antonio del Duca. Often moved by
> divine inspiration, this holy man went to Rome in 1527 to spread
> the cult of these angels, and to find and build them a shrine.
>
> After much fasting and prayer, he merited to know, by
> revelation, that the Baths of Diocletian should be the temple of
> the seven angels, the attendants at the throne of God. The reasons
> for this divine choice were that these famous baths had been built
> by thousands of earthly angels, that is to say, by forty thousand
> Christians condemned to hard labor; that their gigantic
> construction had lasted seven years; and that among all these
> martyrs, seven shone with a more brilliant brightness: Cyriacus,
> Largus, Smaragdus, Sisinius, Saturninus, Marcellus, and
> Thrason, who encouraged the Christians and tended to their
> needs.
>
> This revelation having been recognized, the Sovereign
> Pontiffs Julius III and Pius IV ordered the purification of the

baths and their consecration in honor of the seven angel attendants at the throne of God, or of the Queen of Heaven surrounded by these seven angels. Michelangelo was tasked with this work. With the rich materials of the voluptuous baths of Christians' greatest enemy, the celebrated architect built the splendid church [of St. Mary of the Angels and the Martyrs] that is still admired today. It was on August 5, 1561, that Pius IV, in the presence of the sacred college and the entire Roman court, solemnly consecrated it and honored it as a titular church.[4]

The *Thrones* finish the hierarchy of *the attendant* angels, and the *Dominations* begin the hierarchy of the *administrators*.

The *Dominations* have their name because they dominate all the angelic choirs tasked with executing the orders of the great King. They indicate and command what they must do. The *Principalities*, whose name signifies *leaders according to the sacred order*, are princes of the nations they lead to the fulfillment of the divine plan. The *Powers* are charged with removing obstacles to the execution of the divine orders, by repelling the evil angels who besiege the nations to divert them from their end. The *Virtues*, whose name means *strength*, exercise their empire over material creation, rule the maintenance of the laws which govern it, and preserve the order that we admire in it. When the glory of God demands it, the Virtues suspend the laws of nature.

"Among the blessed spirits," says Bossuet, "there are some called Virtues, of whom it is written: *Angels of the Lord, bless the Lord; bless the Lord, you His Virtues or His Powers...* It is perhaps of these Virtues or these Powers that it is written: *under whom they stoop that bear up the world.*"[5]

The *Archangels*, whose name means superior angels, are charged with fulfilling important missions to men, of watching, under the command of St. Michael, over the Church, of presiding over the government of provinces, dioceses, and communities.

St. Anselm exclaims:

The magnificence of the Archangels is yours, O sweet Jesus! They are the ministers of Your goodness; you have not despised the infirmity of the world, since you send these glorious satraps from your palace to bring help to our littleness, to us who have been likened to mud, and compared to dust and ashes. By their ministry, you administer the great affairs of our salvation, and make known to us the decrees of your supreme counsel; through them, you restore health to men; through them, you govern the kingdoms and empires of the world.[6]

Since all the heavenly spirits are messengers of divine thoughts, the name *angel* is shared by all of them. Since the angels of the last choir in the last hierarchy add nothing to the common role of envoy and messenger, they simply have the name *Angel*s. It is among these last ones that are found the guardian angels of men.

We know the offices confided to each choir; we shall see how they fulfill these offices in the following chapters.

Let us only add that it is a Christian duty to admire and praise here God's august greatness. What earthly monarch ever had a court similar to His! Indeed, His works are raised above the heavens!

CHAPTER 6:

THE VIRTUES, GUARDIAN ANGELS OF MATERIAL CREATION.

Every visible thing in this world has an angelic power placed over it.
– St. Augustine[1]

Matter is inert by nature; no one can deny this. "However," says St. Thomas, [as paraphrased by Mgr. Jean-Joseph Gaume,]

> we see matter in motion everywhere. Movement can only be communicated to it by naturally active beings. These beings are and can only be spiritual powers who, superimposed over each other, receive their movement from angels and ultimately from God Himself, the principle of all movement. From this, these words of St. Augustine: *All bodies are ruled by the rational spirit of life*; and these words of St. Gregory: *In this visible world, nothing takes place without the agency of the invisible creature.* Thus, the entire world of bodies is made to be ruled by the world of spirits.[2]

Thus, it is the angels who set material creation in motion. Furthermore, they preserve it by watching over the perpetual maintenance of its admirable laws. They are to corporeal beings what the soul is to the body.

Universal tradition, poetry, and the arts portray them to us watching over all of creation. Some tend to the celestial bodies, others to the earth and its elements; others to its produce: trees, plants, flowers, and fruit. To some is confided the government of the seas, rivers, and springs, and to others the conservation of animals. In his treatise *Against Celsus*, Origen states:

> We indeed also maintain with regard not only to the fruits of the earth, but to every flowing stream and every breath of air, that

the ground brings forth those things which are said to grow up naturally, — that the water springs in fountains, and refreshes the earth with running streams, — that the air is kept pure, and supports the life of those who breathe it, only in consequence of the agency and control of certain beings whom we may call invisible husbandmen and guardians.[3]

The Angelic Doctor, in his responses to the doctor John of Vercelli, adopts the sentiment of Origen, which he says to be also that of St. Denis and St. Augustine.[4] The latter says, "Every visible thing in this world has an angelic power placed over it."[5] Elsewhere, he states we should recognize the activity of the angels in

those corporeal things which are done in the order of nature in a perfectly usual series of times, as *e.g.*, the rising and setting of the stars, the generations and deaths of animals, the innumerable diversities of seeds and buds, the vapors and the clouds, the snow and the rain, the lightnings and the thunder, the thunderbolts and the hail, the winds and the fire, cold and heat, and all like things;... also those which in the same order of nature occur rarely, such as eclipses, unusual appearances of stars, and monsters, and earthquakes, and such like.[6]

Thus, there is not a creature, however great or small it might be, that would not have an angelic power tasked to watch over it. From the blade of grass in the valley to the star in the heavens, all is confided to their government. Under the orders of the great King, they direct the immense globes that compose the brilliant army of the heavens. Despite the frightful speed they communicate to these gigantic masses, they maintain them in their orbits, making each travel its route with mathematical precision. In the last days, this magnificent harmony will be broken. Cornelius a Lapide says that at the approach of the Sovereign Judge, when all creatures will arm themselves against guilty man, the mighty conductors of the stars will upset the magnificent harmony of the planetary system. Then the nations will be overcome with fear in anticipation of what is to happen.

This teaching of the government of the world by angelic powers is found as far back as the ancient philosophers such as Aristotle and Plato. The pagans, among whom are found so many scraps of primeval revelation, believed that God had assigned a divinity to tend to the movements of the heavenly spheres and to the maintaining of plants and animals. Even today, says Fr. Faber, this teaching indisputably lives on in popular belief. Milton alludes to it in the tenth book of his *Paradise Lost*.

Scripture itself implies this doctrine when it speaks of the angel of the waters, the angel of fire, the angel of the winds, the angel of the sun, and the angel of the earth.

Such is the ministry confided to the Virtues, as we indicated in the previous chapter.

What obligations we have to these heavenly spirits! It is therefore our duty to thank them, to invoke them, and to have them invoked in public and private prayers, in times of famine, war, or plague, during times of epidemic diseases and other needs, for dryness and rain, for the grains of the earth, and in all kinds of public necessities.

The marvelous power of the Virtues is Yours, O Jesus, Virtue of the Eternal Father, we shall say with St. Anselm! It is through their ministry that you make everything the world admires; and for this reason the Prophet let forth a cry of admiration at the sight of your wonders, and said, "Whatsoever the Lord hath pleased he hath done, in heaven, in earth, in the sea, and in all the deeps" (Ps 134:6 [135:6]).

CHAPTER 7:
THE ARCHANGELS, GUARDIANS OF THE CHURCH.
– THEY CONTRIBUTED TO HER FOUNDING.

All the ancients believed that the angels were involved in all the Church's activities.

– Bossuet

God was not content with confiding the angels the government of material creation. He also appointed them, according to an expression of Lactantius, the watch and cultivation of mankind. Sublime ministry! Ministry raised above the first, inasmuch as spirit is raised above matter! Numerous and varied ministries according to the needs of their countless wards!

Mankind is, in fact, composed of the multitude of men who inhabit our earthly globe; and this multitude is wisely ordered, so as to maintain with all the members composing it a mutual subordination, whether considered from a spiritual or temporal point of view. It is thus that individuals coming from a common stock form a family. Families united under a single pastor form a parish.; these latter, united in turn, form dioceses, and the totality of dioceses compose the Universal Church, into which all men are called.

In the temporal order, one distinguishes the sometimes very populous cities which are divided into multiple parishes, the provinces which often form multiple dioceses, the kingdoms which are formed sometimes from the conglomeration of multiple peoples, and the peoples who, sometimes also on account of their exceedingly great multitude, form multiple kingdoms.

At the head of each of these divisions, God, according to universal belief, has placed guardian angels. Let us first speak of the angels appointed to watch over the Church.

The Church began in the earthly paradise. Now, following its course throughout the centuries, one sees the angels intervening in everything

24

which concerns her. They come to announce God's decrees to the patriarchs: Adam, Noah, and Abraham, the father of the chosen people. They protect Jacob, the father of the Hebrews, in all dangers; and this patriarch, on his deathbed, commends his children to their vigilant protection. One of them, in God's name, sends Moses to deliver His people and, as St. Stephen and St. Paul attest, give them on Mount Sinai the law written by God on two stone tablets.

After the Savior returns to His Father, they contribute to the establishment of the Catholic Church and come to the aid of the apostles in their labors. Many a time, the apostles are transported by the angels from one place to another, whether to preach the Gospel or to consult each other about difficulties they encounter. St. Luke recounts in the Acts of the Apostles one incident of this kind: The deacon Philip had just baptized the eunuch of Queen Candace, and immediately, an angel took Philip away and transported him from the Gaza road to Azotus, where he preached the Gospel (Acts 8:38-40). Moreover, if to give a little food to Daniel, an angel transported the prophet Habakkuk to Babylon (Dn 14:32-38), it is not surprising then that, through a similar miracle, the apostles were transported to the places where they were to preach Jesus Christ, make known His divinity, and establish the Universal Church for the salvation of mankind.

We see them coming to help the apostles in their dangers. Twice Peter, the head of the Church, is put in prison, and twice God sends His angel to break his chains and set him free. St. Luke says:

> Peter was sleeping between two soldiers, bound with two chains: and the keepers before the door kept the prison. And behold an angel of the Lord stood by him: and a light shined in the room: and he striking Peter on the side, raised him up, saying: Arise quickly. And the chains fell off from his hands. And the angel said to him: Gird thyself, and put on thy sandals. And he did so. And he said to him: Cast thy garment about thee, and follow me. And going out, he followed him, and he knew not that it was true which was done by the angel: but thought he saw a vision. (Acts 12:6-9)

The doors opened on their own, and Peter was delivered from the hand of Herod.

St. Paul, the tireless apostle, also felt the effects of their protection. Aboard a ship that was taking him to Rome, a tempest rose. All seemed hopeless. St Paul said to the sailors:

> For an angel of God, whose I am and whom I serve, stood by me this night, saying: Fear not, Paul, thou must be brought before Caesar; and behold, God hath given thee all them that sail with thee. Wherefore, sirs, be of good cheer: for I believe God that it shall so be, as it hath been told me. (Acts 27:23-25)

And Paul arrived safe and sound in the capital of the world.

Not content with coming to the aid of the apostles in their dangers, the angels intervene to convert the firstfruits of the Gentiles.

> [Cornelius] saw in a vision manifestly, about the ninth hour of the day, an angel of God coming in unto him and saying to him: Cornelius. And he, beholding him, being seized with fear, said: What is it, Lord? And he said to him: Thy prayers and thy alms are ascended for a memorial in the sight of God. And now send men to Joppa: and call hither one Simon, who is surnamed Peter…. He will tell thee what thou must do. (Acts 10:3-6)

And Cornelius, faithful to the angel's word, was baptized with numerous other Gentiles "in the name of the Lord Jesus Christ" (Acts 10:48).

Mary of Agreda recounts that an angel, on the orders of the Mother of the Savior, "executed the mandate of his Queen and Mistress, and in the shortest space of time the rich and famous temple of Diana, the establishment of which had consumed many ages, was shattered to the dust: so sudden was the destruction and ruin of it, that it roused the astonishment and fear of the inhabitants of Ephesus."[1]

This Blessed Virgin "charged her angels to take care of all the Apostles and disciples, to console them in all their tribulations and to haste to their aid in all their difficulties."[2] Mary of Agreda adds that these sublime creatures, as ministers of the Most Hight, would contribute to the establishment of the Church.

The angels have continued fulfilling this glorious mission. "All the ancients," Bossuet says, "believed that the angels were involved in all the Church's activities."[3] Moreover, as a formidable army defends a besieged city, they protect, under the command of St. Michael, the city of their King, the Holy Church, in its perpetual war against the powers of darkness.

This sublime ministry of the holy angels was revealed to Hermas[4] in a vision that the writer reported in the first book of *The Shepherd.* The Church appeared to him in the form of a tower "built of square shining stones."[5] It was being built in a square by six young men. Thousands of men were bringing stones. Some drew them from the depths of the earth; others were lifting stones from the ground and carrying them to the six young men. These latter were receiving them and building. The extracted stones were polished and fitted together so well that one could not see where they joined. Thus, the tower looked as if it were built with a single stone. Those who brought the stones taken from the earth cast some of them aside and used the others for construction. Many of these stones were thrown far from the tower. Among them, some were full of asperities, others were cracked, and still others were round and unfit for any construction. Others that were thrown very far from the tower were falling onto the road and were soon rolled into a deserted place. Finally, others were thrown into the fire.

"Who are the young men who are building?" Hermas asked.

He was given the answer, "They are the angels God has established over all creatures; it is through them that the tower's construction will be completed."

"And the others who are bringing stones, who are they?"

"They are also the angels of God, but they are less elevated in dignity than the first. When the construction of the tower (that is to say, of the Church) is finished, all will rejoice around this edifice, and will bless God for the completion of its construction."

"And these stones, what do they signify?"

"Those which are squares and perfectly joined together represent the apostles, bishops, doctors, and all other ministers who have worked before God's elect. Those drawn from the inside of the earth represent those who suffered for the cause of God and died. The stones taken above the earth and used in construction are the new faithful ones in the faith; guided into the good by the angels, there is no sin in them. Those which are rejected and placed near the tower represent those who have sinned but will, after having done penance, enter into the construction. The children of iniquity, represented by the stones thrown onto the road and into the fire, cannot be used for the building's construction—impenitent sinners, they are going, in the company of Satan, to wander the deserts, to then fall into the eternal flames."

Travel throughout the earth, holy angels, go to the extremities of the world to seek the stones, that is to say, the souls who must enter into the construction of the edifice of the Church. Vigilant sentinels, take care that the enemy of everything good not come disperse them and throw them onto the road, so as to hurl them into the flames of hell. As in the first days of Christianity, help the apostolic men who are going to proclaim the good news to the four winds of heaven; console the friends of God in their prisons; support those who die for the faith,[6] and defend the Church of Jesus Christ against the incessant attacks of hell.

CHAPTER 8:
THE PRINCIPALITIES, GUARDIAN ANGELS OF PEOPLES. – THEIR MISSION.

He established the bounds of the nations
according to the number of the angels of God.
– Deuteronomy 32:8[1]

There are guardian angels appointed to execute the designs of Providence with respect to different peoples. Guided by the Fathers and exegetes, let us consult our Holy Books and see how we should view this teaching.

We read in Psalms 65:7 [66:7] that the Lord's "eyes behold the nations," and in Proverbs 15:3: "The eyes of the Lord in every place behold the good and the evil." And in 2 Chronicles 16:8-9, the prophet Hanani says:

> Were not the Ethiopians and the Libyans much more numerous in chariots, and horsemen, and an exceeding great multitude: yet, because thou trustedst in the Lord, he delivered them into thy hand? For the eyes of the Lord behold all the earth, and give strength to those who with a perfect heart trust in him.

Similarly, in Zechariah 4:10, there is mention of the "seven eyes of the Lord, that run to and fro through the whole earth." Finally, Revelation 5:6 states that the Lamb has "seven horns and seven eyes: which are the seven Spirits of God, sent forth into all the earth." Morris states:

> This last text seems to show that though the seven gifts of the Spirit rest upon the Lamb, yet also there are seven angelic Beings, who go forth from Him and run to and fro in the earth: and so would seem to point out how the language of Zechariah may be understood of the seven Gifts of the Spirit, though not in

such way as to exclude the intervention of ministering Spirits. For though the Word Himself is said to run very swiftly (i.e. by His operations), yet [seven eyes] is more naturally understood of Beings than of operations.... St. Ephrem gives both senses.... The passage of Chronicles might seem to imply that the nations should no longer be restrained from falling upon [the king of Judah] through the instrumentality of these Eyes, which run to and fro through the earth.... And with these passages before us, we may be inclined to think that the words of [Psalms 65:7 [66:7]] imply something as to the mode in which God exercised His superintendence over the nation—viz. through the instrumentality of angels, or *Eyes* of the Lord.[2]

All the Fathers since St. Clement of Rome have professed this teaching, and, to support it, they have not ceased to repeat this text from Deuteronomy: "When the Most High divided the nations, when he scattered the children of Adam, He established the bounds of the nations according to the number of the angels of God" (Dt 32:8).[3] Severus of Antioch says:

> If God has appointed an angel to be beside each man, why would He not also, and with greater reason, appoint one to guard nations, peoples, and cities? For as Moses says: "The Most High, having divided the peoples and set the bounds of each, appointed to watch them an equal number of angels."[4]

The Archangel Gabriel, speaking to the prophet Daniel in a vision, gives to these angels the title of princes: "But the prince of the kingdom of the Persians resisted me... and Michael, one of the chief princes, came to help me.... [T]here appeared the prince of the Greeks coming" (Dn 10:13, 20).

This belief in the existence of spirits placed to watch over peoples was not foreign to the pagans. The Persians, Syrians, and Greeks believed that beings of a superior order were stationed and appointed in various places. Plato, in his book *The Laws*, expresses the following:

Cronus was of course aware that, as we have explained, no human being is competent to wield an irresponsible control over mankind without becoming swollen with pride and unrighteousness. Being alive to this he gave our communities as their kings and magistrates, not men but spirits, beings of diviner and superior kind, just as we still do the same with our flocks of sheep and herds of other domesticated animals: we do not set oxen to manage oxen, or goats to manage goats; we, their betters in kind, act as their masters ourselves. Well, the god, in his kindness to man, did the same; he set over us this superior race of spirits who took charge of us with no less ease to themselves than convenience to us, providing us with peace and mercy, sound law and unscanted justice, and endowing the families of mankind with internal concord and happiness.[5]

Any man who reflects will see nothing objectionable in this teaching. Inasmuch as it is shown to be Catholic, it will clearly appear to possess that marvelous attribute characteristic of all Catholic truths, which is that of satisfying the desires of human nature, of making manifest the pagan systems and giving them the reality of which they only had a shadow. The erroneous systems are only imitations of the true system; they are erroneous because they are only incomplete revelations of the truth or because they are but products of diabolical prophecies. In both cases, it is only the Catholic belief which can stand on its own amongst them and test the spirits to recognize whether they are of God.

What is the dignity of the angels placed at the head of peoples and kingdoms? St. Basil says, "Just as a nation or an entire people outranks a single man, so does the dignity of an angel presiding over a nation outrank the angel appointed to guard a single man." The Principalities and Powers, which belong to the second hierarchy of angels, and form the fifth and sixth choirs, are charged with this ministry. This is the opinion of Isidore of Pelusium and Theodoret.

What is the objective of their mission?

"It might [be]," Morris says, "that so far as [different nations have retained different amounts of true doctrine], a good angel interfered in order to secure to them that amount of truth which they have preserved."[6]

Eusebius attests that they expend their efforts to lead peoples to the truth:

> Shepherds and leaders of nations, the angels unceasingly stirred men, whose coarseness could neither attain the One Who is beyond the senses, nor lift themselves up to Him on account of their weakness, to consider the bodies which appear in the sky: the sun, the moon, and the stars. Their brilliance amidst the world's beauties, their elevation, and the place they occupy, as in the vestibules of the great king, drew their gazes and revealed, through their greatness and their beauty, the knowledge of the Creator of the universe; for the invisible perfections of God, the Apostle says, as well as His eternal power and divinity, have become visible through the knowledge His works give us.[7]

But there is one name that must be called upon to be saved. Now, St. Paul says, "How then shall they call on him, in whom they have not believed? Or how shall they believe him, of whom they have not heard? And how shall they hear, without a preacher?" (Rom 10:14). We therefore see angels getting apostles to announce the good news to peoples entrusted to them. It is the guardian angel of Macedonia, the exegetes say, who appeared to St. Paul in the figure of a Macedonian and said to him, "Pass over into Macedonia, and help us" (Acts 16:9). It was again an angel dressed as an Indian who, fourteen centuries later, came to visit St. Francis Xavier and powerfully exhorted him to travel into the vast regions of the Far East.

They are still leading peoples and kingdoms to fulfill the divine plan. The four angels of whom St. John speaks in the ninth chapter of Revelation, who are placed at the Euphrates, are, St. Epiphanius says, as many nations placed on the banks of this river: They are the Assyrians, the Babylonians, the Medes, and the Persians. Daniel lists, in this order, these four empires. The Assyrians reigned first, followed by the Babylonians; the Medes came afterwards, and finally, the Persians, of whom Cyrus was the first king. Now, according to the testimony of Moses cited above, the nations are subject to the angels. It is with good reason, then, that the "voice from the four horns of the great altar, which is before the eyes of God, [says] to the sixth angel, who had the trumpet: Loose the four angels, who are bound in the great river Euphrates" (Rv 9:13-14). They have been retained there so that the nations fight amongst each other, until the time when God wants to use them to avenge the injustices done to His saints.

CHAPTER 9:
GUARDIAN ANGELS OF DIOCESES, PARISHES, CHURCHES, COMMUNITIES, AND HOUSES.

The seven stars are the angels of the seven churches.
– Revelation 1:20

There are angels appointed to watch over dioceses; this is the common teaching of the ancient Fathers, who saw in the seven angels of the churches of Asia, to which St. John received the order to write, not only the seven bishops, but also the guardian angels of these dioceses. "Two guardians and two guides," St. Ambrose says, "are appointed to each church: one visible, who is its bishop, and the other invisible, who is its guardian angel." Eusebius teaches the same thing, and St. Gregory Nazianzen, in one of his discourses, said to his people: "The care of this city has been entrusted to the angels, and I cannot doubt that it is the same for all the other churches, as John's Apocalypse teaches this to me."

The role of this angel is to assist the bishop in running his diocese. This is what St. Francis de Sales teaches us in a conversation he had one day with Mademoiselle de Blonay, who was later to be one of the first mothers of the Visitation. "God and the angels are here," he said to her,

> to delight in the good resolutions we make together and confirm them. You should know that God has given me two angels to help me: the one for Francis de Sales specifically assists me when it is a matter of correction, personal improvement, and the progress of my soul; and *the one for the Bishop of Geneva assists me when I am working for the good of the souls committed to me*; and right now, my dear daughter, I very much sense that both of my angels are assisting me, because, in working for your good, I am also working for my own.[1]

It was also believed that the provinces were entrusted to the watch of angel protectors. Upon entering the Chablais, which he was to evangelize, St. Francis de Sales greeted this land's guardian angel and asked him to come to his aid.

Our parishes and the churches of our parishes also have their faithful guardians. Every Sunday, after the aspersion,[2] we address this prayer to God: "Vouchsafe to send Thy holy angel from heaven to guard, cherish, protect, visit, and defend all that are assembled in this place." St. John Chrysostom, on the feast of the Savior's Ascension, told his faithful:

> The angels are here. Do you want to see them? Open your eyes of faith and consider the sight. For, if the open air is populated with angels, how much more this church. What does the Apostle say? That the women must have a veil over their heads on account of the angels of God... And Jacob: I saw the camp of the angels. But why camps and legions of angels on the ground? Just as a king places troops in all his cities to protect them from the enemy's attacks, so does God set His angels against the barbarous and cruel demon enemies of peace ever ready to incite wars, so that they hold them back as soon as they appear and obtain peace for us. That is why the deacons say, "Pray to the angel of peace."

Mary of Agreda recounts in her *Mystical City of God* that the Blessed Virgin recommended to the holy angels to watch over the holy places, witnesses of the sufferings and death of the Savior, and to assist with holy inspirations the faithful who would visit these places with devotion, in order that they know and appreciate the inestimable benefit of the redemption which had been worked there. She also commended to the holy angels the defense of these shrines; and if the temerity and sins of men had not prevented this favor, it is certain that the holy angels would have sheltered them from the profanations of the infidels; and still, up until the present day, they have often preserved them from threats.

The guardian angels of the temple in Jerusalem gave sensible signs of their protection by chastising the sacrilegious Heliodorus. Let us listen to Scripture:

> And these [the priests] indeed called upon almighty God, to preserve the things that had been committed to them, safe and sure for those that had committed them. But Heliodorus executed that which he had resolved on, himself being present in the same place with his guard about the treasury. But the spirit of the almighty God gave a great evidence of his presence, so that all that had presumed to obey him, falling down by the power of God, were struck with fainting and dread. For there appeared to them a horse with a terrible rider upon him, adorned with a very rich covering: and he ran fiercely and struck Heliodorus with his fore feet, and he that sat upon him seemed to have armour of gold. Moreover, there appeared two other young men beautiful and strong, bright and glorious, and in comely apparel: who stood by him, on either side, and scourged him without ceasing with many stripes. And Heliodorus suddenly fell to the ground, and they took him up covered with great darkness, and having put him into a litter they carried him out. So he that came with many servants, and all his guard into the aforesaid treasury, was carried out, no one being able to help him. (2 Mc 3:22-28)

This was how the guardian angels of Jerusalem's temple protected it from plundering.

Shortly before the destruction of this same temple, the priests heard a great noise and commotion, then the voice of a great multitude saying all at once: "Let us go out from here." It was the angels abandoning its protection.

The altars themselves have angels who guard them. Multitudes of these blessed spirits go before the tabernacles where God in the Eucharist reposes, in order to pay court there to their Sovereign. Numerous saints have seen them before the tabernacle adoring Him Who is their King and ours.

It is to these angels that we must often have recourse, in order that they supply for our neglect, our lukewarmness, and our little respect before the God of infinite majesty, and so that they appease His anger so justly aroused by so many acts of irreverence committed in our churches.

Open, O pure intelligences, open the eyes of those Christians who pay so little attention to the respect owed to the holiness of our temples.

Let us honor and make ourselves pleasing to the guardian angels of our parishes and temples. The holy bishop of Geneva, to inspire his Philothea to become "very familiar with the angels," recounts the following:

> The great Peter Faber, a first priest, preacher, and theology professor of the holy Society of Jesus, and a companion of Blessed Ignatius, its founder, returning from Germany, where he had done great service for the glory of Our Lord, and traveling through this diocese, the place of his birth, related that, having passed through many heretical places, he had received a thousand consolations for having greeted, upon approaching each parish, the angel protectors of those places, whose favors he had sensibly received, whether in escaping the ambushes of heretics, or in finding souls so mild and so docile to receiving the doctrine of salvation.[3]

Father Brydaine, the great missionary of the last century, never failed to greet, upon arrival, the guardian angel of the parish and church where he went to preach.

A fairly common custom in the old monasteries teaches us that the angels were considered guardians and protectors of these places. To cite just one example, the monastery of Saint-Riquier, which was surrounded by walls, had three gates; at each one of them there was an oratory in honor of the holy guardian angels. When St. Francis de Sales reestablished the Hermits of Mont Voiron, he prescribed to them the daily recitation of the Litany of the Holy Angels, and placed them under the protection of the choir of Principalities.

Fr. [Paul] de Barry of the Society of Jesus, in his book on devotion to the angels, recounts an incident which shows us that communities and congregations also have angels who take care of them.

As a young man from the city of Eu was very ill, two angels, full of majesty and beauty, appeared to him and consoled him until the moment of his death. One of these angels revealed to him that he was his guardian angel, and the other, the guardian of the Congregation of the Most Holy Virgin established at this city's college. The angel of the congregation told him, moreover, that he was sent on the orders of the Mother of God to assist him; it was, he added, the reward for his patience in bearing the poor treatment of his father and mother, and for his fidelity in observing the rules of the congregation.

Is there an angel appointed to guard our houses? The Church implies it when she blesses them: "We beseech you Lord Jesus… to order your angels to guard it and to drive away the enemy," meaning Satan… "Graciously hear us, Holy Lord, Almighty Father, Eternal God, send from heaven your holy angel to preserve and protect all those who live in this house."

Not even the nuptial bed is outside of what the Church confides to the guardianship of the angels.

There is one habitation subject to a thousand dangers, a thousand pitfalls, and which, more than any other, needs vigilant protection. Thus, the Church addresses this prayer to God: "Send from heaven Your angel, so that he protect against all dangers this boat, this ship, and all those it carries; make it to arrive happily at its desired port."

O God, what solicitude! And it is man who is the object of this solicitude!

CHAPTER 10:
THE GUARDIAN ANGELS OF MEN.
– OUR DUTIES IN THEIR REGARD.

For he hath given his angels charge
over thee, to keep thee in all thy ways.
– Psalms 90:11 [91:11]

If the smallest creature in the physical order, an insect or a blade of grass, lives under the protection of the angels, then man, the king of creation, must be the object of a proportional solicitude.

Therefore, each man, however small or frail he might be, has a guardian angel.

The pagans had imagined divinities appointed to watch over children; and one of their philosophers said that God gives to each man, from the moment of his birth, a spirit to initiate him into life's mysteries. As for us, says Tertullian, we believe that these are the good angels.

We find this belief among the Jews and first Christians. After Peter was miraculously freed from prison and knocked at the gate of the house of Mary, mother of John, everyone exclaimed: That cannot be he! It is his angel! (Acts 12:15).

Nothing is more explicit than the teaching of the Fathers of the Church. "With each one of us who are in the Church,"[1] Origen says, "is present a good angel who directs us, governs us, corrects us, and presents God our prayers."[2] St. Hilary uses the same expressions. "Great is the dignity of souls," St. Jerome exclaims, "for each one to have an angel deputed to guard it from its birth[!]"[3] We all have our angels close to us, St. Basil says, unless, by our evil works, we force them to go away.[4] Finally, St. Thomas Aquinas comes to add his testimony: We are, he says, like children who need masters to enlighten and direct them; God has seen to this by giving us the angels as tutors and guardians.[5]

Our Lord Himself taught us this doctrine, when, speaking of little children, He said: "Their angels in heaven always see the face of my

39

Father who is in heaven" (Mt 18:10). And the Psalmist sings, "The angel of the Lord shall encamp round about them that fear him" (Ps 33:8 [34:7]).

To which order of the heavenly militia do these angel protectors belong? According to St. Gregory the Great and St. Thomas Aquinas, they belong to the third hierarchy. It is, however, more likely, adds the Angelic Doctor, that more elevated spirits are given as guardians to souls destined for a more sublime perfection. But these are secrets which it is not yet given us to know.

Let us make ourselves worthy of their benevolent protection and be careful not to grieve them by our resistance to their inspirations. Let us say with St. Bernard: O incomprehensible charity! God was not content to send us His Son with His Spirit, He has sent His angels to serve us! These angels, these such pure spirits, so superior in power to all the kings of the earth! It is not an exhortation he gives them, it is a command he gives them, a *charge*!

What is this order then? This order to watch not only over the salvation of empires, but over us; "He hath given his angels *charge over thee*" (Ps 90:11 [91:11]), over us, dust, nothingness, miserable creatures, ungrateful and disloyal sinners!

And to what extent must their care for us be? It must extend to all the circumstances of our life, from the crib to beyond the grave. God wants them to guard us *in all our ways* (ibid.), and, when needed, for them to *bear us up in their hands* (Ps 90:12 [91:12]), like a mother carries her infant. And why? It is a little thing that a stone be in the way, and yet it is for fear that we might *dash our foot against it* (ibid.)!

O God, what solicitude for sinners who are so ungrateful, we who are little mindful of these faithful guardians' generous devotion! At what moment are they given to us? St. Jerome says:

> Before birth, the child attached to his mother's womb is in a way a part of the mother, like a fruit hanging from a tree is still part of the tree. It is therefore probable that it is the mother's guardian angel who guards the child enclosed in her womb, like one who guards a tree guards its fruit. However, through birth, is the child

not separated from the mother? Immediately, a distinct angel is sent to guard him.[6]

Let us consider in what manner they fulfill, in our regard, the ministry with which God has tasked them.

These kind guardians never depart from us in this valley of miseries and tears. The angels, St. Augustine says, enter and exit with us, and always have their eyes fixed on us and on all our works. If we stay in one place, they stop there; if we go for a walk, they accompany us; if we change countries, they follow us. Let us go wherever we like, on land or sea, they are always with us. Should a solitary withdraw into a hermitage, his good angel stays there with him; should a traveler continuously change countries, his good angel follows him everywhere.

O excessive goodness! During sleep, they watch over us and are always at our side.

That is not all: They show us the way that leads to salvation. God tells us, as He told the Jewish people long ago: "Behold, I will send my angel, who shall go before thee, and keep thee in thy journey, and bring thee into the place that I have prepared" (Ex 23:20). Wherever we are, they are at our side. If we sense some inspirations, some attractions to God's service, we ought to thank our charitable guardian.

These spirits protect us against the obstacles we encounter on the way of salvation. Like Raphael, they enchain the demons, so that we can "walk upon the asp and the basilisk" (Ps 90:13 [91:13]). As with Lot, they exercise a kind of forcefulness to pressure us to leave dangerous situations.

Let us listen to St. Basil:

> If your works are worthy of angelic protection, if your mind is lifted in contemplation through progress in the virtues, they are the fruits of these faithful friends' good care. However, to appreciate the happiness of being led by such spirits, consider well their nature; it is so powerful that a single angel is worth an entire army, a fortified encampment, a walled enclosure. These are in fact the expressions of the Holy Books, and their aptness

is worthy of attention. What purpose is an armed camp in the vicinity of a besieged city? What purpose are the walls surrounding it? They are a shield against the surprises of the enemy. Such is the protection of our guardian angel. He surrounds us in such a way that our enemies know not how to find in us an entrance. The arrows our adversaries shoot at us will lose their edge against this impenetrable wall.[7]

They offer God our prayers. Bossuet says:

When you offer God your prayers, what an effort it is to raise your minds to Him! Amidst what tempests you articulate your desires! How many vain imaginings, how many vague and disordered thoughts, and how many temporal concerns continuously assert themselves to interrupt them! Being thereby hindered, do you believe they can rise to heaven and that this feeble and languishing prayer that, amidst the many troubles frustrating it, was barely able to come forth from your hearts, might have the power to pierce the skies and reach the heights of the heavens? Christians, who could believe it? Certainly, they would fall to the ground from their own weight if God did not provide. I know well that Jesus Christ, in Whose name we offer them, makes them acceptable. But He has sent His angel, whom Tertullian calls the "angel of prayer." Thus, Raphael said to Tobit, "I offered thy prayer to the Lord" [(Tb 12:12)]. This angel comes to gather our prayers, and they ascend, St. John says, from the angel's hand to the throne of God.... They ascend from the angel's hand because this angel, joining us and giving help to our feeble prayers, lends them his wings to raise them, his strength to support them, and his fervor to animate them.[8]

That is not all. They also offer our alms, present our good works, and collect even our desires and our thoughts.

But who can describe the joy with which they carry to God tears of repentance and works of penance! It is then that goes up amongst them a cry of jubilation, and heaven, Bossuet says, resounds with their joy and with the admirable canticle through which they glorify God for the conversion of sinners. "Finally, this hardened rebel has laid down his arms, this haughty head has humbled itself, and this blind one has opened his eyes to the disorders of his past life!" O penitent soul, consider with what joy they celebrate your conversion!

Finally, the pilgrimage is over, death arrives, and it is going to strike its victim. O holy angel, defend in this terrible moment the one whom you have protected since he was in his crib. Redouble your solicitude to hold back the fury of his enemies.

Boudon says:

> Our Lord has revealed that the souls who had a special devotion to the holy angels during life received from them extraordinary assistance at the time of death, and this is quite just; for Our Lord, the God of all eternity, rewards at that moment the worthy reception of His ambassadors; His honor has an interest in this; for the good or bad treatment one gives the ambassadors of a king returns to his person, and the doctors regard as legitimate grounds for war the affront an ambassador receives. Now, the holy angels are the ambassadors of the King of Kings; what then do those people deserve who barely looked at them, barely thought about them, barely thanked them, but treated them with the utmost ingratitude…? My God, how this moment of death will teach us some things![9]

The soul leaves its body, and its angel follows it to God's tribunal. He stands near it to plead its case. If it is condemned, his ministry is over. However, if this soul descends into purgatory to expiate its neglect and cowardice in the flames, its angel visits it, consoles it, and inspires holy souls to apply to it their suffrages, that is to say, their prayers and good works.[10] On the day when it is finally purified, he will take it to heaven.

The body will also be the object of its care. A cruel tyrant had the body of the illustrious deacon St. Vincent thrown into the sea; however, informed by some angels from heaven, some seamen retrieved it and gave it burial. St. Catherine was interred by the angels on Mount Sinai.[11] But it happens sometimes that this charity that is so tender, benevolent, and obliging is found extinguished due to a long resistance, and then these charitable guardians become, according to Bossuet's expression, persecutors.

Far be it from us to dare claim that they have no compassion for the sinner. There is no help they do not bring to pick him back up. Let us run for the remedies, they say, let us stop the bleeding, let us close the wounds: "Take balm for her pain, if so she may be healed" (Jer 51:8). However, if the remedy is scorned, oh, then we will soon hear the language changed! "We would have cured Babylon," they say, "but she is not healed. Let us forsake her," abandon her; "her judgment hath reached even to the heavens" (51:9). The angels thus leave this soul prey to the demons. Even more, they urge just vengeance for the crimes it has committed: "Sharpen the arrows, fill the quivers" (51:11).

It is also the teaching of Scripture and the tradition of the Holy Fathers that the angels will declare, on the day of judgment, the crimes of the sinner.

> It is they who will one day be presented against us, as irreproachable witnesses; it is they who will confront us to convict our disloyalty. The books will be opened, Scripture tells us (Rv 20:12), the holy angels will be shown us, and in their mind and memory will be read, like in living records, an exact journal of our actions and our sinful life. It is St. Augustine who says it: that our sins are written as in a book, in the mind of the heavenly spirits who are destined to punish our sins…. Judge, judge, brethren, how horrible our sins will appear when in a single view is revealed the shame of our life and the incorruptible beauty of these pure spirits, who calling to mind their assiduous care for us, will so powerfully display the enormity of our crimes that not only heaven and earth will be angry with us, but even we will no longer be able to put up with ourselves—this is what I have gathered from St. Augustine.[12]

O you, who have long afflicted this faithful guardian by your hardness of heart, hasten to gladden him with your repentance. Do not close your ear to the voice that calls you, allow yourself to be moved by grace.

What have we done up to this point to recognize this solicitude, this zeal that is so pure, so tender, and so constant?

Let us respect the presence of our guardian angel, it is God Himself Who commands this of us: "Take notice of him… and do not think him one to be contemned" (Ex 23:21). And why? "My name is in him" (ibid.). Let us therefore, as St. Bernard says, not do in front of him what we would not dare do in front of a person we must respect.

In return for his services, let us show him our gratitude and love, since being ungrateful is forbidden us. Let us imitate the young Tobias, who did not know what proof of gratitude he could give to his guide.

Finally, let us place our confidence in him; we can depend on him; he is *prudent*, *faithful*, and *powerful*. — He is prudent; he cannot be deceived, drawing his light from the source of truth. — He is faithful without fail, for he loves us, for the sake of God by Whom we are loved, for the sake of ourselves in whom he finds the image of God, and for his own sake, since he sees us as his brethren and coheirs.

A practice of the holy bishop of Geneva will show us the value he attached to devotion towards the guardian angels, and will encourage us to imitate him. When this tireless apostle would speak with heretics, he would greet their good angels and commend himself to their protection. When he preached, he would make a long pause after the Hail Mary and look over his entire audience; and one of his canons having asked him the reason one day, he replied, "I greet the angels of each of my listeners, and I ask them to prepare the hearts of those they guard; I have received very great favors through this practice."

CHAPTER 11:

WAYS OUR GUARDIAN ANGELS TAKE CARE OF US, EXPLAINED WITH SOME EXAMPLES TAKEN FROM SCRIPTURE. – LOT. – HAGAR. – ELIJAH. – TOBIAS.

The Lord hath sent me to heal thee.
– Tobit 12:14

God decided to destroy Sodom. On the eve of that infamous city's last day, Lot, the only just man, received at his home two angels in the figure of two young men. The crowd surrounding his home demands these strangers with great cries. Lot refuses. They violently attack him, he is going to be crushed by this wicked multitude; but the angels strike with blindness those who are outside, from the least to the greatest.

Let us listen to the sacred writer:

> All that are thine, [the angels said to Lot,] bring them out of this city. For we will destroy this place; because their cry is grown loud before the Lord, who hath sent us to destroy them. So Lot went out, and spoke to his sons-in-law that were to have his daughters, and said: Arise: get you out of this place, because the Lord will destroy this city. And he seemed to them to speak as it were in jest. And when it was morning, the angels pressed him, saying: Arise, take thy wife, and the two daughters which thou hast; lest thou also perish in the wickedness of the city. And as he lingered, they took his hand, and the hand of his wife, and of his two daughters; because the Lord spared him. And they brought him forth, and set him without the city. And there they spoke to him, saying: Save thy life: look not back, neither stay thou in all the country about: but save thyself in the mountain, lest thou be also consumed. And Lot said to them: I beseech thee, my Lord, because thy servant hath found grace before thee, and thou hast magnified thy mercy, which thou hast shewn to me, in

saving my life, and I cannot escape to the mountain, lest some evil seize me, and I die: There is this city here at hand, to which I may flee. It is a little one, and I shall be saved in it. Is it not a little one, and my soul shall live? And he said to him: Behold, also in this, I have heard thy prayers, not to destroy the city for which thou hast spoken. Make haste and be saved there, because I cannot do any thing till thou go in thither. (Gn 19:12-22)

What tender solicitude! "Save your soul," our guardian angel says to each one of us; but in the eyes of a great number, he seems to be speaking "in jest"!

Look at Hagar, that poor servant woman whom Abraham had just cast out. She is in a scorching desert; her son, her dear Ishmael, is going to perish. "I will not see the boy die," she cried; and, leaving him under a tree, she goes to sit at a distance to weep. Now God, Scripture says,

heard the voice of the boy. And an angel of God called to Hagar from heaven, saying: What art thou doing, Hagar? Fear not: for God hath heard the voice of the boy, from the place wherein he is. Arise, take up the boy, and hold him by the hand: for I will make him a great nation. And God opened her eyes: and she saw a well of water, and went and filled the bottle, and gave the boy to drink. (Gn 21:17-19)

Here, Ishmael is the image of the man who is dying because he lacks the water that springs to eternal life. But his angel, through his good inspirations, leads him to the fountain of salvation.

Elijah the prophet has fled the fury of Ahab. He goes to Beersheba; from there, he moves across the desert of Arabia. After a day of walking, discouraged by the sight of his people's decadence, he

sat under a juniper tree, he requested for his soul that he might die, and said: It is enough for me, Lord, take away my soul; for I am no better than my fathers. And he cast himself down, and slept in the shadow of the juniper tree. And behold an angel of the Lord touched him, and said to him: Arise and eat. He looked, and behold there was at his head a hearth cake, and a vessel of water. And he ate and drank; and he fell asleep again. And the angel of the Lord came again the second time, and touched him, and said to him: Arise, eat; for thou hast yet a great way to go. And he arose, and ate, and drank, and walked in the strength of that food forty days and forty nights, unto the mount of God, Horeb. (1 Kgs 19:4-8)

The doctors have seen in this bread that feeds and strengthens the prophet a symbol of the Holy Eucharist. If we experience the desire to nourish ourselves with this bread, let us give thanks to our angel.

Tobit wanted to send his son to Rages, in the country of the Medes, to reclaim from Gabelus, who lived in this city, a sum of money which he lent him.

Tobias answered his father, and said: I will do all things, father, which thou hast commanded me. But how I shall get this money, I cannot tell. He knoweth not me, and I know not him. What token shall I give him? Nor did I ever know the way which leadeth thither. Then his father answered him, and said: I have a note of his hand with me, which when thou shalt shew him, he will presently pay it. But go now, and seek thee out some faithful man, to go with thee for his hire: that thou mayest receive it, while I yet live. Then Tobias going forth, found a beautiful young man, standing girded, and as it were ready to walk.

And not knowing that he was an angel of God, he saluted him, and said: From whence art thou, good young man? But he answered: Of the children of Israel. And Tobias said to him: Knowest thou the way that leadeth to the country of the Medes? And he answered: I know it; and I have often walked through all the ways thereof; and I have abode with Gabelus our brother, who dwelleth at Rages a city of the Medes, which is situate in the mount of Ecbatana. And Tobias said to him: Stay for me. I beseech thee, till I tell these same things to my father. Then

Tobias going in told all these things to his father. Upon which his father being in admiration, desired that he would come in unto him.

So going in he saluted him, and said: Joy be to thee always. And Tobit said: What manner of joy shall be to me, who sit in darkness, and see not the light of heaven? And the young man said to him: Be of good courage; thy cure from God is at hand. And Tobit said to him: Canst thou conduct my son to Gabelus at Rages, a city of the Medes? And when thou shalt return, I will pay thee thy hire. And the angel said to him: I will conduct him thither, and bring him back to thee.

And Tobit said to him: I pray thee, tell me, of what family, or what tribe art thou? And Raphael the angel answered: Dost thou seek the family of him thou hirest, or the hired servant himself to go with thy son? But lest I should make thee uneasy, I am Azarias, the son of the great Ananias. (Tb 5:1-18)

Azarias, son of *Ananias*, means in Hebrew *God's help born of God's grace*. Raphael was speaking truly. Moreover, he had taken on the features of a young Israelite who bore these names and whose family was well-known.

And Tobit answered: Thou art of a great family. But I pray thee be not angry that I desired to know thy family. And the angel said to him: I will lead thy son safe, and bring him to thee again safe.

And Tobit answering, said: May you have a good journey; and God be with you in your way; and his angel accompany you. Then all things being ready, that were to be carried in their journey, Tobias bade his father and his mother farewell: and they set out both together. And when they were departed, his mother began to weep, and to say: Thou hast taken the staff of our old age, and sent him away from us. I wish the money for which thou hast sent him, had never been. For our poverty was sufficient for us, that we might account it as riches, that we saw our son.

And Tobit said to her: Weep not. Our son will arrive thither safe, and will return safe to us; and thy eyes shall see him. For I believe that the good angel of God doth accompany him, and doth order all things well that are done about him,[1] so that he shall return to us with joy. At these words his mother ceased weeping, and held her peace. (5:19-28)

The two travelers arrived in the evening by the Tigris River. Tobias

went out to wash his feet: and behold a monstrous fish came up to devour him. And Tobias being afraid of him, cried out with a loud voice, saying: Sir, he cometh upon me. And the angel said to him: Take him by the gill, and draw him to thee. And when he had done so, he drew him out upon the land: and he began to pant before his feet. Then the angel said to him: Take out the entrails of this fish, and lay up his heart, and his gall, and his liver for thee. For these are necessary for useful medicines.... If thou put a little piece of its heart upon coals, the smoke thereof driveth away all kind of devils, either from man or from woman, so that they come no more to them. And the gall is good for anointing the eyes, in which there is a white speck: and they shall be cured. (6:2-5, 8-9)

The fish's flesh, which they salted, was used as food during the journey. When they arrived near Ecbatana,

the angel... said: Here is one whose name is Raguel, a near kinsman of thy tribe. And he hath a daughter named Sarah.... Ask her therefore of her father, and he will give her thee to wife. Then Tobias answered, and said: I hear that she hath been given to seven husbands, and they all died. Moreover I have heard, that a devil killed them.... Then the angel Raphael said to him: Hear me, and I will shew thee who they are, over whom the devil can prevail. For they who in such manner receive matrimony, as to shut out God from themselves, and from their mind, and to give themselves to their lust, as the horse and mule, which have not understanding: over them the devil hath power. But thou when thou shalt take her, go into the chamber: and for three days keep thyself continent from her, and give thyself to nothing else but to prayers with her. And on that night lay the liver of the fish on the fire: and the devil shall be driven away.... And they went to Raguel, and Raguel received them with joy. (6:11, 13-14, 16-19; 7:1)

Recognizing Tobias by his resemblance to his father, he embraced him weeping and said, "A blessing be upon thee, my son, because thou art the son of a good and most virtuous man" (7:7).

Tobias then made his request. Raguel was seized with fright thinking of Sarah's seven husbands, but the angel reassured him: "Be not afraid to give her to this man, for to him who feareth God is thy daughter due to be his wife. Therefore another could not have her" (7:12). The father then consented to the marriage.

The angel himself went to ask Gabelus for the money he owed and brought him to Tobias's wedding. — After some days, it was time for Tobias and Sarah to leave. Raguel delivered Sarah into Tobias's hands, with half of all he possessed in servants, livestock, and money. The father and mother tenderly embraced their daughter, giving her wise advice, and they wished the travelers all kinds of prosperity.

Since the young Tobias had delayed in returning at the appointed time, his parents were overwhelmed with grief. His mother, especially, was inconsolable: "Woe, woe is me! My son, why did we send thee to go to a strange country, the light of our eyes, the staff of our old age, the comfort of our life, the hope of our posterity?" (10:4). She daily went to sit on a nearby hill in order to catch sight of his return from afar. One day, she finally did see him in the distance and ran to tell her husband: "Behold thy son cometh" (11:6). At that moment, the angel said to Tobias:

As soon as thou shalt come into thy house, forthwith adore the Lord thy God; and giving thanks to him, go to thy father and kiss him. And immediately anoint his eyes with this gall of the fish, which thou carriest with thee. For be assured that his eyes shall be presently opened, and thy father shall see the light of heaven, and shall rejoice in the sight of thee.

Then the dog, which had been with them in the way, ran before; and coming as if he had brought the news, shewed his joy by his fawning and wagging his tail. And his father that was blind, rising up, began to run, stumbling with his feet: and giving a servant his hand, went to meet his son.

And receiving him kissed him, as did also his wife. And they began to weep for joy. And when they had adored God, and given him thanks, they sat down together. Then Tobias taking of the gall of the fish, anointed his father's eyes. And he stayed about half an hour: and a white skin began to come out of his eyes, like the skin of an egg. And Tobias took hold of it, and drew it from his eyes. And immediately he recovered his sight. And they glorified God both he and his wife and all that knew him....

Then Tobit called to him his son, and said to him: What can we give to this holy man, that is come with thee? Tobias answering, said to his father: ...But I beseech thee, my father, to desire him, that he would vouchsafe to accept of one half of all things that have been brought....

Then [the angel] said to them secretly: Bless ye the God of heaven, give glory to him in the sight of all that live, because he hath shewn his mercy to you.... Prayer is good with fasting and alms: more than to lay up treasures of gold.... When thou didst pray with tears, and didst bury the dead, and didst leave thy dinner, and hide the dead by day in thy house, and bury them by night, I offered thy prayer to the Lord.... And now the Lord hath sent me to heal thee.... For I am the angel Raphael, one of the seven, who stand before the Lord.

And when they had heard these things, they were troubled: and being seized with fear they fell upon the ground on their face. And the angel said to them: Peace be to you. Fear not. For when I was with you, I was there by the will of God: bless ye him, and sing praises to him…. It is time therefore that I return to him that sent me: but bless ye God, and publish all his wonderful works.

And when he had said these things, he was taken from their sight. (11:7-16; 12:1-2, 4, 6, 8, 12, 14-18, 20-21)

What a charming story! Each line contains a precious lesson. The young Tobias represents the child who has just been born. The way he must travel is life. The route is long, difficult, and unknown; moreover, it is sown with dangers. A guide is needed to reach the destination, one who is trustworthy and faithful. Raphael represents the guardian angel appointed to each man. The young Tobias escapes all dangers and completes a blessed journey which for him is the source of all kinds of happiness. But he was faithful in following all of Raphael's instructions. Alas, if so many men perish on the journey, it is not the fault of their angels—they refuse to listen to their counsels; and, despite repeated warnings, they are killed by the demon, like the seven husbands of the young Sarah. The young Tobias finally returns to his father and mother, led by Raphael, who never abandoned him. Everyone together blesses God and sings a canticle of thanksgiving. This is a figure of the Christian who, shown into his father's house, in heaven, begins singing with the one who guided him the unending *Alleluia.*

CHAPTER 12:
JACOB'S LADDER. – THE ANGELS BRING MEN GOD'S ORDERS. – THEY ARE THE EXECUTORS OF HIS WILL.

And he saw in his sleep a ladder standing upon the earth, and the top thereof touching heaven; the angels also of God ascending and descending by it.
– Genesis 28:12

Jacob fled from his brother Esau's anger. Arriving in a place where he wanted to rest after sunset, he took a stone, placed it under his head, and went to sleep. And he saw in a dream a ladder standing on the earth and whose top reached heaven, and the angels of God were going up and down it. And the Lord was leaning upon the ladder.

Why are these angels going up and down? And what is meant by this mysterious ladder linking earth to heaven? Is this not a representation of the continuous back and forth between heaven and earth to execute God's orders? Bossuet says:

> They go down from God to men, they go back up from men to God; because the holy alliance they have renewed with us tasks them with a double ambassadorship. They are God's ambassadors to men, and they are men's ambassadors to God. St. Bernard says, "What a marvel! Christians, can you believe it? They are not only the angels of God, but also the angels of men."[1]

God is sufficient unto Himself: His greatness makes Him present everywhere; His wisdom extends from one end of the universe to the other; His providence effortlessly directs all beings towards their end, and nothing resists His will. However, since He wanted it thus and since this determination entered into the plan He established in creating the worlds, He made use of the angels, and He makes use of them still to execute the designs of His providence.

54

Thus, besides that ordinary ministry of which we have already spoken, God confides to them, so to speak, an extraordinary ministry which consists in carrying, interpreting, and executing His orders either for salvation or for chastisement.

Scripture is filled with examples which prove this truth.

Moses drives his father-in-law Jethro's flock to the inner parts of the desert. The Lord sends His angel. He appears in a flame of fire out of the midst of a bush. "Come," he says to Moses in God's name, "I will send thee to Pharaoh, that thou mayst bring forth my people, the children of Israel out of Egypt" (Ex 3:10). Later, in accordance with St. Paul's testimony,[2] he calls him amidst thunder and lightning from Sinai, saying to him, "Stand thou here with me: and I will speak to thee all my commandments, and ceremonies and judgments. Which thou shalt teach them, that they may do them in the land, which I will give them for a possession" (Dt 5:31). Scripture, it is true, says that God Himself gave Moses His laws; however, St. Denis explains the sense of these words. This doctor states:

> If someone means that God revealed Himself immediately and by Himself to pious personages, let that person know, through positive assertions from Scripture, that no one on earth has either seen or will see the inmost essence of the Godhead, but that God appeared to the saints in the manner suitable to them and through visions they could bear. Now, since these visions relay an image of the divinity, at least as much as that which has a form can resemble that which is above all forms and thereby raise to God those to whom they are granted, theology, in its wisdom-filled language, calls them theophanies.... Now, our glorious ancestors received through the ministry of heavenly powers the understanding of these divine visions.[3]

St. Augustine teaches the same thing in his book *On the Trinity*:

> All apparitions with which the Lord deigned, according to times and circumstances, to favor the Patriarchs and the Prophets, took

place through the mediation of creatures. I certainly would not know how to explain how God employed His angels in these, but I do not hesitate to say that they worked these different apparitions. And in saying this, I am not speaking on my own…. Here, in fact, I am relying on the authority of the Holy Scriptures.[4]

It is the angel of the Lord who comes to draw the plan of attack on Jericho. It is also he who, later, sends Gideon to deliver his people from the yoke of the Midianites: "The Lord is with thee, O most valiant of men…. Go… and thou shalt deliver Israel out of the hand of Midian. Know that I have sent thee…. I will be with thee" (Jgs 6:12, 14, 16).

We also see the Lord's angels come to announce to Abraham the birth of Isaac, to the wife of Manoah the birth of Samson, to Zachary the birth of John the Baptist, the precursor of the Messiah, and to Mary the birth of the Savior of men.

But now the great mysteries of grace are going to be accomplished: The Eternal Word is going to come down to earth to unite Himself to humanity. The angels will be present and will glorify, honor, and serve this humanity divinized in the Word. We see them, in fact, appear in the principal events of Jesus's life. On Christmas Day, they go find the shepherds of Bethlehem, purified by the repose and silence of solitude, to announce to them the Savior's birth, and immediately, Scripture says, a numerous army of the heavenly militia begins singing in the air this well-celebrated hymn: "Glory to God in the highest, and on earth peace to men of good will" (Lk 2:14). "Jesus Himself," St. Denis says,

> the superessential cause of the super-heavenly substances, in taking our nature, without alteration of His divine nature, did not scorn accepting the order of things established for humanity; He submitted Himself to the instructions His Father prescribed Him through the ministry of the angels.[5]

It is, in fact, at the order of an angel, that He goes into exile and stays in Egypt for long years. It is also at the order of an angel that the divine

Exile returns to His homeland. "I do not need to remind you," St. Denis says,

> that an angel strengthened Jesus in His agony, and that Jesus Himself was called the Angel of Great Counsel when, to happily work our redemption, He took rank among the interpreters of the Godhead; for, as He Himself said as a messenger and angel, everything He learned from the Father He has shown to us.[6]

Messenger of the glory of the risen Jesus, they appeared to the holy women who had come to give their Divine Master one last token of their love; and, on the day when the Man-God enters into the glory He acquired by His sufferings, they announce that this Jesus will come in the same manner that they saw Him go up, in order to judge men.

Ministers of the graces of God, the angels are also the executors of His vengeance.

They expel Adam and Eve, and a cherubim is assigned to guard the entrance and to forbid access to guilty man.[7] God wants to punish the five infamous cities, and He tasks His angels with dropping the fire of His anger upon them. The *exterminating* angel, to punish the obstinacy of Pharaoh, strikes in one night all the firstborn of the Egyptians. When David had sinned, the Eternal One sent pestilence to Israel, and seventy thousand men died of it, from Dan to Beersheba. The angel whom God sent to strike the people with this plague, raised between heaven and earth, was already stretching his sword over Jerusalem—David saw him and lowered his face to the ground, and with him all the ancients of the people. And the Lord, moved with compassion, said to the angel, "It is enough. Now hold thy hand" (2 Sm 24:16). It is again the angel of the Lord who, in one night, kills one hundred eighty-five thousand warriors of the army of Sennacherib, the king of Assyria, and who strikes Herod Agrippa when he wants to be honored like a god.

One cannot read without trembling the listing of chastisements by which the angels of God will punish the earth, as St. John reports in the Apocalypse. There are first seven angels to whom are given seven trumpets:

And the first angel sounded the trumpet: and there followed hail and fire, mingled with blood: and it was cast on the earth. And the third part of the earth was burnt up: and the third part of the trees was burnt up: and all green grass was burnt up.

And the second angel sounded the trumpet: and, as it were, a great mountain, burning with fire, was cast into the sea. And the third part of the sea became blood. And the third part of those creatures died which had life in the sea: and the third part of the ships was destroyed.

And the third angel sounded the trumpet: and a great star fell from heaven, burning as it were a torch. And it fell on the third part of the rivers and upon the fountains of waters: And the name of the star is called Wormwood. And the third part of the waters became wormwood. And many men died of the waters, because they were made bitter.

And the fourth angel sounded the trumpet: and the third part of the sun was smitten, and the third part of the moon, and the third part of the stars, so that the third part of them was darkened. And the day did not shine for a third part of it: and the night in like manner. And I beheld: and heard the voice of one eagle flying through the midst of heaven, saying with a loud voice: Woe, Woe, Woe to the inhabitants of the earth, by reason of the rest of the voices of the three angels, who are yet to sound the trumpet!

And the fifth angel sounded the trumpet. (Rv 8:7-9:1)

Then the pit of the abyss is opened, smoke rises from it, and the sun and the air are darkened. Locusts coming from this smoke go throughout the earth and torment for five months the men who do not have the sign of God on their foreheads.

"And the sixth angel sounded the trumpet" (9:13), and the four angels who are bound upon the great river of the Euphrates are loosened "for an hour, and a day, and a month, and a year: for to kill the third part of men" (9:15).

Finally, another angel appeared. "And he set his right foot upon the sea, and his left foot upon the earth... And when he had cried, seven thunders uttered their voices" (10:2-3).

St. John says elsewhere:

> And I heard a great voice out of the temple, saying to the seven angels: Go and pour out the seven vials of the wrath of God upon the earth.
>
> And the first went and poured out his vial upon the earth. And there fell a sore and grievous wound upon men who had the character of the beast: and upon them that adored the image thereof.
>
> And the second angel poured out his vial upon the sea. And there came blood as it were of a dead man: and every living soul died in the sea.
>
> And the third poured out his vial upon the rivers and the fountains of waters. And there was made blood....
>
> And the fourth angel poured out his vial upon the sun. And it was given unto him to afflict men with heat and fire. And men were scorched with great heat: and they blasphemed the name of God....
>
> And the fifth angel poured out his vial upon the seat of the beast. And his kingdom became dark: and they gnawed their tongues for pain....
>
> And the sixth angel poured out his vial upon the great river Euphrates and dried up the water thereof....
>
> And the seventh angel poured out his vial upon the air. And there came a great voice out of the temple from the throne, saying: It is done. And there were lightnings and voices and thunders: and there was a great earthquake, such an one as never had been since men were upon the earth. (16:1-4, 8-10, 12, 17-18)

On Judgment Day, God will make use of His angels to work the resurrection. St. Paul says, "As soon as the signal will be given by the voice of the Archangel and by the sound of the trumpet of God, the Lord will descend from heaven and will appear with His angels, ministers of His power"[8] and of His justice, as Our Lord Himself declared: "The Son of man shall send His angels... [who] shall separate the wicked from among the just... and they shall gather out of his kingdom all scandals, and them that work iniquity. And shall cast them into the furnace of fire: there shall be weeping and gnashing of teeth."[9]

CHAPTER 13:

THE DEMONS. – THEIR EXISTENCE. – THEIR NAMES. – THEIR SIN. – THEY ARE CAST FROM HEAVEN. – THEIR DWELLING PLACE.

Michael and his angels fought with the dragon.
– Revelation 12:7

Before speaking of the power of the angels over demons, it is useful to go into some details about the *gods of this world*,[1] as St. Paul calls them. In learning about them, we will learn to fight them and fear them.

There are evil spirits that we call demons—this is a dogma of the Faith supported by the clear evidence in Holy Scripture and by the Church's infallible verdict.

It is also a truth recognized by the unanimous assent of nations and peoples. Tertullian expresses it this way:

> We say then that there are a certain kind of spiritual substances existing in nature, which go by the name of demons, and the name is not of a modern stamp; the name and the thing being both well known to the philosophers, for Socrates undertook nothing without the privy council of his demon. And no wonder, when this familiar is said to have kept him close company from his childhood to the conclusion of his life, continually, no doubt, injecting dissuasives from virtue. The poets likewise talk of demons, and even the illiterate vulgar frequently apply to them when they are in the cursing mood; for by a secret instigation on their minds when they invoke these demons, in their imprecations, they do in effect invoke Satan, who is the prince of the evil spirits.[2]

In all times, people have believed in the devil, as he is made known in revelation, and people feared him. For our ancestors, the devil was not an allegory or a myth, but rather a real and personal being. He was not an inoffensive, powerless being, but rather a harmful being, *unceasingly prowling around us to devour us.*[3] Thus, the first fright of the child like the final fear of the elderly person was the devil. But today, according to [Pierre] Nicole, "men are so vain in their blindness that they take pride in not fearing [the demons] and almost in not believing in them. It is a weakness of the mind, according to many, to attribute to the demons some effect, as if they were in the world to do nothing in it."[4]

The devil's goal is to make himself denied, for whoever denies Satan, denies Christianity; whoever denatures Satan, denatures Christianity; whoever makes a joke of Satan, makes a joke of the Church; and whoever denies Satan's evil activity over men and creatures accuses mankind of mental derangement and destroys history.

Let us try to make Satan known, in the light of the Faith and of reason.

To name is to define. To define is to express the distinct qualities of a person or thing. Let us ask Scripture what names suit this evil spirit.

Scripture calls him *dragon* and *great dragon*. This term designates an animal monstrous in its size, terrible in its cruelty, frightful in its form, and formidable in its swiftness of motion and in its penetrating sight. The dragon of Scripture is all of this, and this dragon is the fallen angel.[5]

Scripture calls him *serpent* and *old serpent*. A serpent by way of craftiness, a serpent by way of venom, a serpent by way of strength, and a serpent by way of the power of fascination, he "seduceth the whole world" (Rv 12:9) and makes himself worshipped in this form, in antiquity among the great peoples, as today among the blacks of Africa.[6]

Scripture calls him a *vulture* and *bird of prey*.[7] A vulture due to the region he inhabits, due to the skillfulness and promptness with which he discovers his prey and takes it into his nest, due to the cruelty with which he sucks its blood and devours its flesh.

Scripture calls him a roaring *lion*, always seeking prey. Pride, vigilance, might, and cruelty—such is the lion, and such is the fallen angel.[8]

The Hebrew calls him the unclean *goat,* because he spreads an odor of death. It is ordinarily in this form that he presents himself to the gaze and adoration of conjurers.

Scripture calls him *beast,* the beast par excellence, who unites all the characteristics of the different animals in which we have just personified the fallen angel.

He is called *murderer,* murderer par excellence, murderer of the Incarnate Word, murderer of the angels, murderer of the saints, murderer of man in general, a murderer always, a murderer by desire and in fact, a murderer of the body and of the soul.

To indicate Lucifer, the sacred oracles say the *demon.* This name signifies intelligent, knowing, and seeing. His frightening knowledge of natural things and his no less frightening knowledge of man and of each man have given him this name.

He is called *devil,* or rather *the devil.* Odious above all, this name signifies *calumniator.* Calumniator through lies, of which he is the father (he is the living lie), calumniator through the outrage and blasphemy he unceasingly launches at the face of the Word made flesh and of all those belonging to Him.

He is called *Satan,* meaning adversary, enemy of God, of angels, of man, and of all creatures; he is a formidable and implacable enemy.[9]

Such is the fallen angel.

Since God is good, everything which comes from his hands can only be good. Nothing is evil except by its own fault. Thus, the evil angels were free. Yes, they were tested, and they fell.

Let us listen to a great theologian:

> Lucifer, in considering the beauty, nobility, and dignity of his nature, and his superiority over all creatures, forgot God's grace, to which he owed everything. Moreover, he disregarded the means of achieving the perfect felicity God reserves for His friends. Bloated with pride, he strove for this supreme felicity, and for the highest of the heavens—the lot destined for human nature which was to be united hypostatically to the Son of God. He envied this place which in Scripture is called the right hand

of God, was jealous of human nature, and communicated his
desire to all the angels, whose leader he was by nature.

Just as he was superior to the [other] angels by reason of his
natural gifts, he also wanted to be superior in the supernatural
order. He thus insinuated to them to choose him as the mediator
and means of arriving at supernatural beatitude, in place of the
Incarnate Word, Who was predestined from all eternity for this
mission. Such is the meaning of these words [from Isaiah 14:13-
14]: *I will ascend into heaven. I will exalt my throne above the
stars of God. I will sit in the mountain of the covenant, in the
sides of the north. I will ascend above the height of the clouds. I
will be like the Most High.*[10]

And a portion of the angels, one third of them according to exegetes,
answered to these cries of revolt against God.

However, faithful to his creator, "Michael and his angels fought,"
and the dragon, Scripture says, "was cast unto the earth" (Rv 12:7, 9).

What is this earth? St. Peter, speaking of the fall of Lucifer and his
accomplices, says that God cast them into hell where they are tormented
and held in reserve until Judgment Day (2 Pt 2:4). Elsewhere, he tells
us they unceasingly prowl around us to devour us (1 Pt 5:8).

St. Paul calls Satan the "prince of the power of this air" (Eph 2:2)
and warns us to put on the armor of God so that we can resist his attacks
(Eph 6:11).

Despite this apparent contradiction, the two apostles are right. St.
Thomas gives us, after all the doctors of the Church, the reason for this
double abode:

> But man's welfare is disposed by Divine providence in two
> ways: first of all, directly, when a man is brought unto good and
> withheld from evil; and this is fittingly done through the good
> angels. In another way, indirectly, as when anyone assailed is
> exercised by fighting against opposition. It was fitting for this
> procuring of man's welfare to be brought about through the
> wicked spirits, lest they should cease to be of service in the

natural order. Consequently a twofold place of punishment is due to the demons: one, by reason of their sin, and this is hell; and another, in order that they may tempt men, and thus the darksome atmosphere is their due place of punishment.

Now the procuring of men's salvation is prolonged even to the judgment day: consequently, the ministry of the angels and wrestling with demons endure until then. Hence until then the good angels are sent to us here; and the demons are in this dark atmosphere for our trial: although some of them are even now in hell, to torment those whom they have led astray; just as some of the good angels are with the holy souls in heaven. But after the judgment day all the wicked, both men and angels, will be in hell, and the good in heaven.[11]

CHAPTER 14:

HIERARCHY OF DEMONS. – THE SEVEN EVIL SPIRITS. – NUMBER OF DEMONS. – THEIR QUALITIES. – THEIR POWER.

> *Then he goeth, and taketh with him seven*
> *other spirits more wicked than himself.*
> *– Matthew 12:45*

The mutual subordination between the angels, St. Thomas says, was, before the fall, a natural condition of their existence. Now, when they fell, they lost nothing of their condition or natural gifts. Thus, all remain in the superior or inferior orders to which they belong.[1] Consequently, the actions of some are subject to the actions of others, and there exists among them a veritable hierarchy or natural subordination; however, "that the inferior are subject to the superior, is not for the benefit of the superior, but rather to their detriment; because since to do evil belongs in a pre-eminent degree to unhappiness, it follows that to preside in evil is to be more unhappy."[2]

Satan is the *ape of God*, St. Bernard says. Attending Lucifer are seven demons, ministers of the seven capital sins. They immerse their intellects within the depths of his malice, set ablaze their hatred within his own fire, and transmit to the inferior demons the orders of the master.

Although the fallen angels, according to the Angelic Doctor, are less numerous than the good angels, spiritual creatures almost infinitely surpass material creatures in number, which means that the demons are incomparably more numerous than men. Cassian says:

> Their number is such that we should bless Providence for having hidden them from our eyes. The sight of their multitudes, their terrible movements, and the horrible forms they take at will, when it is permitted them, would jolt men with an unbearable fright. Such a spectacle would either make men die or make them eviler each day. Corrupted by their examples, they would

imitate their perversity. Between men and these hideous powers of the air would form a familiarity and relations which would result in universal demoralization.[3]

Having fallen from so high, the demons' natural abilities have not in any way been harmed. Everything in them remains intact. Bossuet says, "That sharp and vigorous action, that strong constitution, that delicate and powerful intellect, and that vast array of knowledge remain with them."[4]

Let us then regard as considerably significant advantages in the eyes of God the knowledge, the great intellect, and the other gifts of nature that He has left to His most cruel enemies.

The demons cannot err in any science; error is only possible for them in things of a supernatural order.

St. Thomas says, "Many things concerning Divine mysteries are made known by the holy angels to the bad angels, whenever the Divine justice requires the demons to do anything for the punishment of the evil; or for the trial of the good."[5]

As for the future, the demons' knowledge far surpasses our own. They know in their causes, with certainty, things that will necessarily happen. Through conjecture, they know contingent future events that happen most often, all the more surely since they know causes more universally and more perfectly. But the knowledge of strictly fortuitous future events is reserved for God alone.

There are no distances for the demons. Within the blink of an eye and at will, they are present at the most opposite points in space. Thus, when God asks Satan, "Whence comest thou?" Satan answers, "I have gone round about the earth" (Jb 1:7). Would it be possible to deny the agility of these spiritual beings when electricity, in the blink of an eye, transports our thoughts and our words to all corners of the world?

Just as the body is subject to the soul, the visible world is subject to angelic power. Beneficial in the good angels, this power is essentially evil in the demons.

This evil action is recognized by tradition and experience. "Genuine evidence for this belief," Mgr. Gaume says, "shows itself in each page of mankind's religious, political, and domestic history. To treat it as fable would be folly. To see crazy people everywhere is to be crazy oneself."[6]

Porphyry says:

> The demons delight in everything that is disordered and incoherent—they enjoy our errors. The bait they use to draw in the crowd is the inflaming of the passions, sometimes through the love of pleasures, sometimes through the love of riches, of power, of voluptuousness, or of vainglory. This is how they incite seditions, wars, and everything that follows from them.[7]

CHAPTER 15:
DEMONS APPOINTED TO EACH NATION, CITY, MAN, AND CREATURE. – NATURE AND SCOPE OF DEMONIC ACTIVITY. – IT IS REGULATED BY GOD'S POWER.

Woe to the earth and to the sea, because the devil is come down unto you, having great wrath.
– Revelation 12:12

We have seen that holy angels are appointed to each nation, city, man, and creature in order to watch over them, and to lead them to their final end. Satan, in his implacable malice, also appoints to each nation, city, and man, from the moment they exist, an individual demon, tasked with perverting them.

This Satanic dispatching is a fact of universal history. The pagans had full knowledge of it. Moreover, they knew that by means of certain mysterious formulas they could invoke these demons, which they called tutelary gods, and draw them into the enemy camp. Hence, the custom among different peoples of the east and west of chaining statues, so that the invocation might not draw them from their shrine or from the city placed under their protection. Plato, Pausanias, Plutarch, and Macrobius report incidents which leave no room for doubt.

Furthermore, it is a truth recognized not only by the Church, but also by pagan antiquity, that each man has an individual demon.

Scripture is frightening when it gives the nomenclature of demons destined to foment each passion. It names, among others: spirits of divination, *spiritus divinationis*; spirits of jealousy, *spiritus zelotypiæ*; spirits of evil, *spiritus nequam*; spirits of lying, *spiritus mendacii*; spirits of storms, *spiritus procellarum*; spirits of vengeance, *spiritus ad vindictam*; spirits of fornication, *spiritus fornicationis*; unclean spirits, *spiritus immundi*; and spirits of illness, *spiritus infirmitatis*.[1] Among the demons, the roles are shared.

Scripture also speaks of demons of the day and of the night. There are some that the prophets call satyrs, lamias, birds of the night, ostriches, and hedgehogs.[2] The psalms name others as asps and basilisks.[3] The New Testament calls others lions, scorpions, dragons, and princes of the air.

There is no visible creature that would not have a demon specially appointed to hold it captive. The devil, Tertullian says, likes to repose in the waters, hidden springs, lakes, and underground streams.[4] Porphyry, as quoted by Eusebius, says:

> It should be known that every dwelling is full of them. That is why we purify it by driving them away every time we want to pray to God. Moreover, all bodies are filled with them; for they particularly relish certain kinds of food. Thus, when we go to eat, they do not only assume a place near our persons, they also attach themselves to our bodies. Hence, there is the custom of lustrations, the principal goal of which is not so much to invoke God as to drive away the demons. They especially delight in blood and impurities.[5]

This was said by a pagan, a prince of pagan theology. Among all the truths that shine in this passage, let us say with one modern writer[6] that there is one we wish to highlight in passing: the profound philosophy of saying grace before eating, and the no less profound stupidity of those who despise doing so.

The Angelic Doctor teaches, according to St. Augustine, that "demons are enticed through various kinds of stones, herbs, trees, animals, songs, [and] rites."[7] They pretend to be the souls of the dead,[8] and they appear often in the form of animals which designate their qualities.[9]

Tertullian says they make oracles out of children, goats, and boards.[10] Have we not seen, in our own time, turning tables and other practices causing a stir in both the Old World and the New World?

What is more famous, in history, than this wood which comes to life and renders oracles? What is better authenticated than the oak trees of Dodona?

However, on this matter, let us consult the most competent authority, the surest and most authoritative voice of orthodox doctrine, the most authentic monument of tradition: the Roman Ritual. The Ritual opens with exorcisms on the newborn who is presented for baptism, and on the elements that are to serve for the child's regeneration. The Church exorcises the water and blesses it. She exorcises and blesses bread, wine, oil, fruit, houses, fields, and flocks. Why, if not to free them from the powers of darkness?

If to the Roman Ritual we join the Roman Pontifical, another monument of the Catholic faith, we shall understand the Satanic action over man and over the world. What is it, in fact, that is taught in these books?

That the demons can contaminate the air and the water, and spread pestilence;

That they can stir up storms, send cyclones, waterspouts, hail, lightning, or in a word, put the elements at the service of their eternal hatred;

That they can infest houses, pollute them, and make staying in them painful and dangerous; that they can also infest solitary places, making them the hearth for contagious illnesses, or the theatre for disturbing molestations;

That they can attack man in his body, bind him with visible and invisible bonds, sweep down on him in great numbers, and appear to him in the form of ghosts and phantoms;

That they can lend man their evil power, take possession of him and dwell in him, communicate to his mind knowledge and to his body superhuman powers and abilities;

That they can harass him in a terrible manner in his final moments; and fight against his soul's passage to blessed eternity upon its leaving the body.

The human mind, Bossuet says, is the only retreat where Satan appears to refresh himself. This old adulterer, St. Augustine says, has no delights other than corrupting chaste souls. Given that the majesty of God is inaccessible to his anger, Satan shoots at us, living images of our Creator, all the arrows of his fury—just as a powerless enemy who is unable to get the one he is after is seen satisfying his vengeance by ripping up that person's picture. This is how Satan acts. He stirs up heaven and earth to incite enemies against God and to make them imitators of his audacious and temerarious rebellion. To destroy all, after having ruined himself, to envelop the world with him in a common ruin, this is the goal of his efforts.

This power is restrained and overseen by God. "God regulates the demon's power," says [Pierre] Nicole, "and does not allow him to always make use of it as he pleases."[11] The devil, it must be pointed out, is naturally man's tempter. He tempts even when he is sent to punish. However, his intention is other than that of God Who sends him—the devil punishes out of hatred and jealousy, whereas God sends him to avenge the rights of divine justice.

This permission from God adds nothing to the demons' power; it only unleashes it and determines its use. Through the mediation of the good angels, God indicates to them in which places and to which persons they are to make their dreadful presence felt, and the type or limit of chastisements or trials of which they are to be the ministers.

Scripture and Church history provide us a multitude of proofs for this double role of the demons: punishing and testing.

Let us cite some examples:

An evil spirit from the Lord came upon Saul and troubled him to punish him for having wanted to exercise priestly functions (1 Sm 16:14; 18:10).[12] — A spirit of lying was also sent by God to deceive Ahab, as punishment for his hypocrisy (1 Kgs 22:20-23).

The Lord told Satan one day, concerning Job, "Behold, all that he hath is in thy hand; only put not forth thy hand upon his person" (Jb 1:12). Everyone knows how Satan used this permission from God; everyone also knows Job's admirable patience. — The devil received a similar mission with respect to St. Paul. This great apostle said, "And lest the greatness of the revelations should exalt me, there was given me a sting of my flesh, an angel of Satan, to buffet me" (2 Cor 12:7).

Church history presents a thousand shining examples of the same delegation. Is anything more famous than the temptations of St. Anthony and the desert fathers? God allowed Satan to act in order to show the world the proven virtue of His faithful servants.

What power! Is this not enough to terrify our souls? Therefore, God has not left us alone—He has given us powerful means to fight our terrible adversary. We shall see so in the following chapter.

CHAPTER 16:

THE DEVIL DEFEATED BY THE ANGELS. – WAR OF THE ANGELS AND DEMONS IN THE DEFENSE OF MAN.

And he laid hold on the dragon… and bound him.
– Revelation 20:2

"God is faithful," St. Paul says, and "will not suffer you to be tempted above that which you are able" (1 Cor 10:13). He will even have you draw profit from temptation in order to ensure your perseverance. St. Ephrem, to elucidate this consoling truth, expresses it this way:

> If the potter knows how much cooking his vases require so that he leaves them in the oven for only the exact time needed to give each one its appropriate solidity and beauty, all the more reason God will only leave us in the fire of temptation for the time required to purify and embellish us.[1]

Lucifer's fierce war against us will turn to his shame and to our glory. "Do you see him," St. Athanasius exclaims, [as paraphrased by Mgr. Jean-Joseph Gaume,] "this such proud dragon trampled underfoot by Anthony like a sparrow, daring not to make a move or bear his appearance!"[2]

But it will be especially through the help of the holy angels that we shall succeed in vanquishing Satan. St. Thomas Aquinas says that the power of the angels is such that the least among them orders Lucifer himself and makes him obey him.

Scripture provides us multiple examples as proof of this truth.

It is recounted, in the book of Tobit, that the Archangel Raphael, having seized the demon that was tormenting the young Sarah, took him to the desert of Upper Egypt, where he bound him (Tb 8:3).

According to the apostle St. Jude's testimony,[3] the devil, in his efforts to lead the Israelites into idolatry, wanted to display the body of

Moses, in order to get this people to render him divine honors. But he was vanquished, the holy fathers say, and the body of the great lawgiver was buried by the angels in a place which has never been discovered.

St. John saw descending from heaven an angel "having the key of the bottomless pit and a great chain in his hand. And he laid hold on the dragon... and bound him.... And he cast him into the bottomless pit and shut him up and set a seal upon him" (Rv 20:1-3).

The same apostle shows us, in the sixteenth chapter of Revelation, seven angels pouring out the seven vials of the wrath of God. The fifth angel, he says, "poured out his vial upon the seat of the beast" (of Satan) "and his kingdom became dark" (Rv 16:10).

The Church recognizes the angels have this power. In her prayers, she beseeches the Lord to send them to put to flight the malignant spirits infesting the dwellings of men. "Send," she says,

> Thy angel Raphael, who of old expelled from Sarah and Tobias the death-giving demon; have him again expel him very far from all souls who piously honor the true God, far from beds, rooms, cellars, stables, and every apartment in this house, in which dwell and repose Thy faithful servants; have him expel him so that he can no longer fill with terror, or vex in any manner, those Thou hast anointed with the unction of Thy holy chrism.[4]

And elsewhere: "Surround, Lord, this house, and confide it to the guardianship of Thy angels... so that the son of iniquity cannot do harm to Thy servants."[5] And also: "May Thy holy angels dwell in this house, may they expel the persecuting angels, and may they preserve in peace its faithful inhabitants."[6] These invocations, the Church does not tire of repeating them again and again, trusting in the power of the angels to vanquish Satan.

One cannot read Psalm 90 [91] without admiring the goodness of God. The infernal powers will be unable to harm the man who puts his trust in the Lord, neither through their snares nor their attacks. All the arrows they shoot at him will fall at his side, without doing him any harm. He will walk with impunity upon the asp and the basilisk, figures of demons, because God "hath given his angels charge over [him], to keep [him] in all [his] ways. In their hands they shall bear [him] up, lest [he] dash [his] foot against a stone" (Ps 90:11-12 [91:11-12]).

We find details of the greatest interest in the writing of Mary of Agreda concerning the conflict between men's guardian angels and the tempting demons:

> This defense [by the holy angels], like the persecution of the devil, commences from the womb in which we receive being, and continues until our souls are presented at the tribunal of God to be adjudged to the state merited by each one. At the moment in which a human being is conceived, the Lord commands the angels to stand guard over it and its mother.[7] Afterwards, at the right time, He assigns a particular angel as its guardian.... From the very beginning the angels enter into violent combat with the demons for the protection of the souls committed to their care. The demons contend that they have jurisdiction over the creature, because it is conceived in sin, a child of malediction, unworthy of grace and divine favor.... The angel refutes them by maintaining that it was conceived according to the laws of nature, over which hell has no power; that, if it is conceived in sin, it was due to its human nature, by default of the first parents and not of its own free will; and that, even if conceived in sin, God has created it to know, praise and serve Him, and, by virtue of his Passion, to merit eternal glory; and that these high ends are not to be frustrated by the mere will of the demons.
>
> These enemies also argue, that in the begetting of the human being its parents had not the proper intention or rightful purpose, that they committed excess and sin in the act of generation.[8] This is the strongest argument which the devils can advance for their right over human creatures yet in the womb; for without a doubt, sins make the child unworthy of divine protection and justly hinder its conception. Yet, although this latter often happens and a number of human beings are conceived without ever seeing the light, ordinarily the holy angels prevent such a sad result. If they

are legitimate children, the angels allege that the parents have received the Sacraments and blessings of the Church; likewise, that they have some virtues, such as having given alms, being kind, having practised some devotions or good works. The holy angels avail themselves of these things as powerful arms to ward off the devils and defend their charges. Over illegitimate children the combat waxes more difficult; the enemy exercises a greater right, because in the begetting of such children, wherein God has been so grievously offended, the enemies obtain a greater right and the parents justly deserve rigorous chastisement. Hence, in defending and preserving illegitimate children, God manifests his most liberal mercy in a special manner. The angels base their arguments against the demon on this mercy, and that, after all, the children are the results of natural causes, as I have said above. If the parents have no merits of their own, neither any virtues, but are sullied by sins and vices, then the holy angels refer to the merits found in the forefathers of the child, in its brothers or relations; to the prayers of its friends and acquaintances, and that it is no fault of the child if the parents are sinners or have committed excess in its generation. They also contend that those children, if they live, may reach a high degree of virtue and holiness, and that the demon has no right to hinder them from arriving at the knowledge and love of their Creator....

The persecutions of the demons and the defense of the angels continue at the birth of the child. At that hour the mortal hatred of this serpent exceeds itself, especially with those children who might receive Baptism; because he strives to hinder it by any means in his power.... [I]t seems, that the angels, after the child has left the shelter of its mother's womb and is unable either to protect itself or to secure from its elders sufficient protection against so many perils, are filled with great anxiety and thus begin to solicit for it direct interference of God. Hence the care of the elders is very often supplemented by that of the holy angels, shielding the child in its sleep, when alone, and in other situations, in which many children would perish, if they were not protected by their angels....

Words cannot describe what and how great are the astuteness and diligence of the demon in order to ruin man by inducing him to commit some sin, as soon as he comes to the years of discretion and the use of reason.... Not less active is the diligence and care of the holy angels to prevent such damage and defend us from the devil.... In conducting this defense they enter into great disputes with the demons; because those malign spirits allege all the sins of the parents against the children and likewise the wrongful doings of the children themselves; for if they are not guilty, the demons claim that their actions are the result of his own activity and therefore that he has a right to continue them in their souls. If the child, on coming to the use of reason, commences to sin, they put up a great fight to prevent the good angels from withdrawing them from evil. The good angels on their part allege the virtues of the parents and forefathers, and the good actions of the children themselves. Even if it were no more than that of having pronounced the name of Jesus or Mary as taught them by their parents, they bring this as a defense as their having begun to honor the name of their Lord and of their Mother; and likewise, if they practice other devotions, or know the Christian prayers and recite them. Of all this the angels avail themselves as serviceable arms in our defense against the demon; for with each good action we rob the devils of some of the right acquired over us by original sin, and still more by actual sin.[9]

As soon as man enters into the use of his reason the battle between the demons and the angels becomes still more bitter.... [The holy angels] defend us against the rabid fury of the demons and set in motion against them all that the intellect of an angel or of a blessed spirit can devise, and all that their power and their most ardent charity can command for our safety.[10]

Mary of Agreda gives some additional details on the struggle between the angels and demons according to the different states of souls.

Then speaking of depraved souls who have not performed one good work during their life, she says the demons

> point out to the good angels all the sins, wickedness and vices of such souls, which of their own free will serve such evil masters. What then passes between the angels and the demons is incredible and indescribable; because the demons exert all their fury to prevent such souls from receiving inspirations and helps. As they cannot resist the divine power, they seek at least with all their power to hinder them from attending or yielding to the call of heaven. With such souls ordinarily it happens, that whenever God himself or through his holy angels sends them a holy inspiration or movement, these demons must first be put to flight.... This defense the angels usually conduct with the words, which I have quoted above: "Who is like unto God, that dwells on high? Who like Christ, at the right hand of the eternal Father? Who is like to the most holy Mary?" together with other sayings, before which the infernal dragons take flight; sometimes they are thereby hurled back into hell, although, not abating in their fury, they again return to the conflict.
>
> The hellish foes also strive with all their force to induce men to multiply their sins, in order that the measure of their sins may so much the sooner be complete and their time of penance and of life may come to an end; for then the demons would be enabled to carry them off to eternal torments. But the angels, who are rejoiced by the repentance of sinners, even though they may not be able to bring them to repentance, labor diligently to do away with occasions of sin and to lessen the number of sins or prevent them altogether. And when, with all their efforts, unknown to mortals, they cannot bring back the souls from sin, they resort to the intercession of the most holy Mother of God.... In order to move her merciful kindness the sooner, they induce the souls of sinners to practice some special devotion or perform some service in honor of the great Lady.... In these different ways an infinite number of souls come out of their sinful ways and are snatched from the claws of the dragon.[11]

What fury on the part of the spirit of darkness fiercely working for our ruin! What solicitude on the part of our guardian angels to save us! It is a combat during which there is no respite. On both sides, everything is done to gain or keep the upper hand.

What precious lessons! How fathers and mothers must examine their intentions with respect to the generation of their children! No, however averse one might be to the revelations, no one can find here any exaggeration. Whoever studies our society will easily be convinced that all the evil comes from this side.

How important still it is for parents to carefully examine their lives and how they educate their children!

Let us also remember, according to the counsel of a well-known writer,[12] that every day and on our account, great struggles are waged beside us, both just and sinners. He says that

> on the right hand, see your victorious Leader, Jesus Christ, with His most holy Mother, the Virgin Mary, and her beloved husband, Joseph, and countless hosts of Angels and Saints, especially St. Michael the Archangel; on the left hand, behold the Devil from beneath, with his followers, ready to kindle the passion in question, and to entice you to yield to it.
>
> Then you shall seem to hear a voice, as of your guardian Angel, saying unto you, "You have today to fight against this enemy and against others too. Let not your heart sink, and do not lose courage; nor yield from fear or on any other account, for our Lord, your Captain, stands beside you, with all His glorious hosts with Him; and He will fight for you against all your enemies, and will not permit them to prevail against you either by force or oppression."[13]

It is on our will, and on our courage, that the struggle's outcome depends.

CHAPTER 17:

THE ANGELIC WORLD HELPS US TO UNDERSTAND THE POWER, GREATNESS, AND PROVIDENCE OF GOD. – TESTIMONY OF APULEIUS. – A PAGE FROM CHATEAUBRIAND.

The creatures are but umbratile (if I may so speak) and arbitrary pictures of the great Creator, [which]... give the intellect rise and occasions to take notice of and contemplate the divine originals.
– Robert Boyle[1]

What an immense horizon is open before us! What magnificent ideas concerning the greatness, power, and providence of God!

No, the King of Heaven is not solitary. Around His throne stand countless legions of resplendently beautiful princes. One prophet, enlightened with divine light, and as though transported amongst the angels, saw "thousands of thousands ministered to him, and ten thousand times a hundred thousand stood before him" (Dn 7:10), doing nothing but adoring and admiring His greatness. Count, if you can, the sands of the sea, or the stars of heaven, those you see and those you do not, and realize that you have not yet reached the number of the angels. It costs you nothing, O God, to multiply the most excellent things, and that which is most beautiful is, so to speak, what you lavish the most!

Such perfect creatures have been drawn out of nothingness like others. God, Who is a pure spirit, wanted to create pure spirits like Himself, who bear within themselves the imprint of a divine character. But since all the perfections we have admired in the angelic nature are but reflections of the divine perfection, they belong to God like solar rays dispersed in space belong to the luminous fire from which they emanate. The Seraphim burn, St. Bernard says, but it is with a divine fire; they love, but not as much as Love Himself. The Cherubim possess knowledge, but not as much or in the same manner as He Who is the Truth. The Thrones are seated, and judge in peace, but not in the measure of Him Who is the "peace which surpasseth all understanding" (Phil 4:7). The Dominations and Principalities govern, but they are ruled in turn by the One Whom all obey. The might of the Powers exceeds everything we can imagine, but what is it before the One Who is Might Himself? The Virtues do wondrous works, but it is You alone, O my God, Who work miracles! You are God, "Who alone doth great wonders" (Ps 135:4 [136:4]). The Angels and Archangels are present to us, but You are yet more present, You Who are in us! Let us not be surprised at this: All corresponding perfections between the Creator and the creatures, without exception, are separated by an infinite abyss.

And yet what does Scripture not tell us about the state of these wondrous creatures! Both the prophet Daniel, whom it seemed no vision ought to surprise after having already been favored with so many brilliant ones, and St. John, whose eagle eyes taught him to see clearly into the dazzling splendors of the Apocalypse, put their faces to the ground upon seeing a single angel, and adored him as if the light from God had suddenly shone before their eyes and thrown them into ecstasy. Similarly, Tobit remained immersed for three hours in a holy rapture when Raphael, upon departing, permitted him to see for an instant the ravishing beauty of a blessed spirit. It would be difficult then for us to exaggerate the spiritual and intellectual superiority that raises the angels above us. And yet, how does Holy Scripture portray to us the bearing of these heavenly spirits in the presence of God? They veil their faces with their wings! The Thrones tremble and the Powers quiver! Their powerful and glorious nature is shaken to its foundations; its depths are moved and troubled; their life, their strength, and their control over themselves seem to have abandoned them. Deeper and vaster than the seas of the earth, these oceans of life seem as if they would dry up in the presence of this sun of glory, and the very simplicity of the angelic nature seems unable to withstand the effects of this fire that penetrates everywhere to purify everything.

But that which, more than anything, gives me an idea of your infinite greatness, O my God, is that amongst these blessed spirits, the Seraphim, who are the most sublime and whom You place at the head of all the heavenly squadrons nearest You, dare not, however, raise their eyes to Your face. Your prophet, who attributes to them six wings, to signify the loftiness of their thoughts, says two of them are for covering Your face and two for covering Your feet [(Is 6:2)]; there is nothing in You that is not incomprehensible. The purest spirits cannot withstand the splendor of Your face. If there is some place in You where You seemed to have made Yourself more accessible to them, and if we can for this reason call it Your feet, they still cover it with their wings and dare not look at it. Of the six wings, they use four of them to shield themselves from Your impenetrable and inaccessible light, and to adore the incomprehensibleness of Your being; and but two wings are left to them to flutter around You [(ibid.)], if one dare say it, without ever being able to enter into Your depths or fathom this immense abyss of perfections, before which they barely flap their trembling wings and can almost not hold themselves up before You.

O God, I adore You with them! And not daring to mingle my impure lips with these immortal mouths which echo Your praises in all heaven, I wait for one of these heavenly spirits to come touch me with the fire from the coals burning before Your altar. What greatness You show me in these purifying spirits, and yet You reveal to me that these spirits who purify me are so little before You![2]

But what gives us here below the greatest idea of God is the consideration of angelic grace. Let us look at what St. Francis de Sales says:

The angels, as the great St. Augustine and St. Thomas confirm, receive grace according to the variety of their natural conditions. Now, they are all a different species or at least of different conditions, since they are distinguished from one another.

Therefore, for as many angels as there are, there are as many different graces. And although with men grace is not given according to their natural conditions, nevertheless the divine sweetness taking pleasure, and in a manner of speaking entertainment, in the production of graces, diversifies them in infinite ways, so that this variety makes itself the beautiful sheen of its redemption and mercy.... Now, this variety in grace, or this grace in variety, yields a most sacred beauty and sweetest harmony which rejoices all the holy city of the heavenly Jerusalem.[3]

Fr. Faber states:

How they [the angels] must have drunk torrents of grace, as the thirsty earth drinks in the thunder-shower of the torrid autumn! Yet they were filled, and to overflowing, and were inebriated with their abundance. Some theologians say that the grace of each angel is separate and different from the grace of the rest; so that the kinds of herbs and flowers on earth are but the faintest shadows of the diversity of the angelic graces. If each single leaf of the crowded forests of earth's historical five thousand summers were a separate kind, it would hardly represent the multitude of those celestial graces.... Try to fathom this universe of angelic grace, in its kind, its degree[,] its variety; and you will sink down in sheer amazement, and a silence that will hardly dare to think.[4]

But does the infinite and almighty God not diminish His greatness by making use of these spirits, finite like all creatures, for governing all of creation? — It is a principle and law of political science that, in the governing of a people, the authority must not be communicating directly with its subjects. Thus, it is true that the authority, under all its forms and all its nuances, has always and everywhere governed through intermediaries or ministers. The minister is a man of all countries, centuries, and governments; we find him everywhere and always, with the invariable role of serving as an intermediary or mediator between the authority and the people, of transmitting to the people the authority's wishes and benefits, and to the authority the people's wishes and, if needed, grievances.

Now, this ancient and universal law is reproduced in divine government. God, Who is the highest authority in the world, the authority that is the most powerful and most independent, God Himself also, in the ordinary plan of His providence, generally only acts through intermediaries or ministers.

Apuleius, a pagan philosopher of the second century, understood that this had to be so. He says:

> If it is unfitting for a king to do everything and rule everything by himself, it is indeed more so for God. In order then to preserve all his majesty, it must be believed that he is seated on a sublime throne, and that he rules all parts of the universe via the heavenly powers. It is in fact through their care that he rules the inferior world. For this, he needs no effort or calculations, things which man's ignorance and weakness require.
>
> Thus, when the king and father of beings, whom we can see only with the eyes of the soul, wishes to set in motion the immense machine of the universe, resplendent with stars, shining with a thousand beauties, and directed by his laws, he does, if it is permitted to speak thus, what is done at the moment of a battle. The trumpet sounds. Alerted by its blares, the soldiers move. One takes his sword, the other his shield; those their breastplates and helmets; this one harnesses his horse, and this other fastens his steeds to the quadriga. Each one zealously prepares. The infantry soldiers form ranks, the leaders inspect them, and the knights assume command of them. Each one tends to his role. However, the entire army obeys a single general, whom the king places at its head.
>
> It is no different with the government of divine and human things. Under the orders of a single leader, each one knows his duty and fulfills it, although he does not know the secret force

making him act, and this power is invisible to the eyes of the body. Let us take one example of lesser order. In man, the soul is invisible; however, it would be crazy to deny that everything man does comes from this invisible principle. It is to this principle that human life is indebted—the fields and their cultivation, the produce and their use, the arts and their practice—in a single word, all that man does.[5]

Yes, the superior world is something, or rather is everything. The material world and the moral world are under the permanent action of the spiritual world. God, like a king ruling his kingdom through his ministers, or better, like a father ruling his family through his servants, rules the universe through his angels, in such a way that neither man nor any creature, from the blade of grass in the valley to the highest star, is left to chance.

Yet, if this teaching is food for Christian piety, it also provides a vast field to the imagination of the poet and the painter. [François-René de] Chateaubriand understood this when he wrote, in his *The Genius of Christianity*, this passage full of poetry:

> In the hierarchy of the *angels*, one discovers a doctrine as ancient as the world, and a thousand scenes for the poet. Not only do the messengers of the Most High carry his decrees from one end of the universe to the other, not only are they the invisible guardians of men and do they assume the loveliest forms to reveal themselves to them, but religion also permits us to associate tutelary angels with beautiful nature, as well as with virtuous sentiments. What an innumerable host of divinities come then to instantaneously populate the worlds!
>
> Among the Greeks, heaven ended at the summit of Olympus, and their gods rose no higher than the vapors of the earth. The Christian *wonderful*, which is in accord with reason, the sciences, and the edification of our souls, extends from world to world, universe to universe, into spaces where the frightened imagination trembles and backs away. In vain do telescopes scan

every corner of heaven, in vain do they pursue the comet beyond our system, as the comet ultimately escapes them; but it does not escape the *Archangel* who propels it to its unknown aphelion, and who, at the appointed time, brings it back by mysterious ways into the hearth of our sun.

The Christian poet is the lone initiate into the secret of these wonders. From globe to globe, from sun to sun, with the *Seraphim*, the *Thrones*, and the *Ardents* who govern the worlds, the wearied imagination finally comes back down to earth as a river which, via a magnificent cascade, pours forth its golden streams like a radiant sunset. One then goes from images of grandeur to sweetness: beneath the shade of the forests, one travels the empire of the *Angel of Solitude*; one finds in the brightness of the moon the *Spirit of the Reveries of the Heart*; one hears his sighs in the trembling of the trees and in the laments of Philomela. The roses of the dawn are but the hair of the *Angel of Morning*. The *Angel of Night* reposes in the middle of the heavens, where he resembles the moon sleeping upon a cloud. His eyes are covered with a band of stars; his heels and his forehead are somewhat reddened by the purples of dawn and dusk; the *Angel of Silence* precedes him, and the *Angel of Mystery* follows him. Let us not insult the poets by thinking they consider the *Angel of the Seas*, the *Angel of Tempests*, the *Angel of Time*, and the *Angel of Death* as spirits offensive to the Muses. It is the *Angel of Holy Loves* who gives virgins a heavenly gaze, and it is the *Angel of Harmonies* who presents them graces; the good man owes his heart to the *Angel of Virtue*, and his speech to the *Angel of Persuasion*. Nothing prevents granting these beneficent spirits attributes proper to their offices: the *Angel of Friendship*, for example, might wear a wondrous scarf where one sees cast, by a divine operation, consolations of the soul, sublime devotions, secret words of the heart, innocent joys, chaste embraces, religion, the charm of the tombs, and immortal hope.[6]

CHAPTER 18:
DEVOTION TO THE HOLY ANGELS. – HONOR. – IMITATION.

All that is the object of our veneration must be the model of our life.
– Bossuet

After all we have said about the nature, power, and so numerous and sublime ministries of the holy angels, and about their relations with us, is it not natural to conclude that devotion to these heavenly spirits is legitimate and advantageous?

What is more legitimate than honoring those whom God Himself honors, by singling them out amongst all His creatures with such excellent gifts, such radiant glory, and such sublime ministries?

What is more advantageous than honoring those whom God has established as ministers of His court, mouthpieces of His will, our guides on the way of salvation, and our defenders against all the dangers with which we are surrounded?

Every Catholic knows that this veneration does not at all go against the worship we owe to God. Theodoret says that we in no way call them gods, and that we do not render them divine worship; God alone receives our adoration. St Ambrose says that we honor them with an honor of charity and fraternal association which is none other, to use the words of a council, than that with which "we anticipate one another by marks of deference and respect, in relation to the dignity with which we are invested."[1]

The Church herself invites us to this when she celebrates feasts in honor of the guardian angels and of the Archangels Michael, Gabriel, and Raphael.

The Holy Virgin, Mary of Agreda says, celebrated each year, with a singular devotion, the feast of the holy angels:

In order to celebrate the excellences and holiness of the angelic nature[,] She prepared herself for some days by exercises such as mentioned for some of the other feasts, adding new songs of glory and praise and retracing in them the work of the creation of the angels, and especially their justification and glorification with all the mysteries and secrets known to Her of all of them and of each one in particular. When the day She had assigned for this feast arrived, She invited them all. Many thousands of the celestial choirs and orders descended and manifested themselves in wonderful beauty and glory in her oratory. Then, forming two choirs, one of which was our Queen and the other all the supernal spirits, the Lady and the angels sang songs of celestial harmony in alternate verses during that entire day. If it were possible to make known to the world the mysterious canticles composed on those days by the most blessed Lady and the angels, they would no doubt be reckoned among the great miracles of the Lord and astonish all the mortals. I cannot find words nor time to describe what I have come to know concerning this mystery; for they began by praising the essence of God in Himself; and in all his perfections and attributes known to them. Then the Queen proceeded to bless and magnify Him for having manifested his Majesty, Wisdom and Omnipotence in the creation of so many and beautiful spiritual beings; for having favored them with so many gifts of nature and grace, and appointed them as ministers and executors of his will in the government of men and of all the lower and visible creation. The angels on their part responded by due and thankful acknowledgment of their obligation, and all of them sang to the Almighty wonderful songs of praise for having created and chosen for his Mother a Virgin so pure, so holy, so worthy of his greatest gifts.... This day was one of admirable joy and jubilee to the Queen, and of accidental joy to the angels.[2]

Let us imitate Mary. Let us praise God first, for having created these heavenly spirits and exalted them; let us then congratulate the angels, for having been predestined to such great glory. However, if we wish to enhance the value of this honor, let us join to our praises the imitation of the virtues which shine in these sublime creatures.

Bossuet says, "This is the rule of Christianity that I beseech you to fix in your memory. The Christian must imitate all that he honors. All that is the object of our veneration must be the model of our life."[3]

Moreover, we are called to take our place among them in heavenly beatitude. According to the teachings of St. Augustine in his *The City of God*, of St. Anselm in his *Why God Became Man*, and of St. Isidore in his *Sententiarum libri tres*, we are destined to fill the empty places made by the defection of the evil angels; it is fitting then that we should exhibit in ourselves the virtues of those amongst whom we are to take our place.

This will also, according to the thinking of Origen, be a means of "making them favorable to us, and of leading them to do everything we can hope from them."[4]

However, is it possible to imitate such perfect creatures, these pure spirits who have nothing of our infirmities?

Oh, if, like the Apostle, we could be taken up for a few moments into the palace of the King of kings, into the sight of those blessed spirits who are transported with love for God and occupied with singing His praises, we would learn to live only for Him.

Let our heart burn with the sacred fire of a pure charity free of all self-interest, so that we become ablaze like the Seraphim. After the example of Sister Minima of Jesus of Nazareth, let us offer the divine majesty the love of the first choir of Seraphim, in reparation for all the outrages committed in the world.

If we want to be similar to the Cherubim, let us seek the light that enables discernment of heavenly inspirations and even of the smallest sins.

Let us exercise justice and fulfill our duties, and we shall become the Thrones of the earth.

Let us practice the angelic virtue par excellence, that purity that subjugates the flesh and the affections in us excited by earthly objects, and we shall become similar to the Dominations.

The Principalities will teach us to practice the divine virtue of obedience.

The Powers will find us their imitators if we resist Satan's suggestions and if we subdue our sensual appetites.

Finally, let us be compassionate, always ready to render services to our brethren, and we shall become the Virtues, Archangels, and Angels of the earth.

Let us learn from all these heavenly spirits to never speak of the secrets of the divine nature with such levity and irreverence. The prophet Isaiah, recounting that vision full of majesty that opened heaven to his gaze, after having spoken of the angels as heavenly spirits occupied in serving God and arranged around His throne to form His court, portrays them to us as veiling their faces with their wings, and thereby testifies that they cannot withstand the dazzling rays of His glory, nor look directly at the brightness of His terrible majesty. How then could we, sinful men whom an infinite distance separates from the Creator, think that we have enough power in the mind and purity in the heart to penetrate the admirable mysteries of this incomprehensible nature!

Let us also learn from the holy angels the way in which we must honor God and extol His praises. The Church, in her liturgy, gives us their example and offers them to us as models.

At Holy Mass, she mingles her voice with that of the angels when she repeats this canticle, this angelic hymn which resounded in the heavens on the day of the Savior's birth: *Glory to God in the highest, and on earth peace to men of good will.*

The act of the august sacrifice at the altar is going to begin. The Church then, through the mouth of the priest, invites the faithful to lift up their hearts, *Sursum corda,* and to give thanks for the astounding miracle that is going to take place. But alas, feeble creatures that we are, where do we go to find words capable of praising, in a sufficient manner, the majesty of the God Whom we adore? Let us listen:

> It is truly meet and just, right and profitable for us, at all times, and in all places, to give thanks to Thee, O holy Lord, Father almighty, eternal God, through Christ our Lord. Through Whom the angels praise, the dominations adore, the powers, trembling with awe, worship Thy majesty: which the heavens, and the forces of heaven, together with the blessed seraphim, joyfully do magnify. And do Thou command that it be permitted to our

lowliness *to join with them* in confessing Thee and unceasingly to repeat: Holy, holy, holy, Lord God of hosts. The heavens and the earth are full of Thy glory. Hosanna in the highest. Blessed is He that cometh in the name of the Lord. Hosanna in the highest.[5]

However, even more than in the Latin Church, the Greek Church and the Armenian Catholic Church, in the prayers of the holy and divine Mass, unite their voices to those of the angelic spirits. In their liturgies, we see reflected, so to speak, the purity and the beauty of the Eastern sky. When they address themselves to God, they always see Him surrounded by His angels. Let us take a closer look.

Among the Armenians, when the celebrant dons the sacred vestments, the clerics chant the following in the middle of the choir: "O profound and incomprehensible mystery, without beginning! Above us Thou hath illuminated the Principalities in the nuptial chamber with inaccessible light, and Thou hath surrounded the choirs of Angels with incomparable glory."[6]

The celebrant subsequently advances towards the altar and says aloud, "In the Tabernacle of holiness, and in the place of praise, the habitation of Angels,... prostrated at the foot of the holy altar, we adore with trembling, and glorify Thy holy, admirable and victorious resurrection."[7]

The clerics then chant melodies according to the mystery of the day, most of which mention angels.

"The children of the Hebrews sing the song of the Cherubim: the multitude of the Gentiles rejoice with the inhabitants of the skies."[8]

"To-day the battalions of the Angelic choirs of Heaven harmoniously modulate songs of praise."[9]

In the liturgies of St. John Chrysostom and St. Basil, the [priest],[10] in a low voice, recites a prayer called the Prayer of the Entrance of the Holy Gospel: "O Master, Lord, our God, who hast appointed in the heavens ranks and armies of Angels and Archangels, for the ministry of thy glory; cause that with our Entrance, there may be an entrance of holy Angels, ministering together with us, and with us glorifying thy goodness."[11]

Whilst the Armenian celebrant incenses the altar, the clerics sing the incensing hymn: "Through the intercession of Your heavenly armies, always keep the Armenian Church unshakeable...."[12] The priest then says in a low voice: "O Lord our God, who hath ordered in Heaven, choirs and battalions of Angels and Archangels for the service of Thy glory, grant that the holy Angels may enter with us...."[13]

Then comes the prayer of the thrice-holy hymn: "Holy Lord... to whom the Seraphim gives praise in the Song of Trisagion; to whom the Cherubim gives glory, and all the heavenly hosts the tribute of adoration; Thou who... didst not abandon [man] when he became a sinner...."[14]

Among the Armenians, the clerics chant the hagiology, according to the mystery of the day. In almost all the chants, we again find the angels mentioned: "An innumerable Choir of Angels and of the heavenly hosts descended from Heaven with the king, the only Son, singing and saying: This is the Son of God."[15] "Thou who sittest majestically enthroned in light, O ineffable Word of God, descending from the celestial heights for Thy creatures, Thou hast deigned this day to sit at table with Thy disciples. Seized with astonishment and amazement, the Seraphim and Cherubim stood around, and the principalities of the heavenly hosts shouted: Holy, Holy, Holy, Lord God of Hosts."[16] "At the miracle of Thy Resurrection, the Virtues sing praises, the Seraphim are filled with dread, the Cherubim tremble, and the Heavenly Powers and Principalities, ranged in joyous groups, cry with a loud voice and say...."[17]

The moment of the consecration approaching, it is then that one must unite with the angels. The deacon sings, "You who with faith surround this sacred and royal altar, behold Christ the King seated there, surrounded by the Heavenly Hosts." The clerics respond, "...We bless Thee with the Angels...." The deacon later says, "Give thy benediction, Lord Priest." The priest says, "To sing with one voice, with the Seraphim and Cherubim the songs of hagiology...."[18]

In the liturgies of St. John Chrysostom and St. Basil, the priest recites in a low voice a prayer very similar to our [Roman rite] preface, the ending of which is: "For thee do praise Angels, Archangels,

Thrones, Dominations, Principalities, Authorities, Powers, and the many-eyed Cherubim: about thee stand in a circle the Seraphim, one with six wings, and another with six wings; and with twain they cover their faces, and with twain their feet; and with twain flying, they cry one to another, with unceasing mouths, with never silent doxologies." The priest then says aloud, "Singing, vociferating, crying, and saying the triumphal Hymn." Then the choir sings, "Holy, Holy, Holy…."[19]

After the consecration, the deacon prompts the people to ask God for the special graces they need. Among these petitions, we call attention to the following one: The deacon says, "An Angel of peace, a faithful guide, a guardian of our souls and bodies, let us ask of the Lord." The choir then responds, "Grant, O Lord."[20]

Following the consecration in the Armenian liturgy, one still finds a great number of prayers mentioning the angels. But what we have already cited suffices to show how much the Eastern churches, united to the Latin Church, are keen to excite the devotion of the faithful towards the angelic spirits, and to offer them for their imitation.

It is again to imitate the angels, and to join ourselves with their choirs, that the Church has her priests recite the divine office of the breviary. "To be able to join with the nine choirs of angels, in the night office," Durand says, "we sing God's praises in a novena of antiphons, psalms, versicles, lessons, and responses."[21] "The Church," one author adds, "desires that on earth we endeavor to exercise, even during the night, what the angels practice unceasingly in heaven, praising and blessing the most holy, most infinite, and most incomprehensible Trinity."[22]

This is also the thinking behind the institution of novenas, practices of piety spread amongst the faithful.

CHAPTER 19:
CONTINUATION OF THE PRECEDING CHAPTER.
– INVOKING THE HOLY ANGELS.

Employ their help and assistance in all affairs.
– St. Francis de Sales

Let us invoke the holy angels. Invoking them is to call them to one's assistance, to obtain that they intercede for us before God and that they come to help us.

Jacob implored the angel with whom he wrestled to give him his blessing (Gn 32:26). On his deathbed, he asked the same grace for his grandsons Ephraim and Manasseh from the angel who had led and protected him (Gn 48:16). It was also her angel to whom Judith appealed to save her people.[1]

St. Francis de Sales recommends this devotion to his Philothea:

> Make yourself very familiar with the angels, often see them invisibly present in your life! And particularly love and revere the angel of the diocese in which you are, the angels of the persons with whom you live, and especially your own angel. Pray to them often, praise them regularly, and employ their help and assistance in all your affairs, whether spiritual or temporal, so that they may cooperate with your intentions.[2]

Here again, we take for our model the Church, which, in a multitude of circumstances, and through the mouths of her ministers, invokes these blessed spirits.

On Sundays, before High Mass, she addresses this prayer to God: "Graciously hear us, O Holy Lord, Father Almighty, Eternal God; and vouchsafe to send down from heaven Thy holy angel, that he may watch over, foster, safeguard, abide with and defend all who dwell in this house."

At the holy sacrifice, after the consecration, the priest says this prayer:

> We humbly beseech Thee, almighty God, to command that these our offerings be borne by the hands of Thy holy angel to Thine altar on high in the presence of Thy divine Majesty; that as many of us as shall receive the most sacred Body and Blood of Thy Son by partaking thereof from this altar may be filled with every heavenly blessing and grace.

Bossuet says:

> What better thing could one do than again ask the company of the holy angel who presides at the prayer, and in him that of all the holy companions of his beatitude, so that, our offering being presented in this blessed company, it ascends promptly and more agreeably to the heavenly altar?[3]

Compline, as we know, finishes the divine office for the day. It is the prayer of a soul who, after having finished the day with the help of God, and before taking rest, seeks shelter from all kinds of dangers and temptations. "The devil, as a roaring lion, goeth about seeking whom he may devour" (1 Pt 5:8). The soul thus puts before God the promises He has made us and which are expressed in magnificent Psalm 90 [91]:

> He that dwelleth in the aid of the Most High, shall abide under the protection of the God of Heaven…. There shall no evil come to thee: nor shall the scourge come near thy dwelling. For he hath given his angels charge over thee, to keep thee in all thy ways. In their hands they shall bear thee up, lest thou dash thy foot against a stone. Thou shalt walk upon the asp and the basilisk: and thou shalt trample under foot the lion and the dragon. (Ps 90:1, 10-13 [91:1, 10-13])

Assured by such magnificent promises, the Christian makes this prayer:

"Visit, we beseech Thee, O Lord, this dwelling, and drive far from it the snares of the enemy; let Thy holy angels dwell herein to preserve us in peace, and let Thy blessing be always upon us." There is a final salutation to the Queen of the Angels, and the Christian can then repose in peace. His angels shall watch over him. He whom God protects is well-protected!

It was on our mother's knees that we began to babble this other prayer that we address to our guardian angel when, in the mornings and evenings, we give our heart to God: "Angel, my protector, do not abandon me; enlighten my mind; guide my steps; procure my salvation, O divine protector! Inspire in me always the desire to do good."

Each morning, we also make this invocation: "Angel of heaven, my faithful and charitable guide, obtain for me to be so docile to your inspirations that I never stray from the path of my God's commandments."

It is indeed interesting to consider the care the Church takes to have us ask the help of these heavenly spirits in our different actions and in the important circumstances of our life.

Is one embarking on a journey? The Church has us ask God to give us as a traveling companion the angel Raphael, who will bring us back home in peace, health, and joy. "May the Angel Raphael be with us along the way, that we may come to our home again in peace, and health, and gladness."[4]

If God desires to give Himself in viaticum to a dying person at his home, or if He deigns to grant the person the grace of Extreme Unction, the minister of Jesus Christ says this prayer: "Deign, Holy Lord, Almighty Father, Eternal God, to send from heaven Thy holy angel, to guard, keep, protect, visit, and defend this ill one and all those who dwell in this house."

How the Church redoubles her prayers and invokes all the angelic choirs for the Christian soul that is going to leave his body! Luther himself found this devotion so salutary that he recommended it to the dying. "Let no one," he rightfully said, "omit invoking the Blessed Virgin, the *angels*, and the saints, so that they intercede for him at that critical moment."

Finally, the Christian has breathed his last breath. Is everything finished? No, the Church will invoke the holy angels even up to the grave.

Do you see this coffin? A body lies inside, and it is to return to the earth from whence it came. But before this, it is taken into the house of God: The Church exclaims as it receives him, "Come to his assistance, ye saints of God! Meet him, ye angels of the Lord. Receive his soul and present it to the Most High…. May the angels lead thee into the bosom of Abraham."[5]

The sacrifice is finished; the mortal remains will be taken to their final resting place. O holy religion, how great you are! How you raise the soul up to God! How you inspire us with confidence! There is only a dead body here; it came from dust and shall return to dust. But man is not only matter; he is spirit, he has a soul, and this is why, O Church, my mother, you sing, up to the edge of the grave, this admirable prayer that one cannot hear without being moved: "May the Angels lead thee into Paradise…. May the choir of angels receive thee, and with Lazarus, once a beggar, mayest thou have eternal rest."[6]

Finally, there is one last prayer while the grave is sealed: "May Thy tender mercy give him place above, among the angel choirs."[7]

There is yet another prayer, a sublime summary of all the prayers that earth addresses to heaven, and particularly to the holy angels. Litanies, in fact, have been composed in honor of these heavenly spirits, in which one delights in enumerating the principal titles credited to them, upon which we rely as pledges of our deliverance. Such is this prayer, we say with [Auguste] Nicolas, that rises up from the hearts of the faithful multitudes when, to this chant so admirably expressing a melancholic and plaintive seriousness in each invocation, they answer each repetition with that "pray for us" which, like the blows of a battering ram battering the different sides of a tower, shakes and ultimately averts the divine justice poised against us due to sin.

We wish to conclude by pointing out a devotion that St. Mary Magdalene de' Pazzi practiced towards the angels. She learned it while in ecstasy.

VISIT TO THE NINE CHOIRS

I shall go to the choir of the Angels and ask them for the spirit of humility. From there, I shall go to the choir of the Archangels and petition them for an inviolable purity. I shall ascend to the choir of the Principalities, to obtain through their merits a perfect obedience, not only to God, but to every creature, for God's sake. I shall ascend to the choir of the Powers and beseech them to dispose their divine Master to grant me the grace to subdue my sensual appetites. I shall respectfully approach the choir of the Virtues and solicit, from their generous charity, steadfastness and progress in the good. I shall run to the choir of the Dominations and ask for their powerful intercession to obtain a genuine command over my passions and over the affections that earthly objects excite in me. I shall visit the choir of the Thrones and solicit from their love for the Incarnate Word all the dispositions that can make my heart a pleasing dwelling for His Holy Majesty. I shall go to the choir of the Cherubim to seek the light that enables discernment of heavenly inspirations and of even the smallest sins. Finally, I shall dare to approach the choir of Seraphim to obtain there the fire of a pure charity that is free from all self-interest. I shall then guard against admitting anything into my heart that might diminish the purity of my love. *Amen. Amen.*

"O God, Who dost in wonderful order dispose the ministries of angels and men, mercifully grant that our lives be fortified by those who continually stand in Thy presence and minister before Thee in heaven."[8]

CONCLUSION OF PART ONE

Love and devotion for the holy angels, such is the conclusion we ought to draw.

Therefore, O men, O Christians, love the heavenly spirits!

Love them, apostolic men; they are the divine missionaries from paradise.

Love them, preachers and doctors; they are the savants of the science of heaven, of the beautiful and grand eloquence of eternity.

Love them, priests of Jesus Christ; it is through their hands that the august sacrifice is carried to the foot of the throne of the divine majesty.

Love them, you who are hidden in the cloister or who live in solitude. These sublime spirits are always hidden in God, immersed in God, and never lose sight of Him.

Love them, you who appear in public, who live amidst the noise of the world; these pure intelligences dwell there with you and are at your side.

Love them, you who live in the holy state of matrimony; Raphael, leading Tobias, shows you, in an admirable manner, the delicate care they have for your state.

Love them, widows and orphans; they are the protectors and support of those who are in suffering.

Love them, O virgins. O virgins, once again, fervently love the holy angels. You possess, in fragile vessels, an inestimable treasure, preferable to crowns and empires, for the preservation of which there is no life one ought not lose, no pain one ought not suffer, and no pleasure one ought not forego. This precious treasure, this virginity, you, as feeble creatures, live it on earth, like they, perfect creatures, live it in heaven.

Love them, just ones; they are the guides on the paths of holiness.

Love them, sinners; they carry your repentance to God.

Love them, you who are afflicted; they will dry your tears and be your consolation and refuge.

Love them, rich ones, powerful ones, and great ones of the world;

they will make you understand that all passing things are contemptible, and that the only object worthy of your ambition is blessed eternity.[1]

PART TWO: ST. MICHAEL THE ARCHANGEL

INTRODUCTION TO PART TWO

It was necessary, in order to well understand the greatness and glory of St. Michael, to first know the nature and prerogatives of the angelic world, inasmuch at least as we are able from the lights of reason supported by faith. St. Michael, in fact, is one of these pure spirits created by God in the beginning; he possesses the same nature, participates in the same happiness, and shares the same duties.

However, what is more, this archangel bears a name, possesses prerogatives, and fulfills sublime duties which are reasons for his own particular greatness and glory. We shall endeavor to make them known.

In order to proceed with order and clarity, we shall divide this second part into three books. In the first book, we shall explain the prerogatives and glorious ministries of St. Michael; in the second book, we shall address devotion to this great archangel; finally, in the third book, we shall recount the principal apparitions of this prince of the heavenly militia, and we shall make known some of the places sanctified by his presence and renowned for his benefits.

BOOK ONE: ST. MICHAEL'S PREROGATIVES AND GLORIOUS MINISTRIES

CHAPTER 1:
ST. MICHAEL. – HIS NAME. – HIS RESOUNDING VICTORY. – HIS GLORY IN HEAVEN.

Who is like God?

The name Michael comes from the Hebrew phrase *mi-cha-el*, which means, "Who is like God?" We take pride in a name won on a battlefield, a name that will remind posterity of a signal victory. It was on the first and most terrible field of battle that this name was won by the greatest fighter against God's enemies. St. John says, "There was a great battle in heaven: Michael and his angels fought with the dragon, and the dragon fought, and his angels" (Rv 12:7). It was a great battle, *praelium magnum*. Gaume says:

> It is indeed great from whatever point of view it is considered: great due to the number and power of the combatants, great because this battle was the beginning of all others, great due to its immense and eternal results, and great because of the truth that it concerned. In order to divide heaven into two irreconcilable camps, to drive into the abyss a third of the angels, and to forever ensure the felicity of the others, the truth that was in dispute had to have been a fundamental dogma.[1]

The Holy Fathers and the theologians after them claim it pertained to the mystery of the Incarnation, and consequently to the exaltation of

104

human nature in the God-Man and the Virgin Mary, above the angelic nature.

"I protest!" exclaimed Lucifer, this Lucifer who, in the judgment of St. Jerome and St. Augustine, had been the highest work to have come from the hands of the Creator; and immediately, a third of the angels uttered the same cry: "We protest!"

Mary of Agreda says:

> Saint Michael, burning with zeal for the honor of God and armed with divine power and with his own humility, resisted the arrogant pride of the dragon, saying: "Worthy is the Highest of honor, praise and reverence, and of being loved, feared and obeyed by all creation. He is mighty to work whatever He desires. He that is increate and without dependence on any other being, cannot seek anything that is not most just. To us He gave grace such as we have, creating us and forming us out of nothing. He can create other beings, as many and in what manner He pleases. It is reasonable that we, submissive and prostrate in his presence, adore his Majesty and kingly grandeur. Come then, ye angels, follow me, let us adore Him, and extol his admirable and secret judgments, his most perfect and holy works. God is most exalted and above all creatures, and He would not be the Most High, if we could attain or comprehend his great works. Infinite He is in wisdom and goodness, rich in the treasures of his benefits. As Lord of all and needing none, He can distribute them to whomsoever He wishes, and He cannot err in the selection. He can love and confer his favor to whomsoever He chooses, and He can love whom He likes; He can raise up, create and enrich according as it is his good pleasure. In all things He will be wise, holy and irresistible. Let us adore and thank Him for the wonderful work of the Incarnation which He has decreed, and for his favors to his people and for its restoration to grace after its fall. Let us adore this person endowed with the human and the divine nature, let us reverence It and accept It as our Head; let us confess, that He is worthy of all glory, praise and magnificence, and, as the Author of grace, let us give Him glory and acknowledge his power and Divinity."

[Lucifer responded:] "Unjust is God in raising the human nature above the angelic. I am the most exalted and beautiful angel and the triumph belongs to me. It is I who am to place my throne above the stars and who shall be like unto the Highest; I will subject myself to no one of an inferior nature, and I will not consent that any one take precedence of me or be greater than I." In the same way spoke the apostate followers of Lucifer. But St. Michael answered: "Who is there like unto the Lord, who dwells in the heavens, or who to compare himself to Him? Be silent, enemy, cease thy dreadful blasphemies, and since iniquity has taken possession of thee, depart from our midst, wretch, and be hurled in thy blind ignorance and wickedness into the dark night and chaos of the infernal pains. But let us, O spirits of the Lord, honor and reverence this blessed Woman, who is to give human flesh to the eternal Word; and let us recognize Her as our Queen and Lady."[2]

And the prince St. Michael, with this invincible utterance, "Who is equal to God?" cast from heaven Lucifer, "that great dragon…, that old serpent, who is called the devil and Satan, who seduceth the whole world. And he was cast unto the earth: and his angels were thrown down with him" (Rv 12:9).

The angels, Mary of Agreda says, still repeat the cry of St. Michael when they fight the demons, and this cry puts them to flight.

A text that is sung in the Diocese of Coutances and Avranches, on feasts of the leader of the heavenly armies, extols this great victory:

> *We consecrate this day to the celebration of the feast of the angels, and especially to singing St. Michael's praises.*
>
> *Lord, Thou hast made the heavenly spirits Thy servants; how glorious is this servitude for which the reward is God Himself!*
>
> *Full of pride, Lucifer's audacity goes so far as to aspire to the supreme domination that belongs to God alone; he does not want to acknowledge any dependence.*
>
> *His companions unite with him, burning to shake off their yoke; they try to incite all heavenly spirits to revolt with them.*

Immediately armed with a sword that casts lightning, Michael advances against them: Who is like God? At this utterance, battle wages in the middle of heaven.

Surrounded by the holy cohort, he charges the wicked troop; he encourages his own to combat by showing them eternal glory.

The outcome of this amazing battle is not doubtful; immediately, the proud legion precipitously falls from the heights of heaven.

God satisfies with eternal happiness those He has made vanquishers; He punishes the vanquished for eternity with all kinds of torments.

The Church again recalls this glorious victory in the Vespers hymn for the great archangel's feast day:

Thee, O Christ, the Father's Splendour,
Life and virtue of the heart,
In the presence of the Angels
Sing we now with tuneful art:
Meetly in alternate chorus
Bearing our responsive part.

Thus we praise with veneration
All the armies of the sky:
Chiefly him, the warrior Primate
Of celestial chivalry:
Michael, who in princely virtue
Cast Abaddon from on high.

By whose watchful care, repelling,
King of everlasting grace!
Every ghostly adversary,
All things evil, all things base;
Grant us of Thine only goodness
In Thy paradise a place.[3]

According to the thinking of one writer who is believed to be St. Ambrose, St. Michael, in this glorious fight, is the figure of Christ: Michael fought with the dragon for the salvation of all the elect; Christ, through His preaching, His sufferings and death, fought for the salvation of mankind. The angels of Michael fought alongside him; and the apostles of Christ fought against the dragon by preaching, working miracles, and dying in the end for the name of Jesus.

The dragon and his angels fought Michael; and Satan with the multitude of demons also fought against Christ, pressing the Jews to put Him to death. But it was not just against the archangel that the dragon directed his attacks; it was also against the other faithful angels. Similarly, by means of the Jews and the pagans, Satan persecuted until death Christ's apostles.

On earth as in heaven, Satan was the weaker. He could defeat neither Christ nor His apostles; and the means he believed would assure him victory were the cause of his defeat. Thus, through the preaching of the apostles, he was expelled from that which represents heaven on earth: the heart of the elect.

God, to reward the zeal of His archangel, made him prince of the heavenly host. The Church gives him this title in the offices she has composed in his honor. *St. Michael, most glorious prince of the heavenly armies.* What a dignity! What glory! When one wants to celebrate the greatness of an earthly prince, one describes the vast extent of his empire, the incalculable number of his subjects, the multitude and invincible strength of his armies, his glorious conquests, the prosperity his peoples enjoy beneath the shadow of his scepter, the respect and love with which he is surrounded, after having himself loved his subjects like his own children and poured into their bosom the largesse of his royal magnificence. Illustrious archangel, your greatness is without equal! The boundaries of your kingdom are those of heaven. Your subjects are more numerous than the stars of the firmament and the sands of the sea; a prophet who saw them spoke only of myriads, of legions, of millions, and of hundreds of millions; a single one is worth the most numerous and most well-trained army; under your command, they have conquered heaven where they enjoy all blessings. Faithfully obeyed and tenderly loved, you enjoy a glory whose splendor is impossible for us mortals to comprehend!

Where, in fact, does one go for paintbrushes capable of depicting this archangel? Daniel says:

> And in the four and twentieth day of the first month, I was by the great river which is the Tigris. And I lifted up my eyes and I saw: and behold a man clothed in linen, and his loins were girded with the finest gold. And his body was like the chrysolite, and his face as the appearance of lightning, and his eyes as a burning lamp: and his arms and all downward even to the feet, like in appearance to glittering brass: and the voice of his word like the voice of a multitude. And I Daniel alone saw the vision: for the men that were with me saw it not: but an exceeding great terror fell upon them, and they fled away and hid themselves. And I being left alone saw this great vision: and there remained no strength in me, and the appearance of my countenance was changed in me, and I fainted away and retained no strength. And I heard the voice of his words: and when I heard, I lay in a consternation upon my face, and my face was close to the ground. (Dn 10:4-9)

And the one who appeared to Daniel in the form of a man was an angel.

St. John reports, in the Apocalypse, that he saw an angel light up the earth with the rays of his glory. He says: "And I saw another mighty angel come down from heaven, clothed with a cloud. And a rainbow was on his head: and his face was as the sun, and his feet as pillars of fire" (Rv 10:1).

At the beginning of the Apocalypse, he gives us the description of the one who came to reveal to him the mysteries contained in this book.

> I was in the spirit on the Lord's day and heard behind me a great voice, as of a trumpet, saying: What thou seest, write in a book.... And I turned to see the voice that spoke with me. And being turned, I saw seven golden candlesticks: And in the midst

of the seven golden candlesticks, one like to the Son of man, clothed with a garment down to the feet, and girt about the paps with a golden girdle. And his head and his hairs were white, as white wool and as snow. And his eyes were as a flame of fire: and his feet like unto fine brass, as in a burning furnace. And his voice as the sound of many waters. And he had in his right hand seven stars. And from his mouth came out a sharp two-edged sword. And his face was as the sun shineth in his power. And when I had seen him, I fell at his feet as dead. (Rv 1:10-17)

The one who appeared in the form of the Son of Man was, says Bossuet with the exegetes, an angel sent at His order and in His form. What majesty! What brilliance! And this glory is nothing before that of the angelic nature!

In the judgment of St. Anselm, the beauty of the least of the angels is so radiant that it is capable of effacing as many suns, if they existed, as there are stars in the firmament. How then does one speak of the glory of the illustrious archangel prince of the heavenly armies? There is no angel in heaven whose glory surpasses that of St. Michael, and, according to St. Basil and several other Fathers, there is not one who even equals him.[4] This opinion is very reasonable, says St. Alphonsus Liguori, since Michael was chosen to strike down the pride of Lucifer and all the rebel angels by casting them out of paradise.

One reads in the life of St. Francis of Assisi, and in that of St. Frances of Rome, who died in 1440, that Lucifer belonged to the order of the choir of the Seraphim; from this, St. Alphonsus Liguori says, we can assume that St. Michael was inferior in rank to the apostate angel whom he was chosen to cast into the abyss that the latter's pride had just hollowed.

Yes, says Cornelius a Lapide, St. Michael is the first of the Seraphim because he stood as the general of the faithful army against Lucifer; and in the same way that Lucifer is the first of the demons, St. Michael, in turn, is the first of the angels. And because he is the first one in this angelic order whose prerogative is love, he loves God with an incomprehensible love. Faber says, "The gigantic intelligence of St.

Michael has been fathoming the depths of divine love through countless cycles of revolving ages, longer far than even those seemingly interminable geological epochs which men of science claim, and he has reported no soundings yet."[5]

The qualification of "archangel" which St. Paul and St. Jude give to St. Michael[6] does not mean that he is of the order of the Archangels, but that he is at the head of and prince of the Archangels. Such is the sentiment of the Greeks and of the commentators, among others the savant Willem Hessels van Est. The Greek doctors, particularly St. Basil the Great, call St. Michael the *Archistrategos*, meaning "leader of armies." The Latin doctors St. Jerome, Pope St. Gregory the Great, St. Bernard, St. Thomas, St. Alphonsus Liguori, and the celebrated theologians Suárez, Salmerón, and Cardinal Bellarmine are of this sentiment.[7]

The deacon Pantaleon of the Church of Constantinople says, "St. Michael is the greatest and most radiant star of the angelic order, and holds the most distinguished rank among those thousands and myriads of angels who populate the blessed abode and who safeguard frail humanity with a benevolent solicitude during the short moments of its pilgrimage in the land of exile."

CHAPTER 2:
ST. MICHAEL, ANGEL PROTECTOR OF THE CHURCH OF GOD. – HOW HE FULFILLED THIS MINISTRY IN THE TIME OF THE PATRIARCHS.

The angel that delivereth me from all evils, bless these boys.
– Genesis 48:16

The angels, we said in the first part of this work, contribute to the governance of the spiritual and material world. It is to St. Michael that the most important mission belongs: the governance of the Church of God. It belongs to him to defend her in the battles in which hell engages her, to separate the children of God from the children of Belial, and to preserve them in fidelity to the laws of their Creator.

However, to better understand what we have to say about this great mission of the Archangel, it is necessary to know what is understood by the word "Church."

The Catholic Church, in its entirety, is the society of God with angels and faithful men. The angels were called first. Created good, but free, God put them to the test. At one moment, there was schism and heresy in heaven; however, St. Michael reaffirmed the good, and, by God's command, cast the evil to the bottom of the abyss. The Church in heaven was saved.

To fill the places left by the fallen spirits, God created man. But on earth, as in heaven, the struggle between good and evil was to exist. To St. Michael was again confided the mission of preserving faithful adorers for God, a mission he has fulfilled with an unfailing zeal, as we shall see, in whatever age one considers the Church, whether in the time of the patriarchs, in the time under the written law, or in the time under the law of grace.

Moses, recounting the beginnings of the Church, never speaks of St. Michael; the Hebrew people, always inclined to idolatry, would have been tempted to render this archangel divine honors. However, based on the phrase in our Holy Books that "no man hath seen God at any time" (Jn 1:18), the Holy Fathers and commentators teach that God made use of His angels to work the apparitions spoken of in the Sacred Letters. They thus attributed to the heavenly host's leader everything relating to the preservation of God's Church on earth.

"And the Lord God," Scripture says, "took man" whom he had created, "and put him into the paradise of pleasure" (Gn 2:15). The Fathers and commentators[1] explain the word *tulit* [or "took"] in the sacred text by saying that God made use in this circumstance of the ministry of His angel St. Michael. It was in fact fitting that the one who would be tasked later with the honorable role of bringing the souls of the saints into heaven would bring the father of the human race into the earthly paradise, a figure of the paradise awaiting us.

As he brought man into this delightful abode, the angel of God made known to him the end for which he had been created; in the name of God, he gave him "instructions, and the law of life for an inheritance. He made an everlasting covenant with [him], and he showed [him] his justice and judgments" (Sir 17:9-10).

Created in a state of holiness, justice, and innocence, man was perfect according to nature and grace. God was pleased with him. He deputized his angel who, in human form,[2] came "walking in paradise" (Gn 3:8).

Soon, however, seduced by the evil spirit, man transgressed the divine laws. What will you do, O great archangel? The one who was to be the father of the children of the Church is worthy of death! Fulfill then your mission; announce to man the mystery that you first proclaimed before the angelic peoples: the mystery of the Incarnation. God did in fact make known to repentant man through His angel the coming of a Redeemer. At the same time, He had man expelled from the delightful garden[3] so that he would go to work in cultivating the earth. He "placed before the paradise of pleasure Cherubims, and a flaming sword, turning every way, to keep the way of the tree of life" (Gn 3:24).[4]

Men became perverted as they multiplied. Knowledge of the true God threatened to disappear from among the peoples. The sons of God took to themselves wives from the daughters of men.[5] Amidst the general corruption, one man alone was "just and perfect" (Gn 6:9). The angel of God goes to him. He says, "Make thee an ark.... Behold I will bring the waters of a great flood upon the earth, to destroy all flesh, wherein is the breath of life, under heaven. All things that are in the earth shall be consumed. And I will establish my covenant with thee, and thou shalt enter into the ark: thou and thy sons, and thy wife, and the wives of thy sons with thee" (Gn 6:14, 17-18).

Noah obeys, and soon the vessel which enclosed the Church, led by her protecting angel, was majestically sailing over the sea that covered the world's ruins.

Later, idolatry invades the world. One can scarcely find any adorers of the true God. God then sends His angel to the one who is to be the father of His people. Michael says to him, Abraham, speaking in the name of God, "Go forth out of thy country, and from thy kindred, and out of thy father's house, and come into the land which I shall shew thee. And I will make of thee a great nation" (Gn 12:1-2). Multiple times he renews to him the promise of a great posterity. "Look up to heaven and number the stars, if thou canst," he says to him in another circumstance. "So shall thy seed be" (Gn 15:5), his seed being the children of the Church.[6] Despite these promises repeated so many times, Sarah, the wife of Abraham, was sterile, and, moreover, she had become advanced in years. One day, three angels in the form of three young men go down to the valley of Mamre. Abraham offers them hospitality and treats them with the most moving kindness and the greatest generosity. Then the Archangel Michael,[7] the one of the three who appeared the greatest, told Abraham that he would return to him one year later and that his wife Sarah would have a son. The event fulfilled the promise.

With what solicitude he watches over this patriarch's grandchildren, over Jacob! He appears to him during his sleep, on the way to Haran. He says to him, "I will be thy keeper whithersoever thou goest, and will bring thee back into this land: neither will I leave thee, till I shall have accomplished all that I have said" (Gn 28:15).

When the time comes for him to leave the house of his uncle Laban, he appears to him again. "And the angel of God said to me in my sleep: Jacob? And I answered: Here I am. And he said:... I am the God of

Bethel,[8] where thou didst anoint the stone, and make a vow to me. Now therefore arise, and go out of this land, and return into thy native country" (Gn 31:11-13). The angel assures Jacob of his protection, and Jacob obeys.

And the angels of God come to meet him (Gn 32:1), as though to tell him to fear nothing on the part of his brother Esau. St. Michael is at their head.[9] Soon, Esau lays down his arms, and the brothers are reconciled.

This great patriarch Jacob, lying on his deathbed, recognized the services of his powerful protector and beseeches him to continue them with his grandsons: "The angel that delivereth me from all evils, bless these boys" (Gn 48:16).

St. Michael heard this prayer and showed himself the zealous protector of the sons of him whom he had given the name Israel.

CHAPTER 3:
ST. MICHAEL, ANGEL PROTECTOR OF THE CHURCH
UNDER THE WRITTEN LAW.

But at that time shall Michael rise up, the great
prince, who standeth for the children of thy people.
– Daniel 12:1

The promises of the archangel to the patriarchs had finally been fulfilled. The descendants of Abraham, Isaac, and Jacob had multiplied "as the stars of heaven, and as the sand that is by the sea shore" (Gn 22:17). They formed a great people. Led into Egypt, at the request of Joseph, by their father Jacob, the Hebrews groaned for a great number of years under the tyranny of the pharaohs, when God, according to the testimony of St. Stephen,[1] sent His angel to raise up for them a liberator.

One day when Moses was pasturing his flock, this angel "appeared to him in a flame of fire out of the midst of a bush" (Ex 3:2) and said to him,

> I have seen the affliction of *my people* in Egypt, and I have heard their cry: because of the rigour of them that are over the works.... For the cry of the children of Israel is come unto me: and I have seen their affliction.... But come, and I will send thee to Pharaoh, that thou mayst bring forth *my people*, the children of Israel out of Egypt. (Ex 3:7, 9-10)

Scripture says nothing about the name of this angel, but St. Gregory of Nyssa and the most renowned commentators[2] call him St. Michael. It is in fact reasonable to attribute to this archangel one of the greatest marks of protection that has been granted to those he was able to call *his people*.

Moses obeys the order given him. Protected by this angel, he surmounts countless difficulties, works the most astounding miracles,[3] and rescues the children of Israel from the severest and most humiliating of slaveries.

But who will lead this people? Before them are vast, uncharted deserts! Behold a sure guide: "And the Lord," Moses says, "went before them" in the person of His angel, "to shew the way by day in a pillar of a cloud, and by night in a pillar of fire: that he might be the guide of their journey at both times. There never failed the pillar of the cloud by day, nor the pillar of fire by night, before the people" (Ex 13:21-22) for forty years, meaning until the day of the children of Israel's entrance into the promised land.

But the Egyptians regret letting the Hebrews leave, and they pursue them with a great multitude of chariots and a numerous cavalry. At the sight of this, Israel cries out to the Lord.

> And the angel of God, who went before the camp of Israel, removing went behind them: and together with him the pillar of the cloud, leaving the forepart, stood behind, between the Egyptians' camp and the camp of Israel. And it was a dark cloud, and enlightening the night, so that they could not come at one another all the night. (Ex 14:19-20)

"Stretch forth thy hand over the sea," the angel, in the Lord's name, says to Moses (Ex 14:16), and when Moses stretched forth his hand, the angel of God[4] suddenly parted the waters and the Hebrew people "went in through the midst of the sea dried up…. And the Egyptians pursuing went in after them, and all Pharaoh's horses, chariots and horsemen" (14:22-23). However, the glorious archangel "overthrew the wheels of the chariots, and they were carried into the deep" (14:25). He then unleashed God's lightning and thunder against them. The Egyptians cried out, "Let us flee from Israel, for the Lord fighteth for them against us" (ibid.). But it was in vain. The angel spoke, Moses stretched forth his hand, and the waters returned to their original place so that not a single man in Pharaoh's army could escape. Moses and the children of Israel then sang hymns to the Lord, "for he is gloriously magnified: the horse and the rider he hath thrown into the sea" (15:1).

What a great spectacle is now presented to our gaze at Mount Sinai! "Thunders began to be heard, and lightning to flash, and a very thick cloud to cover the mount. And the noise of the trumpet sounded exceeding loud, and the people that was in the camp, feared.... And all Mount Sinai was on a smoke: because the Lord," represented by His angel, "was come down upon it in fire, and the smoke arose from it as out of a furnace. And all the mount was terrible. And the sound of the trumpet" of the angel "grew by degrees louder and louder, and was drawn out to a greater length.... The Lord," in the person of St. Michael, "came down upon Mount Sinai, in the very top of the mount: and he called Moses unto the top thereof" (Ex 19:16, 18-20), and gave him the written law on two stone tablets. This is the great event St. Stephen recalls to the Jews in his admirable discourse. Moses, he said, when the people were assembled in the desert, was "with the angel who spoke to him" on behalf of God "on Mount Sinai" and "received the words of life to give to us" (Acts 7:38). St. Paul, in his epistle to the Galatians, teaches in clear terms that the law was given through the ministry of the angels (Gal 3:19).[5]

Protected by their angel, the Israelites crushed all peoples who dared oppose them on their route to the promised land. Balak, the king of Moab, feared a similar fate and dared not resort to arms; he found Balaam, a celebrated soothsayer, and said, "Come therefore, and curse this people, because it is mightier than I, if by any means I may beat them and drive them out of my land. For I know that he whom thou shalt bless is blessed, and he whom thou shalt curse is cursed" (Nm 22:6). But the angel of God, holding a drawn sword, went before Balaam. Three times he stopped the ass on which Balaam was riding, and three times Balaam, becoming angry, beat his animal with increasingly vehement blows.

> And the angel said to him: Why beatest thou thy ass these three times? I am come to withstand thee, because thy way is perverse, and contrary to me. And unless the ass had turned out of the way, giving place to me who stood against thee, I had slain thee, and she should have lived.... Go... and see thou speak no other thing than what I shall command thee. (Nm 22:32-33, 35)[6]

And Balaam returned after having blessed three times those whom he had come to curse.

But one enemy, more formidable than the Egyptians and the Moabites, soon threatened God's people. Moses, the savior of Israel, the man admitted into the counsels of the divinity, had just died; the holy archangel, by the Lord's command, had buried him in a place hidden from the Jews. Lucifer, to lead the people to adore the body of the prophet with sacrifices and to make them fall into idolatry, wanted to make known the place of his burial. However, St. Jude says,[7] to preserve his people, St. Michael fought the demon and prevented him from revealing the sepulchre.

St. Michael's mission was not limited to having the people of God enter the promised land. With his counsels, he assisted Joshua, the successor of Moses. He found Gideon and sent him against the Midianites who were oppressing his people. Later, as is recounted in the book of Daniel, when Israel was in captivity in Babylon, he removes the obstacles preventing the people's return to their homeland. Gabriel said, "The prince of the kingdom of the Persians resisted me one and twenty days: and behold Michael, one of the chief princes, came to help me" (Dn 10:13). Finally, at the time of the war of independence, we see this "great prince, who standeth for the children of [God's] people" (Dn 12:1), visibly come to the aid of the brothers Maccabee.

However, before being able to provide his people such effective help, St. Michael had to have recourse to prayer; this is what a vision of the prophet Zechariah teaches us. It was the second year in the reign of Darius. The prophet says:

> I saw by night, and behold a man riding upon a red horse: and he stood among the myrtle trees that were in the bottom: and behind him were horses, red, speckled, and white. And I said: What are these, my lord? And the angel that spoke in me said to me: I will shew thee what these are. And the man that stood among the myrtle trees answered and said: These are they whom the Lord hath sent to walk through the earth. And they answered the angel of the Lord that stood among the myrtle trees, and said: We have walked through the earth, and behold all the earth is

inhabited and is at rest. And the angel of the Lord answered and said: O Lord of hosts, how long wilt thou not have mercy on Jerusalem and on the cities of Judah, with which thou hast been angry? This is now the seventieth year. (Zec 1:8-12)

St. Jerome, explaining this vision, says that this horseman, standing among the myrtle trees, is Michael, leader of the Lord's armies and principal defender of God's kingdom. Behind him are the angels of the nations, who report to him and receive God's orders through him. He is mounted on a red horse to perhaps indicate the prompt and bloody vengeance God will exact from Babylon, which, at that moment, is contemplating revolt against Darius. After the angels of the nations have reported to him that all the inhabited earth is at peace, he intercedes before God for Jerusalem, which is deserted and oppressed, and the Lord shows Himself responsive to his prayer by ending the captivity.

But of all the most signal marks of protection, it was the zeal with which this holy archangel worked to bring his people back to God, by rescuing them from the most dreadful captivity, from the most shameful slavery, the slavery of sin. Among the most propitious means for arriving at this goal, one must include suffering. One Holy Father says, "Tribulation… opens the ear of the heart, which this world's prosperity too often closes."[8] Nothing is truer; no people has demonstrated the truth of this saying like the Jewish people. Almost from the moment they have prosperity, and almost from the moment their enemies, ministers of divine vengeance, cease to weigh them down with an oppressive yoke, they forget God and return to idolatry. But when an extreme misery sweeps down upon them, they stop, consider the enormity of their sins, confess them before God, and throw themselves into the arms of His mercy. It would take a long time to recount to the reader the history of all the chastisements through which this "stiff-necked people"[9] were led back to God; for, the Jews' existence for close to seventeen centuries, that is to say from the passage through the Red Sea to the coming of Jesus Christ, is but a long alternation between successes and defeats, prosperity and setbacks, according to which this people served God or strayed from Him. It was you, O Michael, who, in all these circumstances, drew your sword from its sheath or placed it back inside, like on the day when you appeared to David during the pestilence that punished his pride!

The Jews in our day still invoke the holy archangel as the most steadfast defender of the synagogue against all kinds of enemies. On the Feast of the Atonement, they recite prayers in the form of litanies, composed by Rabbi Eleazar ben Kalir. They conclude with an invocation to St. Michael, an invocation that Zanolini, a renowned professor from the University of Padua, interprets this way: "Michael, prince of mercies, pray for Israel that he may reign in the heavens, and in the light coming from the face of the King seated upon the throne of mercies."

It is in vain, O unfortunate people, that you today invoke the one who, in other times, gave you such sensible signs of protection. You are no longer *his people*, not since the day when you killed Him Who is the Truth. Numerous nations from the four winds of heaven have been called, in your place, to form the true Church of God. It is there, only, that are found the protégés of the archangel. Enter the fold of her who wants to be your mother, and you shall again find your protector.

CHAPTER 4:

ST. MICHAEL, MINISTER OF THE MAN-GOD AND OF HIS MOST HOLY MOTHER. – HE IS THE GUARDIAN ANGEL OF THE EUCHARIST.

And there appeared to him an angel from heaven, strengthening him.
– Luke 22:43

The time had arrived for the Synagogue to be replaced by the Catholic Church. In place of the law of *fear*, written by the angels with the fire from Sinai, was going to be the law of *grace* and love, written with the blood of the Man-God. The Messiah, the Angel of the Great Counsel, was going to be given to the world through the mediation of a virgin mother.

Was St. Michael's mission finished? Far from it. Everything we have seen up to this point was only the preparation for a yet more glorious ministry.

Mary of Agreda says,

> By the continual enlightenments, favors and instructions of this great prince, I have understood great sacraments and mysteries of the Lord and of the Queen of heaven; for this angel was one of those who guarded and assisted Her and who were delegated from the angelic choirs…. He was a special witness and faithful minister of the mysteries of the Incarnation and Redemption.[1]

What the Venerable Mother says here very much conforms to St. Michael's character. In heaven, he had defended these mysteries against the pride of Lucifer; it was fitting that he be tasked with the great mission of being their minister on earth.

God had given His archangel as a protector to the ancestors of the Man-God; one should not then be surprised that He also gives him to His Holy Mother. "The Almighty destined him as a special ambassador of Christ our Lord and to act in some of the mysteries as the defender of his most holy Mother."[2] During Mary's journey to Bethlehem, St. Michael

> remained at the right side of his Queen without leaving Her even for a moment; several times, when She became tired, he led Her by the arm along the way. Whenever the Lord permitted, he also shielded Her against the weather and performed many other services for the heavenly Queen and the blessed Fruit of her womb, Jesus.[3]

Holy Ark, infinitely more precious than the one built by Moses, did she not deserve heaven's protection? Could angels do less for her than they do for the rest of men? "In their hands they shall bear thee up," Scripture says, "lest thou dash thy foot against a stone" (Ps 90:12 [91:12]).

When Mary gave birth to the Savior, St. Michael and St. Gabriel "received [the Incarnate Word] in their hands with ineffable reverence" and "presented to the divine Mother of God her glorious and refulgent Son."[4]

After having adored the Redeemer, the prince of the heavenly militia descended into limbo. He told the patriarchs and the prophets

> how the Onlybegotten of the eternal Father was already born into the world and was resting, humble and meek, as they had prophesied, in a manger.... It was the most consoling and joyful day, which this great gathering of the just and the saints had yet had during their long banishment.[5]

It was again St. Michael, says the Oratorian Fr. [Denis] Amelote, who announced to the shepherds in the outskirts of Bethlehem the news of this birth, these "good tidings of great joy that shall be to all the people" (Lk 2:10).[6] According to one tradition, he also announced to the Magi this blessed birth, and led them, by means of a star, to the foot of the manger.

Thus, the archangel who had been the first to recognize the Incarnate Word, and who, as a "first apostle," had announced Him at the Spirit of God's prompting to all the angelic peoples, is also the one who first announces Him to men in both this life and the other.

The archangel [Gabriel] had told Mary: You will give to the one born of you the name Jesus (Lk 1:31). The moment had arrived when the Son of God made man was to be given this name forever blessed, which makes bend every knee in heaven, on the earth, and in hell (Phil 2:10). Let us listen to Mary of Agreda.

On the day of the Circumcision, countless hosts of angels descended from heaven; they were

> clothed in shining white garments, on which were woven red embroideries of wonderful beauty. They had palms in their hands and crowns upon their heads and emitted a greater splendor than many suns. In comparison with the beauty of these holy princes all the loveliness seen in this world appeared repulsive. But pre-eminent in splendor were the devices or escutcheons on their breasts, on each of which the sweet name of Jesus was engraved or embossed. The effulgence which each of these escutcheons emitted exceeded that of all the angels together.... The chiefs of these heavenly cohorts were the two princes, saint Michael and saint Gabriel, shining in greater splendor than the rest and bearing in their hands, as a special distinction, the most holy name of JESUS, written in larger letters on something like cards of incomparable beauty and splendor.
>
> The two princes presented themselves apart from the rest before their Queen and said: "Lady, this is the name of thy Son, which was written in the mind of God from all eternity and which the blessed Trinity has given to the Onlybegotten Son and our Lord as the signal of salvation for the whole human race; establishing Him at the same time on the throne of David. He shall reign upon it, chastise his enemies and triumph over them, making them his footstool and passing judgment upon them; He

shall raise his friends to the glory of his right hand. But all this is to happen at the cost of suffering and blood; and even now He is to shed it in receiving this name, since it is that of the Savior and Redeemer; it shall be the beginning of his sufferings in obedience to the will of his eternal Father. We all are come as ministering spirits of the Most High, appointed and sent by the holy Trinity in order to serve the Onlybegotten of the Father and thy own in all the mysteries and sacraments of the law of grace. We are to accompany Him and minister to Him until He shall ascend triumphantly to the celestial Jerusalem and open the portals of heaven; afterwards we shall enjoy an especial accidental glory beyond that of the other blessed, to whom no such commission has been given."[7]

Thus spoke St. Michael and St. Gabriel, according to Mary of Agreda. On the day of the Annunciation, Gabriel had already spoken to Mary in somewhat similar language.

Not until the day of the Savior's agony does the venerable sister of St. Francis say anything to us about the special mission of the prince of the angels. However, was it not he who told Joseph to leave for Egypt and who protected him during this journey?[8] Was it not also he who came, on behalf of God, to announce that his exile was finally over and that he was to return to Nazareth? From what we have said concerning this archangel's predestination, it is very reasonable to attribute this mission to him.

But behold the Savior in His agony, as He was praying for the third time. The eternal Father

sent the archangel Michael to the earth in order to comfort Him by a sensible message and confirmation of what He already knew by the infused science of his most holy soul; for the angel could not tell our Lord anything He did not know, nor could he produce any additional effect on his interior consciousness for this purpose. But, as I related above, Christ had suspended the consolation, which He could have derived from his human nature from this knowledge and love, leaving it to its full capacity for suffering, as He afterwards also expressed Himself on the Cross. In lieu of this alleviation and comfort, which He had denied Himself, He was recompensed to a certain extent, as far as his human senses were concerned, by this embassy of the archangel. He received an experimental knowledge of what He had before known by interior consciousness; for the actual experience is something superadded and new and is calculated to move the sensible and bodily faculties. Saint Michael, in the name of the eternal Father, intimated and represented to Him in audible words, what He already knew, that it was not possible for those to be saved who were unwilling; that the complaisance of the eternal Father in the number of the just, although smaller than the number of the reprobate[,] was great.[9]

When Our Lord descended into limbo, His

> most holy soul... betook itself in the company of innumerable angels, who gave glory, fortitude and Divinity to their victorious and triumphant King. In accordance with his greatness and majesty they commanded the portals of this ancient prison to be opened, in order that the King of glory, powerful in battles and Lord of virtues, might find them unlocked and open at his entrance.[10]

How exceedingly jubilant St. Michael must have been, at the head of his sacred battalion, as he came to proclaim the fulfillment of the promise of which he had been the messenger on the day of the birth of the Incarnate Word! With what joyful eagerness he must have obeyed the Divine Majesty when God ordered him and his angels to remove from that place all the souls yearning for their deliverance! You began, O great archangel, that glorious mission of bringing souls before God. "May the standard-bearer, St. Michael, lead them into the holy light!"[11]

After the Ascension of the Savior, our illustrious prince continued to watch over Mary during those years God wanted to leave the Church on earth this invaluable treasure. Finally, when the time of this great Queen's pilgrimage was completed, he transported her to heaven.[12] With what joy he escorted her into glory! With what eagerness he prostrated himself at the foot of the throne of her whom he had proclaimed, so many ages before, his Mistress and his Queen! Did he not share any of the honor with the Man-God of placing on Mary's head her royal crown? In this way, the Queen would be crowned both by men and by angels: by men in the person of Jesus Christ, and by angels in the person of St. Michael.[13]

Before the Savior ascended into heaven, He told His apostles, "I will not leave you orphans" (Jn 14:18) and "I am with you all days, even to the consummation of the world" (Mt 28:20). Indeed, Jesus is always among us, in the sacrament of the Eucharist. It was natural then that the angel minister of the Man-God during His mortal life would also be the guardian angel of His Eucharistic life. St. Michael, it is attested, declared in a revelation to the hermit St. Eutropius that he had been chosen to fulfill this duty, which had been entrusted to him since Holy Thursday. There are multiple other accounts of revelations made by him to various saints pertaining to worship of the Blessed Sacrament.

Illustrious head of the guard of honor for the Eucharistic Jesus, banish bold profaners from our temples; draw pure hearts to the foot of the altars of Him Whose court you adorn; inspire souls with a tender love for and noble devotion to the interests of Jesus and Mary, Whose faithful minister you are in heaven and on earth.

CHAPTER 5:

ST. MICHAEL, ANGEL PROTECTOR OF THE CATHOLIC CHURCH. – TRADITION ATTRIBUTES THIS ROLE TO HIM. – NOVENAS IN ROME. – HE MAKES USE OF EMPEROR CONSTANTINE TO GIVE PEACE TO THE CHURCH. – HE COMES TO THE AID OF APOSTOLIC MEN.

Blessed Michael... mightily drives out the ancient enemy from the Church's domain.
– Hugh of St. Victor[1]

"The dragon," St. John says in the Apocalypse, "persecuted the woman" (Rv 12:13). What woman is it then who is the object of this persecution? Mgr. Gaume says that it is the woman par excellence, it is the mother of the Son par excellence, it is the woman of whom it was said to the dragon himself, immediately after his first victory: "I will put enmities between thee and the woman, and thy seed and her seed: she shall crush thy head, and thou shalt lie in wait for her heel" (Gn 3:15). Do you wish to know who she is? Listen to the voice of past and present centuries: all repeat the name of Mary.

But how is it that Mary, whose time on earth was accomplished in a few years in an obscure corner of Palestine, can be the object of such a persecution lasting centuries and covering the entire globe? Mary is the immortal woman. Forty centuries before her birth, she lived in Eve, and Satan knew this. For the last eighteen centuries, she has been living in the Church, and Satan knows this also.

Mary, indeed, lives in the Church, who is her daughter and her likeness. We say her daughter because the divine blood that gave birth to the Church is the blood of Mary. We say her likeness because, like Mary, the Church is simultaneously virgin and mother. Virgin, because error has never sullied her, and mother, because she gives birth to as many Christs as she gives birth to Christians. *The Christian is another*

128

Christ. Thus, the woman, object of the dragon's eternal hatred, is the Church, or rather Mary living in the Church.

What characterizes this hatred most is its *implacability*. Incapable of loving, and needing to hate—this indeed is the mystery of Satan's life.

This hatred is incarnated in living humanity. It is called revolution, meaning that thing that has at its heart, as its life essence, hatred for the Church. My ideal, it exclaims, is always the same; my ideal is Voltaire, from atop a pedestal, sneering over the ruins of Christendom; it is the new humanity repeating, or practicing rather, the master's motto: *Crush the infamous thing!* It is myself finally smothering in my arms my eternal enemy, the Catholic Church. Hatred for the Church is the rallying point for all opinions, sects, schools, presses, and doctrines that qualify as revolutionary. Hatred for the Church is the very essence of this dark spirit that shakes the world today and threatens to crush it; it is the universal protestation of Satan against the Word, and against Mary.

The defender of Mary, and of the Church, in which Mary lives, is still the one who makes heard this cry in heaven: "Who is like God?" Vanquisher in heaven, he is also this on earth. When God judges it expedient for the salvation of His children, St. Michael comes down from heaven with a long chain; he binds the dragon and casts him into the abyss, which he seals so that he no longer seduces the nations. When the time is fulfilled, he loosens him once again, for a little time, until the day when he will be "cast into the pool of fire and brimstone, where the beast and the false prophet shall be tormented day and night for ever and ever" (Rv 20:1-3, 7, 9-10).

The ecclesiastical writers delighted in celebrating this mission of St. Michael.

Let us look in particular at a sermon of Hugh of St. Victor for the feast of the great archangel:

> Let us have great confidence in St. Michael and his angels. We sing on this day's solemnity, "The sea was moved and the earth quaked, when the Archangel Michael descended from heaven."[2] The sea is the demons, and the earth is evil men. The demons are represented by the sea because, like it, they are full of

bitterness, swollen, and always in motion. The wicked are represented by the earth because they scorn the things of heaven to attach themselves to the earth. But there, where Michael descends from heaven, the sea is moved and the earth quakes, because this archangel curbs the temptations of the demons and the perversity of the wicked, in order to deliver the faithful of Jesus Christ.[3]

Bossuet notes the universality of this belief. He says:

One must not hesitate to recognize St. Michael as the defender of the Church, as he was for the ancient people according to St. John's testimony (Rev. 12:7), in conformity with the testimony of Daniel (10:13, 21; 12:1). The Protestants who, through a gross error, always believe they are taking away from God whatever they give to His saints and angels in the fulfillment of His works, want St. Michael to be in the Apocalypse Jesus Christ Himself, the prince of the angels, and apparently in Daniel to be the Word eternally conceived in the bosom of God; but will they ever accept Scripture's straightforward meaning? Do they not see that Daniel speaks to us of the prince of the Greeks and the prince of the Persians, simply meaning angels who preside over these nations by God's command; and that St. Michael is called in the same way *the prince of the synagogue*, or as the archangel St. Gabriel explains to Daniel, *Michael, your prince*, and as more explicitly stated elsewhere, *Michael, the great prince, who standeth for the children of thy people*? And what does St. Gabriel tell us of this great prince? *Michael*, he says, *one of the chief princes*. Is it that the Word of God, equal to His Father, the creator of all the angels and sovereign of all these princes, is only one of the first among them? Is that a characterization worthy of the Son of God? That Daniel's Michael is only an angel, that of St. John's, who is clearly the same one spoken of by Daniel, cannot be otherwise. If the dragon and his angels war against the Church, it is not at all surprising that St. Michael and his angels defend her.[4]

Such has always been the Church's belief. Thus, when persecution makes itself felt, when the tempest threatens to engulf the barque of Peter, everyone, sailors and passengers, turn to the glorious prince of the heavenly militia.

More recently, in the name of Pius IX, the cardinal vicar invited the Roman people to the foot of the archangel's altars in these terms:

> If, on the one hand, the ungodly of our day have dared to honor the prince of darkness, whose sons and imitators they have become, the faithful, for their part, have endeavored to increase the veneration and trust that the Catholic Church has always placed in St. Michael the Archangel, the first vanquisher of the accursed spirit.
>
> Now, since the struggle of rebellious thought against the Most High has rekindled, since hell has redoubled its dark efforts against the supports of divine reasons, we have witnessed a more universal and solemn expansion of preparation for the feast of the holy archangel. And this preparation is prescribed us by the Holy Father this year (1868), for we have no less need than at other times of being protected by the glorious victor over the demons.
>
> The invincible leader of the angelic legions wants to see and recognize his brave soldiers at the foot of his altars, as of old he saw around his banner the angels armed against the proud Lucifer. Let us hasten with confidence beneath the wings of St. Michael, and let us implore his favors, so that he expel Satan from the world as he in the past expelled him from heaven! "Now is the judgment of the world: now shall the prince of this world be cast out" [(Jn 12:31)].

This appeal by the Roman Pontiff is founded on centuries of experience. How many times, in fact, has the prince of the angels come to the aid of the Church when she was attacked! When God was cementing the edifice of His Church with the blood of the martyrs, St. Michael was assisting the generous confessors of Jesus's name, in prisons, before tyrants, and upon scaffolds; he helped the apostles and their successors to overcome the obstacles opposed to the preaching of the good news and the spread of Christianity. On the day marked by God, when the Christian name seemed condemned to disappear from the world, he sought out a still pagan warrior, Constantine, gave him the cross as a standard,[5] and led him to Rome after a brilliant victory. The Church came out of the catacombs.

According to the interpretation of Bossuet, St. John had announced this victory in the twelfth chapter of Revelation.

> *And there was a great battle in heaven...* As the demon foresaw *that he hath but a short time*, and that the Gentiles, who were converting en masse, would soon lose him the Roman Empire, he makes his last efforts against the Church; the angels, for their part, fight with greater intensity. *Michael and his angels fought with the dragon, and the dragon fought, and his angels.* Each army had its leader. *Michael, the great prince, who standeth for the children of thy people.* One sees here then that St. Michael is the defender of the Church, as he was the defender of the Synagogue.
>
> *And they prevailed not, neither was their place found any more in heaven....* This fall happened to them when Galerius, who was the originator of the persecution, was himself constrained on his deathbed, by a horrible illness very much appearing to result from divine vengeance, to issue an edict giving peace to the Church in the year 311 A.D.; and this edict was supported by Constantine, who grew more powerful each day....
>
> *And I heard a loud voice in heaven.* This was the saints' song of thanksgiving for the victory over idolatry, and the peace given to the Church by Constantine. *The accuser of our brethren... who accused them before our God.* One can hear here the calumnies with which the demon inspired the pagans against the faithful; but this phrase *before our God* takes us back to what happened in the person of Job, when he was delivered to Satan,

who boasted he would overcome his constancy. Similarly, to test the patience of His Church, God permitted the demons to incite persecutors against her.

Woe to the earth and to the sea. Woe to the entire world and to all men! And the cause of this woe in all the earth is, St. John continues, that *the devil is come down unto you, having great wrath* against the Church, which he will persecute with a new fury…. *Knowing that he hath but a short time:* something he easily saw from the conversions that were multiplying, from the Gentiles' very acclamations that were to the credit of Christians and their God, and finally, because Constantine, so favorable to the Church, was manifestly advancing to sovereign power more than all the other emperors at the time. Here St. John declares to us most explicitly that this implacable wrath, which makes the demon exert his final efforts against the Church, is a woe for the entire world. It is even more of a woe for the persecutors than for the persecuted Church, for even though she still has much to suffer on account of the demon unleashing upon her this *great wrath* with which he is filled, those in whom he operates and whom he makes instruments of his wrath are in an incomparably more deplorable condition.[6]

But the Church, after this triumph, was not to live in peace. Christ promised her persecution and war. Like fruit crushed in a press, she is at times crushed under the weight of suffering: "in the world you shall have distress" (Jn 16:33). The kings and powerful ones of the earth have allied themselves against her; the wicked have wanted to conspire to undermine her foundations; they have even seized, multiple times, the city to which her fate is tied; however, after the example of Clement VII fleeing the fury of the Spanish, the Roman Pontiffs took refuge behind the shield of St. Michael,[7] and the archangel, hitting these enemy armies with the tip of his sword, scattered them.

Sometimes, however, help has seemed to delay. But here, as everywhere, we see the finger of God. In the Church, there must be heroes and martyrs; there must be illustrious souls; there must be generous men who get crushed and slain for justice's sake. Now, it is war that makes heroes. Peace weakens courage and softens hearts—this is the complaint St. Cyprian made amidst the peace the Church enjoyed in the fourth century. But war shakes off people's torpor, raises up souls, and fortifies character. This is the secret of the life of the Church, always young and always beautiful: suffering is the blood that carries life to all her members. Like the giant in the fable who, each time he touches the earth, acquires new powers, the Church, after each persecution, always gets back up more brilliant and more radiant.

Yes, O Church of Jesus Christ, you live and will live until the end of the ages without the gates of hell ever able to prevail against you! Let the impious rejoice, let them strike twice as hard the unshakable rock, and let them proclaim with great pomp its coming destruction! The fools! They fulfill without realizing it the promise of the Divine Founder! But when their work is over, they will break themselves, like their predecessors, against the sword of the glorious vanquisher of Satan, and against the rock that they try to overcome.

But St. Michael is not only in charge of defending the Church; he also enters her ministry of assisting the apostolic men who work for her extension. This is the sentiment of ecclesiastical writers.

Hermas, a writer in the first century of the Church, explains in his book *The Shepherd* the mystical construction of the Church and the ministry of the angels. The Church first appears like an aged woman, because she was created before all things, and the world was made for her. These are the words of the revelation. But she is principally represented as a tower that is built on an immense, square-shaped foundation that is Jesus Christ. Six principal angels preside over the construction; countless other angels bring and prepare the stones, which are the faithful. Among these angels are identified the angel of penitence, the angel of chastisement, the angel of equity, and even the angel who has power over the animals. But the one who has received authority over both the angels and the men for building the Church is the archangel St. Michael. He enters into his ministry to examine the use made of the Divine Law by those to whom it has been given.

This sentiment is also that of Origen.

Moreover, St. Michael himself has given visible proofs of his intervention. Let us cite some examples.

It was the third century. The martyr St. Erasmus had just been put into a narrow cell where he was bound with strong chains. An angel appeared and said to him, "I am the angel Michael, sent to you to lead you into the province of Campania and teach the people." And, having him exit the prison, he had him travel from Asia Minor to Campania. The martyr went into the city of [Formia],[8] where for seven years he evangelized this people; one legend adds that the angel of the Lord provided him bread each day.

In the sixteenth century, we see St. Michael coming to assist St. Francis Xavier when this apostle was evangelizing the peoples on the island of Moro.

We shall let one of his biographers, Fr. Bouhours, tell the story. This was on September 29.

> On that day, which is consecrated to St. Michael's honor, the Christians were assembled in very great numbers, and Father was saying Mass. In the middle of the sacrifice, the earth was so violently shaken that all the people chaotically exited the church. Father feared that the altar would overturn; however, he did not leave it and finished celebrating the sacred mysteries, thinking, as he himself said, that the blessed archangel was then expelling to the depths of hell the demons of the island, and that these infernal spirits were making all of this commotion due to the resentment they had in seeing themselves banished from a place where they had reigned for so many centuries.[9]

At the beginning of the last century, Fr. Cavallero, a Spanish religious, was evangelizing numerous tribes in South America. One day, he set up a rural altar at the foot of a tree; he placed the image of St. Michael close to the Savior's cross and the image of Mary, then addressed some words to his dear neophytes. They fell on their knees and cried out in one voice: "Jesus, our Savior, you are our father! O, Mary most holy, you are our mother! O, powerful St. Michael, you are our protector!" Then all this people, in an exhilaration of joy whose transports they could not contain, began doing dances in front of the altar. And the missionary cried out to the Lord for being sufficiently rewarded for his work and sacrifices through the consolation he experienced at that moment.

Even in our own time, St. Michael comes to the aid of the missionaries announcing the good news to the peoples of North America.

The following was written on March 20, 1868, by Fr. Genin of the Oblates of Mary Immaculate:

> In the center of Sioux territory, from where I am writing, is a lake until now called Devil's Lake (*Mini-Wakan*) for reasons I will tell you…. On Friday, March 6, I solemnly blessed it and renamed it St. Michael's Lake…. The Sioux equally adore God, under the name of *Wakan-Tanka* (the greatest Spirit), and the demon under the name of *Wakan-Citca*. All while acknowledging the existence of a good God, they would fear the anger of the manitou if they did not make some sacrifices to please him. At certain times, one therefore sees them cutting their own living flesh, mainly around the heart, offering the blood to Satan so that he will spare them. For the same purpose, they plant large poles into the ground, tie a rope at the top, then, piercing a hole in their side, they run the other end of the rope through it and pull until their flesh tears into shreds. Some of them become weak to the point of losing consciousness; but then a relative comes to throw cold water on their face and, coming to, they continue the work started. Do you find in any Christian mortifications anything so cruel as the mortifications Satan inspires in his victims? Poor people! How I suffer seeing them act so bravely to please their enemy!
>
> The great St. Michael's Lake, formerly called *Mini-Wakan* (Devil's Lake), was the specific place for these kinds of sacrifices. There, in fact, the demon sometimes showed himself in a hideous form.

The same missionary states that the Sioux now show excellent dispositions for learning, knowing, and practicing the religion of Jesus Christ. Driven away by the powerful arms of St. Michael, Satan, let us hope, will no longer dare to reappear among this people he had made his own.

CHAPTER 6:

ST. MICHAEL MAKES USE OF FRANCE TO PROTECT THE CHURCH. – HE IS THE ANGEL PROTECTOR OF THE FRENCH PEOPLE.

The angel St. Michael told me of the great distress in the Kingdom of France and how I should hasten to help my king.
– Deposition of Joan of Arc

Saint Michael assuredly can, by his power alone, help the Church in all her necessities. However, like God, of Whom he is a perfect image, he makes use of peoples and individuals to fulfill the decrees of Divine Providence.

It is in this way that we see him make use of the French people, whose protector he has declared himself to be.

This people, in fact, is bound to the Church by such a close and necessary tie, that their special mission is to serve the preservation, defense, and development of the Church.

Oh, may they always understand this sublime mission and execute it faithfully!

They did so when their first Christian king showed himself, in his time, to be the only Catholic king in the entire world. The Pope wrote to Clovis:

> Glorious and illustrious son, be the consolation of your mother; to support her, be for her a pillar of iron... for our barque is battered by a raging storm. But we hope against all hope, and we praise God for having rescued you from the power of darkness to give to His Church, in the person of so great a king, a protector capable of defending her from her enemies. May the Lord also deign to continue to grant you, to you and your kingdom, His divine protection; may he order *His angels* to guard you in all your ways, and may He give you victory over all your enemies.

The French people understood and fulfilled their mission when, under Charlemagne and succeeding kings, they took charge of

138

defending the interests of the Holy See and showed themselves its most constant support.

They understood and fulfilled their mission when, through the Crusades, for which they had the initiative, they drove back the Muslim barbarism in Asia, and delivered the holy places from their profaners.

They understand and fulfill this sublime mission still, when they crisscross all the seas of the globe with their missionaries, who go to bring the light of the Gospel to the peoples sitting in the shadow of death.

St. Michael has come to the aid of France in the fulfillment of this sublime mission. Such has perpetually been the belief of the princes and peoples since Clovis and Charlemagne, who had depicted on their standards the image of the archangel vanquisher of Satan. Certainly, this belief has been confirmed in an obvious manner by the mission of Joan of Arc. Was it not the archangel who came, in the name of God, to announce to her what she should do? Was it not he who led her and supported her in her glorious and painful mission? And what was this mission, if not that of saving French nationhood when it was on the brink of perishing?

But let us listen to Joan herself recounting before her iniquitous judges how she knew her providential mission:

> It was a summer day, around noon. I was about thirteen years old, and I was in my father's garden. I heard a voice on the right, from the side of the church; I saw at the same time an apparition surrounded by a great light. It had the appearance of a very good and very virtuous man; it had wings and was surrounded on all sides by many lights and accompanied by angels from heaven; for the angels often come towards Christians without them noticing; I myself often see them among them. It was the Archangel Michael. He seemed to me to have a very respectable voice; but I was still a young child; I was very afraid of this apparition, and I had much doubt it was an angel. It was only after having heard this voice three times that I recognized it as his. He taught me and showed me so many things that I finally believed firmly that it was he. *I saw him, him and the angels, with my own eyes, as clearly as I see you, my judges, and I*

believe what he said and did with as firm a faith as I believe in the passion and death of Jesus Christ our Savior, and what makes me believe him are the good teachings, the good counsel, and the help with which he has always assisted me.

The angel told me that above all else, I must be a good child, behave well, and go often to the church, and that God would support me. *He told me of the great distress in the Kingdom of France and how I should hasten to help my king....* When St. Michael and the angels come to me, I have a great joy of not being in mortal sin; for, if I were, I think they would leave me on the field.... When they would part from me, I would kiss the ground where they stood, and I would bow before them.

This was how Joan recounted the miraculous manner in which God ordered her to take up the sword for her king and her homeland. She steadfastly upheld the truth of these apparitions, despite every suffering and every threat; and she upheld this truth with a loud voice, in the flames, when she was being burned at the stake.

Shortly before, St. Michael had secured the days of Charles VII, to whom Joan had come to return the kingdom. [When a floor collapsed in a meeting hall in][1] La Rochelle, a large rock fell on the [soon-to-be] king's head, without doing him any harm. Attributing this protection to "the favor of St. Michael, to whom he was strongly devoted,"[2] he brought this rock to Mount Tombe. This votive offering, for a long time, remained hanging in the nave by an iron chain.

"Since the Christian era, is there a people in the world," we ask with Cardinal de Bonnechose, "for whom God has employed such means and worked such wonders?"

Should one be surprised if our ancestors had a great devotion to the holy archangel?

Bishop Bravard says:

His cult is impregnated in our customs and our mores; our revolutions were unable to efface its marks.

It is on the date of St. Michael celebrations, on Michaelmas still, that tenant farmers schedule their entry onto estates whose operations they are assuming, or their arrival in houses of which they are taking possession.

It is on this same date that creditors require payment of their rents, on the same occasion that the most significant markets and most notable fairs[3] have been established, which accomplish a number of the most important acts of family and social life, not only in Normandy, but elsewhere throughout Europe.

The kings of France had taken St. Michael as their protector. They were obligated during their reign to visit his shrine built *at the peril of the sea.*

An old prediction made by an abbot, Richard Toustain, and formerly preserved in the abbatial archives of Mont Saint-Michel, threatened with the greatest misfortunes, down to the third generation, the posterity of the king who neglected to make a pilgrimage to St. Michael and Our Lady.[4] "This prediction," Fr. Orsini says, "has only been too verified."[5]

They no longer desired, these kings, to recognize the protector of their fathers; and the protector disowned them as leaders of his people.

But for you, O France, who have not wanted to renounce the religion of your ancestors, remember that you are the right arm of the angel protector of the Catholic Church. This mission calls today for your energy and your generosity. The fury of the Church's enemies is at its full: danger is imminent. The Vicar of Jesus Christ, besieged and affronted by ungrateful children,[6] is threatened from everywhere. It belongs to you, O France, to fly first to his aid, to reestablish by force of arms, and under the protection of St. Michael, the age-old conditions of his security and independence—it belongs to you to make him a bulwark of your devotion.

CHAPTER 7:

ST. MICHAEL PROTECTS THE JEWISH AND CHRISTIAN ARMIES FIGHTING FOR THE DEFENSE OF THE CHURCH.

I am prince of the host of the Lord.
– Joshua 5:14

Saint Michael is the angel of battle. At the first battle, at the head of the most valiant army, he fought the most formidable enemy. Glorious vanquisher, God made him head of the heavenly militia—a countless army of invincible soldiers worthy of the leader who commands them!

It is still, in battles without number, that the archangel defends, on earth, the Church of God.

But why speak of war when today one only hears the word peace: *League of Peace! Congress of Peace!* Utopians, who speak and act as if war were not a plague God uses to punish the sins of peoples! They put the blame on sovereigns: Horace says playfully, "By the madness of kings, the peoples are punished."

However, Jean-Baptiste Rousseau says with greater seriousness and true philosophy:

> *It is the wrath of kings that makes the earth rush to arms,*
> *It is the wrath of Heaven that makes the kings rush to arms.*

Joseph de Maistre says:

> When sins, and especially sins of a certain kind, have accumulated to a given point, the exterminating angel unconstrainedly hastens his indefatigable flight. Like a burning torch revolving rapidly, the great swiftness of his motion makes him simultaneously present at all points of his fearsome orbit. He strikes all the peoples of the earth at the same moment; other times, as the minister of a precise and infallible vengeance, he is bent on particular nations and bathes them in blood. Do not

142

expect them to make any effort to escape their judgment or shorten it. We believe we see these great guilty ones, enlightened by their consciences, who ask for the punishment and accept it to find atonement therein. As long as blood remains, they come to offer it; and soon thereafter, a sparse youth will be told of these desolating wars produced by the sins of their fathers.[1]

War in itself is therefore divine.

It is also divine in its results. There are wars that degrade nations, and degrade them for centuries; other wars exalt them, and perfect them in every way. Such is the spectacle that the history of the Church presents to us. Let us not then be surprised if we see the Envoy of the God of armies punishing guilty peoples through war, and strengthening the assailed Church by this same means.

He did so for the Jewish people.

Joshua, the valiant leader of the Hebrews, had just passed over the Jordan. And when he was

> in the field of the city of Jericho, he lifted up his eyes, and saw a man standing over against him, holding a drawn sword. And he went to him, and said: Art thou one of ours, or of our adversaries?
>
> And he answered: No: but I am prince of the host of the Lord, and now I am come.... Behold I have given into thy hands Jericho, and the king thereof, and all the valiant men. Go round about the city, all ye fighting men, once a day: so shall ye do for six days. And on the seventh day the priests shall take the seven trumpets, which are used in the jubilee, and shall go before the ark of the covenant: and you shall go about the city seven times, and the priests shall sound the trumpets. And when the voice of the trumpet shall give a longer and broken tune, and shall sound in your ears, all the people shall shout together with a very great shout: and the walls of the city shall fall to the ground. And they shall enter in every one at the place against which they shall stand. (Jos 5:13-14; 6:2-5)

The event soon unfolded as promised.[2]

Later, we see him again with Gideon. He says to him, "The Lord is with thee, O most valiant of men.... Go in this thy strength: and thou shalt deliver Israel out of the hand of Midian. Know that I have sent thee.... I will be with thee: and thou shalt cut off Midian as one man" (Jgs 6:12, 14, 16). Gideon then gathered a numerous army. "The people that are with thee are many, and Midian shall not be delivered into their hands. Lest Israel should glory against me, and say: I was delivered by my own strength" (Jgs 7:2). The Hebrew warrior then dismissed most of his army and kept only three hundred men. It was an invincible army, for it was supported by an assistance that nothing could overcome. Soon, there was disorder in the camp of the Midianites, who turned their swords against themselves and killed each other.

But one of the most admirable deeds of the great archangel was the defeat of the army of Sennacherib, the king of Assyria. Everyone knew this proud prince's message, full of blasphemy, to the inhabitants of Jerusalem:

> Let not Hezekiah deceive you: for he shall not be able to deliver you out of my hand. Neither let him make you trust in the Lord, saying: The Lord will surely deliver us; and this city shall not be given into the hand of the king of the Assyrians.... Who are they among all the gods of the nations, that have delivered their country out of my hand, that the Lord may deliver Jerusalem out of my hand? (2 Kgs 18:29-30, 35)

But the king of Judah cried out to heaven. And at night, the *angel of the Lord* went into the camp of the Assyrians and slew one hundred eighty-five thousand of the strongest men and the leader commanding them. And Sennacherib, at the sight of all those dead bodies, went away in disgrace.

Multiple times, during the war of independence, St. Michael came to the aid of the army commanded by the intrepid Maccabees. Scripture tells us that when Antiochus was preparing a second journey into Egypt,

> it came to pass that through the whole city of Jerusalem for the space of forty days there were seen horsemen running in the air,

in gilded raiment, and armed with spears, like bands of soldiers. And horses set in order by ranks, running one against another, with the shakings of shields, and a multitude of men in helmets, with drawn swords, and casting of darts, and glittering of golden armour and of harnesses of all sorts. Wherefore all men prayed that these prodigies might turn to good. (2 Mc 5:2-4)

Judas Maccabee assembled seven thousand men, telling them that their enemies

trust in their weapons and in their boldness: but we trust in the Almighty Lord who at a beck can utterly destroy both them that come against us and the whole world. Moreover he put them in mind also of the helps their fathers had received from God: and how under Sennacherib a hundred and eighty-five thousand had been destroyed. And of the battle that they had fought against the Galatians in Babylonia: how they, being in all but six thousand, when it came to the point and the Macedonians their companions were at a stand, slew a hundred and twenty thousand, because of the help they had from heaven. (2 Mc 8:18-20)

It was in this way that this valiant defender of his oppressed brothers attributed to the *angel of the Lord* the success of his weapons, and deserved, by this recognition, new favors. Shortly thereafter, when he was advancing against Lysias,

there appeared at Jerusalem a horseman going before them in white clothing, with golden armour, shaking a spear. Then they all together blessed the merciful Lord.... So they went on courageously, having a helper from heaven.... And rushing violently upon the enemy, like lions, they slew of them... and put all the rest to flight.... And Lysias himself fled away shamefully. (2 Mc 11:8-12)

Protector of the Jewish armies, St. Michael is still so for the Christian armies, who fight for the defense of the Church and what is right.

For the first three centuries of the Church, no army had been raised to avenge oppressed Christianity. The Christians, rather than defending their faith with arms, preferred, like St. Maurice and his companions, to be killed and to shed their blood.

The time marked by God to make the faith triumph over the pride of the Caesars had finally arrived. Three centuries of persecutions had sufficiently made known that all the powers of earth and hell conspiring against the Church could not overcome her. It was time for God to show the world a no less stunning miracle, in the person of emperors subject to the law of a crucified God and adoring His cross. St. Michael was tasked with this mission.

In Rome, there reigned a notorious tyrant, Maxentius; Constantine hastened to overthrow him. Maxentius, at this news, consulted demons who promised him victory. But the leader of God's armies protected Constantine and made him victorious. This is what we learn from a revelation St. Michael later made to Constantine: "It was I," he said, "who, when you were fighting against the impiety of the tyrants, made your weapons victorious."

This victory was only the prelude to a great number of other no less glorious victories, winning multitudes of peoples, enemies to the Christian name.

We learn from an ancient inscription visible in Rome that Pope Leo IV, after winning a signal victory over the Saracens and expelling them from Rome's port, had constructed, in thanksgiving for this benefit, a temple at the Vatican, under the name of the Commander of the Armies of God. This was around the year 849.[3]

Indeed, St. Michael, far better than the fortification cannons bearing his name, struck the enemies of the Eternal City. What enemy peoples Rome saw encamped around its walls! They were called Huns, Vandals, Saracens, Lombards, etc. They came from the four winds of heaven! Some of them were even rebellious children! Some of them may have appeared victorious for a moment, but soon afterwards, as though expelled by an invisible power, one saw them disappear.

Scatter again today, O great archangel, an implacable enemy who has been working for so many years to eliminate the patrimony of St.

Peter, so necessary for the Church's freedom. Support the small but valiant army that has come to make a bulwark of its devotion to the Roman Pontiff. It has chosen you as its patron.[4] Lead it, again, to victory; and, all together, we shall bless the name of the *God of armies.*

It is not only in Rome, but everywhere that the cause of the Church is in danger, that St. Michael intervenes.

It was the fifth century. The inhabitants of Naples, still pagan, declared war on the inhabitants of Siponto and Benevento. These latter, who were Christians, asked, following their bishop's advice, for a three-day truce. During this time, they devoted themselves to fasting and prayer and implored the support of St. Michael. On the third night, the archangel appeared to the bishop and told him that their prayers had been heard and that they would obtain victory. He gave the order to attack the enemy at the fourth hour of the day. When the Sipontans rushed to attack, Mount Gargano quaked, lightning shot from heaven, an obscure, dark cloud covered the entire top of the mountain, and more than six hundred enemies died by the sword of Christians and by arrows of fire falling from the sky. Forced to acknowledge the power of the archangel, the Neapolitans abandoned the errors of idolatry and submitted themselves to the Christian faith.

It was in this same region that six centuries later, he came to the aid of the emperor St. Henry, against the Saracens who were threatening to advance to Rome. The multitude of these barbarians was incalculable; however, St. Michael scattered them, one author says, like he long ago killed the one hundred eighty-five thousand men of the blasphemer Sennacherib's army.

When the Crusaders, commanded by the valiant Godfrey of Bouillon, were battling for the deliverance of the Holy Sepulchre, and when the Christian armies, encamped for a long time around the Holy City, were performing marvels of bravery to expel the Muslims, a heavenly vision was seen on the side of the Mount of Olives; it was a horseman signaling to approach the city and seize it. Comforted by this vision, the Christians waged an attack and entered as victors into Jerusalem.

According to the belief of William of Tyre, Cardinal Baronius, and the Bollandists, it was again St. Michael who, in 1146, saved the

Crusader army.[5] The Crusaders had advanced into enemy territory and found themselves in such an unfortunate position that retreating was their only safe option, but to escape the Saracens who were closing off their routes, it was necessary to know the detours, and they had no guide. Nevertheless, the army began their march, and immediately one saw at the head of the vanguard an unknown knight mounted on a white horse, covered in shining armor, and holding a red standard in his hand. He led them through shorter routes where they found an abundance of water, and, in three days, they arrived at Gadara, which they would not have reached without him in five days of marching. This knight disappeared each evening and reappeared in the morning when it was time to depart. The army was saved by St. Michael from an almost certain ruin.

Later still, in the sixteenth century, he helped the Spanish battle the Moors in Africa. The great Cardinal Jiménez de Cisneros, in his extreme old age, sensing the misfortunes these barbarians would inflict on his homeland and on all of Christendom, thought to quash piracy at its base, and to establish a presence there to prevent its reemergence. He traveled to Africa; and, trusting more in help from heaven than in his weapons, this great man shut himself up inside St. Michael's Church, in Mers-el-Kébir, in order to implore the archangel's help. During this time, Pedro Navarro took the city of Oran, and shortly thereafter marched from victory to victory.

It has not only been against enemies of the Christian name that St. Michael has showed the power of his arm.

In the fifteenth century, France fell to the power of the English! Was the nation God used to do great things[6] thus going to perish? No, behold a savior led by the angel of battles: it is Joan of Arc. What the most experienced and most intrepid of warriors—the La Hires, the d'Illiers, the Dunois, and the Xaintrailles—were unable to do in seven months, it took but seven days, nay, only three days, for this young eighteen-year-old girl to accomplish. Orléans, the city loyal to its king, was freed; Jargeau was no longer under the English; and the fields of Patay were strewn with corpses. A frightful giant who had been crushing our homeland was gone. The English army disappeared; its most renowned leaders were dead or held as prisoners; the rest had fled. Joan no longer fought; she flew from victory to victory. And who did all these things? The veil hiding the divine action here was transparent. Beneath this young girl's armor, it was the angel of battles who fought; his power was in her. When heaven spoke to her, this poor little shepherdess, who did not know A from B, had all the sublimity of genius and all the authority of inspiration. The war leaders, assembled in council, hid from Joan due to an awareness of their inferiority; and the young girl, banging her spear against the hall door, almost made the Gaucourts and the Xaintrailles turn pale. "You have been at your council, and I at mine."

[In the thirteenth century],[7] another nation, well-known for its attachment to the Church and to France, received, from the same archangel, proofs of a miraculous protection. Lithuanian hordes were ravaging Poland and bringing the fire and sword everywhere. All seemed hopeless when Leszek [the Black], the [high duke][8] of this country, reassured by an apparition of St. Michael whom he had called to his aid, defeated the enemy multitudes with a handful of soldiers. Poland was saved. Grateful for this signal blessing, the prince erected a shrine to the glory of the angel of battle.

Illustrious prince of the angels, this Poland that you rescued four centuries ago is presently persecuted by a ruthless tyrant. It is no longer her autonomy whose destruction is sought today, but her heretofore unshakeable faith. The soil of this Catholic country is covered in ruins and strewn with corpses; her bishops and most of her priests are sent into exile; those who remain can no longer preach freely. Listen to the lamentations made not long ago for this unfortunate country by the great Pontiff who rules the Catholic Church; come to the aid of the persecuted faithful; like the glorious bishop of Krakow, Stanislaus,[9] give them the courage to profess their faith, even, if necessary, to the shedding of their blood.

CHAPTER 8:
ST. MICHAEL, ANGEL OF PRAYER, OBLATION, PARDON, AND PEACE.

*And another angel came and stood before
the altar, having a golden censer.*
– Revelation 8:3

B esides the extraordinary means through which we have seen St. Michael protect the Church of God, means which are material and human, there are others which are purely spiritual and divine; and these are ordinary means. The archangel, in fact, does not make use of nations and armies every day, but every day he does make use of prayers made by the faithful for the Church's prosperity. Powerful and invincible arms, especially when presented to God by the pure hands of the archangel.

St. John saw an angel who "stood before the altar, having a golden censer: and there was given to him much incense, that he should offer of the prayers of all saints, upon the golden altar which is before the throne of God. And the smoke of the incense of the prayers of the saints ascended up before God from the hand of the angel" (Rv 8:3-4).

The apostle does not tell us who this angel is; however, the Church, in agreement with the exegetes, has recognized him as St. Michael, the same one who appeared at Mount Gargano, as history relates, and who *stood at the altar of the temple, having a golden censer in his hand.*[1] At the offertory for Solemn High Mass, the priest says, "By the intercession of blessed MICHAEL the archangel, *who standeth at the right hand of the altar of incense,* and of all His elect, may the Lord vouchsafe to bless this incense, and to receive it for an odor of sweetness."[2]

But what does this smoke rising to God signify? Bossuet gives us the explanation. In holocausts,

the rising smoke would mix with the clouds, and seemed to want to ascend up to the throne of God. The prayers joined to it also seemed to go with it; therefore, David says, "Let my prayer be directed as incense in thy sight" (Ps 140:2 [141:2]), meaning like the smoke from the burning victim, for this is what the word *incensum* means here, although we have appropriated our word "incense," which comes from it, to that kind of fragrance which is called *thus* in Latin. Therefore, this angel from the Apocalypse appears with a censer in his hand; and it is said that "the smoke of the incense," meaning the holy prayers coming from a heart set ablaze by the Holy Ghost, "ascended up before God from the hand of the angel" (Rv 8:4), meaning that they were pleasing to Him. This is also what is called, in Scripture, a pleasant-smelling sacrifice before the Lord, when the oblation is made with a pure heart and the prayer, coming from an innocent conscience, rises to God with the smoke of the holocaust.[3]

St. Michael is thus the *angel of prayer*; it is to him then that must be attributed what the most ancient Fathers said of the angel who presided at prayer. "Examine," Origen says, "how you might be admitted into the company of St. Michael, who *unceasingly offers to God the prayers of the saints.*"[4] "This," St. Gregory the Great says, "is the Archangel Michael, prince of the angelic hosts... and *his prayer leads to the kingdom of heaven.*"[5]

At Holy Mass, after the consecration, the priest says this prayer: "We humbly beseech Thee, almighty God, to command that these our offerings be borne by the hands of THY HOLY ANGEL to Thine altar on high." Most exegetes say that this holy angel is Jesus Christ. But Bossuet, diverging from this sentiment, sees in this angel the same one who is called the angel of prayer. He says:

> To understand the essence of this prayer, and to overcome all the difficulties we might find in it, we must ever remember that these things of which we are speaking are in truth the Body and Blood of Jesus Christ; but that they are this Body and this Blood with us all, and with our petitions and our prayers, and that all of these together comprise one same oblation which we want to make in all aspects pleasing to God, with respect to Jesus Christ

Who is offered, and with respect to those who are offering Him and who are also offered with Him. In this design, what better thing could one do than again ask the company of the holy angel who *presides at the prayer*, and in him that of all the holy companions of his beatitude, so that, our offering being presented in this blessed company, it ascends promptly and more agreeably to the heavenly altar? It will be useful here to remark that whereas our canon speaks only of a single angel, the Ambrosian canon speaks of all the angels, to explain the holy union of all these blessed spirits, who all in fact do by consent what one of them does by action and special designation.[6]

According to this sentiment, it is thus to St. Michael that this glorious ministry must be attributed, a ministry, moreover, which is but the natural consequence of his ministry as protector of the Church. Is it not in fact for the needs of the Church that the Divine Victim is offered each day on our altars? "We humbly pray and beseech Thee... to receive and to bless these gifts, these presents... which we offer up to Thee, in the first place, for Thy holy Catholic Church, that it may please Thee to grant her peace"[7] over all the earth, despite the efforts of all her enemies; to deliver her from the persecutions of tyrants and from all wars, from which spring so many troubles and disorders. We beseech Thee to "guard"[8] her and support her against the efforts of heretics and all her visible and invisible enemies who attack the foundations of her faith; to "unite"[9] her, to preserve her from heresies and schisms, and to "guide her, throughout the world."[10]

This sentiment is also that of Cardinal Bona, in his ascetical treatise on the celebration of the holy sacrifice of the Mass. "When you are bowed down," he tells the priest, "beseech God that He command this sacrifice to be borne by the hand of His holy angel. Then, excite yourself to a great humility; ask the blessed spirits, and namely St. Michael, to come to your assistance."[11]

Carry then, O holy angel, to the "altar on high," the divine oblation offered for the peace and prosperity of the Church. But perhaps our sins make us unworthy to have our prayers heard? Carry then the accusation of our sins and the expression of our repentance. We "confess to...

[you], blessed Michael the Archangel... that [we] have sinned exceedingly;... pray to the Lord our God"[12] that we be granted pardon.

But why is St. Michael, rather than any other angel, invoked in this circumstance? St. Jerome gives us the reason. "None other than God," this doctor says, "can grant the grace of forgiveness; when He wants to promise it, he sends St. Michael, whose name signifies, 'Who is like God?'"[13]

Church history shows him fulfilling this mission in two solemn circumstances.

When David had offended God by conducting a census of his people, he was punished by a pestilence that took seventy thousand men of Israel. "And David said to God: Am not I he that commanded the people to be numbered? It is I that have sinned.... Let thy hand be turned, I beseech thee, upon me, and upon my father's house: and let not thy people be destroyed" (1 Chr 21:17). The angel, whom the commentators call Michael, then ordered built an altar to the Lord, on which to offer holocausts and peace offerings. After David obeyed, St. Michael was seen putting his sword back into the sheath, as a sign of pardon (1 Chr 21:27).

It was in this way that he appeared in Rome, atop Hadrian's mole, at the time of St. Gregory the Great. He announced that the Roman people's prayers and fasting had appeased God's anger, and that they would finally see an end to the famine and the plague.

Where sin reigns, there is war; where purity and holiness reign, there is peace. Thus, when we ask St. Michael to obtain us pardon for our sins, we are asking him for peace: peace with God and peace with ourselves. Sweet peace, which is not given the world to know! For this reason, St. Michael is given the name the "angel of peace." He earned it when he expelled from heaven the one who sought to bring war there.

> *Angel of peace*, may Michael to our dwelling
> Down from high Heaven in mighty calmness come,
> Breathing serenest peace, wild war dispelling
> With all her sorrows to the infernal gloom.[14]

CHAPTER 9:

ST. MICHAEL'S MISSION AT THE END OF THE WORLD. – HE WILL COME TO THE AID OF ELIJAH. – HE WILL BE TASKED WITH AVENGING THE AFFRONTS TO JESUS AND MARY, AND EXTERMINATING THE ANTICHRIST. – IN THE NAME OF GOD, HE WILL WORK THE MIRACLE OF THE RESURRECTION.

At that time shall Michael rise up.
– Daniel 12:1

Protected in every age of her earthly sojourn, the Church will be protected in a yet more striking way at the end of time.

The prophet Malachi, speaking of the time before the "great and dreadful day," says that God will send Elijah the Tishbite (Mal 4:5). This prophet "shall turn the heart of the fathers to the children, and the heart of the children to their fathers" (Mal 4:6). What does this mean? Who are these fathers, and who are these children? The fathers, as Theodoret explains, are the Jews, who first knew the truth; the sons are the Gentiles, who recognized Jesus Christ and abjured their errors; they thereby took the place of those who had been called first. But at the end of time, and this will be one of the precursory signs, these fathers, hardened until this point, will abandon their errors at the voice of Elijah, and will unite with the Christians to form but one heart and live according to the faith and piety of the ancient patriarchs.

This glorious mission, the prophet will fulfill with the help of St. Michael. Such is the meaning given by Theodoret to this passage of Daniel: "But at that time shall Michael rise up, the great prince, who standeth for the children of thy people: and a time shall come such as never was from the time that nations began even until that time. And at that time shall thy people be saved, every one that shall be found written in the book" (Dn 12:1). Admirable protection of the holy archangel! The people that had been entrusted to him rejected the truth; however, despite the numerous centuries of hardness, he still works for the salvation of his wards.[1]

Mary of Agreda speaks of an angel

> through whom God will avenge with an especial and dreadful chastisement the injuries committed against his most holy Mother.... As the most holy Trinity has pledged Itself to honor and exalt this Queen of heaven above all human creatures and above the angels, placing Her in this world as a Mirror of the Divinity and as the special Mediatrix of mortals, God has taken it in a particular manner upon Himself to avenge the heresies, errors, outrages, and all injuries committed against Her, since thereby men have not glorified, acknowledged and adored Him in this tabernacle and have not made use of this incomparable mercy.[2]

Which angel might this be, if not he who was the first in heaven to defend Mary's honor against the blasphemies of Lucifer? This is indeed what the venerable sister recounts elsewhere:

> The prince of the heavenly hosts saint Michael appeared in order to defend the cause of the incarnate Word and his most blessed Mother; and by the arms of the understanding they began another battle with the dragon and his followers. Saint Michael and his angels hurled at them the convincing arguments of old, reproaching them with their pride and disobedience in heaven and with their temerity in persecuting and tempting the incarnate Word and his Mother, and contending with those in whom they had no part or right whatever, since they could accuse Them of no sin, injustice or imperfection. Saint Michael justified the works of the divine justice, declaring them most righteous and unblamable chastisements for the disobedience and apostasy of Lucifer and the demons. Anew they anathematized them and confirmed the sentence of their damnation, confessing the Almighty as holy and just in all his works.[3]

But the great mission of the archangel, at the end of time, will be defending the Church against the attacks of the Antichrist. The Fathers of the Church, and the commentators of Holy Scripture after them,[4] explain to us the manner in which he will fulfill this mission.

According to the prophet Daniel, a king will rise up at that time who will cover the world in ruins. This king, in whom is recognized the Antichrist, for whom

> arms shall stand on his part, and they shall defile the sanctuary of strength, and shall take away the continual sacrifice: and they shall place there the abomination unto desolation.... And the king shall do according to his will, and he shall be lifted up and shall magnify himself against every god: and he shall speak great things against the God of gods and shall prosper till the wrath be accomplished. For the determination is made. And he shall make no account of the God of his fathers: and he shall follow the lust of women and he shall not regard any gods: for he shall rise up against all things.... And he shall fix his tabernacle Apadno between the seas, upon a glorious and holy mountain: and he shall come even to the top thereof, and none shall help him. (Dn 11:31, 36-37, 45)

This is indeed the Antichrist, the son of perdition who, at the end of time, will raise himself up above all that is called God, to the point of sitting in the temple of God and passing himself off as God (2 Thes 2:3-4). He will wage such a violent persecution against the elect "such as never was from the time that nations began even until that time" (Dn 12:1).

But at that time shall Michael rise up, the great prince protector of the children of the people of God. He will then mark the foreheads of the true servants in order to preserve them, says [G. Henry] Wouters, from the final tempest. St. John says in Revelation:

> I saw another angel ascending from the rising of the sun, having the sign of the living God. And he cried with a loud voice to the

four angels to whom it was given to hurt the earth and the sea, saying: Hurt not the earth nor the sea nor the trees, till we sign the servants of our God in their foreheads. And I heard the number of them that were signed. An hundred forty-four thousand were signed, of every tribe of the children of Israel. (Rv 7:2-4)

He will then send his angels to assist the true servants of Christ, those whose names will be found written in the book of life. Then, faithful to the command of the Lord Jesus, he will go straight to the Antichrist, topple his throne set up on Mount Zion or the Mount of Olives, this mountain that witnessed the glory of Christ, and will kill this man of pride, lying, and blasphemy.

It is true that St. Paul says, in his second letter to the Thessalonians, that "the Lord Jesus shall kill [the Antichrist] with the spirit of his mouth" (2 Thes 2:8), but all commentators have understood this word "spirit" in the sense of a command that Christ will give to His archangel.[5]

Every day, numerous antichrists rise up against the Church of Jesus Christ. Scatter them, O powerful archangel, and do not allow them to seduce God's elect.

It is also through the ministry of St. Michael that God will work the great miracle of the general resurrection. St. Paul says, "For the Lord himself shall come down from heaven with commandment and with the voice of an archangel and with the trumpet of God: and the dead who are in Christ shall rise first" (1 Thes 4:15). This archangel that is mentioned, Bernadine a Piconio says, is St. Michael, prince of the angels. It is according to his orders, orders which he has from Jesus Christ Himself, that the angelic spirits "shall gather together [God's] elect from the four winds" (Mt 24:31; Mk 13:27). He cries out, St. John Chrysostom says, he cries out to all who have been sent: "Make everything ready, for the Judge is at hand!"[6]

O holy archangel, the thought of this day plunges my soul into dread and terror! What will be my fate, when the sound of your trumpet comes to shake the dust from the tombs and has our bodies leave them to summon them before the throne of the Judge of the living and the dead?[7]

I invoke, even today, your protection, so that on the great day of judgment, you recognize me as one of your servants, and give me a place among the elect of God.

CHAPTER 10:
VISION OF HERMAS. – ST. MICHAEL HAS UNDER HIS CARE THE OBSERVERS OF THE DIVINE LAW. – HE IS TASKED WITH GATHERING CONVERTED SINNERS. – APPARITION TO ST. EUDOCIA.

He visits them to whom he has given the law, to see if they have kept it.
– The Shepherd of Hermas[1]

We have spoken until now of the glorious ministries St. Michael fulfills with respect to the Church in general. He has other ministries he performs with respect to each of those who make up the Church.

The first is that of examining the manner in which each one of the faithful keeps the divine law. This is what was revealed to Hermas, as this writer recounts in the third book of *The Shepherd*. We have spoken elsewhere of how much the Fathers of the Church, principally St. Irenaeus and Clement of Alexandria esteemed this work, which they called "divine."

We shall try analyzing this long passage. Hermas says that the shepherd

> shewed me a willow which covered the fields and the mountains, under whose shadow came all such as were called by the name of the Lord. And by that willow stood an angel of the Lord very excellent and lofty, and did cut down boughs from that willow with a great hook, and reached out to the people that were under the shadow of that willow little rods, as it were about a foot long. And when all of them had taken them, he laid aside his hook, and the tree continued entire, as I had before seen it. At which I wondered, and mused within myself. Then that shepherd said unto me, forbear to wonder that that tree continues whole,

notwithstanding so many boughs have been cut off from it; but stay a little, for now it shall be shewn thee what that angel means, who gave those rods to the people. So he again demanded the rods of them, and in the same order that every one had received them, was he called to him, and restored his rod; which when he had received, he examined them. From some he received them dry and rotten, and as it were, touched with the moth; those he commanded to be separated from the rest, and placed by themselves. Others gave him their rods dry indeed, but not touched with the moth; these also he ordered to be set by themselves. Others gave in their rods half dry; these also were set apart. Others gave in their rods half dry, and cleft; these too were set by themselves. Others brought in their rods, one half dry and the other green, and these were in like manner placed by themselves. Others delivered their rods two parts green, and the third dry, and they [too] were set apart. Others brought their rods two parts dry, and the third green, and were also placed by themselves. Others delivered up their rods less dry, (for there was but a very little, to wit, their tops dry) but they had clefts, and these were set in like manner by themselves. In the rods of others there was but a little green, and the rest dry, and these were set aside by themselves. Others came and brought their rods green as they had received them, and the greatest part of the people brought their rods thus; and the messenger greatly rejoiced at these, and they also were put apart by themselves. Others brought their rods not only green, but full of branches; and these were set aside, being also received by the angel with great joy. Others brought their rods green with branches, and those also some fruit upon them. They who had such rods were very cheerful; and the angel himself took great joy at them; nor was the shepherd that stood with me, less pleased with them.

Then the angel of the Lord commanded crowns to be brought; and the crowns were brought made of palms; and the angel crowned those men in whose rods he found the young branches with fruit; and commanded them to go into the tower.

He also sent those into the tower, in whose rods he found branches without fruit, giving a seal unto them. For they had the same garment, that is, one white as snow; with which he bade them go into the tower. And so he did to those who returned their rods green as they received them: giving them a white garment, and so sent them away to go into the tower. Having done this, he said to the shepherd that was with me, I go my way, but do thou send these within the walls, every one into the place in which he has deserved to dwell; examining first their rods, but examine them diligently that no one deceive thee. But and if any one shall escape thee, I will try them upon the altar. Having said this to the shepherd, he departed. After he was gone, the shepherd said unto me, let us take the rods from them all and plant them; if perchance they may grow green again. I said unto him, sir, how can those dry rods ever grow green again? He answered, that tree is a willow, and always loves to live. If therefore these rods shall be planted, and receive a little moisture, many of them will recover themselves. Wherefore I will try, and will pour water upon them, and if any of them can live, I will rejoice with him; but if not, at least by this means I shall be found not to have neglected my part.... And after he had planted them all, he poured much water upon them, insomuch that they were covered with water, and did not appear above it. Then when he had watered them, he said unto me, let us depart, and after a little time we will return and visit them. For he who created this tree, would have all those live that received rods from it....

I said unto him, sir, tell me what this tree denotes? for I am greatly astonished, that after so many branches have been cut off, it seems still to be whole; nor does there any thing the less of it appear to remain, which greatly amazes me. He answered, hearken. This great tree which covers the plains and the mountains, and all the earth, is the law of God, published throughout the whole world. Now this law is the [S]on of God who is preached to all the ends of the earth. The people that stand under its shadow, are those which have heard his preaching, and believed. The great and venerable angel which you saw, was MICHAEL, *who has the power over this people, and governs them. For he has planted the law in the hearts of those who have believed; and therefore he visits them to whom he has given the law, to see if they have kept it. And he examines every one's rod; and of those, many that are weakened: for those rods are the law of the Lord. Then he discerns all those who have not kept the law, knowing the place of every one of them.* I said unto him, sir, why did he send away some to the tower, and left others here to you? He replied, those who have transgressed the law which they received from him, are left in my power, that they may repent of their sins; but they who fulfilled the law and kept it, are under his power. But who then, said I, are those who went into the tower crowned? He replied, all such as having striven with the devil, have overcome him, are crowned: and they are those who have suffered hard things, that they might keep the law.[2]

According to the vision of Hermas, it is therefore under the watch of St. Michael that are placed the observers of the Divine Law. The Fathers, and particularly Origen, adopted this sentiment. "Those who embrace the Faith," Origen says, "are immediately subject to St. Michael, but they lose this patronage as soon as they abandon themselves to their inordinate desires." The archangel then confides them to the care of the shepherd so that the latter leads them back to observance of the Law.

O Christian, you who have received the Divine Law, have you not deserved through your infidelities to lose the patronage of the great archangel? Is not the branch you received withered and dried-up, when you could have made it produce flowers and fruit? Oh, if such is the case, hurry to place yourself under the direction of the shepherd who, by his assiduous care, will make your dried-up branch green once more. On the day of inspection, you will be recognized as worthy to be among the great archangel's protégés. This is what is subsequently shown us in the vision of Hermas.

Hermas states that the shepherd led him back to the place where he had planted the rods. The archangel was already there; he had the same brightness and majesty as the first time. Having assembled all the penitents, he told each one to fetch his rod and bring it to him. They again offered the various kinds of branches previously mentioned. The archangel then sorted them as he had before: some received crowns, others marks of distinction, others only a white robe, but these were all sent into the tower. For the others, they remained outside, to be confided again to the shepherd, who then said to Hermas: "You see how patient and merciful the Lord is, but woe to those who do not profit from this, for, when death comes, they shall forever perish."[3]

We read in the *Acta Sanctorum* [*Acts of the Saints*], compiled by the Bollandists, an incident that confirms the vision of Hermas. This incident is taken from the life of the martyr Eudocia (March 1).

This woman, of Samaritan origin and an idolater, lived in Heliopolis, under the reign of Trajan, in the most scandalous disorders. Converted by a holy monk named Germanus, she shut herself in her room for six days to weep over the many enormous sins of which she was guilty, when a light, brighter than that of the sun, suddenly surrounded her. She saw before her a young man, of majestic bearing, whose clothing was white as snow. "This young man," Eudocia recounted, "took my right hand, and raised me up with him into the air." (This was a spiritual rapture.) "I arrived at an immense, wonderful light, where there was a countless multitude of people, whom I nevertheless saw in a single glance. They were all dressed in white and appeared very joyful. As soon as they saw me, they came to me in throngs, and greeted me no less amicably than if I were their sister.

"Shortly afterwards, I saw a horrible giant, black as coal; he approached, gnashing his teeth, and wanted to snatch me from the hands of my guide. Violently pushed away, he said with a voice that made the air resound: 'What, you want to take this woman into heaven, she who polluted the earth with her harlotry, and corrupted so many men through her artifices? But if you take her from me, who will you leave me then?' The one who held my hand cast a scornful look at him, then stared at me with a gentle smile. I then heard a voice coming from the light, which said, 'Such is My merciful will for the children of men, that those who do penance, after great sins, be received like the others into the bosom of Abraham.' Then, addressing my guide, the voice added, 'Michael, guardian of My testament, take this woman back to the place from which you took her, so that she may continue to atone for her sins; I will be with her during all the days of her earthly life.' He did take me back, in fact, to my room, and said to me, 'Peace be with you, Eudocia, servant of God; be of good courage, the grace of God is with you, and will never be taken from you.' Encouraged by these sweet words, I had the confidence to ask him his name. He answered me, 'I am the prince of the angels. To me is confided the mission of gathering converted sinners, and of ushering them to the blessed city, for you must know that God is a good father who does not want His children to perish. Therefore, when a sinner passes from the quagmire of his vices to the pure light of penitence, His heart is satisfied, and the holy angels share His joy.' Having said this, he blessed me and disappeared."

O benevolent archangel, strengthen the pastors of souls in their zeal for stray sinners.

CHAPTER 11:

ST. MICHAEL, ANGEL PROTECTOR OF A HAPPY DEATH. – HE PRESENTS SOULS TO GOD, WEIGHS THEIR WORKS IN THE BALANCE, AND USHERS THEM INTO HEAVEN. – HIS MISSION TO THE SOULS IN PURGATORY.

Let Michael, the holy standard-bearer, bring them into the holy light.
– Offertory of the Mass for the Dead

Saint Michael is the governor of heaven, of the palace of the King of kings, *"the viceroy of paradise;"*[1] it is he who ushers into this holy light that God promised of old to Abraham and his seed, the souls over whom he had guard on earth, and who observed the Divine Law.

A glorious mission entrusted to him by God Himself. *"Michael Mine Archangel,"* He said to him, *"I have appointed thee for a prince over the ingathering of souls."*[2] Faithful to this order, he comes with the multitude of the angels to lead into paradise, where they tremble with joy, the souls of the saints God entrusted to him, and he stays with them all the way to Christ's tribunal.

A terrible and solemn moment it must be when we are summoned before the tribunal of God! But a yet more terrible and solemn moment must be the one preceding it, since it will decide our eternity! Oh, it is in that moment especially that hope and strength will be needed: hope to fix our eyes towards heaven, and strength to resist the final assaults of hell, which is bent on our destruction.

Who then will be our help? Each morning, in his preparation for the august sacrifice of the Mass, the celebrated Archbishop of Canterbury, St. Anselm, would recite this prayer: "St. Michael, archangel of God, guardian of heaven, come to my aid at the moment of my death, be my defense against the malicious enemy, and lead my soul into the paradise of everlasting jubilation."

The Church invites us to recite a similar prayer when she puts on the lips of her children these words we read in the offices of the prince of the angels: "Holy archangel Michael, defend us in battle: that we perish not in the dreadful judgment."[3]

This is also the cry that escapes all hearts at the sight of the archangel's venerable shrine *at the peril of the sea.* Do you see these long lines of pilgrims advancing across our shifting shorelines? The distance prevents you from making out the individual persons, but a chant that rises to heaven reaches your ears. Men, women, children, everyone, young and old, repeat, and repeat again, *"Holy archangel Michael, defend us in battle, that we perish not in the dreadful judgment."* And this cry touches the depths of one's soul, filling it with indescribable emotion.

The help comes. Those who have solicited it and waited for it have never had their hopes disappointed.

Let us cite some examples.

A chronicle says that when St. Caprasius, abbot of Lérins, had come to the end of his time in this land of exile and tears, St. Michael came to bring him the news. The holy abbot received it with great joy, for nothing could be more pleasing to him. He yielded his beautiful soul to God, which St. Michael ushered into heaven on June 1, 430, the day we celebrate his feast.

St. Michael did the same for St. Arnulf, bishop of Soissons. This holy prelate was gravely ill when the prince of the angels appeared to him, accompanied by a countless number of blessed spirits. "Arnulf," he said to him, "have courage. I will soon come for your soul, to take it to heaven." St. Arnulf, in accordance with the words of the archangel, died shortly thereafter, on Sunday, August 15, 1087, and went to celebrate in heaven the glorious assumption of the Queen of the Angels.

St. Anselm recounts in his work *De similitudinibus* that the same archangel came to help a monk at his monastery in Bec at the time of his death.

St. Wilfrid, bishop of York, was granted the same favor. Unexpectedly falling ill at Meaux, recounts Eadmer, a monk from Canterbury, the holy bishop went four days without taking food or drink, and without speaking a word or hearing a sound, when finally, on the fifth day, all his people weeping as though he were dead, God sent the archangel St. Michael to give him back his former health. He said:

Wilfrid, why do you remain lying on this bed? Arise, for although you are already counted among the number of heaven's citizens, the prayers of your children, and the merits and prayers of the Blessed Mary, Mother of God, have postponed the hour of your death. This Virgin has prayed for you because your works have been pleasing to her. Thus, you will be called back to life and to health. However, be prepared, for in four years, I will come back to visit you.[4]

And the angelic vision disappeared. Wilfrid, as though coming out of a deep sleep, got up, and everyone gave glory to God. When the time announced by the angel had elapsed, the holy bishop fell ill. St. Michael, faithful to his promise, returned to the servant of God, to take his soul to heaven.[5]

To his role of presenting souls to God, tradition, the theological savant Eckius says, joins another role: that of weighing their works in the balance.[6] One must not understand this, Molanus says, in the sense that those who obtain eternal life have good works outweighing bad ones, nor that those who are abandoned to the devil have bad works outweighing good ones, but rather that our judgment will be made according to equity. Scripture mentions this balance. When Belshazzar, in a sacrilegious orgy, profaned the sacred vessels of the temple in Jerusalem, "there appeared fingers, as it were of the hand of a man, writing over against the candlestick upon the surface of the wall of the king's palace" (Dn 5:5), and this hand was that of an angel,[7] whom we believe to be St. Michael, writing, "MANE, THECEL, PHARES" (5:25). And this is how Daniel the prophet interpreted these three words: "MANE: God hath numbered thy kingdom and hath finished it. THECEL: *Thou art weighed in the balance and art found wanting.* PHARES: Thy kingdom is divided and is given to the Medes and Persians" (5:26-28). A terrible sentence, which filled the king and the court with dread.

May our works, O holy archangel, one day be found of sufficient weight before God. "Let him weigh me in a just balance, and let God know my simplicity" (Jb 31:6). For this reason, I want, after the example of St. Denis and according to the counsel of St. Augustine, to examine my own works myself in the scales of justice.

The soul, after its judgment, goes to heaven, purgatory, or hell. If its works merit heaven, St. Michael ushers it amidst the choirs of all the heavenly spirits. If this soul is condemned to hell, the archangel surrenders it to the power of the demons; his ministry is finished. But if it must still expiate for a time the stains which prevent it from appearing before the God of all purity, oh, it is then that the leader of the heavenly militia will redouble his solicitude until he can open the eternal courts to this new member of the elect. He will pray to God, for his prayer leads to the kingdom of heaven. The Church will also pray, and ask Our Lord to allow His standard-bearing archangel, St Michael, to usher it into the holy light, this light promised to Abraham, father of the children of God, and to all his seed: *"Let Michael, the holy standard-bearer, bring them into the holy light which Thou once didst promise to Abraham and his seed."*[8]

BOOK TWO: DEVOTION TO ST. MICHAEL

CHAPTER 1:
IN WHAT DEVOTION TO ST. MICHAEL CONSISTS.
– HONOR. – INVOCATION. – IMITATION.

Arise, Michael, stand up for our children.
– Office of St. Michael

The consideration of the sublime ministries by which God has desired to honor His great archangel should cause us to value and practice devotion to this glorious prince of the angels.

Moreover, this devotion, as we shall see, has always been practiced by peoples, saints, and religious orders of every country.

Today, as in the past, it is even considered necessary. The illustrious bishop of Poitiers, Monseigneur Pie, recently wrote to the Reverend Father Superior of the Missionaries of Mont Saint-Michel: "*The Church and France have greater need than ever of the Holy Archangel's powerful patronage.* I gladly accept the duty of invoking him more faithfully, each day, as protector of the Church and our nation, and as advocate of my soul before the Sovereign Judge."

Let us examine in what this devotion consists.

The devotion we give the saints is summed up in these three words: honor, invocation, and imitation.

St. Michael has the right to our honor and veneration. St. Gregory the Great, in the preface he composed for the dedication of the archangel's basilica, expresses it this way:

It is truly meet and just, and profitable unto salvation, that we should at all times, and in all places, give thanks to Thee, O Holy

Lord, Father Almighty, eternal God, by celebrating the merits of the archangel St. Michael. Although it is our duty to honor each angelic sublimity who stands in the presence of Thy majesty, we ought still more willingly to render honor to him who merited to be placed at the head of all the heavenly militia.

St. Lawrence Justinian also says,

Although we should honor all the angels, *let us venerate more particularly the glorious St. Michael,* as head of all the heavenly spirits, on account of his sovereign grace, the singular prerogative of his office, his invincible power, and the unshakable constancy he showed in the battle he had to wage against the infernal demon and his desperate adherents.[1]

Moreover, by honoring St. Michael and singing his glory, we shall be following the example of the Church. Three times per year, on May 8, September 29, and October 16,[2] this mother gathers her children to the foot of the altar and invites them to thank God for the glory He has conferred upon His archangel. For this purpose, she has composed hymns and canticles in which she expresses the sentiments she desires to sow in Christian hearts.

The first of these sentiments is the confidence manifested through prayer.

But why address our prayers to St. Michael and have them carried by an intermediary to the foot of God's throne?

It is a principle and law of political science that in the governing of people, the authority should not communicate directly with its subjects, but through intermediaries or ministers. This is the ancient law of human government as well as of divine government. God could in fact have given us existence without the aid of another, as He did in the earthly paradise, but today He leaves this care to our parents. He could directly provide for the needs of the destitute man and provide him food like he does for the small bird, but He prefers to leave the initiative to the alms of the rich benefactor whom He has made the minister of His providence. In the intellectual order, He could make Himself the teacher for our ignorance, but He sends us to savants. It is the same in the supernatural order. The Christian child of God does not reach his perfection and arrive at his goal except through intermediaries; I do in fact see mediators between God and the soul, necessary mediators whose intervention is required for the salvation of man and God's regular intervention. I open Holy Scripture, which contains the history of the religious relations of man and God, and, from the first pages, I see a prince from the east, Abimelech, who has made himself guilty before Abraham, and only obtains deliverance for himself and his house through the prayer of the patriarch. Let us listen to what God says to Abimelech: "Now therefore restore the man [Abraham] his wife, for he is a prophet. And he shall pray for thee, and thou shalt live: but if thou wilt not restore her, know that thou shalt surely die, thou and all that are thine" (Gn 20:7). The patriarch was generous; he prayed, and the king was saved along with all his house. One day, the prophet Ezekiel, seated on the bank of a river, was weeping at the thought of the crimes and misfortunes of his homeland; and while he wept, a dreadful vision unfolded before his eyes. He saw ravaged countryside, cities on fire, smoking ruins, people fleeing in terror, and God hovering over this immense devastation and casting an encompassing gaze full of concern and pity; and God said, "Jerusalem, Jerusalem, you who have shed blood within your walls, you who have demeaned My priesthood and profaned My sanctuaries to prostrate yourself at the foot of vile altars, tremble, for the day of My wrath has come, and your ruin is near. Heaven is My witness that I had wanted to save you. I have long waited for a man to rise up within you to place himself as a living barrier and hedge between you and My anger, a man who would dare take your defense and resist Me to the face, but I have not found such a man. This is why My justice must run its course, and I will spread over your children the last waves of My indignation; I will release against them the fire and the sword, and hunger and pestilence, and terror, and tempest, and death, and I will devour them all to the last one, because no one has been found to intercede for them before My mercy."[3]

This man whom God sought out with a kind of anxiousness was never found, and Jerusalem was destroyed and annihilated.

What should be concluded from these two incidents, if not that there are evidently circumstances when individual, isolated prayer is without power and efficaciousness. King Abimelech had prayed, and he had been condemned. Jerusalem had prayed, and the divine wrath did not hover any less over the city with all its threats and chastisements.

It follows therefore that prayer, instead of going alone and directly to God, should be preceded and recommended by the intercession of the just and of the saints. We therefore cannot evade this law of divine government without fault and without danger.

Let us then emerge from our weakness and infirmity to lean on those who are stronger than we.

Let us turn to St. Michael.

He is God's minister in the governing of the Church. Let us beseech him then to come to her aid, and that he rescue her—not in the sense that she could perish since she has eternal promises, but that he bring a stop to the persecution, a cause of the fall and ruin of so many weak souls.

He has defeated the demon.

Let us ask St. Michael to protect us against the deadly wiles of Satan. "Let us not be afraid," the Church tells us. "He who valiantly upheld the rights of God makes himself our defender and places in our hands the faith's powerful weapons.

"Supported by such assistance, do not permit it, Lord, that we stray from You; do not allow us to succumb to the snares of our enemies."[4]

St. Michael is the angel of prayer. Let us entrust to him our own prayers to carry to the foot of God's throne; presented by such pure hands, they will be more pleasing to the Divine Majesty.

Let us especially ask him to have our repentance accepted. Is it not to him that we confess each day? "I confess to almighty God, to blessed Mary ever Virgin, to *blessed Michael the Archangel...* that I have sinned exceedingly."[5]

But the precious grace we ought to desire above all is that of a holy death. Let us fervently ask for it through his intercession.

And invoking him should be frequent, according to the author of *The Spiritual Combat*: "Never let a day go by without having recourse multiple times... to your guardian angel, and to St. Michael the Archangel."[6]

But the means par excellence of proving our devotion to him consists in the imitation of the virtues that set him apart.

Imitation, in fact, is the proof of love. Love cannot exist without resemblance: there is nothing in the world that it does not put down, no pleasure it does not forego, and no profit it does not scorn in order to make itself similar to the one it loves. It is then that love is reciprocal. Is not the child who most resembles his mother the one who is the most loved?

Moreover, to imitate the virtues of the archangel is to imitate the Incarnate Word, and thereby to merit His love. Nicolas says:

> The saints are, in relation to Jesus Christ, like prisms in relation to the light; they dissect the brightness of His holiness into various colors loved by the eyes, into diverse perfections accommodated to our nature. Jesus Christ refracts Himself in the saints, as in so many stars of the firmament of holiness, as in so many flowers of the garden of the Church, in order that, according to our inclinations and characteristics, we might find in them examples to collect, contemplate, and imitate, and, through this secondary and partial imitation, raise ourselves up to the heavenly original of all perfection.[7]

Like St. Michael, let us show a prompt obedience to the Lord's commandments. He was the first to submit to divine orders; and this submission merited him to be placed at the head of the heavenly militia.

Guardian of the Incarnate Word and of His Holy Mother, he fulfilled this ministry with joy and love. After his example, let us show a great love for Jesus and Mary, a love which manifests itself through works.

We will not forget the Church which he has loved, which he loves and guards like an army arrayed in battle. O Holy Church, "let my right hand be forgotten, let my tongue cleave to my jaws, if I do not remember thee" (Ps 136:5-6 [137:5-6])!

St. Michael is the consolation of the souls in purgatory. He is like the prince of that kingdom, to whom Mary has delegated the regency.

Desirous of fulfilling this sweet mission which the Church attributes to him, he receives, like a homage rendered to himself, each act of charity made in favor of the holy souls confided to his care. Let us do something for these souls, and we shall become servants of St. Michael and the guardian angels of this beautiful but sad region where souls suffer and wait.

"Lord Jesus Christ, deliver from the pains of purgatory the souls of all the faithful departed.... May the prince of the angels, St. Michael, lead them into the heavenly light which you promised of old to Abraham and his posterity."[8]

But the glorious archangel will especially be our model in the great combat we must wage against the temptations of the powers of darkness. Let us listen to St. Francis de Sales:

> When the wretched army of diabolical spirits revolted against its Creator and wanted to draw into its ranks the holy company of blessed spirits, the glorious St. Michael stirred his companions to the fidelity they owed their God, crying in a loud voice (but in an angelic manner) in the heavenly Jerusalem, "Who is like God?" And through this utterance, he overthrew the treacherous Lucifer with his following, who wanted to make himself equal to the Divine Majesty; hence, as it is said, the name was given to St. Michael.... And when love for created things seeks to inordinately draw our minds to them to make ourselves disobedient to the Divine Majesty, if great divine love is found in the soul, it firmly resists, like another St. Michael, and forcefully directs its powers and energy to the service of God by this firm utterance: "Who is like God?"[9]

Lucifer led in revolt against God a third of the angels; but Michael appealed to all those who wanted to remain faithful, and, at the head of this "Holy League," marched against the impious army, which he expelled from heaven.

The revolutionary cry resounded from one end of the world to the other: "I will ascend! I will topple God!" Let us appeal to generous and faithful souls, and, arrayed beneath the banner of St. Michael, let us resist impiety and march to the enemy with this war cry: "Who is like God!"

According to Our Lord's word, the children of darkness are prudent: they have understood the power of association. United in one same mind and one same will, under the presidency of Satan, they have joined together in solidarity.[10] "Dying in the hatred of God and of the Church," this is their motto!

Therefore, today, more than ever, there is a need for the children of light, in turn, to join together, form an association, and unite in solidarity to combat hell and the works of hell. "Dying in the *love* of God and of the Church," such must be their motto. The presidency of this association must belong to St. Michael. Honored by this mark of trust, the powerful archangel, for the happiness and peace of the souls who have been entrusted to him, will again strike down the enemy of God and men.

We shall see in the following chapters of this second book how this devotion has been understood and practiced.

CHAPTER 2:
DEVOTION OF PEOPLES, KINGDOMS,
AND CITIES TO ST. MICHAEL.

*Thou art the glory of Jerusalem, thou art the joy
of Israel, thou art the honour of our people.*
— *Judith 15:10*

We can say of devotion to St. Michael what Lacordaire said of
devotion to the Rosary: "Whenever a thing attains universality
and perpetuity, it necessarily contains a mysterious harmony with the
needs of man."[1]

Devotion to St. Michael has in fact attained universality and
perpetuity: it began with the Church, it spread among all peoples and
under all conditions, and it has perpetuated itself to our own day.

The Christians of Phrygia and Pisidia, provinces in Asia Minor,
cultivated, from the first centuries of the Church, this devotion to such
excesses that the Council of Laodicea was constrained, out of prudence,
to prohibit invoking the angels. Despite this prohibition, Theodoret
stated that "one still sees in our day, among them and their neighbors,
oratories to St. Michael."[2]

A canonist cited by Bossuet, Alexis Aristenus, makes known to us
the error that gave rise to the Laodicea canon:

> There were some teaching… that we must not say we had access
> to God through Jesus Christ, but only through the angels, for
> Jesus Christ, they said, was too great for us. To say that was to
> renounce under the pretext of humility the order established by
> God for our salvation.[3]

Those who support this, the canonist adds, "let them be anathema, as
having abandoned Jesus Christ and approaching the sentiments of
idolaters."[4]

Without falling into the errors of the Phrygians, the Eastern Church, from the first centuries, gave St. Michael a special veneration; she established two very solemn feasts in memory of two apparitions which had taken place, one in Colossae and the other in Rhodes.

Constantinople, capital of the Eastern Empire, stood out among all the cities. Within its walls, there were fifteen churches erected in honor of the archangel, and all of them had imperial foundations. Emperor Justinian alone had six of them built; and he liked to repeat that if he had the support of the prince of the angels, he had nothing to fear from barbarian invasions. But not content erecting temples of stone, the emperors also placed their persons under his protection.[5]

St. Michael, for his part, rewarded this trust. Painters have depicted various miracles worked by this archangel in favor of this city and its inhabitants. They in fact show us him preserving Constantinople against an attack from the Persians, and saving a child from the abyss of the sea. He also prevented a church dedicated to him from being inundated by a flood.

Rome, capital of the old empire, could not let itself be outdone by its young rival; it could not forget him who, according to the testimony of Pantaleon, deacon of Constantinople, shields it with his protection, and along with it, the Universal Church, of which it is the head. Temples were built,[6] charitable establishments were founded,[7] and feasts were instituted.[8] Drepanius Florus,[9] the most ancient of Christian poets, confirms that in his time, in this city, a solemn feast in honor of St. Michael was celebrated.

Docile in following the example of the Eternal City, all of Italy has offered the prince of the angels a veneration worthy of the high prerogatives with which God invested him. One witnessed multitudes hastening onto the roads to Mount Gargano, to go honor at his shrine him who revealed his presence by numerous striking miracles.

Naples, which was indebted to him for abjuring the errors of paganism, has offered him a special veneration. More recently, it has added him to the number of its patrons, and a silver statue of him in the Treasury Chapel appears next to that of St. Januarius. Parma, Pisa, Pavia, Florence, Turin, Cagliari, etc., the most important and flourishing cities of Italy, erected shrines in his honor.

At the same time as Italy, the cult of St. Michael made great progress in France. The most Christian people took this archangel for their defender, and the kings placed themselves under his patronage. From then on, the Gallican Church celebrated St. Michael's feast day with an unusual solemnity.[10] More numerous still than those of Italy were the multitudes who hastened from all regions of France to the *Jerusalem of the West*.

The cities rivaled each other in zeal to erect temples to the leader of the heavenly army, but none distinguished itself more than the city of Paris.[11] The city named streets, bridges, fountains, and charitable establishments after St. Michael.

After France, England distinguished itself for its devotion to the great archangel. Here is what is written in the *Laws Ecclesiastical*, published in 1014 by Ethelred, the King of England:

> And we ordain, that every Christian who is of age, fast three days in bread and water and raw herbs before the feast of St. Michael, and let every man go to confession and to church barefoot.... And let every priest with his people go in procession three days barefoot;... and let every one's commons for three days be prepared, without any thing of flesh, as they themselves were to eat it, both in meat and drink, and let all this be distributed to the poor. And let every servant be excused from labour these three days, that he may the better perform his fast; [or] let him work what he will for himself. These are the three days, Monday, Tuesday, and Wednesday next before the feast of St. Michael. If any servant break his fast, let him make satisfaction with his hide; let the poor freeman pay thirty pence; the king's thane a hundred and twenty shillings; and let the money be divided to the poor.[12]

From this strict ordinance, we can see with what solemnity the feast of St. Michael was celebrated in England. The *Anglo-Saxon Chronicle* and the *Anglo-Saxon Menologium*, both from the ninth century, designate this feast as one of the high feast days. In later times, we see several kings of England undertake, at the head of their peoples, the pilgrimage to Mont Saint-Michel *at the peril of the sea.*

May the glorious archangel deign to bring back into the bosom of the Roman Church this people who were in times past so devoted to him, and may he bring to completion what was done under his patronage in 1850 when Pius IX, on September 29 of that year, reestablished the ecclesiastical hierarchy in England.[13]

Germany did not lag behind. It took St. Michael for its patron. One then saw its pilgrims going in countless throngs to Mount Gargano and Mount Tombe. Their number was sometimes so prodigious that amazed scholars, seeing entire cantons depopulated by these peregrinations, published works in order to put an end to these distant voyages. But the more they wrote, the more the number of these pilgrims seemed to increase. These men were stopped neither by the thought of being so far from the homeland nor by the difficulties of the journey. The routes they followed were for them the way to heaven, and they were only too happy to be able to travel to the venerated shrine.

To support them in their generous resolutions, they often had noble examples. Otto [III], the [Holy Roman] Emperor,[14] made a pilgrimage barefoot to Mount Gargano, and in 1777, one saw at Mont Saint-Michel [future Holy Roman] Emperor Francis II, [also to be known as Emperor Francis I of Austria].[15]

In moments of calamity, Germany and Belgium have had recourse to the prince of the angels. In 1524, an epidemic disease plagued these two countries with such fury that in Antwerp alone, close to five hundred persons succumbed to it within three days. The frightened Senate made a public petition to St. Michael the Archangel, whose feast the Church was celebrating on that day. From that moment, the plague ceased to inflict its ravages. Hence, there is a customary procession in this city on the Sunday preceding September 29.

Brussels rivaled Antwerp's zeal and, in 1674, showed how dear devotion to the prince of the angels was to it. It was a custom to have a procession on September 29 and to carry there, with the Blessed Sacrament, the image of St. Michael. Alphonse de Berge, the Archbishop of Mechelen, wanted to forbid this practice as something contrary to the rules of the Church. The city was so troubled by this news that the magistrates refused to appear at the procession, according to custom. It was necessary, in order to overcome their resistance, to bring back the image of the archangel.

This devotion still flourishes in Germany in our own day. Everyone knows how much the Confraternity of St. Michael, which counts among its members the most illustrious names, works for the propagation of the faith and lends its assistance to supporting the chair of St. Peter.

One also saw Spain, Portugal especially, Catholic Ireland, Sweden, and Norway uniting their chorus of praises to those peoples we have already mentioned.

The Far East, in its turn, wanted to join its tribute of homage to that of Old Europe. The mission in Japan, so flourishing in times past and so persecuted today, but still unshakable in the faith, placed itself under the patronage of St. Michael. The Japanese faithful have continued, despite the misfortunes of the times, to invoke the great archangel and to put themselves under his protection.[16] This confidence, let us hope, will not be disappointed; it will soon bear fruit and contribute to making better days shine on these unfortunate islands.

Even the most distant islands of Oceania have eagerly accepted the protection of the prince of the angels. In September 1868, tuberculosis was working frightful ravages among the populations of the Gambier Islands. A missionary at the time wrote, "We are making a novena to St. Michael, the glorious protector of our missions, to ask for an end to the plague."

In Canada, this land that is so French, numerous associations have been formed under the patronage of St. Michael. One Franciscan wrote:

> At the Christian Brothers in Montreal, I preached to some young people gathered together under the patronage of the glorious archangel. Since that time, my devotion to St. Michael has greatly increased. I also attended a blessing of a bell, by Bishop Bourget, which was dedicated to St. Michael.

And this is not only in the Catholic Church. We also find this devotion among the Russian schismatics,[17] and even among the Muslim infidels. The followers of Muhammad also venerate St. Michael, and, in a book titled *Muhammad's Doctrine*,[18] they designate him secretary of the divinity.

We have stated elsewhere the devotion of the Jews to the archangel.

Thus, always and everywhere, at the Church's birth as in our own day, in the Old World and in the New World, from the city of Arkhangelsk, seated on the icy banks of the White Sea, to San Miguel de Tucumán, built in South America amidst groves of orange, fig, and pomegranate trees,[19] countless multitudes from all classes and every condition have honored and invoked the great archangel, the commander-in-chief of the armies of God.

CHAPTER 3:

DEVOTION OF THE SAINTS: POPES, BISHOPS, FOUNDERS OF RELIGIOUS ORDERS, KINGS, AND VIRGINS.

God gives us in the saints what is needed to instruct and move us.
– Rev. Louis Bourdaloue, S.J.

It has been a great glory for St. Michael to see so many peoples and such numerous multitudes having recourse to his benevolent protection. But these peoples and multitudes have only been following the example of illustrious personages around whose heads the halo of sanctity shines.

What is a saint? According to St. William of Paris, a saint is a real, visible, palpable, and substantial idea of all evangelical perfection. When God places a saint before our eyes, He tells us as He did to Moses, "Look and make it according to the pattern" (Ex 25:40). In other words, "Behold what you must do." What you have difficulty perceiving in the law, what seems obscure to you in the books, what all the words of men only expound upon imperfectly, is placed before your eyes, and clearly expressed in the example of My elect. See what has led them to holiness, *look and do according to the model.*

Did the saints know about devotion to St. Michael? Yes, all, certainly; but among those raised to the highest sanctity, a great number distinguished themselves in this devotion. We shall mention some names, among the most well-known, taken from different conditions.

All the Sovereign Pontiffs, from St. Peter up to the glorious Pius IX,[1] have honored and invoked St. Michael as their special protector[2] and as the defender of the Holy Church. It was undoubtedly to this archangel that St. Peter owed seeing his chains come off in the Jerusalem prison, thereby delivering him from the hands of the Jews; it was probably also by St. Michael's powerful arm that St. Leo the Great twice stopped at the gates of Rome the barbarian peoples who were upsetting Europe and Africa.[3] St. Gelasius, for whom Dionysius

Exiguus made a magnificent eulogy, who was raised to the chair of St. Peter and can be counted among the number of great popes,[4] composed an office in honor of the prince of the angels, and established a feast day commemorating the apparition at Mount Gargano. St. Gregory the Great saw St. Michael above Hadrian's mole, and obtained by his prayers the end of the terrible plagues decimating the Roman population. This illustrious pope built the church of Sant'Angelo in Borgo Pio and put the finishing touches on the prayers of the office that we recite today. In the ninth century, the formidable Saracen army, which seemed would destroy Italy and turn Christendom's capital into a Muhammadan town, fell apart upon encountering the courage of another St. Leo, Pope Leo IV.[5] In thanksgiving for this victory, the holy pope had a temple built in the Vatican in honor of him who is the leader of the armies of God and the great protector of the Church. The renowned St. Gregory VII also asked St. Michael for help and protection against the fury of the hostile Henry, the emperor of Germany. His hope was not disappointed, for soon rushed in warriors, sons of a people known for its devotion to the prince of the angels,[6] who delivered the common Father of the faithful.

The most holy and illustrious bishops of the East—St. Basil, St. Gregory of Nyssa, St. Gregory Nazianzen, St. John Chrysostom, etc.— professed for the glorious archangel a devotion that they preached to the faithful confided to their care. We saw in the preceding chapter the East's devotion to St. Michael.

Among the bishops in the Western Church, two merited to be honored by an apparition of him whom they regarded as the most perfect image of the divinity. They were St. Lawrence, bishop of Siponto or Manfredonia, and St. Aubert, bishop of Avranches. The first saw St. Michael at Mount Gargano, and the second at Mount Tombe. By the orders and with the assistance of the archangel, the latter devised a plan and laid the foundations for the abbey and shrine that would become the Wonder of the West. [Historian Fr. Émile-Auber] Pigeon says:

> The venerated bishop had in the basilica of the archangel a small marble altar on which he often liked to celebrate the holy mysteries. During his visits, Aubert busied himself propagating

devotion to St. Michael and the holy angels. Since October 16 simultaneously called to mind the apparition of the archangel, the dedication of his church, and the reception [of the relics] from Mount Gargano, the bishop wanted this day to be a solemn feast each year in his diocese. He even encouraged pilgrimages to the holy mountain, and granted numerous indulgences in perpetuity to all those who would visit it with devotion and go there to pray to St. Michael. A historian assures us that he also composed several pious prayers in which he petitioned the angels to defend us in all our ways and to procure our salvation.[7]

St. Aubert preached this devotion with a zeal which earned him the title of "Apostle of the Angels." It was also to this place sanctified by such an august presence that he ordered the confiding of his mortal remains.

One of his successors, Norgod, whom some have given the title of saint, resigned from his episcopal office to come to this same place to sanctify the rest of his days with prayer and penance.

It was undoubtedly at Mont Saint-Michel that two renowned holy men who passed through the school of Avranches, and successively became Archbishop of Canterbury, Blessed Lanfranc and St. Anselm, to whom the Church has given the title of doctor, came to draw a tender devotion towards St. Michael. The latter had the custom of celebrating with pomp in his cathedral church the feast of the glorious archangel, and as we learn from a letter addressed to the prior Ernulf, it was a great regret for him, when on a trip to Rome, to be unable to return to England by September 29.

This great bishop placed his most important affairs under the protection of the prince of the angels. Driven from his see by William Rufus [also known as William II], he wanted to stop on the route of his exile to celebrate the feasts of Holy Week and Easter in the famous monastery of Sacra di San Michele. Upon returning to his diocese, he gathered the English bishops in council to address faith and morals. It was on St. Michael's feast day that he wanted to open these solemn conferences, as the new Saxon chronicler tells us.

He frequently commended the hour of his death to St. Michael. He would say, "Come to my aid, defend me against the malicious spirit at my final moment, and lead my soul into the paradise of everlasting jubilation."

St. Romuald, the founder of the Camaldolese Order, also showed himself very devoted to the great archangel, whom he seemed to especially honor as the *angel of pardon*. St. Peter Damian informs us that around the year 1002, Emperor Otto III had the Roman senator Crescentius killed, contrary to the assurance he had given him; to this crime, he had added another by dishonoring the widow of the unfortunate senator. Moved to repentance, this prince went and threw himself at the feet of St. Romuald, who prescribed that he should go barefoot from Rome to Mount Gargano to visit St. Michael's shrine, and to petition this archangel to carry his repentance to the foot of God's throne. It was also on the advice of St. Romuald that Peter Orseolo, the Doge of Venice, went away to do penance for his numerous sins in the monastery of Saint-Michel-de-Cuxa. The *angel of pardon* had God accept the repentance of this famous man, whom the Church declared a saint.

Each year, on September 29, St. Bernard recommended to his monks in Clairvaux devotion to St. Michael and the holy angels, a devotion which was later rewarded miraculously, as the following chapter will tell us.

St. Peter Damian, cardinal-bishop of Ostia and doctor of the Church, honored the archangel as vanquisher of the demon and of the Antichrist. He composed this prayer:

> Hasten, O Michael, prince of the heavenly militia. You, who at the end of the world are to put to death the Antichrist, who will boldly raise himself up against God, overthrow him who even now expends his efforts to reign in my heart. While my soul lives in its body, deliver it from temptation, so that when it separates from this body, you may present it worthily to its Creator.

The seraphic St. Francis [of Assisi] prepared himself for the feast of St. Michael by a forty-day fast. It was this, no doubt, that merited him, two years before his death, one of the most signal favors God has granted to his saints on earth. Let us listen to what St. Bonaventure says happened to St. Francis during this forty-day fast:

> When, therefore, by seraphic glow of longing he had been uplifted toward God, and by his sweet compassion had been transformed into the likeness of Him Who of His exceeding love endured to be crucified,—on a certain morning about the Feast of the Exaltation of Holy Cross, while he was praying on the side of the mountain, he beheld a Seraph having six wings, flaming and resplendent, coming down from the heights of heaven. When in his flight most swift he had reached the space of air nigh the man of God, there appeared betwixt the wings the Figure of a Man crucified, having his hands and feet stretched forth in the shape of a Cross, and fastened unto a Cross. Two wings were raised above His head, twain were spread forth to fly, while twain hid His whole body. Beholding this, Francis was mightily astonied, and joy, mingled with sorrow, filled his heart. He rejoiced at the gracious aspect wherewith he saw Christ, under the guise of the Seraph, regard him, but His crucifixion pierced his soul with a sword of pitying grief. He marveled exceedingly at the appearance of a vision so unfathomable, knowing that the infirmity of the Passion doth in no wise accord with the immortality of a Seraphic spirit. At length he understood therefrom, the Lord revealing it unto him, that this vision had been thus presented unto his gaze by the divine providence, that the friend of Christ might have foreknowledge that he was to be wholly transformed into the likeness of Christ Crucified, not by martyrdom of body, but by enkindling of heart. Accordingly, as the vision disappeared, it left in his heart a wondrous glow, but on his flesh also it imprinted a no less wondrous likeness of its tokens. For forthwith there began to appear in his hands and feet the marks of the nails, even as he had just beheld them in that Figure of the Crucified.... [Francis's] right side, moreover, was—as if it had been pierced

by a lance—seamed with a ruddy scar, wherefrom ofttimes welled the sacred blood, staining his habit and breeches.[8]

The seraphic Order of Friars Minor is convinced that this Seraph was St. Michael.

Another St. Francis, no less renowned for his heroic virtues than the order he founded, Francis of Paola, received from the prince of the angels, whom he honored with a special devotion, the coat of arms and escutcheon of his order. It was the word "CHARITAS," meaning charity, written in letters of heavenly gold, surrounded by gold rays, and on an azure background.

The two celebrated apostles of Germany and England, St. Boniface and St. Augustine of Canterbury, had no more powerful helper in their battles against idolatry than the glorious vanquisher of Satan; they showed their gratitude to him by building churches and monasteries in his honor.[9]

St. Francis Xavier, the great apostle to the Indies and Japan, also merited by his devotion to the archangel, as he himself liked to acknowledge, special signs of protection.[10]

St. Francis de Sales imitated his illustrious patrons. This great bishop of Geneva made every effort to inculcate this precious devotion in others. We read in the constitutions he gave to the Hermits of Mont Voiron: "On ferial and working days, following the thanksgiving after dinner, the hermits will go to the church to recite the litanies of St. Michael and the Holy Angels." In several of his writings, he recommends imitating the holy archangel and uttering at the moment of temptation his war cry, *"Who is like God?"* a cry, he says, which puts the demon to flight.

We could still mention a multitude of other names, the most renowned in monastic glory's splendor, but we shall make known some of them in the following chapter.

Among the sovereigns whose sanctity raised them to the altars, there are two who are especially illustrious: St. Henry, Emperor of Germany, and St. Louis, King of France. The first was favored at Mount Gargano with an apparition of the archangel, who miraculously protected him in a war against the barbarians. In thanksgiving for this blessing, this prince had built, in the city of Bamberg, a monastery dedicated to St. Michael. St. Louis, in the year 1236, the same year he came of age, went to Normandy's Mont Saint-Michel to place his person and his kingdom under the protection of St. Michael. This confidence was rewarded by the greatest and most beautiful reign, as well as by a holy death. We could add to these two names that of Charlemagne, whom some have given the title of saint. This great emperor of the West had the image of St. Michael depicted on his standards, and had multiple churches built in his honor, among others one in Rome bearing the name St. Michael in Sassia.[11] This church today serves as the residence for the Confraternity of the Blessed Sacrament in the service of the Vatican, instituted by Paul III.

Christian virgins have also had recourse to the protection of the glorious archangel. Their confidence has not been disappointed. Blessed Oringa and some of her companions were departing the city of Lucca to go on pilgrimage to Mount Gargano. St. Michael protected them from some wretches who sought to despoil their honor, and lavished them with the most attentive care.

After the example of St. Francis of Assisi, St. Elizabeth, an abbess in Germany, prepared for the feast of the heavenly army's leader by fasting for forty days on bread and water.

But it is impossible to mention here all the saints devoted to the archangel.[12] The number of those we have just made known, who belong to all conditions, is sufficiently large, their names are sufficiently illustrious, and the graces they received are sufficiently evident to make us resolve to imitate them.

CHAPTER 4:

DEVOTION TO ST. MICHAEL FLOURISHES IN MONASTERIES AND RELIGIOUS ORDERS: THE BASILIANS, BENEDICTINES, PREMONSTRATENSIANS, CAMALDOLESE, CARMELITES, FRANCISCANS, MINIMS, ETC.

Thy children [shall be] as olive plants.
– Psalms 127:3 [128:3]

The religious orders are to the mystical body of the Church what the heart and entrails are to the natural body. Heirs of the spirit of their holy founders, they unceasingly invoke over the people of God the protection and graces they need; like other Moseses, they stretch their hands towards heaven and obtain, for those who fight against the errors and scandals of the age, the courage and strength they need to attain victory.

St. Jerome thus rightly calls the initial founders of monastic life the pillars of the Church; they are in fact her support and glory. They have edified her by their examples, they have honored her by the holiness of their lives, they have supported her by the fervor of their prayers, and they still are the firmest support through the generations of saints who live by their spirit and according to the example of their eminent virtues.

It is in fact in the religious orders that have been formed so many holy bishops and so many illustrious defenders of the faith who, in their retreat, have drawn abundant lights, a generous freedom, and an intrepid courage; it is there that the exercises of monastic life have prepared them for the works and combats of their holy ministry. Voltaire admits, "One cannot deny that there have been very great virtues in the cloister. There is still hardly a monastery that does not contain some admirable souls who do honor to human nature."

But the religious orders, like all the works of God, have been attacked with all the rage that is distinctive of Satan. What we read in the lives of St. Dominic and St. Macarius can give us some idea of it.

Lacordaire recounts the following story he borrows from [the Dominican hagiographer] Dietrich of Apolda:

> One day when Dominic, a vigilant sentinel, was going around the monastery, he encountered the demon prowling about the enclosure like a raging beast. He stopped him and said, "Why are you prowling about like this?"
>
> The demon responded, "Because of the profit I find in it."
>
> The saint said to him, "What profit do you get in the dormitory?"
>
> The demon answered, "I take sleep from the friars, I persuade them not to get up for the office, and, when it is permitted me, I send them dreams and phantasms."
>
> The saint led him to the choir and said, "What do you gain in this holy place?"
>
> The demon answered, "I make them come late, leave early, and forget themselves."
>
> Asked about the refectory, he answered, "Who does not eat more or less than is necessary?"
>
> Led to the parlor, he said laughingly, "This place belongs to me; this is the place for laughter, vain noises, and useless talk."
>
> But when he was in the chapter, he started wanting to flee, saying, "This place is abhorrent to me, I lose here everything that I gain elsewhere; it is here that the friars are admonished for their faults, that they accuse themselves, do penance, and are absolved."

To defend their institute and their monasteries from the attacks of the evil spirit, a good number of holy founders placed them under the protection of St. Michael. Their confidence was not disappointed: these orders preserved their primitive spirit and multiplied with surprising rapidity.

We shall mention some of the most renowned examples.

The Basilian Order (of St. Basil the Great) chose as its special patron St. Michael the Archangel. This order enjoys so much esteem in the East that no one can be raised to the dignity of patriarch, archbishop, bishop or even pastor of a simple parish if he is not a religious of the order of St. Basil or of St. Anthony. But the latter is less widespread.

It is again under the protection of the archangel that a new congregation of St. Basil flourishes in our day, whose motherhouse is in Annonay, in the French diocese of Viviers. Called in 1852 by Bishop de Charbonnel, their former student, the Basilians established a minor seminary in Toronto, Canada, dedicated to their patron St. Michael, which is very prosperous today.

St. Benedict, the father of Western monasticism, also bequeathed to his countless children a special devotion to St. Michael. Of the twelve monasteries he built for his numerous disciples, he placed two of them under the protection of the great archangel; he called the first one Holy Angel and the second St. Michael. The latter one was located above the famous cave to which this seraphic soul so often went to converse with God.

The Benedictines, following the example of their father, erected numerous abbeys for which they made St. Michael the patron.[1]

Cluny, Cîteaux,[2] Clairvaux, and Sacra di San Michele distinguished themselves among all the monasteries governed by St. Benedict's Rule.

In Cluny, above the entrance door inside the basilica, one noticed with keen curiosity a St. Michael chapel, largely enclosed within the massive wall, but jutting out six feet and ending in a cul-de-lampe within the church, in such a way that it seemed suspended inside the large nave, like organs in our own day. By way of a double spiral stairway hidden inside the wall, one could go up to this chapel, which faced east.

The disciples of Blessed Berno thus wanted to unite their voices to the angelic voice which gave them the pitch, so to speak, to worthily celebrate the Lord's praises. At the same time, they confided to the archangel the guarding of this basilica, which was one of the architectural wonders of France.

After the establishment of the congregation of Cluny, the most significant one to be erected next was that of Sacra di San Michele, at the entrance of the Alps, in the Kingdom of Piedmont. An Auvergnat, Hugh the Unsewn, Lord of Montboissier, was its founder. This lord having gone to Rome to obtain absolution from the Pope for a sin he had committed, promised, in expiation for his offense, to have a monastery built.

Passing through Suze, Hugh made known to one of his friends the reason for his voyage and the promise he had made to God and to the Sovereign Pontiff. This friend advised him to ask the bishop of the city for a church this prelate had erected in honor of St. Michael on Mont Epicare. Through several dreams, God made known to Hugh and his wife that it was His will to place this monastery under the protection of the *angel of pardon.*

After obtaining the permission of the bishop and lord of the place, some cells were built on the mountain, as many as the irregularity of the place allowed. But soon, recognizing the unsuitability of the place, Hugh obtained a small property called Clusa, and built there the celebrated monastery which is now known as Sacra di San Michele.

Emperors, kings, and princes gave it great privileges and considerably increased its revenue. The Sovereign Pontiffs granted the abbots all the prerogatives enjoyed by generals and heads of orders. The bull of confirmation, given by Innocent III in 1216, makes known to us that more than one hundred forty churches and abbeys depended on this monastery.

This abbey, which was of the Order of St. Benedict, was first governed by elected abbots who distinguished themselves by their merit and their holiness. It was subsequently ruled by abbots whose titles made them respectable, mostly cardinals and princes, or at least other highly prestigious title holders.

The French Benedictine congregation of Marmoutier was also strongly devoted to St. Michael. It received this devotion from St. Maurus, its founder. This illustrious disciple of St. Benedict had confided the guardianship of his monastery in Glanfeuil to the archangel, by building him a chapel at its entrance.

The glorious archangel was also the object of a special veneration in Clairvaux. The reason for it was this: It was the vigil of the feast of St. Michael in the year 1597. Being attacked by a Calvinist army of forty-five thousand men, the monks of Clairvaux addressed their prayers to the Blessed Virgin and to "Monseigneur St. Michael." The Calvinists had already made a bridge when, according to a contemporary account,

> their planks and weapons were hurled, at which time multiple enemies were injured and thrown into the water, which caused them to retreat in shame; and a great number of them fell into the water, who were lost and drowned, as the river was high and moving rapidly. One of the enemy leaders, who was extremely enraged, swore he would neither drink nor eat until he had burned down the abbey church and roasted all the monks alive; however, thanks to God, he died an unfortunate death that same night, without having spoken to anyone…. In thanksgiving, they have the custom at Clairvaux of doing a general procession every year on September 29, the feast day of the blessed archangel St. Michael, protector of the Church, leader of the troops of the God of armies, and invincible defender of the faithful.

The Premonstratensian Order did not distinguish itself any less for its devotion to the prince of the angels. St. Michael's in Antwerp was one if its first and most eminent abbeys. St. Norbert, after having destroyed the abominable heresy of Tanchelm, founded it in 1124[3] with assistance from Godfrey of Bouillon, the Duke of Lorraine, who placed in the church a miraculous image of the Virgin,[4] and twelve canons to serve there. This abbey shortly became the motherhouse of three others.[5] It kept the spirit of its founder so well that, one hundred years later, the Sovereign Pontiffs confided to the abbot of this monastery the mission of putting an end to the relaxation in other houses of the order.

The Order of Prémontré, having disappeared like so many others in the winds of the revolutionary storm, has just been reestablished in France. It is under the invocation of St. Michael that the first monastery has been placed.[6] May the glorious prince of the heavenly militia deign to protect this nascent order, and give to the Church apostles filled with zeal for the glory of God and the salvation of souls!

In 1212, Camaldolese religious, sons of St. Romuald, so devoted to St. Michael, went to found a monastery on a small island between

Venice and Murano. The government of Venice gave them an ancient church located on this island and dedicated to St. Michael the Archangel. These religious built a new monastery and a new church consecrated by Cardinal Hugolino around the year 1221. There, a congregation was formed comprising multiple monasteries and which took the name St. Michael of Murano.[7] Protected by the great archangel, this order gave the Church several distinguished prelates, some of whom were cardinals.

A great number of monasteries of Camaldolese daughters are subject to the jurisdiction of the superiors of the St. Michael's monks congregation.

If the holy order of Carmel has given our France souls admirable for their holiness, we owe it, Boudon says, to St. Michael. Mademoiselle Acarie, the prime mover for everything great that was done for the good of the Church in France at the end of the sixteenth century, initially tasked Monsieur de Santeuil to go to Spain to bring back some of St. Teresa's daughters; however, he was unable to succeed. After yet a second fruitless attempt, she put Monsieur de Bérule in charge of this undertaking. Despite the opposition from the demon, despite the traps this evil spirit set up for him on the way and the dangers of death into which he threw him, Monsieur de Bérule returned to Paris, bringing with him six nuns filled with the spirit and zeal of their holy foundress. This success was due to St. Michael, who appeared to Venerable Anne of St. Bartholomew, fully armed like a warrior who had come from battle. He wanted to make known by this that he had won the victory over hell's opposition and over the obstacles set up by men.

After the example of their seraphic father, the Franciscans have professed a singular devotion with respect to the prince of the angels. Let us listen to Mary of Agreda, a daughter of St. Francis:

> Among all those who have most favored and obliged this monastery[8] are the great prince of the heavenly armies and patron of the Holy Church, the Archangel St. Michael, and our seraphic father St. Francis, prince of the evangelical poor…. O Queen of Virtues,… we pray to you from the bottom of our heart

to give us and appoint to us as special protectors and copatrons of this family your two favorites, St. Michael and St. Francis, in whose devotion we wish to distinguish ourselves; commending us to their protection, so that they may defend us from our enemies in the perils of this life, enlighten us in the darkness of night, teach us in ignorance, enliven us and bring us to practice all that is more holy and more perfect; may the Holy Archangel present us, on the last day of our life, free from all sin, before you and before the Sovereign Judge....

...Great prince St. Michael, remember these humble religious, devoted admirers of your holiness, and accept our zeal for your devotion; it is to testify to it that we perpetually celebrate your three feast days with a very special sentiment of joy and consolation; we will fast on the vigils of these feasts, and those who can do so, after the example of our seraphic father, will fast during the lent instituted in your honor; we will continue to invoke you, as we do each day, and we will always have a firm confidence in your protection, on account of your holiness and what you owe the Most High, having you to defend the glory and truth of His ineffable name.[9]

The Minims, faithful to the motto brought them from heaven by the prince of the angels, are also faithful to imitate their model and father, St. Francis of Paola. It is on the feast day of St. Michael and under his protection that takes place, every year, one of the most important acts for a religious order: the election of a superior for each house.

The Society of Jesus, the Congregation of the Sacred Hearts of Jesus and Mary, the Hospitaller Order of St. John of God, and the Congregation of Christian Brothers also honor St. Michael with a special veneration. The Jesuits placed a great number of their houses under the patronage of the archangel, and the Christian Brothers spread among the youth, principally in Canada, this salutary devotion.

Among the female congregations, we can mention the Daughters of Charity and the Daughters of Wisdom, who profess a special devotion to St. Michael.

A good number of religious orders prepare for the feast of the prince of the angels by fasting and penance. The Caloyers, or Greek monks, do an eight-day lent; the monks and nuns of the Brigittine Order fast from the feast of the Exaltation of the Holy Cross until September 29, exclusive; the Angelic and Guastaline religious sisters, as well as a good number of other religious orders, fast only on the vigil of the feast of St. Michael, which they celebrate with great pomp.[10]

Thanks to the archangel's protection, these religious families have multiplied; and while many others have disappeared or have visibly relaxed their original fervor, these, for the most part, have preserved, without need for reform, the spirit that presided at their foundation.

CHAPTER 5:
ST. MICHAEL CHOSEN AS THE PROTECTOR OF MILITARY ORDERS IN PORTUGAL, NAPLES, AND FRANCE. – ORDER OF MERIT IN BAVARIA, ETC.

For the success of war is not in the multitude of the army, but strength cometh from heaven.

– 1 Maccabees 3:19

Saint Michael is the angel of battles. Many times, in fact, since the beginning of the Church, as we have seen, he has given to Christian armies who have invoked him visible marks of his powerful protection.

For this reason, many cities that converted to Catholicism have substituted St. Michael for Mars, the god of war among the Gentiles. Among these cities, we shall mention Antwerp, Liège, Bonn, Lüneburg, Cologne, etc.[1] Continuously beset by incursions from the Turks, Christian Europe wanted to have soldiers always ready to defend her. One thus saw generous men, most bearers of illustrious names, promising with a vow to consecrate their lives to the defense of the Church, the homeland, and what is right; hence, there were the military orders, so celebrated in the Middle Ages. Although all honored St. Michael as one of their protectors, multiple ones were specially established in honor of the glorious archangel. We shall make known some of them.

The Order of the Wing of St. Michael was founded by King Afonso I of Portugal in the year 1167,[2] after this prince won a victory over Albarech, the king of Seville. Afonso was in Santarém when Albarech came with a powerful army into Portugal, to besiege him in this city where he was with a handful of men. Afonso, fearing that the king of León was coming to help the king of Seville, gave the necessary orders to march to the enemy. He was persuaded that God, who had one hundred eighty-five thousand soldiers of Sennacherib's army killed by St. Michael, was no less capable of delivering him from his enemies. He

197

therefore fervently beseeched God to send him an angel to march before him and to bring fear and terror of the power of His arm into the hearts of His name's blasphemers, who had come only to oppress His people and profane His temple. His prayer was graciously heard: He attacked with every possible success. Seeing in the heat of combat that the Moors had taken the great standard of the kingdom, he was visibly helped by St. Michael and rushed into the midst of the enemies, almost all of whom were slain on the battlefield.

As this miraculous victory filled the prince's heart with a just gratitude for his liberator, Afonso was not content merely having a chapel built in his honor in Alcobaça Monastery, but, in order to perpetuate its memory until the end of time, he instituted a military order which he called the Wing of St. Michael, because in battle he had only seen one wing, which covered the entire body of this archangel, only allowing his hand to be seen, with which he indicated all the places he should attack.

Afonso remained thirty days in Alcobaça Monastery to give thanks to God there. It was during this time that he prescribed to the knights of the Wing of St. Michael their obligations. He who was admitted had to swear, between the hands of the abbot of Alcobaça, that he would be faithful to God, to the Pope, and to the King. The abbot of this monastery alone had the power to give the mark of the order. The knights had to recite daily, whether in time of war or peace, the same prayers as the Cistercian Order's converse brothers. They had to contribute to the upkeep of the chapel of St. Michael. On the feast's vigil, they had to be in this abbey to assist at Vespers and Matins. They would take communion at Mass, from the hands of the abbot, clothed in white capes, like the Cistercian converse brothers. Their principal obligation was to be meek and humble, to curb the haughty, to give aid to women, principally nobles, girls, and widows, to defend the law, and to fight its enemies.

King Ferdinand I of Naples also instituted a military order named after St. Michael. The king was its head. The knights wore a white robe lined with ermine. Their collar was a gold chain made up of various O-shaped links joined together, from which hung a medal inscribed with the word *Decorum*.

Some authors claim that this order is the same as the Order of the Ermine, an order instituted by Ferdinand and placed under the protection of St. Michael.

France, so devoted to St. Michael, could not be without an order of chivalry in honor of this glorious archangel. Louis XI acted on the wishes of his father, Charles VII, when he instituted this order. This was around the year 1469, the ninth year of his reign, at Château d'Amboise.

This is the preamble of the letters patent of institution:

> We, to the glory and praise of God, our almighty Creator, and reverence to the glorious Virgin Mary, and to the honor and reverence of Monseigneur St. Michael the Archangel, the first knight, who, for the cause of God, victoriously battled against the envious enemy of the human race, and cast him from heaven, and who has ever guarded, preserved, and defended his place and oratory of Mont Saint-Michel, without it being captured, subject to, or placed in the hands of the ancient enemies of our kingdom, and so that all good, high, and noble men of courage be excited and more moved to all virtuous works, on the first day of August of the year 1469....

He decreed that there would be only thirty-six knights, a number which he never reached under his reign. He gave them a gold collar of shells double strung together on a golden chain, from which hung a medal depicting St. Michael the Archangel vanquishing the devil. They were obligated every day to wear this collar unconcealed, under penalty of having one Mass said and giving an alms of seven sols and six deniers in Tours currency, unless they were serving in the army, traveling, in their home, or hunting. In such cases, they wore only a medal attached to a gold chain or black silk cord, and they could not forsake it in the greatest dangers, even to preserve their life. Brantôme recounts that King Francis I, in his presence, gave a severe reprimand to a knight who, after having been captured in combat, had removed the mark of his order so as not to be recognized and pay a heavy ransom.

These knights could not participate in any war or engage in any dangerous activity without first notifying and consulting the majority of the other knights. Those who were French could not commit themselves to the service of any foreign prince or make long journeys without the permission of the king; the foreign knights could do so by simply letting it be known. A knight of the order could take up arms for the defense of his king when the latter was warring against some prince, unless it was against the king of France; the knight, his subject, then had to excuse himself from serving against the French kingdom; if his prince did not want to accept his excuse and forced him to serve, he could then take up arms against France, but he had to notify the head of the order, and make known to his sovereign that if he took a knight of this order as a prisoner of war, he would free him and do what he could to save his life; if his prince did not want to consent, he had to quit his service.

The king, for his part, was committed to protecting the knights, upholding all their rights and privileges, and not undertaking any war or matter of consequence without first consulting them and taking their advice, except in cases where the matters required much secrecy and prompt execution; and the knights promised and swore not to reveal the undertakings the sovereign put before them for deliberation. According to the same statutes, the knights were to be expelled from the order for heresy, treason, cowardice, or fleeing in combat.

The church of Mont Saint-Michel in Normandy was designated by Louis XI to celebrate there the divine office and to receive the benefits and endowments made in favor of the order.

Louis XII, when he seized the Kingdom of Naples, made multiple Neapolitan lords knights of St. Michael. Francis I sent the ribbon to King Henry VIII of England.

Later, when the kings instituted the Order of the Holy Ghost, they required that the knights of this order first be received into the Order of St. Michael.

Louis XVIII, in 1816, recalled that the Order of St. Michael is specially intended to serve as a reward and encouragement to Frenchmen distinguishing themselves in letters, sciences, and arts, or by discoveries, works, or enterprises useful to the state.

After a lapse of more than thirty-five years, there was in Reims, following the coronation of Charles X, a solemn reception of knights and commanders belonging to the king's orders. It was held in the cathedral on Monday, May 30, 1825.

Before the ceremony, the Dauphin, according to the rule and custom, received as knights of the Order of St. Michael all the knights who were going to be received into the Order of the Holy Ghost. In 1826, there was on September 29, St. Michael's feast day and the anniversary of the birth of the Duke of Bordeaux, a convocation of the chapter of the Order of St. Michael.

This order was de facto abolished by the July Revolution of 1830.[3]

There still exists in our day, in Bavaria, an order of merit of St. Michael, [formerly] called a knightly order. We read the following in Migne's *Dictionnaire des ordres religieux* [*Dictionary of Religious Orders*]:

> Joseph Clemens, the elector of Cologne, instituted this order of chivalry as Duke of Bavaria, in the province of Munich. It was later solemnly confirmed by King Maximilian Joseph of Bavaria in the revision of royal orders on September 11, 1808.
>
> In a decree of April 6, 1810, when the statutes of what was called the Order of Merit of St. Michael were reformed and ratified, the first and principal aims it set for itself were supporting the Catholic religion, defending the divine honor, to which its end obliged it, and assisting the defenders of the homeland.
>
> This order was originally divided into three classes... to which were later joined the fourth class of honorary knights. To be admitted to any of the first three classes, one needed to give proof of nobility....
>
> Pius VII declared in [a] brief... dated February 5, 1802, that ecclesiastics decorated in this order would have the right to wear the clothing of a prelate and enjoy all the privileges of domestic prelates.
>
> On September 14, 1846, King Ludwig I... published a royal decree by which he ruled that the Order of Merit of St. Michael would from then on consist of thirty-six grand crosses, sixty commanders, and three hundred knights.

The dignity of grand cross is conferred on one who is a prince by blood, with the consent of the king. On the shield of St. Michael, on the front of the decoration, one reads the following epigraph: *Quis ut Deus?* [*Who is like God?*].

On the four parts of the cross are the initials P. F. F. P., which stand for *pietas, fidelitas, fortitudo,* and *perseverantia,* or piety, fidelity, strength, and perseverance. On the reverse side is the legend "*Dominus potens in prælio,*" or "The Lord mighty in battle."[4]

In 1617, three gentlemen brothers of Spello, Italy, from the Petrignani family, devised the plan of instituting a military order under the name of the Blessed Virgin Mary, Mother of God, and under the rule of St. Francis of Assisi, for the defense of the Catholic faith, the exaltation of the Holy Church, and opposing the incursions of the Turks. This order was confirmed by Urban VIII in 1623 and placed under the protection of St. Michael.

The general standard of the order was to be white. On one side, there is the image of Jesus crucified; to the right of the crucifix is the Blessed Virgin compassionating the sorrows of her Son; and on the left is St. Michael the Archangel, piercing with a cross-shaped lance in his left hand the defeated dragon beneath his feet and holding a sword in his right hand where these words are written: *Quis ut Deus?*

Around their necks, the knights wore a blue enameled cross, one side having a representation of Mary's conception and the other having an image of St. Michael as he was depicted on the banner.

The following is part of the formula for the vows:

> I, N., do vow and promise to Almighty God, the Blessed Virgin Mary, St. Michael the Archangel... to combat by land and sea the infidels and enemies of the Holy Roman Church when it is commanded me by the grand master.... I shall apply myself to the propagation of the Catholic faith, to the recovery of the Holy Land.... I shall always uphold the truth of the Immaculate Conception of the Virgin Mary... according to the opinion of the Roman Church.[5]

It belonged to Mary's guardian angel to be the protector of an order committed to defending the most beautiful title given to this Most Holy Virgin.

To all these orders of chivalry, we can add a great number of others that professed a very special devotion to St. Michael and regarded him as one of their principal protectors. Such orders include the Knights of Alcántara in Spain, the Order of Amarante in Sweden, the Order of Angelics (or Order of Constantine) in Rome and the East, the Knights of Avis in Portugal, the Knights of the Bath in England, the Knights of the Band in Castile, the Knights of St. Bridget in Sweden, the Knights of Calatrava in Spain, the Knights of Christ in Portugal, the Knights of Cyprus on the island of the same name, the Knights of the Overthrown Dragon and Knights of the White Eagle in Germany,[6] the Teutonic Order, the Order of St. John of Jerusalem, of Rhodes, and of Malta, etc., etc.

Most of these chivalric orders were established to combat the enemies of the Christian name, principally the Moors. They preserved Europe from devastation and plunder, by going so far as to fight the enemy on his own turf. Clad with armor from head to toe, with a coat of arms over the breastplate, a heavy scimitar hanging at the side, and a long spear in the hand, the knights were seen wherever the danger was the greatest, the fighting the fiercest, and the conflict the thickest. Never did they ask how many enemies there were, but only where they were. They trusted in the protection of the angel of battles. Often, a small number of them made an enemy ten times more numerous flee. It was you, O Michael, who was protecting them!

However, their mission being fulfilled, most of these military orders have disappeared; and if some remain today, they are now only made up of members admitted for honorary reasons, as a reward for services rendered to religion or the homeland.

CHAPTER 6:
CONFRATERNITIES OF ST. MICHAEL.

The truth counsels men to seek the fellowship of the holy angels.
– St. Augustine[1]

" Again I say to you, that if two of you shall consent upon earth, concerning any thing whatsoever they shall ask, it shall be done to them by my Father who is in heaven. For where there are two or three gathered together in my name, there am I in the midst of them" (Mt 18:19-20).

These words of Jesus, which reveal the power of association in prayer, have been understood by the Catholic Church's faithful. In the first centuries, all Christians, having but one heart and one soul, lived animated by the spirit of faith and piety. However, when the charity and zeal of a great number grew cold in the ages that followed, it was necessary to find means to warm and maintain them. One of the principal means, after religious orders, was confraternities. In these associations, one has no other goal than to work for the glory of God, the honor of His saints, and one's own sanctification, through prayer, alms, penance, and good works. The fruits that many of them produced were wonderful, and the Church was pleased to favor them with special graces and privileges. St. Francis de Sales says of these confraternities, "One can gain everything in them, without losing anything."

Among the associations established in honor of the saints, St. Michael had some in the past and still has multiple today. These confraternities offer their members the most precious benefits with regard to piety, charity, and salvation. We shall make some of them known.

One of the oldest on record is the Confraternity of the Dying, established in Lille. The explanation of the establishment, rules, and customs of this confraternity were published in the same city in 1706.

René Lebreton de Gaubert, in his brief history of Saint-Similien,[2] speaks of a confraternity of St. Michael established in Nantes in 1642, in the chapel of Notre-Dame-de-Miséricorde.

In 1836, pious lay people from Évreux, in Eure, formed an association whose aims were the following:

1. Have a Solemn Mass celebrated the Monday following the feast of St. Michael (September 29), for which confraternity members carry in procession a statue of St. Michael decorated with flowers and a banner and torches having images of St. Michael and the Blessed Virgin, from the hamlet of Saint-Michel to St. Taurin Church. This Mass is true homage paid to the cult of St. Michael to enjoy his intercession. After the Gospel of the Mass, prayers are recited for the relief of the souls of confraternity members who died during the year.

2. On the following day, have a Requiem Mass celebrated for the repose of the souls of all deceased confraternity members.

3. After the death of each member, have a Requiem Mass celebrated particularly for that individual.

The members assist at the burials and Masses with their banner and torches.

These offices are celebrated by means of an annual contribution which is specific to each member.

The administration of the confraternity consists of:

1. A *trustee* or *director*, who is responsible for keeping the books and treasury, having the confraternity's religious services celebrated, and maintaining the order of things observed since the foundation;

2. A *bâtonnier*, commonly called *king of the confraternity* due to the very direct participation he assumes in receiving from the Church the statue of St. Michael, which he keeps for one year, from September 29 until the same date in the following year;

3. A *dauphin*, meaning a person committed to assuming the office of *bâtonnier* after the current one;
4. *Four members* who control the management of the confraternity.

This confraternity today has close to six hundred members in the city of Évreux and its surrounding area. These details come to us from the current director of this confraternity, who, with a charming simplicity, describes himself as a "poor, little, very lowly farmer, who trusted only in his loyalty, integrity, and good faith to accept this office."

On October 16, 1867, Monseigneur Bravard, the Bishop of Coutances, established a confraternity at Mont Saint-Michel whose purpose is to honor the holy angels, especially the archangel St. Michael, and to obtain through their intercession:

1. Heaven's special protection over the Church, the Sovereign Pontiff, and France;
2. The grace of a happy death, and preservation from a sudden, unforeseen death;
3. The deliverance of souls in Purgatory.

This confraternity was approved by a brief of the Sovereign Pontiff, which he enriched with indulgences. At the time of this writing, it already counts more than four thousand members. Mgr. Pie, the bishop of Poitiers, was himself one of the first to become a member of this confraternity. He said, "I shall gladly learn that my example has imitators around me."

A society was also canonically established a short time ago in the Archdiocese of Bourges by its archbishop; its purpose is to pray for the admission into heaven of the souls in purgatory.

Besides these confraternities we have just mentioned, and which were established to obtain, through the intercession of St. Michael, a precious death before the Lord, and to deliver the suffering souls, others have been erected to plead for the Church's victory over heresies, and, in general, over all the enemies of Catholicism. Such is the great confraternity of St. Michael in Germany, which counts among its members the most distinguished personages of the country.

In the Middle Ages, individuals practicing the same art or profession formed confraternities or corps for the purpose of mutually defending themselves and watching over the maintenance of their privileges. Each corps was placed under the patronage of a saint, which it honored with a special devotion, and whose altar was decorated at the expense of the association. Sometimes the same patron was shared by multiple professional corps; sometimes also the same professional corps, established in different cities, had different patrons.

The corps of tailors and merchants in certain cities of Lorraine, the parchment makers of Rennes, and the *oublie*[3] makers of Paris honored St. Michael as their protector.

Each confraternity had its own banner on which an image of the archangel was depicted, and the confraternity would participate with it in processions that took place on solemn feast days.

In 1552, in Rome, the church of San Michele Arcangelo del Torrione alle Fornaci was built. This church is outside of the city, but a short distance from the Porta Cavalleggeri. It was erected in the vicinity of vast tower ruins by laborers who worked in the nearby clay quarries. Their confraternity paid half of its expenses, the other half coming from the Chapter of the Vatican, which continues to appoint its parish priest.

Another church in the same city, St. Michael in Sassia, serves as a residence for the Confraternity of the Blessed Sacrament, instituted by Paul III and at the service of the Vatican. There was also there a community made up of a hundred priests and twenty clerics, established in 1631 under the patronage of St. Mary of the Conception and St. Michael, to support each other through mutual aid. One indeed could not choose more beautiful models: Mary, who was without sin, and Michael, who supported the faithful angels against Satan.

We are quite far from having mentioned all the confraternities established in honor of the prince of the angels. In the Middle Ages, when pilgrims would establish confraternities in their parishes upon their return from Mont Saint-Michel in Normandy, they were countless.

We have contented ourselves to mention those honoring St. Michael under different titles which we have attributed to him in the first book, and which ask of him particular graces of which he has always been considered a dispenser. He is thus invoked in Italy, Germany, and France as protector of the Church, the Catholic priesthood, and France; he is considered the guardian angel of the Eucharist; and he is asked for a precious death before God, as well as for the deliverance of the souls in purgatory.

The great archangel, let us hope, will carry to the throne of God the prayers of these multitudes who are enlisted under his banner, and will obtain for them the graces they ask.

CHAPTER 7:

ST. MICHAEL AND WORKS OF REPARATION.

*There is no better means of putting
the devil to flight than praising God.*
– St. Francis de Sales

Satan, as we have already said, began in heaven a fight which he
continues on earth. The seductive and blasphemy-filled discourse
which made the first man fall in the earthly paradise was not at all an
isolated incident; it was a permanent act which will endure as long as
man. It is no longer, of course, in the outward form of a serpent, whose
instincts he has preserved, that he presents himself today; he knows how
to clothe himself in other seductive forms. "Woe to the earth and to the
sea," St. John exclaims, "because the devil is come down unto you,
having great wrath, knowing that he hath but a short time" (Rv 12:12).
Engaging man in his fight against God, making him an accomplice to
his crime, such is the aim of Satan's unceasing efforts. Thus, on earth
as in heaven, today and until the end of the world as in the beginning,
there are the same combatants, the same weapons, and the same goal.
Here is the entire philosophy of history, past, present, and future.

But who could list all the means of seduction employed by this
infernal spirit? He diversifies them according to times, places, and
circumstances; and, very often, alas, he makes man similar to himself,
by making him a man of blasphemy and revolt.

Today, seemingly unleashed, he redoubles more than ever his fury
to ruin souls and destroy the Church. Rationalism, sensualism,
Caesarism, and hatred of Christianity—these are his means, and these
are what we find everywhere today.

Rationalism, or the emancipation of reason from any divine
authority in matters of faith. — *Sensualism*, or the emancipation of the
flesh from any divine authority in matters of morals. — *Caesarism*, or
the emancipation of society in matters of government through

centralizing all spiritual and temporal powers into the hands of a single man who is both emperor and pontiff, and answers only to himself. — *Hatred of Christianity*, meaning hatred of the God of Christians. After the past century, what blasphemies are still left to utter against the Incarnate Word? — *Hatred of his ministers.* In the paroxysm of his fury, did he not say that he wanted to use "the last entrails of the last of the kings to strangle the last of the priests"?[1] — *Hatred of true Catholics*, whom he oppresses in their true freedom, in their right to property, and in their conscience. — *Hatred of the dogmas and morals* of Christianity, scorn for its laws, the profanation of Sundays, the sanctification of Mondays, the abandonment of prayer and the sacraments, infernal hatred, whose last word is to smother Christianity in the mud—this is what Satan preaches through his anti-Christian men, books, brochures, and newspapers, the oracles of the masses. He floods cities and countryside with these wicked products, he has them enter the hut of the poor and the palace of the great, into the workshop of the laborer and into the sanctuary of science. Each day, he devises new attacks which appear to him to have greater chances of success. It is still the same cry as in heaven: *I will ascend.*

What is to be done to hold back Satan? What is to be done to repair the glory of our God Who has been outraged?

Let us listen to St. Francis de Sales:

> When this wretched spirit abandoned the obedience he owed to his Creator, saying, "*Similis ero Altissimo,*" that he would become like Him, notice that he became the devil only because he did not want to praise God; seeing this, the great St. Michael cried out, "*Quis ut Deus? Quis ut Deus? Who is like God? Who is like God?*" He repeated this multiple times and was followed by all the other blessed spirits, who in chorus responded with this holy anthem, "*Who is like God?*" thereby putting the wretched Lucifer and his accomplices to flight, all of whom were cast into hell for not wanting to intone this divine anthem, by which the other angels were so much confirmed in grace that they could never fall from it. *Thus, it is most certain that there is no better means of putting the devil to flight than praising*

God, because that wretch cannot bear seeing God adored and praised by men.[2]

To the cries of revolt, let us answer with the war cry of the great archangel: *Quis ut Deus? Who is like God?* They propose to us the emancipation of reason and the flesh; they want to push society far from God; they designate for our hatred the God of Christians, His ministers, true Catholics, dogmas and morals. Behold our response: *Who is like God?* — They want to lead us into blasphemy! Let us imitate St. Michael, our leader. St. Jude says, "When Michael the archangel, disputing with the devil, contended about the body of Moses, he durst not bring against him the judgment of railing speech, but said: The Lord command thee" (Jude 1:9)! If then, St. Jerome observes, St. Michael dared not blaspheme the devil, who was certainly worthy of malediction, how much should we be free from this sin! Satan deserved to be cursed, but the blasphemy was not to come from the archangel's mouth.

But in order to most fully repair the glory of our God Who has been outraged, in order to more effectively fight the evil, let us imitate St. Michael, who united around him the faithful angels to protest Satan's rebellion. Let us bring together faithful souls and form associations, as they possess a power which nothing can resist. The poet[3] says, "All power is weak, unless it be united."

See the drop of water: The least breath makes it disappear. But bring drops of water together and you will have this powerful element, the sea, which breaks the strongest dikes.

The Church was weak initially; it was the small mustard seed; but soon it became powerful against her enemies, against persecutors. To what does she owe this power? To the association of *minds* in one same faith, of *hearts* in one same desire and one same love, of *wills* submitted to one same law, of *persons* in the unity of the same interests, same hopes, and same conduct. Through this union, the Church lives, sheds light, and triumphs over hell.

It is through this same means that it is given us to successfully fight the works of Satan. A union of minds, hearts, and wills to make reparation for blasphemies and the revolt against God, and to combat the deleterious influence of publications coming from the presses of hell.

Associations have been formed under the patronage of St. Michael to achieve this last goal.

For some years now, a work of this kind has existed in Chartres. As of three years ago, it already counted more than 83,000 members.

Under the inspiration and care of Fr. [Célestin Joseph] Félix, a similar work has also been formed in Paris. Let us listen to the eminent preacher of Notre-Dame de Paris make known to us its objective:

> The mounting ravages of perverting and corrupting words demonstrate better than ever, even to the most inattentive, the supreme need to spread and increase the activity of salutary and conservative speech.
>
> The work of St. Michael the Archangel answers this present need. It is not the only one: others with it, and before it, have entered on this path to restore our great ruins, and far from diminishing their influence, it intends to increase it; it is not their competitor, it is their helper....
>
> Our century, so rich in science and inventions, is so poor in the substantial truth that makes nations live. Oh, may our good books come to instruct it, may they come to reillumine before our troubled eyes the torch of pure light.
>
> Our century, so resplendent with luxury and so filled with pleasures, is nevertheless so sad; and so profound today is the melancholy of souls gripped by the evil of ennui and gnawed at by the worm of skepticism. Oh, may good books come to reveal to these desolations, with the sweet mystery of Christianity, the secret of supreme consolations.
>
> In short, our century which so highly praises all its progress, our century so proud of what it calls its virtues, it exhibits the spectacle of such strange degradations, it provides the example of such formalized corruption, and it lets its morals fall into such squalid mire. Oh, may our good books come to convert this prodigal child that is called the nineteenth century; may they

come to sow amidst our corruption and our ruins the seeds of life and resurrection.

And since the Society of St. Michael the Archangel, with so many others, seeks, for its part, to participate in this work of regeneration and salvation, come to its assistance; help it to be born, to grow, and to march on its path of Christian and social restoration....

The work of St. Michael comes to assist all talented persons who have passion for the truth, ambition for the good, and the desire to extend by word the reign of Jesus Christ on earth.... This is the supreme ambition of this new work.

O glorious archangel, take these works under your powerful patronage; give them visible marks of your protection.

For us, we have envisioned the founding of a great *Reparation Archconfraternity* under the protection of St. Michael, the one who was the first to make reparation to God's glory when He was outraged.

Given that the majesty of God is principally outraged by blasphemy, the violation of Sundays, and evil books, the members of this association would commit themselves to the following:

1. Never blaspheming; using one's authority to prevent one's subordinates from doing so; saying each time that one hears blasphemy, "Blessed be God's holy name!" or "Praised be Jesus Christ!"

2. Never working or having others work on Sundays, outside of cases of *absolute necessity*.

3. Never reading bad books, not even buying them or keeping them in one's possession as soon as they are recognized as such; using one's influence to prevent their reading and to promote the diffusion of good books.

4. Praying to St. Michael to obtain through his intercession: 1) heaven's special protection over the Church and France, whose special protector he is; 2) the grace of a happy death, committing oneself to dying in the love of God and of the Church.[4]

May St. Michael deign to raise up a man of God to implement this plan, formed for the greater glory of God and the salvation of souls!

Chapter 8:
St. Michael's glory celebrated through art. – Architecture. – Sculpture. – Painting.

The stone came to life and transformed into an immense poem.
– Théophile Lavallée

In the Middle Ages, one author says,

> All minds were uplifted by the passion of the time: the faith. The arts were born, not modeled after antiquity, but spontaneous and indigenous, all imagination and invention a living expression of the society. This naive and passionate poetry, which superabounded in all minds, diffused its treasures, less in books, which were insufficient to contain it, than in those monuments which personify the Middle Ages: the cathedrals, gigantic works erected by the people and with faith, on which no one would dare put his name, for the work is shared like the God to Whom it is raised. Hence… the pyramidal bell tower rose to pierce the heavens with its audacious spire; the entryways, the galleries, the naves, and the chapels were packed with a profusion of graceful and tremendous details, countless statues, and magnificent stained-glass windows. The stone came to life and transformed into an immense poem, in which the most fecund imagination exhausted all its fantasies.[1]

It is thus the arts, far better still than books, which make known to us the devotion of peoples and religious orders to the glorious archangel. Indeed, throughout Catholic territory, one saw splendid monuments rise. Some have perdured through time; others present to the pilgrim's eye majestic ruins recalling their former splendor.

Among these latter, the ruins of the wealthy abbey of Saint-Michel-de-Cuxa, located very near and to the south of Prades, are the most

215

remarkable that exist in Pyrénées-Orientales. This superb monument was completed in 984. All of the cloister's columns were made of red marble, and multiple entryways, including the entrance to the abbey house, were made of white marble. St-Michel-de-Cuxa was destroyed in 1794. Capitals, column pieces, bases, cornice fragments, and entablatures are found in a great number of gardens and private homes in Prades.

"What still exists of the cloister and abbatial house," one author says, "makes one conceive the highest idea of the wealth and taste that directed the building of these monuments."[2]

Worth mentioning is that most of the monuments built to the glory of St. Michael are located on hills or mountains. They thus seem nearer to heaven, the abode of the blessed archangel.

In Brussels, on the hill called Molenberg, in the northern part of the city, the ancient church of St. Michael, today [St. Michael and] St. Gudula, prominently displays its imposing Gothic facade. One goes up a large, magnificent stairway of thirty-nine steps. The church is Gothic with a regular and imposing architecture; it was built in the form of a cross, with two beautiful side entryways. The frontispiece is vast, loaded with sculptures and bas-reliefs, flanked by two very high, massive square towers which are not yet completed. The interior consists of one nave and two collateral aisles. The choir, separated from the nave by a rood screen, is entirely enclosed, and one can fully go around the outside of it. Attached to each of the columns separating the collateral aisles from the central nave is a colossal statue. The sculpture of its wooden pulpit is worth the focus of one's attention—it is the work of Verbruggen.

In one of the faubourgs of Le Puy-en-Velay, not far from the Borne River, an isolated volcanic mass rises to a height of about eighty meters. At the summit, there is a chapel built in honor of the archangel called Saint-Michel d'Aiguilhe.[3] Mérimée writes:

> In its present state, the chapel occupies the summit of the rock, exactly following all its contours. It consists of a choir... and a semi-elliptical nave... [in which] six light columns arranged in

a semicircle meet the springs of a semicircular groin vault. Other columns, applied along the walls, support veneered arches.... The column's mostly historiated capitals, their rather finished ornamentation, and the lightness of their shafts certainly date them back to the eleventh century.... Its bell tower... despite its quite mediocre architecture, does not fail to impress by reason of its position....

...The chapel's entrance door... is curiously decorated with colored inlays, molding, and rather finely sculpted bas-reliefs. It is something of a little gem for its kind; and whoever would want an idea of the ornamentation particular to Velay's Byzantine architecture could not find a more elegant example....

The interior of Saint-Michel was fully covered with frescoes.[4]

The author of the *Dictionary of Abbeys and Monasteries* writes, "The foundation of this church is one of the marvels that the genius of religion alone seems able to create, because it participates in some way in the power of its Divine Founder."[5]

With great effort, a stairway was carved into the tall rock, its steps abutting the steep edge in many places. Credit for this difficult and costly undertaking goes to a dean of the chapter of Le Puy-en-Velay, Truan, who conceived its design and partially executed it at the end of the tenth century.

On a rock of equal elevation in the middle of the sea, between Normandy and Brittany, stands the monastery and basilica of St. Michael the Archangel [Mont Saint-Michel]. This is *the Wonder of the West* and *the Jerusalem of the West*. We shall try to give a description of it at the end of this work. But everything we can say is but a shadow compared to the reality.[6]

Besides the shrines and monuments we have just mentioned, there are other remarkable ones found in a great number of cities. We shall mention, in France: Bordeaux, Carcassonne, Dijon, Limoges, Marseille, Paris, Toulouse, etc.; in Belgium: Ghent; in the Netherlands: Zwolle; on the island of Sardinia: Cagliari; in Italy: Lucca, Parma, Pisa, Rome, Turin, Venice, etc.; in Spain: Barcelona; in Germany: Hamburg,[7]

Lüneburg,[8] and Munich; in Russia: Moscow,[9] St. Petersburg, and Smolensk.[10]

Architecture did not do everything. Thought, written in arches and pillars, remanifested itself more visibly in the contours, the attitude, and even the clothing folds of statues.

Thus, at the same time as architecture, statuary sought to honor the archangel. [Arcisse] de Caumont writes:

> Of the three archangels Michael, Gabriel, and Raphael, it is St. Michael one most ordinarily finds represented, whether striking down the demon [as one sees on the tympanum of the church of Saint-Michel-d'Entraigues, near Angoulême] or weighing souls in the balance. It is especially in exercising this latter role that one sees him on tableaux of the last judgment, which, in the thirteenth century, so often covered the tympana of our great church doors.[11]
>
> In combat, he carries a shield in his left arm and a spear or sword in his right hand. Outside of combat, he is clothed in a long robe with undulating folds; he holds a balance like a minister of justice, sometimes a globe.[12]

Among the numerous statues of centuries past, some are remarkable for their colossal proportions.

Such is the case for the St. Michael statue in the vast, old parish church of Bono, in Sardinia. This statue passes for a work from the end of the eleventh century.

But most of these statues have been placed at the top of edifices erected by cities devoted to the archangel. St. Michael thus seems to hover above these cities and shield them with his protection.

At the top of the pediment of the beautiful church of San Michele in Lucca, Italy, the inhabitants of this city, in times past a people rather fond of war, placed a colossal statue of the warring archangel, and chose him for their patron. The statue is made of bronze and has its wings outstretched; however, in order that they not offer too much resistance to the wind, the artist, through an ingenious technique, placed their plumes perpendicularly and made them mobile, in such a way that they can open in different directions and allow the air to pass through.

At Mont Saint-Michel, at the top of its spire, which soars into the sky with such grace and majesty, on a point that rotates at the least wind, there appeared the gilded statue of the archangel, transpiercing with his spear the dragon struck down beneath his feet.[13] "This admirable specimen which we miss, but which we could easily put back up,[14] even with the massive tower" that exists today, "has been replicated in multiple places. The most beautiful copy, which still exists, is most certainly the one at the city hall of Brussels, a city so devoted to St. Michael of the Mount that it reminds us of it everywhere, in its churches, its pilgrimages, its martyrologies, and its manuscripts."[15] This city hall's admirable belfry, one of the most beautiful monuments in all of Belgium, is 390 feet high; the statue on top of it, which is gilded copper, is eighteen feet high.

But of all the statues erected in honor of the archangel, the vanquisher of Satan, the greatest and most well-known today is the one atop Castel Sant'Angelo in Rome. It is made of bronze. Raised thus to a great height, it seems to hover over the Eternal City, whose palladium it is, so to speak. It is from the terrace on which this statue stands that, on the Monday and Tuesday of the Easter octave, on June 28 and 29, and for other extraordinary solemnities, they shoot the fireworks, so famous in Rome, and end them with a grand finale of nine thousand rockets, called *girandola*. The effect produced as St. Michael appears in the darkness amidst the flames is indescribable.

Other statues, many regarded as fine works of art, have been erected at a countless multitude of shrines, where some are the object of a special veneration.

Some have been made with the most precious materials: gold and silver. Mont Saint-Michel possessed several in the past, due to the munificence of our kings.

In the year 1311, Philip the Fair placed twelve hundred ducats on St. Michael's altar, which were consecrated to molding a gold leaf statue of the archangel. It was life-size. It was around the altar on which this statue stood that pilgrims came to place their votive offerings.

Another statue made of silver, representing St. Michael's victory over the demon, decorated the altar of St-Michel-du-Circuit. It was donated in 1415 by the Count of Harcourt. One of the members of this family, Louis, who was bishop of Bayeux and patriarch of Jerusalem, took as his motto: "*Nemo adjutor mihi nisi Michael*," or "I have no protector but St. Michael."

A small golden statue was also donated by Louis XI, around 1460. This prince "had always carried it out of devotion, being out of favor with the king, his father."[16]

We have spoken elsewhere of a silver statue which is today venerated in Naples, a city so devoted to the archangel.

We have also been told of a remarkable statue currently found in the vestibule of the chapel of the honorable Brothers Hospitallers of St. John of God in Paris.

Carving has also wanted to celebrate the glory of the prince of the angels. On the mount in Normandy, the tabernacle of the high altar was, like the altar itself, "entirely coated in solid silver, as well as… its tiers, which held a beautiful figure of the exterminating angel."[17] It was of this work that the Marquise de Créquy[18] said, "Benvenuto Cellini never produced anything more striking, more poetically chimerical, or more finely carved than the figure of the dragon coiling and struggling beneath the feet of the archangel."[19]

The archangel's battle with the dragon is the emblem of the combat the leaders of the Christian militia wage against the evil spirit; thus, we see bishops and abbots, in order to recall this combat to the faithful, and to keep it unceasingly before their eyes, having it depicted in their crosiers, the insignia of their jurisdiction.

For the crosier of Robert d'Arbrissel, the abbot of Fontevrault, deposited at the museum of Angers, and for another that exists in the museum of Amiens, the curved part, which forms the crosier, properly speaking, imitates the body of a serpent: the scales covering it are blue enamel, surrounded by a gilded border. St. Michael and the dragon, in the form of a salamander and pierced by his spear, are gilded; the eyes are enamel; the back of the dragon is inlaid with turquoise.

Painting came, in turn, to add the tribute of its homage. On the walls and arches of churches, on glass, and on canvas, it celebrated the great victory spoken of by the Apocalypse.

Raphael, the prince of painting, did a sublime canvas. St. Michael appears striking down the dragon, with a powerful and almost divine calm. Guido Reni, some say, achieved his masterpiece in this subject. Even St. Luke, the painter of the Man-God and His Most Holy Mother, paid his tribute to the prince of the angels, the Copts say. According to their testimony, this painting would be preserved in the church of St. Mark, in Alexandria, Egypt, where it is the object of the veneration of the faithful.

St. Michael has also been depicted on the walls of our churches, as in Saint-Savin in Poitou, in Coutances, and in Saint-Sulpice in Paris;[20] on stained-glass windows, as in Sainte-Perpétue in Nîmes; and on furniture paneling, like the example seen in the Napoleon III Museum, which is credited to the paintbrush of Francisco Signorelli.

Behold then the temple, with its walls covered with paintings, its tableaux, its windows, its statues, its altars, and its bell tower, surmounted by the statue of the archangel. But up to this point the temple has been mute. It shall speak, and the music shall crown the other arts.

> Chants shall rise up amidst the silence of the vaults… and the expression of the liturgical melodies shall conform so beautifully to those of the monument, that you would say that these chants rose from the lips of the statues and the throng of figures in the windows and frescoes like a great choir of supernatural beings.[21]

Hymns, sequences, and canticles have been written in honor of the vanquisher of Satan. It would take too long to cite them here; suffice it to say that, among their authors, we shall mention Adam of St. Victor and the celebrated [Pierre-Daniel] Huet, Bishop of Avranches.

On earth, therefore, nothing has been lacking in the glory of the illustrious archangel.[22]

BOOK THREE: APPARITIONS OF ST. MICHAEL, PILGRIMAGES & NORMANDY'S ST. MICHAEL OF THE MOUNT

CHAPTER 1:
APPARITIONS OF ST. MICHAEL. – MIRACLES. – PILGRIMAGES TO CHONAE, CONSTANTINOPLE, COLOSSAE, MOUNT GARGANO, ROME, AND MONTE FAITO.

A celebrated apparition of the Archangel took place.
– Roman Breviary, St. Michael's May 8 Feast

This universal cult, of which we tried to give an idea in the preceding book, St. Michael asked for it through the mediation of holy personages to whom he appeared; he even demanded it by ordering shrines built to him, and God confirmed His archangel's commands through numerous miracles.

It is of these apparitions, shrines, and miracles that we shall speak in this third book.

Some authors mention an apparition made during the lifetime of Jesus's beloved disciple, St. John. In a time of drought, the archangel made a spring of water gush forth. Due to this signal benefit, his name was thenceforth venerated among all the peoples.

But this apparition is less known than the one in Colossae, which took place, as Simeon Metaphrastes recounts, as far back as the first or second century of the Christian era. The Greek Church established a feast day to celebrate its memory. This is what we read in the ancient Greek menologium: "Sixth day of September, memorial of the miracle worked by the prince of the heavenly militia, St. Michael, in the city of

Colossae, which was later called Chonae." The archangel appeared in human form to a man from Laodicea. The daughter of this man, who was mute, instantaneously regained her speech. At the sight of this marvel, the father and the daughter converted. A temple was soon built, such as the persecution and misfortune of the times permitted. St. Michael protected it from those who sought to profane it. Nicetas, born in Chonae, recounts how the iconoclast Alexios, the emperor of the East, was punished on this occasion.

The historians Sozomen and Nicephorus make mention of an apparition of the prince of the heavenly militia to Constantine the Great from the first year of his reign. All historians, as Baronius relays, agreed in saying that Constantine's victory over Maxentius was promised him by an angel. But that apparition was not the only one.

Sozomen recounts the following:

> According to the general opinion of foreigners and citizens, the most remarkable church [in the vicinity of Constantinople] was that built in a place formerly called Hestiæ.[1] This place, which is now called Michælium, lies to the right of those who sail from Pontus to Constantinople, and is about thirty-five stadia distant from the latter city by water…. This place obtained the name which now prevails, because it is believed that Michael, the Divine archangel, once appeared there. And I also affirm that this is true, because I myself received the greatest benefits, and the experience of really helpful deeds on the part of many others proves this to be so. For some who had fallen into fearful reverses or unavoidable dangers, others with disease and unknown sufferings, there prayed to God, and met with a change in their misfortunes. I should be prolix were I to give details of circumstance and person. But I cannot omit mentioning the case of Aquilinus, who is even at the present time residing with us, and who is an advocate in the same court of justice as that to which we belong. I shall relate what I heard from him concerning this occurrence and what I saw. Being attacked with a severe fever, arising from a yellowish bile, the physicians gave him some foreign drug to drink. This he vomited, and, by the

effort of vomiting, diffused the bile, which tinged his countenance with a yellow color. Hence he had to vomit all his food and drink. For a long time he remained in this state; and since his nourishment would not be quiet in him, the skill of the physicians was at a loss for the suffering. Finding that he was already half dead, he commanded his servant to carry him to the house of prayer; for he affirmed earnestly that there he would either die or be freed from his disease. While he was lying there, a Divine Power appeared to him by night, and commanded him to dip his foot in a confection made of honey, wine, and pepper. The man did so, and was freed from his complaint, although the prescription was contrary to the professional rules of the physicians, a confection of so very hot a nature being considered adverse to a bilious disorder. I have also heard that Probianus, one of the physicians of the palace, who was suffering greatly from a disease in the feet, likewise met with deliverance from sickness at this place, and was accounted worthy of being visited with a wonderful and Divine vision. He had formerly been attached to the Pagan superstitions, but afterwards became a Christian; yet, while he admitted in one way or another the probability of the rest of our doctrines, he could not understand how, by the Divine cross, the salvation of all is effected. While his mind was in doubt on this subject, the symbol of the cross, which lay on the altar of this church, was pointed out to him in the Divine vision, and he heard a voice openly declaring that, as Christ had been crucified on the cross, the necessities of the human race or of individuals, whatsoever they might be, could not be met by the ministration of Divine angels or of pious and good men; for that there was no power to rectify apart from the venerated cross. I have only recorded a few of the incidents which I know to have taken place in this temple, because there is not time to recount them all.[2]

By whom was this church built? Theophanes, in his history of the Council of Nicaea, as well as Cedrenus and Nicephorus, report that it was built by Constantine in memory of an angelic apparition with which he was favored at this place. Nicephorus reports this apparition in the following manner: The emperor having gone to sleep in this place, an angel appeared and said to him, "I am Michael, the master of the heavenly militia and the protector of the faith of the Christians; it was I who, when you were fighting against the impious tyrants, made your weapons victorious." Constantine, upon awaking, ordered the land there to be cleared, and then had a magnificent temple built there, which he decorated with royal magnificence. This historian adds that the frequent apparitions of St. Michael made this shrine very famous to the region's inhabitants and to foreigners. There was no one experiencing serious troubles, pressing difficulties, inevitable dangers, unknown illnesses, or incurable infirmities who did not find help and assistance in this temple.

In the fifth century, near the city of Colossae, in Phrygia, there was a fountain where frequent miracles occurred through the intercession of St. Michael. The renown of these prodigies, the Bollandists report, drew to this place the devotion of the peoples, and as the number of visitors was ever increasing, a magnificent church ended up being built here, dedicated to the great archangel. Ninety years after its construction, a ten-year-old boy named Archippus, born in Hierapolis, came, propelled by grace, to live as a hermit near this holy place. He grew in virtue as he advanced in age, and became a figure of eminent sanctity. Many infidels came to him, drawn by his renown and even more by that of the archangel's fountain, and many wonders and conversions occurred here. Some pagans in the vicinity devised the plan to close the fountain. They therefore came at night, but frightened by flames which came out of it and rushed towards them, they fled. This miracle, however, instead of converting them, only increased their fury. They spent several days deliberating about what to do next. They decided to redirect a stream that flowed down from Mount Cadmus towards the fountain, in the hope that mixing the waters together would despoil the fountain of its special power. The plan was in vain; the flow of the diverged stream spread out so widely that it dissipated over the land. This new defeat, far from discouraging them, inspired them with another plan. They called on all other pagans to help them and they began digging a new channel for the Lycus River in the direction of the church, in order to destroy the building and to drown the hermit, or at least to force him away. But Michael was watching over his temple and the holy hermit. He let the pagans go through the trouble of digging up the earth and amassing the water; however, at the moment they anticipated seeing the water rush onto the church and destroy it top to bottom, he appeared full of glory and forced the water by his power to go back to its normal course. This miracle made the temple more venerated than ever, and this was the most painful punishment for its enemies.

According to Robert du Mont, the celebrated abbot of Mont Saint-Michel, it is also in the fifth century, around the year 494, that we must place the famous apparition at Mount Gargano.

Mount Gargano, today called Monte Sant'Angelo, is a mountain in Puglia, in the Kingdom of Naples, near the city of Siponto or Manfredonia,[3] on the Adriatic Sea. Mount Gargano, Strabo says, is rather high and a difficult climb. It is detached from the Apennines by a graduated elevation, twenty thousand paces long and two thousand wide; its summit then forms as it narrows and ascends to a great height, where fruit trees can still live, however. Its side facing the sea juts and forms a promontory, the circumference of which is two hundred thousand paces; its other sides are steep and difficult to access; its surface is covered in part by forest and in part by pasture, where many medicinal plants are found; an enormous rock caps this beautiful mountain. It is crowned with magnificent trees and contains a deep cave of which we shall speak. Now, there was, James of Voragine says, in this city of Siponto, a man named Gargano who, according to some books, had taken the name of the mountain. Others think conversely that this mountain had taken his name. This man, who was very rich, owned a great multitude of sheep and cattle. As they were grazing along the slopes of this mountain, it happened that a bull left the rest of the herd and went up to the summit. In the evening, not seeing it return with the drove into the stables, the owner took several servants with him to go find it. Finally, they found it at the top of the mountain, near the entrance of a cavern. Angry, the master drew his bow and shot a poisoned arrow at the bull; but the arrow immediately turned around as though pushed by the wind and struck the one who had shot it.

Troubled at the sight of this incident, the inhabitants of the city went to find the bishop to ask him what should be done in such an extraordinary circumstance. The bishop enjoined them to fast for three days and pray to God. At the end of this time, St. Michael appeared to the bishop and said to him, "Know that that man was struck with his spear by my will. I am Michael the Archangel, one of the attendants at the throne of God. I want to honor this place on the earth and guard it; therefore, I wanted to show that I was its vigilant guardian."

Then the bishop and the inhabitants of the city, without delay, went in procession to this place. They did not dare enter the cavern, but they prayed before the entrance.

Shortly afterwards, the inhabitants of Naples declared war on those of Siponto, but Michael came to the aid of the latter and gave them victory. James of Voragine says:

> The Sipontans, returning after having slaughtered their adversaries and winning such a striking victory, doubted whether they should go inside this place (Mount Gargano) and have it consecrated. The bishop then consulted Pope Pelagius about the matter, who responded, "If a church should be consecrated in such a place, it is especially on the day when such a victory has been won, and if St. Michael wants it otherwise, we should pray to him to know his good pleasure."
>
> The pope, the bishop, and the inhabitants of Siponto therefore prayed for three days. Michael then appeared to the bishop and said, "There is no need for you to consecrate the church that I have built; he who constructed it has consecrated it." And he ordered him to go there the next day with the people and pray there; and he said they would find a sign of the consecration, namely that they would see a man's footsteps imprinted on the marble when they turned to the eastern side. On the next day, the bishop and all the people went to this place; they found three altars upon entering the cavern, two of them placed on the western side and a third on the eastern side which was covered with red adornment. Holy Mass was solemnly

celebrated, and everyone having received holy communion, they returned to their homes, filled with profound joy. And the bishop designated clerics and priests to take turns celebrating the holy offices in this place. In this cavern flows a spring of clear water very pleasing to the taste; after communion, the people drink of it, and all those who are sick regain their health. And the Sovereign Pontiff, having learned of these things, ordered that this day be celebrated over the entire earth in honor of St. Michael and the blessed spirits.[4]

The pilgrimage to Mount Gargano became one of the most celebrated in Christendom. According to Baronius, the Norman warriors, when arriving in the south of Italy in 1016, went to visit the archangel's temple. They were fulfilling a vow they had made, and were thus showing themselves everywhere devoted to St. Michael.

By order of Pope Urban II, the poet William of Apulia recounted this expedition of our fathers: "Some of these climbed to the top of Mount Gargano, to fulfill a vow that they had made to thee, O Archangel Michael."[5]

St. Michael gave, throughout the course of different centuries, visible marks of protection to those who undertook this pilgrimage. We shall mention a famous incident that happened in the fourteenth century and which we find in the writings of the Bollandists.

Blessed Oringa left Lucca one day with some companions to go to Mount Gargano. They had been walking for a few days when some thieves, claiming to be pilgrims, offered to accompany them and provide them protection. These young women, timid and inexperienced, believed in the fidelity of such men; they accepted with gratitude. To better deceive them, these scoundrels spoke only edifying words to them. Arriving towards evening at a crossroads where several roads met, their deceptive guides went off the right path and took them on one leading to the place of their lair. The scoundrels already regarded these young women as prey incapable of escape when a young man of majestic stature and resplendent face appeared and said to the women in a severe voice: "Where are you going, young women? Flee, flee; these wretches are after your honor, the demon incites them to ruin your souls." The frightened thieves continued on their way, while Oringa and her companions retraced their steps, following the stranger, a secret instinct assuring them that they had nothing to fear. He first entertained them with his pious discourse, and encouraged them to walk, despite their weariness. He then had them sit by a fountain, presented them a goblet so that they could drink, and gave them fruit to eat. Resuming their walk, he had them return to the public road, led them to the door of an inn, and disappeared before their eyes, leaving them filled with an inexpressible consolation. Who then was this benevolent guide? Oringa learned his identity the next day, for St. Michael appeared to her and made known that he had been her heavenly conductor.

In the sixth century, Arthelais, the daughter of a proconsul of Constantinople, was protected in a no less remarkable manner. Having fallen into the hands of thieves in Dalmatia, she remained in their custody for seven days, without receiving any outrage, being protected by an angel. On the eighth day, this angel freed her, and, in gratitude, she went to Mount Gargano to thank her heavenly protector. The angel appeared to her uncle, Narses, and made known to him the place where he would find his niece.

St. Henry, the emperor, as we said elsewhere, visited this celebrated place of pilgrimage. He had learned that once each week, the angels make their heavenly melody heard inside this church. After having assisted at the divine office, he had himself shut inside the church alone, and remained in prayer until the appointed time, wanting to enjoy, if God permitted it, this ravishing concert. While asking for this grace with many tears, he saw two angels enter into the holy place, who began decorating the altar; a great number of others then arrived, leading with honor a spirit of superior glory, who by all appearances was St. Michael the Archangel. After arranging themselves in the most beautiful formation, they made their magnificent chants heard; then one of these spirits took the book of the Gospels and presented it to the emperor to kiss. The emperor, seized with fear and respect, trembled with all his body. The angel, seeing this, reassured him with sweet words; but as the angel withdrew, he touched the emperor's thigh, resulting in a contraction of nerves which made him limp for the rest of his life.

According to Ado, whom Baronius cites, shortly after the apparition at Mount Gargano, the venerable pontiff Boniface II dedicated to St. Michael a church he built in Rome, in 530, on the summit of the circus plaza; elevated as it is above a crypt, one would say that it is in the clouds. This church is today called Sant'Angelo in Pescheria. It is a collegiate church, a parish, and the titular church of a cardinal-deacon.

The cult of St. Michael in Rome, Baronius says, does not just date to the Mount Gargano apparition. For a long time, they had already been celebrating a feast in memory of an apparition that the archangel made in Rome. This is also what we learn from a sacred hymn composed by Drepanius Florus, the famous ninth-century poet.[6]

At the end of the following century, namely the sixth, Italy was beset with flooding. The waters of the Tiber overflowed, flooded Rome, collapsed a large number of buildings, contaminated the wheat in the stores, and left behind a multitude of snakes, many of them enormous in size. This calamity was followed by a great plague, which took a vast number of people of every rank. Pope Pelagius II was one of the first victims. At the same time, war was at the gates of Rome. In this extremity, the clergy, the senate, and the Roman people unanimously chose the one they considered their only hope: St. Gregory the Great. Gregory assembled the people and called everyone to do penance. For three days, they did a solemn procession. On the third day, St. Gregory saw above the fortress called Hadrian's mole an angel who put his sword back into its scabbard. Through this sign, he was announcing that the people's prayers had appeased God's wrath and that the evil had ceased.

In memory of this apparition, this great pontiff had built the church of Sant'Angelo in Borgo Pio.

From this time until the eighth century, history relates no apparition of the prince of the angels. Then, in 709, there is the famous revelation of St. Michael to St. Aubert, the bishop of Avranches. In 715, the same archangel also appeared in Ireland. We shall speak of these apparitions in the following chapters.

The Bollandists mention, on February 14, an apparition whose date they place in the ninth century.

Near Castellammare, in the Kingdom of Naples, stands a high mountain whose base goes down into the sea, and whose summit is reached by a winding and barely feasible path. Living there together in the ninth century were St. Catellus and St. Antoninus, later abbot of the monastery in Sorrento. One day when they were at prayer, outside of the cave, they saw a candle burning a few paces in front of them. The following night, a young man of ravishing beauty appeared to them and said, "I desire that you build, at the location where you saw a lit candle, an oratory that bears my name."

"We do not know your name," responded the two solitaries.

The unknown man replied, "I am the Archangel Michael."

Both solitaries awoke at this utterance and communicated their dream to each other. They saw it was not permitted them to doubt that St. Michael had truly appeared to them. Getting to work, they used branches to make the small oratory that was asked of them.

As soon as this apparition was made known in the surrounding area, the inhabitants came to pray at the rural oratory and obtained many graces through the intercession of St. Michael. The number of visitors then increased and became very considerable. Some years later, a beautiful church replaced the poor cottage, and the mountain received the name Monte Aureo [now Monte Faito]. This church still existed in the thirteenth century.

St. Michael has thus made his name known throughout the earth. The countless miracles he has worked in these places sanctified by his visible presence have drawn multitudes of pilgrims, hastening from all regions to have recourse to his powerful intercession.

CHAPTER 2:
CONTINUATION OF THE PRECEDING CHAPTER. –
PILGRIMAGES IN ITALY, FRANCE, ENGLAND, AND CHINA.

The celebrated shrines of which we have spoken up to this point were erected by order of the archangel himself, visibly appearing among us. Others were built, in great number, at the initiative of the faithful. St. Michael has deigned to signal his presence in these places, and also to obtain from God numerous graces for those who go there invoking him.

We shall make some of these known.

In Italy, on the summit of a mountain overlooking all of Sabina, stands the celebrated Mentorella Shrine, currently serviced by the Polish Resurrection Fathers. It was around the middle of the second century that this shrine was first built, in memory of the conversion of St. Eustace. For several centuries, St. Michael the Archangel was venerated there, as well as the Most Blessed Virgin. But after the miraculous transfer of the house of Nazareth to Loretto, people have gone there simply to pay homage to St. Michael. Each year on September 29, the inhabitants of Rome do this pilgrimage en masse.

In France, the chapel of Saint-Michel d'Aiguilhe, built atop a tall rock near Le Puy-en-Velay, has also been visited by numerous pilgrims, who have obtained signal graces there.

In the seventeenth century, near the city of Rouen, the venerable [Henri-Marie] Boudon says that "a great number of persons" had the devotion of "going every month to visit a certain chapel built on a high mountain, in honor of St. Michael the Archangel." The writer adds:

> This is how it came about, according to what I learned. Two or three servants of God, going to do their devotions in a celebrated church, where the Most Holy Virgin is invoked under the title of Our Lady of Good Help, felt inspired to do their prayers at the entrance of the aforesaid chapel of St. Michael, which is not very far from there, and, at the same time, were powerfully moved in

seeing this chapel neglected, the devotion there having been great previously, as one could learn from the testimony of the elders, as well as from the very sight of a pathway paved with large rocks, which had specially been made there with much expense and difficulty, and whose vestiges are still noticed. This compelled them to make the resolution to go there from time to time; and having communicated their plan to some other persons, these others joined in easily. Now, it pleased the God of all goodness to so abundantly bless this project that within the course of a few years, not very long after this devotion began, there is such a great number of people on the day designated at the beginning of each month, that the sermon has to be given outside the chapel—one is sensibly moved seeing all these people modestly seated on the top of this mountain, listening in profound silence to the discourse made to the glory of the holy angels; for they do not fail to ensure that there is a preacher for every month, as well as a Mass celebrated there, where a great number of communions are made.[1]

Even in our own day, the archangel has chosen for himself a shrine in the capital of France, on Rue de Sèvres.

The following was written to us three years ago by the Reverend Mother Superior of the Hospitaller Sisters of St. Thomas of Villanova:

In 1855, having to do some repairs in our small shrine dedicated to the Blessed Virgin under the title of Our Lady of Happy Deliverance,[2] we removed a statue of St. Michael that occupied a niche and placed it in the chapel's vestibule. Ladies spontaneously left flowers at its feet, and one of them, having obtained a happy outcome for an important matter, burned candles there.

The Countess of B. offered a lamp, which since then has always been maintained by the faithful. Her husband undertook giving the vestibule the form of an oratory by closing off the sides with glass doors. It was embellished little by little, and the wall behind the archangel was painted in relief, in such a way that the white statue, whose lance, buskins, and clothing edges are gilded, appears to be in a niche with an azure, star-studded background, within a temple supported by colonnades. Tiers are arranged on each side of the pedestal to accommodate vases and flowers, and a rail surrounds the entire display.

In that first year, 1855, a female domestic worker obtained a special grace and wanted, as a token of her gratitude, to leave an ex-voto, which was not permitted her until 1860. Her example found imitators. Today, there are twenty-eight ex-votos and numerous votive hearts in the oratory. A woman laborer who had been out of work for a long time found employment after having commended herself to St. Michael. During the Crimean War, pious soldiers asked for help from the powerful arm of the vanquisher of Satan, and declared, upon their return, that they had experienced perceivable effects of his protection. Since that time, it is not rare to see soldiers kneeling before the statue of St. Michael.

In 1860, a young girl came with childlike confidence to commend herself to the blessed archangel to win some prizes; some weeks later, she triumphantly placed her crowns at his feet, and even wanted to leave her books. Letters are often put on St. Michael's pedestal. Some sick persons, having requested oil from his lamp, have experienced relief; one woman, in particular, who could not walk for a long time, found herself sufficiently well, after rubbing herself with the oil, that she came to thank her heavenly physician. Young people who had placed themselves under his protection before their exams passed them with distinction. Court trials have been won, calumnies recognized, etc., etc., through the intercession of St. Michael.

These special and miraculous graces, however, are not recorded; but what is certain is that devotion to St. Michael is growing each day.

The ex-votos today number thirty-nine; four lamps burn day and night; and a large number of little gold and silver hearts attest that the powerful archangel is always favorable to those who invoke him.

England, so devoted to the archangel, also had its place of pilgrimage. On a rock similar to Normandy's, a church [was built]³ which became celebrated for the great number of pilgrims who visited it. It was called St. Michael of Cornwall [or St. Michael's Mount].

The Far East, in turn, witnessed the rise of a shrine where Catholic multitudes hasten singing hymns. [Historian Fr. Émile-Auber] Pigeon, always so eager to publish what concerns the glory of St. Michael, wrote a short time ago in the *Revue Catholique de Coutances*:

At the entrance of a gulf formed by one of the mouths of the Yangtze River and the important rivers of Qiantang Jiang and Yong Jiang is the island of Zhoushan, surrounded by a crowd of lesser islands which form the archipelago of the same name. The main island contains 250,000 inhabitants. Dinghai, a city of 70,000 souls, is its capital. This place, located amidst the waves of the East China Sea, was simultaneously a center of pagan superstitions, rebellions, and continuous wars. Bishop [Louis-Gabriel] Delaplace had tried to introduce the light of the Gospel there, but all his efforts had produced only feeble results. It was then that he conceived the plan to build a temple to St. Michael, the angel of peace, the vanquisher of Satan and all the spirits of darkness.

In the center of the city of Dinghai is a hill from where one can see the sea and a large part of the island. It was there that the bishop built his church, dominated by a shining statue of St. Michael which is able to greet all the navigators coming from Shanghai, Hangzhou, and Ningbo,⁴ as they pass by Zhoushan to go to Korea, Japan, and the island of Formosa.

The small temple, oriented from north to south according to Chinese tradition, measures only thirty-nine meters long by sixteen meters wide. Its entrance is magnificent and exhibits a large Gothic rose window, which is a replica of the one at Notre-Dame in Paris. From this main entrance, the view is grandiose and captivating. One can see not only the island's volcanic mountains, but an immense sea that comes to appease the fury of its waves on Zhoushan's golden beaches towards the south, all the islands of the archipelago, and, in a marvelous backdrop, these great Chinese cities, these frequented ports of enormous trade, and these industrial hubs which proudly display their fortified castles, their quays, their nine- and ten-story porcelain and terracotta towers, and these pagodas of peculiar, light architecture, near which are already built numerous Catholic churches.

The great feast of St. Michael of Dinghai is celebrated on September 29. On that day, all the Catholics of Zhoushan and the neighboring islands flock to the archangel's basilica singing hymns. The crowds are very considerable, and the celebration is magnificent.[5]

Since the erection of this celebrated church, the wars have stopped, darkness has given way to light, the superstitions are disappearing, and the number of new converts, already very considerable, is ever increasing.[6]

CHAPTER 3:

HISTORY OF THE FOUNDATION OF THE CHURCH AND ABBEY OF MONT SAINT-MICHEL, AT THE PERIL OF THE SEA.

Aubert, the venerable man of the Lord, becoming fully certain of the Archangel's apparition upon its third instance, entered upon the spot with hymns and praises.
– Twelfth-century lectionary

From the shoals separating Normandy and Brittany arises a granite mountain nine hundred meters in circumference and eighty meters in elevation. Atop it, majestically towering into the sky, is the wondrous abbey dedicated to St. Michael.

But what was this mountain before the archangel's apparition and the founding of this illustrious monastery? His Eminence Cardinal de Bonnechose says:

To answer this question, it is necessary to look back and cast a quick glance at the past. Without going back to the furthest extremities of history, we shall note that, from the earliest times, this mountain was the object of the veneration of peoples and of their religious awe.

Here was a temple where druidesses pronounced their oracles and distributed to the Gallic navigators arrows which, when thrown into the tempest, had the ability to appease it. The divinity adored on this rock was the sun, under the name of Belenus. Who cannot see the striking similarity that exists between this name and the Bel of the Assyrians, or the idol Baal of the unfaithful Israelites?

The Romans, having conquered the Gauls, established their cult here and substituted Jupiter for Belenus. Under their rule, the mountain was called *Mons Jovis*, and subsequently *Mont-Joic*. Under this new form, idolatry continued to reign here, until

237

Christianity came to spread its pure light in the forests of the Gauls.

In the sixth century, St. Paternus, or St. Pair, having come from Poitiers and an apostle of the region, converted thousands of idolaters, and founded on this mountain a monastery, which in the ancient chronicles was called *monasterium ad duas tumbas*. The mountain itself, ceasing to bear the name of Jupiter, was now only called *Tumulus* or *Tumba*. In the forests then covering the surrounding lands, lived a number of hermits, withdrawn from the world and praising God in solitude.

About two centuries thus passed when, in 708, a holy bishop of Avranches had a miraculous apparition.

The history of this celebrated apparition was written in the eighth century by a priest of our region, a canon of St. Aubert, the bishop of Avranches. The eighth-century manuscript, written in Latin, no longer exists; but this account had such reverberations during the Middle Ages that copies of it are found in the main libraries of Europe. The Vatican Library in Rome and the Imperial Library in Paris each possess two editions. Spain, England, Germany, and Sweden also have copies of it. One additionally finds texts that are more or less complete in Montpellier, Dijon, Rouen, Le Mans, Angers, Tours, Évreux, Rennes, etc.

Here is the account, translated as faithfully as possible:

> The nation of the Franks, made illustrious far and wide by the grace of Christ, had subdued the proud in the provinces; the most pious prince Childebert vigorously governed the kingdom in all the west, the north, and the parts of the south. Since Almighty God governs through legions of spirits, who are subject to Him, not only in all nations, but also in all parts of the world which He Himself created—and the blessed Archangel Michael, one of the seven who always stand in the presence of the Lord, the same one who is appointed to guard paradise and usher the souls of the elect into the region of peace, already having indicated through an apparition the manner in which he desired to be

honored on Mount Gargano (as one reads in the writings), and the blessed archangel having evidently fulfilled these designs in favor of all the nations illuminated by the grace of Christ in the eastern parts of the Roman Empire—learn now by what signs this same blessed prince of the inhabitants of heaven wanted to show himself the defender of the Western peoples.

He who in times past brought the aid of his defense to the people of Israel, blessed in the patriarchs, this same one was yet to remain the guide and guardian of the children called to adoption. One reads, in fact, in the vision of the prophet Daniel, that an angel spoke to him these words: "None is my helper in all these things, but Michael your prince" [(Dn 10:21)]. He says "your prince," meaning the prince of the Jewish people. But Christ our Lord, having come among His own and having not been received there, and then having ascended to His Father as He had announced, the observance of the old law was then abolished, and the wondrous deposit of Gospel preaching was made firm; and while the message of the apostles spread throughout the earth, the sacred rites were propagated through the ministry of the holy angels.

Ecclesiastical histories in fact say that after the Passion and the Ascension of the Lord into Heaven, after the long-awaited fullness of Israel, when those days of desolation approached which the Savior foretold in advance with His holy speech and human tears, the Church, through a divine notification which was to be announced to the nations at Jerusalem, spread throughout the earth.

When the people, coming from all directions, had been awaiting the feast of Passover, the priests who were observing their customary watch and keeping vigil near the temple suddenly heard voices saying, "Let us go out from these places."

Now, these sudden voices, emitted by the angels who were proclaiming the flight of the blessed spirits, were insinuating that the angelic ministry would be transferred to the Church of the Gentiles.

One obviously concludes that the ministry formerly exercised by blessed Michael to the people of God was confided to him anew for the elect nations.

The sight of signs that have manifested themselves have led the devotion of the faithful to believe that such is the case.

In fact, St. Michael wanted to make himself known to the mortals living in our time, so that mankind would understand that it is called into the company of the angels.

Finally, it should be noted by what mystery he chooses for mortals, in the Western countries, a place where the religious multitude of the faithful can flock from all parts of the earth, coming respectfully to ask for angelic help.

This place, which is called *Tombe* by the inhabitants, emerges from the sands in the form of a tomb, and rises into the air at an elevation of two hundred cubits.

Girded by the ocean on all sides, it exhibits the narrow space of an admirable island, situated at the place where the Sée and Sélune rivers flow into the sea, and yet gives to the inhabitants on both sides a space which is not too constricted. Due to its length, width, and height, it does not differ much, one thinks, from that ark in which mankind was saved. It is a distance of six miles from the city of Avranches; it faces the west and separates the Avranchin from Brittany.

Here, one cannot work on any earthly business; this island, such as it is, is suitable only for those who sincerely wish to adore Christ; and it only receives those whom an ardent love of the virtues lifts towards heaven. One only finds here a great abundance of fish, which often accumulate from the effusions of the rivers and the sea. To those who see it from afar, it appears as nothing other than a spacious, or rather a specious, tower.

But the sea, twice per day through its ebbs, offers a desired route for pious peoples who reach the blessed archangel's doorstep.

Originally, as we were able to learn from truthful narrators, this place was surrounded by a very dense forest, believed to be six miles away from the tide of the ocean, and provided a remote refuge for wild animals. And, as the wilderness's most far-flung places have customarily been much sought after by those who love to penetrate heaven's secrets through contemplation, we know that monks did in times past dwell in this place, where today two churches still exist that were built by ancient hands.

The monks who served God in this place were fed by the munificence of God, Who governs all. A priest of the village presently called Austériac[1] came to their aid in the following manner: When the food without which man cannot live was lacking them, a plume of smoke rushing to and fro and ascending towards heaven gave the signal; then the priest loaded an ass with prepared foods, and, subsequently led by an invisible guide, the animal came and went through places without paths, carrying the Lord's orders and the necessary provisions.

But because, according to God's will, this place was being prepared for a future miracle and for the veneration of His archangel, the sea, which was distant, swelling little by little, leveled with its power all the forest's grandeur, and reduced everything into sand, offering a pathway for the peoples of the earth, so that the marvels of God could be told.

It must now be said how this same prince of the blessed spirits, through an angelic revelation, consecrated the place that we know.

At a certain time, when the very religious and God-pleasing Aubert, the bishop of Avranches, was fast asleep, he was informed by an angelic revelation to build on the summit of the aforesaid place a temple in honor of the holy archangel, so that he whose venerable memory was celebrated on Mount Gargano would be honored with no less jubilation amidst the waves.

But whilst the priest pondered within himself the word of the apostle to "try the spirits if they be of God" [(1 Jn 4:1)], he was told in a new vision to accomplish what he had been commanded.

And since the Spirit of the prophets is not always subject to the prophets,[2] the bishop still delayed the construction; but he asked, for a matter of this kind, that he might recognize the will of the Lord Jesus Christ and of the most blessed archangel. It happened during this time that a man, urged by a perverse instinct, hid on the summit of this rock a bull that he had stolen. The thief planned to derive a shameful profit from it once the bull's owner lost hope of finding it.

Meanwhile, after not having obeyed the two angelic messages, the venerable bishop was urged more severely[3] a third time in order to get him more quickly to the place, from where he was not to leave until after having accomplished what he was commanded.

For confirmation of this fact, there is still to this day a stone exhibited, as though written on by a man's finger, on which the said bishop sat until he had completed his work.

When the bishop asked what place might seem suitable for the construction, an angelic voice answered, "Build the edifice in the place where a bull has been secretly fastened." And as he inquired about the size or extent, the same voice made known to him that he should give the edifice the circular extent that he would see outlined by the trampling of the bull's feet. He was then ordered to return the stolen bull to its owner.

The venerable bishop, very much reassured about the vision, after having arrived at the aforementioned place singing hymns and praises, set out to perform the work commanded.

Having thus assembled a great number of peasants, he purified the place and leveled the ground.

In the middle, two stones stood, which the hands of numerous workers could neither budge nor remove from their positions.

After being at an impasse for a long time and not at all knowing what they could do, that following night, a certain man named Bain, from the village called Itier, had a vision; this man had twelve sons and held the most distinguished rank among his own people. That is why, notified through this dream to go work with the laborers himself, he hastened to the place, with his sons, to do what he was ordered. When he arrived, he was assisted by

St. Michael the Archangel to do what no human power could do, and he so easily moved a mass of such great size that it appeared to be weightless.[4]

Then everyone, together praising God and His archangel, continued their work with greater alacrity.

And as the bishop, again doubtful, was reflecting on the greatness of the edifice he had to construct, on the following night, as long ago for Gideon, as a sign of victory, dew fell onto the mount's summit. There, where the foundations were to be placed, it was dry, and the bishop was told: "Go, and cast the foundations, according to the sign that will be given you."[5] Immediately thanking the Lord Almighty and imploring the assistance of the holy angel Michael, he very joyfully rose and set to work.

He thus built a low, round church in the form of a crypt, which could contain an estimated one hundred persons.

St. Aubert, seeking to match the form of Mount Gargano, of that difficult-to-access mountain, and of that church established according to an angelic apparition made to men for the glory of God, clearly teaches us that we should always ask the angels for the help of divine grace. He further teaches us to look beyond the stars of heaven through the gaze of contemplation, and not to steep our hearts in earthly things or in miry bogs.[6]

CHAPTER 4:
AFTER THE FOUNDING OF MONT ST-MICHEL, ST. AUBERT, BY ORDER OF THE ARCHANGEL, SENDS MESSENGERS TO MOUNT GARGANO. – DEDICATION OF MONT ST-MICHEL. – MESSENGERS FROM IRELAND BRING THE WEAPONS WITH WHICH THE PRINCE OF THE ANGELS HAD KILLED A DRAGON DESOLATING THE COUNTRY. – ACCOUNT OF THIS MIRACLE.

The bishop Aubert was concerned, seeing he was without any pledges from the holy archangel. The blessed Michael then advised him.
— Canon of St. Aubert

The eighth-century author continues:

Shortly after the construction of the basilica, the man of the Lord, the bishop Aubert, was concerned, seeing he was without any pledges from the holy archangel. The blessed Michael then advised him to very promptly send some of his brethren to the place where the memory of the most holy archangel is celebrated with veneration at Mount Gargano, in order that, under his patronage, they could bring back a most precious blessing.

The envoys arrived at Mount Gargano. They were welcomed there with much kindness by the abbot of the place, and, after having changed clothes and rested from the fatigue of such a long journey, they explained everything that had happened in their country and indicated the motive for their visit.

When the abbot of this place had reported these words to his bishop, both addressed abundant praises to Almighty God, Who deigns to accord the assistance of the ministers surrounding Him to men fallen through the fragility of their nature.

Then, keepsakes were taken, with appropriate reverence, in this place where the blessed archangel had confided

244

remembrances of himself, namely a portion of the red cape that the same archangel left at Mount Gargano, on the altar that he had built with his hands, and a part of the marble on which he stood, vestiges of which still exist in this place today. The abbot gave these souvenirs to the brothers from Avranches, to take back to the already consecrated place.

But they agreed, on both sides, that a bond of charity would eternally unite those whom one same revelation had linked together.

The envoys about whom we just spoke were returning, after a long journey, to the place from whence they had come, on the same day of the completion of the church on the mount, already well known in the western regions. They entered as into a new world which they had left full of thorny bushes.

As they were approaching, the priest of the Lord, Aubert, immediately came to meet them, and, amidst praises and hymns, he himself carried to the holy mountain the precious keepsakes which would be of such useful help.[1]

Unspeakable was the joy of the surrounding provinces at this arrival that one could call angelic; they saw that the gift of an inhabitant of heaven was divinely granted them in the presence of the blessed archangel Michael, standard-bearer and prince of the heavenly army.

They also knew the signs and wonders that the Lord works through His minister in favor of mortals. They did not know that, during this journey, twelve blind persons recovered their sight, and that multiple persons afflicted with various infirmities were restored to their original health. But there is one incident that must be added to the preceding ones: A woman deprived of sight and living in the village of Austériac began to follow the most precious relics of the heavenly archangel. As soon as she reached the plain and the sand of the sea, she recovered, in an entirely divine manner, the use of her eyes, and was completely astonished to have so suddenly passed from darkness into light. To this very day, the Lord, through His heavenly minister, does not cease to work similar prodigies in this place, to the praise and glory of His name.[2]

The temple's venerable dedication took place on the seventeenth day before the calends of November (October 16). The man of the Lord, Aubert, after having wisely arranged everything with order, also established clerics to serve the Lord. He wanted there to be twelve in number to persevere continuously, with fixed rules, in the service of the most blessed Michael the Archangel, although the same number of clerics was not maintained by the blessed [Aubert's] successors. At the same time, he gave to those who served in this place his bishopric's villages of Itier, already mentioned, and Genêts.

The same bishop, seeing everything accomplished in proper order, thought it necessary to ask the holy archangel for only that which might seem difficult, namely a source of water so necessary to the life of mortals. Thus, with the flock entrusted to him, he implored the help of the Lord Jesus Christ and that of the holy archangel, so that He Who long ago had given water from the rock to His thirsting people would deign to preserve His servants from a lack of water.

Soon an angelic revelation informed him that, in a place at the foot of a steep rock where a pit is dug, one would find, in a wondrous manner, a great abundance of water which can suffice for the use of the inhabitants. It was proven in diverse manners that this spring water was salutary to those who drank it. It in fact brings quick relief to the feverish every time that they take it.[3]

Such is the account of Mont Saint-Michel's foundation, an account written by a contemporary author in a style that has all the charm of a veritable poem. Reading it, we breathe in a spirit of candor and faith which prevents calling into question its veracity. Such was the judgment of subsequent writers who made it the subject of their narratives.

While all the wonders of which we have spoken were being worked at Mont Saint-Michel, pilgrims, led from Ireland by the glorious archangel, were coming to deposit in the shrine built by St. Aubert the precious pledges of the incomparable love of this great prince of paradise towards the inhabitants of that celebrated island, which today possesses to such a high degree the sympathies of the Catholic world.

The savant Baldric, Archbishop of Dol, who was one day visiting these precious souvenirs, wanted, Fr. Pigeon says, to know their origin. The prior of the abbey recounted to him what he had learned from the elder monks, and the celebrated bishop composed, according to what the monks relayed, a legend which begins as follows:

> Account of Lord Baldric, Archbishop of Dol, regarding the sword and shield admired by the pilgrims in the church of St. Michael that is called Tombe.
>
> At the time of Aubert, there was beyond England, in a far-off region, on that island of Ireland where King Elga reigned, a ferocious serpent whose poisonous breath imparted death. Its head bore a horrible crest, and its mouth spewed a venom which burned the grasses and the shrubs. It also devoured animals and men, and contaminated the air with its noxious breath. The land it inhabited was pillaged and ravaged. Near its dwelling was a very clear spring it had poisoned, as well as the river that came from it. There it reigned supreme, and no one dared approach it. The surrounding peoples were also suffering from its presence, for it stopped the water of the river, and the little that escaped was dissipated by the rays of the sun. What further increased the suffering was that the land itself refused its produce, not only to the animals, but also to men, stripped of all earthly assistance. These unfortunate ones had recourse to God. They addressed their bishop, and through him they relayed their petition to the Author of all things. The bishop ordered a three-day fast, so that the Lord would be moved by these evils. At the same time, they implored God's mercy through prayers and large alms. The bishop finally assembled them on the third day to go attack the serpent and put it to death.[4]
>
> You would have then seen hastening, long before sunrise, pale, fearful, and diversely armed legions.

The clerics marched in the front, carrying crosses and holy relics; the combatants were equipped with swords and spears, and advanced with fright. Despite their trust in God and their holy bishop, it seemed to them that they were going to a certain death.

They finally arrived at the place where the horrible beast usually retired. The region appeared completely ravaged to them and as consumed by fire. Looking in the distance, they recognized the monster and its immense size, which resembled the summit of a mountain. At this sight, they did not know whether they should advance or flee. But suddenly summoning up their boldness, they provoked the serpent by clamoring loudly. Then, adjusting their arrows with their arms bent, they launched them with terrible screams. The monster remained motionless as if it were asleep. They soon recognized that it was dead, and, rushing to its hideous cadaver, they cut it to pieces. While they were reflecting on such an astonishing death, they noticed near the dragon a small shield and a small sword. As these tokens did not appear suitable for combat, they took them for imitation arms. But they were completely unaware of who had defeated the monster, and, in the presence of this prodigy, they gave thanks to God for what had been done; and in order to discover what they did not know, they beseeched the Lord to reveal to them the secret of this victory.

The bishop spent the night in prayer. He penetrated heaven with his prayers and endeavored to sway the Lord through worthy sacrifices. God graciously heard the wishes of His people and informed them of what He had done.

St. Michael, the confidant of the Lord's secrets and the angel of good news, came down from heaven. He appeared visibly to the bishop and made known to him what he had been unable to understand. He said, "I am the archangel St. Michael, always present before the throne of God, where I love to defend and protect you. It was I who destroyed that beast which you could not have defeated by your own power. The arms that you found are mine. I did not need them to obtain victory, but I took them and left them so that you have some remembrance of me, and so that through this means your faith grow and strengthen more and more. But you, priest of the Most High, send these tokens through your clerics to the mount that is dedicated to us beyond the seas, so that the monks of that place rejoice over the graces you have received." The bishop immediately reported this response to his people, and hastened to send the souvenirs into the maritime regions that had been designated to him.

After choosing four of the region's senior clerics, the bishop enjoined them to cross the sea and gave them his final counsel. They embarked and shortly after landed on the continent. Their first thought was to head to Mount Gargano, for they had not yet heard of Mount Tombe, which had just been newly dedicated. They took the route to Italy. But they perceived that their efforts were in vain. After having walked for a long time, they retraced their steps, and in the morning, they found themselves back at the place from which they had parted on the previous day. Astonished at this marvel, they conferred with each other and wondered what they should make of this. We have been traveling for several days and we are not making progress. We were dispatched to the archangel's mount, and we headed for Mount Gargano. Our bishop, however, spoke to us of a place dedicated to St. Michael without adding anything further. Since he expressed himself in such an imprecise manner, why have we so imprudently dared to designate the place? Very near to us, as we have heard it said, is a mount that is called St. Michael. Perhaps it is there that we should direct our steps. Let us therefore consult him who has already helped us. He cannot abandon the members of this tribe he has saved.

In the middle of the following night, an angel, all radiant with light, appeared to them, and in a very distinct voice gave them this response: "You must go to Mont Saint-Michel, which is called Tombe, because this newly consecrated place has become our dwelling. Although our habitation is in heaven, we have places on earth of which we are especially fond. We love to visit them when they are consecrated to God, and to console there those who suffer, because we cannot neglect those who commend themselves to us. This mount is a new house which is called to bear blessed fruits. We shall visit it often, because it is dear to God, because His name is invoked there, and it will be more and more through sacrifices which will be pleasing to Him."

At these words, the angel disappeared. The pilgrims woke and headed to the place that had been indicated to them. As they walked, they recalled what had been said to them, and, fortified by the divine oracle, they proceeded with joy. Arriving at the oratory, they presented the shield and the sword, recounted everything they had seen, and affirmed it by oath. The tokens were received with the veneration appropriate for them and kept as precious mementos. The mount's inhabitants could not doubt the account of these honorable persons who had come from so far. Everyone therefore rejoiced at the visit the angel had promised them, and together they gave thanks to the heavenly court. They had read in the Apocalypse that St. Michael had annihilated the invisible dragon, and they believed in the vanquisher of this invisible serpent, in the defender and protector of the Holy Church.[5]

These precious pledges of the archangel's protection were displayed for the veneration of pilgrims, who saw them and left descriptions of them. [Fr. Henri-Marie] Boudon says, "I had the honor and blessing to see this year, 1667... the shield and the sword that are kept in the treasury. This shield is decorated with small crosses and made of a bronze material, as well as the sword." Arthur du Moustier speaks of them in his *Neustria Pia*: "They are small and made of bronze. The shield is oval-shaped and decorated with four small crosses, and the sword has the form of a dagger."

Why did Ireland not keep these wonderful pledges of the archangel's protection? Why did St. Michael order them to be taken to Mount

Tombe? And why did St. Aubert receive the order to procure relics left at Mount Gargano by the prince of the angels? It is that God was designating our mountain as a place chosen among all to have His archangel honored. Is there indeed a place somewhere that the finger of God has marked in a more miraculous manner? Is there anywhere a shrine dedicated to the prince of the heavenly army that is more worthy of our veneration?

CHAPTER 5:
ST. MICHAEL SIGNALS HIS PRESENCE AT MONT SAINT-MICHEL THROUGH NUMEROUS MIRACLES.

To this very day, the Lord, through His heavenly minister, does not cease to work similar prodigies in this place.

— Canon of St. Aubert

The prodigies worked at the time of the angelic mountain's consecration were only the prelude to countless miracles, worked in the following centuries. More than nine centuries later, in fact, Boudon was able to say, without fear of being contradicted, that one could go to this holy place to obtain all kinds of graces, "but especially to be delivered from temptations and attacks of evil spirits, to obtain there purity of body and mind, and an invincible strength in the ways of salvation."[1]

The manuscripts of Mont Saint-Michel are filled with incidents validated

> by the notes of this abbey's monks, who witnessed most of them, and, having seen them, left them to us in writing with all the testimony one could desire in these matters, in which, under the pretext of piety, a number of falsehoods often creep if one does not take the necessary precautions which we believe we have taken in this book.

Thus says [the seventeenth-century Benedictine historian] Dom [Jean] Huynes.

Let us mention some of these miraculous deeds worked in the fourteenth century. An inhabitant of Fougères who suffered paralysis in all his limbs regained his health as he prayed with all the monks in the archangel's basilica. — In 1333, a woman, who had also lost the use of her limbs, beseeched the pilgrims who were leaving for the mount to

252

invoke the prince of the angels on her behalf, and she suddenly found herself able to accompany them. — A deaf-mute from Caen was healed at the mount on the vigil of the feast of Saints Peter and Paul.

Fr. Feuardent also reports miracles which he qualifies as *certified by public authority.*

A young girl from Saint-Silvain-en-Caux[2] had a hand that was shut by an invisible spirit. On May 4, 1560, "as she was having the Mass said at the mount and the priest made the final elevation of the Body of Our Lord, her hand opened as easily as if it had never been closed." — A Breton from Quintin, "struck with such an illness that he could in no way speak or walk, returned from Mont Saint-Michel perfectly healed."

Numerous votive offerings hanging in the basilica attested to the archangel's power. One noticed among them an enormous rock hanging by an iron chain from one of the pillars of the tower. This rock, which was brought by King Charles VII, had fallen on this prince's head "in the city of La Rochelle, without hurting him, and this, as he believed, through the favor of St. Michael, to whom he was strongly devoted."[3] — To the left of St. Michael's altar, in the nave, one also saw a charming gilded silver seashell, weighing two marks. It was brought from Paris by Jean-François de Mesgrigny. This lord, seeing his wife in imminent danger, made a vow to go on pilgrimage to the mount if it would obtain her healing. Graciously heard at that very instant, he made the journey and showed himself grateful to the archangel. — Two small boats, hanging in the middle of the basilica's large nave, testified to the gratitude of some sailors for the assistance St. Michael gave them amidst the sea's perils.

But of all those who experience the archangel's protection, the possessed were the most numerous. St. Michael has indeed showed himself the vanquisher of Satan everywhere and always.

The glorious archangel was furthermore accustomed to signaling his presence through other extraordinary phenomena. One time it was to Norgod, the bishop of Avranches, who, on the night of St. Michael's feast day, after Matins, looking through his window, suddenly saw the mount resembling a burning furnace:

He called some canons to be witnesses of this spectacle, and they believed that the church with the monastery and the monks had been reduced to ashes. They returned to the church very distressed by such a disastrous event and recited the Office of the Dead for those they already believed to be numbered among the dead. At daybreak, the bishop left to go view and mourn such sad ruins; however, learning that nothing extraordinary had happened, he recognized that the holy angels dwelled on this sacred mount. Just as long ago like Elisha the prophet,[4] this occasioned him to renounce his bishopric and become a Benedictine monk on this same mountain, and serve God here in the company of the holy angels for the rest of his days, which he holily completed on October 15, 1036.

Sometimes it was a miraculous flame illuminating the monastery tower.

Other times, the monks heard in the church choir the divine melodies of the seraphic spirits. In the eleventh century, the monk Bernier heard a divine symphony for close to an hour. The angels were singing the *Kyrie eleison* with their sweet, harmonious voices. Later still, under the prelacy of Richard Toustain, similar chanting was heard again. It was probably in memory of these miracles that, in the fifteenth century, at the time of the construction of the apse of the admirable basilica, the pinnacles were crowned with angels sounding trumpets.

Most of the time, the archangel announced himself through the terrifying splendor of lightning flashes and thunder crashes, through the bellowing of the wind, or through the sudden breaking of the church's doors and windows, which made one think that the entire abbey had been invaded by a legion of evildoers. The monks fasted for three days to obtain the manifestation of the truth.

The annalists recount that in 1270, during a calm night, three crashes of thunder resounded and were followed by a frightful tempest, in the middle of which could be seen, by the high altar, a figure of fire, and, above the main entryway, two sparkling angels each holding a sword.

A similar phenomenon occurred on the night of Pentecost, in the year 1333.

Dom Huynes says the following about all these prodigies:

> During the nights, the angels would fill the church with a very
> bright light and make a divine melody heard. For over five
> hundred years, they have spoken in this area about "St.
> Michael's light." A number of times, in the middle of the night,
> people have seen heavenly lights on this rock which make this
> place as bright as during the most beautiful days. Several
> persons who are still alive assure us they have seen this light and
> add that this marvel ordinarily occurs during times of war.

The archangel, by signaling his august presence in such an
extraordinary manner, has sheltered his shrine from all profanation. He
has also done so by punishing with terrible chastisements the irreverent
actions, slight in appearance, committed by those to whom he had
entrusted the care of his shrine.

Let us mention some incidents reported by Dom Huynes.

> In 1070, two young monks, having been excused from assisting
> at choir due to some mild infirmities, were reciting their office
> in front of the Holy Savior altar, remaining seated and with little
> devotion or reverence. All of a sudden, they saw something like
> a great flame of fire come from the altar and dart straight at their
> heads, heating them so much that they believed they were
> burning. They learned through this visible sign that the angels,
> whom the Psalmist calls flames of fire,[5] are present with us when
> we pray—something to which the angels have attested at various
> times, by making their melodious singing heard in this church,
> as was observed by many people in the year 1263, and by other
> signs.

That miracle came after the one of the monk Drogon, the sacristan
who, in 1047,[6] was chastised in a very divine way at the foot of St.
Michael's altar,[7] before which he passed with little respect, making
neither a bow nor a prayer.

Contrary to the monastic custom, it was forbidden the porter of
Saint-Michel to spend the night in the church to watch it. The reason for

this prohibition was that one often heard the singing of the heavenly spirits, who made frequent apparitions in this august temple. However, a certain person desiring to witness these heavenly apparitions hid in a corner of the church when it was being closed. But as soon as that time came when sleep takes hold of mortals, he was seized with a dreadful fear. The prince of the heavenly host appeared to him in the temple walking with Mary, the pious Mother of Mercy, and the blessed Peter, who holds the keys to the kingdom of heaven. At the sight of the archangel's irritated face, the unfortunate man, having fallen almost lifeless onto the temple floor, started to pray. Then, the blessed Mary and St. Peter asked that he be pardoned. But St. Michael was opposed to this and said, "Such an offense cannot go unpunished." The Blessed Virgin then asked that he be allowed time to do penance, and, addressing the guilty one, she said to him, "Colibert, why did you seek to intrude into heavenly mysteries? Rise, therefore, and go out from this church; make reparation, as much as you are able, for the offense you have given the angelic spirits." — The unfortunate man exited the church, but he did not survive this deadly curiosity; he died three days later.[8]

St. Michael's great miracle is the powerful protection he constantly gave this celebrated rock by sheltering it from the enemies of the Church and of the State. Let us listen to His Eminence Cardinal de Bonnechose:

> Under Charlemagne's weak successors, Neustria fell into the hands of the Norsemen. Before fully and securely possessing it, they brought the fire and the sword throughout the region. Who can recount, in all its truth, the awful ravages of our fierce ancestors? The monasteries that were destroyed! The churches that were burned! The monks that were slaughtered! Our rivers' banks and the sea's shoreline were covered with blood and ruins. However, amidst this universal desolation, Mont Saint-Michel was respected! The church and the clerics who served there remained sheltered from all attacks; moreover, the terrible Rollo and his successors rivaled each other in devotion and generosity towards the shrine of the glorious archangel....
>
> In the fifteenth century, alas, the most disastrous period of our history opened before us. How does one depict the

desolation of this beautiful kingdom beset by civil war, foreign invasion, the royal family divided with its members armed against each other, the unfortunate monarch gone mad and occasionally regaining his reason only to contemplate more bitterly the sufferings of his subjects and the humiliation of France, our homeland, delivered to the English, and their king crowned in Paris? But it was during this time of darkness, humiliation, and sorrows that St. Michael manifested his protection in the most striking manner.

Everything in Normandy was giving way to the English—they had triumphed over all resistance there when the efforts of their ambition were dashed against the rock of Mont Saint-Michel. In vain did more than fifteen thousand of them cover the beaches surrounding us; in vain did they hurl against these walls the thunder of the most formidable artillery; in vain did their warriors multiply their assaults and concentrate their greatest efforts to storm inside. One hundred nineteen knights, whose memory history will forever remember, defended the archangel's shrine, and nothing could shake them. Intrepid, tireless, clearly supported by heaven, and invested with a supernatural power, they night and day repelled the multitude of assailants and forced them to convert the attack into a blockade. The English summoned their fleets, and the sea was covered with vessels which were going to wage a new attack on this bulwark of French honor. [Thomas] Scales and his army already believed themselves sure of victory. However, a hermit warned him that St. Michael would stir up a tempest to defend the shrine placed under his protection. The English disregarded this warning, but the winds broke loose, the waves swelled high, and the scattered vessels disappeared, covering the shoreline with their debris. Thus, when everything in France seemed to have succumbed to English domination, when alas, the enemy flag was waving over all the towers of Normandy, Mont Saint-Michel alone kept the French flag raised in the sky; and never was any human effort able to take it down.

This admirable defense of Mont Saint-Michel by 119 knights, under the command of Louis d'Estouteville, in 1423, had immense reverberations in France and England. Charles VII was deeply moved by this and sent Dunois to communicate his royal congratulations to his valiant knights. The pope conferred the abbey of Mont Saint-Michel to Cardinal d'Estouteville, the brother of its illustrious defender. In memory of this great feat of arms, Charles VII wanted to institute a new order of chivalry, but death prevented him from executing his plan. Louis XI accomplished it. This prince went with great pomp to Mont Saint-Michel. He came to give thanks to the archangel for his protection over France, and again commended to him his person and his kingdom.

At the same time, he instituted the celebrated order of St. Michael, "in honor," he said, "of Monseigneur St. Michael, the first knight of heaven, who, as champion of God's glory, struck down the rebel angels."

It was here, in the magnificent hall that we still admire, and which since that time has been called the Knights' Hall, that Louis XI held the first chapter of the order....

...Never have the enemies of the Church, any more than the enemies of the State, been able to seize it.

In the sixteenth century, the Huguenots tried multiple times, as the English before, to take possession of Mont Saint-Michel, and to raise there the flag of heresy. They were never able to succeed. Nevertheless, what various attacks they directed against this rock and this shrine! Sometimes it was Montgomery who commanded them; sometimes it was Belle-Isle; sometimes they used cunning and trickery, sometimes open force and violence; they were always pushed back by the warriors and the monks, as had been done with the English, until defeated in every encounter and discouraged, they renounced forever their iniquitous enterprise.

Thus, Mont Saint-Michel, by a precious privilege, has always remained free from heresy and foreign domination; it has always remained Catholic and French! Who would not recognize in this double fact a signal protection, that of the powerful archangel who struck down in heaven the first attempt at usurpation and heresy?

To all these clear signs of miraculous protection, let us add the extraordinary protection of a monument that goes back more than eleven centuries. Despite fires recurring eleven times, despite sieges and assaults hellbent on its destruction, it is still there standing, almost as it was at the time of its glory, while time alone has made nearly all its contemporaries disappear!

For seventy years, it is true, this monument dedicated to the angel of pardon was a place of expiation for crime; for seventy years, these vaults which had reverberated with the chanting of God's praises echoed blasphemies; but hardly had the time of captivity elapsed when St. Michael then scattered the profaners of his temple, to call the faithful once again to the holy mountain to give their piety the satisfaction of times past.

CHAPTER 6:
THE JERUSALEM OF THE WEST.

It was called the Jerusalem of the West.
– Bishop Bravard [1]

The pilgrimages to Mont Saint-Michel were countless. Bishops, priests, princes, and simple faithful hastened there from all regions of Europe. How can one be surprised? Reports circulated and proclaimed its so many marvels! One spoke everywhere of the miracles worked through the intercession of the archangel!

But let us listen to Bishop Bravard recount the history of these pilgrimages:

> The pilgrimage destination of Mont Saint-Michel was, for long centuries, one of the most frequented in Christendom. Santiago de Compostela, Notre-Dame-du-Puy, Sainte-Anne-d'Auray, the tombs of the holy apostles, and even the holy places in Palestine did not surpass it in the people's veneration.[2]
>
> It was called the Jerusalem of the West, and people flocked there from the furthest places in the world, as did the Jews to their holy mountain of Zion. And it was not only the simple faithful who went there to bring the homage of their devotion, it was also the world's rich and powerful.
>
> The proud barons, dukes, and counts of Normandy, those of Brittany, those of Burgundy, the lords of all places, and all those who had authority or power, considered it an honor to present there to the archangel their crowns or their valiant swords.
>
> All warriors and all gentlemen who sought out battles, with their glorious dangers, wanted to stand guard on this rock and defend its blessed shrine.
>
> We know the history of these gentlemen, of these heroes, who, during the Hundred Years' War, came to shelter their independence behind the ramparts of the impregnable abbey,

where, for thirty years, they fought with the courage of the desperate against the forces assembled by England on land and sea; then, numbering 119, under the command of Louis d'Estouteville, 7th Captain, and Lieutenant N. Paysnel, they forced their twenty thousand enemies to flee from these shores, which for too long had been bloodied by their odious and futile attacks.

The kings of France and those of England, ours especially, beginning with Childebert III, the last of the Merovingian kings in 710, to the great Charlemagne in the year 800, to St. Louis, to the Count of Artois, who was later Charles X, to the Duke of Orléans, who was Louis-Philippe, all came to visit the archangel; all would regard this journey as a duty, as a necessity for the security of their persons and their states.

The queens, princesses, and great and noble ladies imitated their examples; and they also came in great number to confide to the leader of the heavenly army their concerns, their gratitude for benefits received, or their prayers for desired graces.

In a number of provinces, one could not enter into an inheritance without coming to invoke the archangel on behalf of the soul of the deceased whose property one was going to receive; in other places, young spouses had to visit the mount immediately after their wedding to ask St. Michael for a blessing on their union, which so many causes might make unhappy. In other regions, there were confraternities whose rules required members to make the pilgrimage to our archangelic abbey multiple times during their life.

King Louis XI did more: He required the thirty-six knights with whom he formed the order in honor of "Monseigneur St. Michael" to assemble every year, on the "penultimate day of September with great pomp to hold a solemn feast, chapter, and general assembly in the dwelling of said Monseigneur St. Michael."

Besides obligatory pilgrimages, countless caravans[3] would depart from the most distant regions, arrive at the mount after much fatigue and privations, amidst songs composed in all languages, and then, after having prayed, and after having often rested on the bare rock because there was no more room in the thirty-eight inns, they would set off again with joyful hearts, their bodies sometimes healed of infirmities, supplied with shell necklaces[4] and medals, and their souls filled with pious memories and sweet hopes.

There was even an era when a kind of invincible attraction took hold of the children and filled them with an immense desire to make the pilgrimage to the mount. One would see two or three of them band together, from the furthest part of Germany or from other far-off places, in the middle of their games or of their prayers, then leave, despite remonstrances and supplications, join with other children they encountered on the way, and arrive here numbering five or six hundred. In the heavenly abbey, they poured out the desires of their innocent hearts, and then headed back to rejoin their worried families, hoping that God, an adoptive father to the little birds, would give to them, children of the holy archangel, provisions for their return, just as He had granted them what they needed to make the original journey.

The traffic occasioned by all these pilgrimages was so considerable that it was necessary in the Middle Ages to set up special infrastructure and open roads and pathways at all points leading to the mount. For long centuries, these Mont Saint-Michel routes were thoroughfares for pedestrians, equestrians, and vehicles, as well as for almost all the trade done between the various peoples of France and Europe.

These thoroughfares still exist. We find them on all our coasts, in Genêts, Saint-James, Les Biards, Pontorson, Montviron, and elsewhere; we have even been assured that similar ones exist on the banks of the Rhine, in northern Germany, and that there, as here, they are still known as the "Ways to the Mount," or rather, under the very moving name of "Ways to Paradise."

Such was the great pilgrimage of Mont Saint-Michel, in the Middle Ages, and in times nearer to us.

Besides, could it be otherwise when, by a miracle, children, still at their mother's breast, were asking to be taken to the archangel's shrine? This is at least what fourteenth-century manuscripts, among others, relay to us. Woe to those who wanted to hinder these pilgrimages! Two children from Écouché asked their parents to let them go pray to St. Michael of the Mount; the parents refused this and locked them in a room; the next day, both children were found dead. The archangel had certainly taken to heaven those two young souls who were devoted to him. — One man from Mortain was struck by God for having prevented children he had as boarders from fulfilling a similar desire; he then commended himself to the archangel, who healed him, and he came to the mount accompanied by a priest of the city to obtain forgiveness. — And it was not just those who wanted to prevent these pilgrimages who were struck by God, but also those who mocked them. — One woman, who was hardly Christian, one day made fun of some young pilgrims to the mount, but she was soon struck by an illness which only subsided upon vowing to go to the shrine herself.

Sometimes, heavenly voices made themselves heard to multitudes of faithful, who would leave at that moment for the mount, without even first going back into their homes. One blacksmith, among others, stated that he had left his hot iron on the anvil. Dom Huynes recounts:

> Around the year 1457, there came to this Mont Saint-Michel, from parts of Germany, such a great quantity of men, women, and children of all kinds of nobility, that many prelates, lords, and other persons of nobility in this country and through where they traveled marveled at it and asked the reason for it to the priests leading the groups, who only responded that God inspired in each one of them the desire to make the journey, and sometimes so suddenly, that they left everything to get on their way, and that a number of miracles had occurred in their areas upon invoking St. Michael.

These pilgrims, St. Michael sometimes protected them in the most striking manner on their journey.

One Norman man on horseback who was carried away by the sea, having consecrated himself to the archangel, was swept back onto the shores of Saint-Jean with his faithful steed, which he then had enter the archangel's church in the presence of an enormous crowd, proclaiming that after commending himself to St. Michael, he trusted as though a million men and horses would rush to his aid. — Another man on horseback was swept away by the sea in the vicinity of Pontaubault. Seeing the mount, he cried out, "St. Michael, help me, and I will be at your mercy!" And he was found full of life at Tombelaine, his horse dead beneath him.[5]

But of all the marks of protection, the most famous one is the following. The chroniclers have recounted it for a long time, and Fr. Deschamps sums it up this way in his *Histoire du Mont-St-Michel*:

At the beginning of the eleventh century, a woman from Normandy who was about to become a mother, wanted to go with her husband and some relatives to Mont Saint-Michel, to place herself under the archangel's protection. When they were returning from there at the time of the rising tide, a thick and fast-moving fog suddenly enveloped them in the middle of our very dangerous banks. The tide was surging at the speed of a galloping horse, and death was imminent. This woman, in fear, suddenly went into labor. But the archangel was watching over his devoted servants. All around them, he lifted the water to form high walls, just as the waters of the Jordan and the Red Sea had been parted long ago to make way for the Hebrews. Within this humid enclosure, the mother held her newborn in her arms, and the father, invoking the august Trinity, let the roaring waters splash onto him to clothe him with Jesus Christ. This miraculous child, from its first years, was confided to a teacher capable of instructing him in Sacred Scripture and forming him in piety. Later, he was raised to the priesthood and assigned a parish four miles from Lisieux. The chronicler ends his account by saying,

"He is still alive, and every year he comes to the mount to thank the archangel."

A hundred-foot cross, erected at the location of the miracle, was dedicated to its memory. It was placed between Tombelaine and Saint-Léonard.

Such was this great pilgrimage site.

Closed for seventy years to the piety of Christians, it is open today. May we see pilgrims, led by faith, embarking again in masses on the road to this holy mountain! No, no, the archangel will not remain deaf to the fervent prayers addressed to him. He ever has the same merit before God, and today as in times past, he wants to make use of it in favor of those who have recourse to him.

CHAPTER 7:
MARY, QUEEN OF THE ANGELS.
– OUR LADY OF MOUNT TOMBE.

Hail, Lady of the Angels.
– Church antiphon

We cannot conclude this study on St. Michael and the holy angels without saying a word about the Queen placed at the head of these heavenly spirits. The pilgrims to the mount did not separate the name of St. Michael from that of Mary.

Mary, in fact, is Queen of the Angels by right and by election.

All the graces and all the glories in which the angels were created and the saints edified have their fullness in Mary as in their ocean. She is an abyss of grace, says St. John Damascene, she is higher than the Cherubim and the Seraphim; there is nothing that comes so near to God as she. Indeed, the holiness of Mary surpasses that of all angels and men combined. Pile grace upon grace, glory upon glory; travel through and span all the degrees of grace and glory, the Saints, the Confessors, the Martyrs, the Apostles, the Prophets, and the Patriarchs; ascend beyond all the Angels, Powers, Virtues, Thrones, Cherubim, and Seraphim; and with all these created grandeurs and with all these glories, form a single grandeur, a single grace, a single glory. How far will you still be from Mary? An inexpressible distance.

Mary is the Queen of each angelic hierarchy and each order of sanctity, because, in this plenitude of grace with which she has been filled, she has received all the special graces that constitute the first in each of these orders and hierarchies; and it is through her that all these graces have passed and do pass in their radiance and their application.

St. Paul, wanting to express the greatness of Jesus Christ, said of Him: "Being made so much better than the angels, as he hath inherited a more excellent name than they. For to which of the angels hath [God] said at any time, Thou art my Son?" (Heb 1:4-5). — Who is the angel, we shall say, to whom God has said, "Thou art My Mother"? A Mother, consequently, who is as much above the angels as this name is more excellent than theirs.

The holy angels themselves have chosen Mary for their Queen; and because Lucifer and his angels refused to recognize her, they were cast into the abyss.

According to the testimony of St. Bridget, the angels, from the beginning, conceived such a pure zeal for the interests of Mary that they took more joy in what she was to be than in the fact that they had been created.

On the day of the Immaculate Conception, Mary of Agreda says,

> a thousand angels were chosen from the Seraphim and the lower orders of angels, and thus that City of God was superabundantly fortified against the infernal hosts.
>
> In order that this invincible warrior-troop might be well appointed, saint Michael, the prince of the heavenly militia, was placed at the head, and although not always in the company of the Queen, he was nevertheless often near Her and often showed himself to Her. The Almighty destined him as a special ambassador of Christ our Lord and to act in some of the mysteries as the defender of his most holy Mother. In a like manner the holy prince Gabriel was appointed to act as legate and minister of the eternal Father in the affairs of the Princess of heaven.[1]

It was an archangel who gave to men the most beautiful prayer that has ever been addressed to this glorious Queen. "The angel," Nicolas says,

> intoned the first *Hail Mary*, he gave us the note and the measure for the honor that was due Mary with all the authority of his heavenly nature, and he left us to discharge this office after him with all the submission and all the obligation of our mortal and redeemed nature.[2]

On the day of the death of this Most Holy Mother of the Savior, the angels transported her body to heaven, and all the heavenly court acclaimed her Queen of Heaven and of the Angels.

The Church recalls multiple times, in the office of the feast of the Assumption, the joy that this mystery caused in the angelic world: *"In whose Assumption the angels rejoice, and highly extol the Son of God."*

The title of Queen of the Angels is particularly dear to the blessed spirits, Mary of Agreda tells us. She states,

> I wish to mention, that while I wrote of this, the holy princes asked me why I did not more frequently call Mary the Queen and Mistress of the angels, and they told me not to neglect the use of that title in the balance of this history, since they derived such great delight therefrom. In order to obey and please them I shall use it many times from now on.[3]

The Church addresses and invokes her frequently under this title, principally at the end of the evening office: *Ave, Regina caelorum, Ave, Domina Angelorum.* Hail, Queen of Heaven, Hail, Lady of the Angels.... *Regina caeli, laetare, alleluia.* Queen of heaven, rejoice, alleluia....[4] *Salve Regina, Mater misericordiae,* Hail Holy Queen, Mother of Mercy. One author claims that one night St. Bernard, "getting up carefully for fear of waking his monks asleep in the dormitory very near his cell, went to the chapel, where he learned from angelic voices the *Salve Regina.*"[5]

Mary is thus the Queen of the Angels, and the angels are her servants, but such zealous servants that they await the manifestation of her wishes to execute them at the least sign, with untellable swiftness.

But if the angels honor Mary as their Queen and Mistress, Mary also desires that her servants be honored. Boudon says:

> The love that she has for them... demands... that we love what she loves, that we have profound respect for those she wants honored. Let us therefore praise and bless the holy angels, because the most pure Virgin, the august Queen and Lady of the

Angels, is thereby praised and blessed; but let us praise and bless the Lord, Who has made everything that is great and praiseworthy in the Lady of the Angels and in the holy angels; and this is God alone, God alone, God alone.[6]

Numerous churches have been built in honor of Our Lady of the Angels. There is one, among others, celebrated in all the world, Our Lady of Portiuncula, near the city of Assisi, in Italy.

At Mont Saint-Michel, the most beautiful crypt, the Great Pillars Crypt, whose boldness Vauban admired and which the Marquise de Créquy called the great work of the Benedictines, is dedicated to Mary. The kings of France had to fulfill this pilgrimage at the same time as that of St. Michael. This basilica possessed a statue to which was attributed a miraculous origin. This wooden statue, miraculously preserved in the middle of a fire in 1112, had first been placed in the chapel of Our Lady of the Thirty Candles. It was in this chapel that St. Aubert celebrated the holy mysteries, and it was also here that he received so many extraordinary graces.

Who can say how many pilgrims flocked to invoke Our Lady of Mount Tombe? A declaration signed by a monk on June 20, 1694, tells us there were coming at the time "a great flux of pilgrims and that multiple obtained miraculous effects and healings, through the assistance of the Most Holy Virgin."

Before the Revolution, it was especially visited by long lines of sailors saved from shipwreck. These sons of the ocean, with a fervor which is not rare among them, would intone in one throaty voice, like the noise of the waves, the *Ave Maris Stella*, or that gracious *Salve Regina* which the angels themselves sing on their harps of gold.

May it please God to henceforth have a great throng of pilgrims coming to seek, with a certain preference, the very special graces of Mary.

But someone will stop us and say, "The holy crypt has reopened, but the statue that has been put there is no longer the miraculous ancient statue venerated by our fathers. What guarantees us that heaven will confer it the same power?"

We will answer with Monseigneur Pie, the Bishop of Poitiers:

> No, it is true, this statue is no longer the one venerated by our fathers. Let us not remember what will always be a painful subject of tears; let us rejoice rather in this act of reparation that is accomplished at this moment.... No, this statue is not the same as in times past; however, by coming to take the place of its predecessor, it will inherit all its virtue. Already, the powerful and genuine prayer of the Church has distinguished and separated this inanimate wood from the domain of profane things; holy water has not only purified it, but sanctified and consecrated it to be forever the representation of the Virgin who was the hope of the Gentiles as much as Israel's.... To this blessing of the Church will be joined, if not the consecration of future times which we cannot anticipate, at least the consecration of centuries past. No sooner will this sacred image be installed in its ancient and traditional place than will all the memories of bygone ages and ancient marvels immediately come to invest and penetrate it, gathering over its head like the cloud that hovered over the ark of the covenant and revealed the presence of the divinity. Then, so many tears with which the temple floor has been dampened; so many wishes, so many sighs, and so many prayers which, like a cloud of incense, have attached themselves to the surfaces of the walls and arches; in a word, all that there is of holiness that is spread throughout all parts of this building will come together and amass in this blessed image, impregnate it, and vivify it. And all those generations of holy bishops, holy priests, holy kings, holy confessors, holy virgins, and holy widows who came to invoke the power of Mary in this place, all those legions of faithful servants of Our Lady who are presently in glory, will jointly put forth their hands to make descend from above into this statue the same divine virtue that flowed from the ancient statue for their sanctification.

Lastly, in addition to the Church's blessing, and in addition to the consecration of memories past, this statue will soon possess the consecration resulting from the prodigies and miracles of which it itself will be the channel and instrument.[7]

The great bishop of Poitiers can see the fulfillment of his hopes. Today, as in times past, numerous pilgrims, led by faith, come to invoke Our Lady of Chartres, and today, as in times past, Mary graciously hears those who come to place in her an entirely filial trust.

CONCLUSION OF PART TWO

Let us end this second part like the first, saying: Love and devotion to St. Michael.

Love him, apostolic men; he was the first missionary in paradise; the first one, he supported the rights of God and fought Satan.

Love him, preachers and doctors; placed in the hearth of eternal love, he contemplates up close the divine splendor and draws from there a supereminent knowledge which makes him repeat unceasingly this sublime cry: "*Quis ut Deus?* Who is like God?"

Love him, priests of Jesus Christ; it is through his hands that the divine oblation is carried to the feet of the Eternal One.

Love him, warriors who fight for the Church and what is right; he is your protector and your model.

Love him, you who are zealous for the interests of Jesus, Mary, and the Church; you are his auxiliaries in this sublime mission.

Love him, you whom an ardent charity makes work for the relief of the Church suffering; he is the consoler of the souls in Purgatory.

Love him, sinners; he carries your repentance to God and places in the scales of divine justice your works of penance.

Love him, you who observe the law of God; he will usher you into the paradise of everlasting jubilation.

Amen! Amen!

Appendices

<hr/>

Appendix 1:
Calendar of St. Michael and the Holy Angels.

God, as we have said, makes use of St. Michael and the holy angels to make known to us His will, to protect us in dangers, and, often, to grant us extraordinary graces.

It suffices to read the lives of the saints to be convinced that we have put nothing forward that is not backed up by experience.

But to make understood in a yet more striking manner everything that we can expect from these benevolent spirits, we shall point out, in a few words, the singular favors that they have procured for some of the saints recognized by the Church.

We shall do this according to the *Acts of the Saints* compiled by the Bollandists, the martyrology of the Roman Breviary, *The Golden Legend* by James of Voragine, [*The Lives of the Saints* by] Alban Butler, translated by Godescard, etc.

We shall also recall the names of saints who distinguished themselves by a special devotion towards St. Michael and his angels.

And to provide some daily nourishment for the piety of the faithful devoted to the holy angels, we shall briefly point out the connections with the feasts instituted in honor of Our Lord, the Blessed Virgin, and the saints.[1]

Movable Feasts

2ⁿᵈ Sunday after the Epiphany – Feast of the Holy Name of Jesus. "You will call Him Jesus," an angel said.

Tuesday after Septuagesima – Feast of Our Lord's Prayer in the Garden of Olives. St. Michael came to console the Savior (see pp. 125-26).

Tuesday after Sexagesima – Memorial of the Passion of Our Lord Jesus Christ. The Savior did not want to call the legions of angels for help.

Friday after Ash Wednesday – Our Lord's Holy Crown of Thorns.

1ˢᵗ Sunday of Lent – The gospel of this day recalls that the angels came to serve the Savior.

Friday after the 1ˢᵗ Sunday of Lent – The holy lance and the nails.

Friday after the 2ⁿᵈ Sunday of Lent – The holy shroud. Painters and sculptors depict the angels carrying the instruments of the Passion. This is how ten of them are portrayed on the Ponte Sant'Angelo in Rome.

Friday after the 3ʳᵈ Sunday of Lent – The Five Wounds. The angels adore them in heaven.

Friday after the 4ᵗʰ Sunday of Lent – The Precious Blood of Our Lord. The angels, Mary of Agreda says, collected the blood that the Savior shed in His Passion.

Friday after Passion Sunday – The Seven Sorrows of Mary, Queen of the Angels.

Holy Thursday – Our Lord entrusted to St. Michael guardianship of the sacrament of the Eucharist (see p. 127). The cenacle, Mary of Agreda says, was filled with countless legions of angels who assisted at the admirable works performed by the Savior (also see p. 93).

Good Friday – Legions of angels surrounded the Cross and worked marvels in nature which took place at the Savior's death.

Holy Saturday – The angels guard the body of the Savior in the tomb. – St. Michael, with legions of angels, goes to limbo (see p. 126).

Easter Sunday – The angels announce Jesus Christ's resurrection to the holy women.

Ascension Day – Angels appeared to the apostles, while legions of the heavenly army accompanied the Savior's triumphant entrance into heaven.

Pentecost – The Holy Ghost is the King of the City of Good; the angels are its princes, and they are filled with His grace.

Trinity Sunday – The Most Holy Trinity is the object of the angels' adoration.

Corpus Christi – The Thrones form the Most Blessed Sacrament's guard of honor, whose leader is St. Michael (see p. 127).

Sacred Heart of Jesus – It is the object of the angels' adoration.

—

Month of November – *Dedication of Churches* – The angels are their guardians (see p. 35).

January

1	– Circumcision of Our Lord Jesus Christ. – St. Michael and St. Gabriel bring from heaven the Holy Name of Jesus (see p. 124). – St. Concordius, priest and martyr in Spoleto at the time of Emperor Antoninus, consoled in his prison by an angel.
5	– St. Simeon Stylites. He was often seen conversing with a gloriously radiant angel (Bollandists).
6	– Epiphany of Our Lord. An angel led the Magi by means of a star, and revealed to them the wickedness of King Herod. – Birth of Joan of Arc, her interactions with St. Michael (see pp. 139-40).
7	– The child Jesus returns from Egypt. St. Michael protects His return. – St. Cedd, bishop. The angels announced his death to him. – St. Raymond of Pennafort. He had frequent communications with an angel (Bollandists).
8	– St. Gudula, patroness of Brussels. An angel foretold her future sanctity to her mother (Bollandists).
9	– St. Julian of Antioch, assisted in his martyrdom by three angels. The judge Marcian saw them place on his head a crown as resplendent as the sun (Bollandists).

10	– Blessed Oringa, protected by St. Michael (Bollandists, see pp. 228-29). – St. Paul, first hermit. The angels were seen by St. Anthony taking his soul to heaven amidst a numerous troop of apostles and prophets (Roman martyrology). – St. Aldo, honored as a confessor at St. Michael's in Pavia, where his body is (Roman martyrology).
11	– At Castel Sant'Elia, near Monte de San Silvestro, the monk St. Anastasius and his companions, called by an angelic voice, entered into the joy of the Lord (Roman martyrology).
13	– St. Viventius, protected by an angel, escaped his persecutors' pursuits, 4th century (Bollandists). – St. Yvette, in a rapture she saw eighteen angels clothe her in golden fabric and jewels of precious stones, 13th century (Bollandists). – St. Veronica of Milan, warned by an angel that the thought of withdrawing into the wilderness conformed neither to God's will nor to her salvation, 15th century (Bollandists).
14	– St. Felix of Nola, freed from his prison by an angel, brought help to his bishop, 3rd century (Bollandists). – St. Peter Orseolo, Doge of Venice, died at the monastery of St-Michel-de-Cuxa, where he had gone to do penance for his numerous sins.
15	– St. Eudocia (see pp. 163-64). – St. Alexander, founder of the Acoemetae Order, he and his disciples were fed by a visible angel (Bollandists). – St. Ita, of Ireland, assisted multiple times by an angel, built a monastery in a place the angel indicated to her, 6th century (Bollandists). – St. Habakkuk, transported to Babylon by an angel.
16	– St. Fursey, in ecstasy he saw a great number of angels, 7th century (Bollandists).
17	– St. Anthony saw the angels multiple times taking the souls of saints to heaven. He also saw the heavenly spirits come down from heaven to take his own soul there, 4th century (Bollandists).
18	– St. Prisca. After her martyrdom, two angels guarded her body from ravenous beasts, 3rd century (Bollandists).

19	– St. Bassian saw, on the day of his baptism, his guardian angel present him a white robe, 5th century (Bollandists).
20	– St. Sebastian. Jesus Christ appeared to him on the eve of his martyrdom surrounded by seven angels, one of whom clothed him in a mantle of light (Cornelius a Lapide). – St. Neophytus, of Nicaea, withdrew to Mount Olympus and was fed for five years by an angel, 6th century (Bollandists).
21	– St. Agnes, virgin and martyr. An angel blinded a brazen man who dared to cast indecent looks at her, 3rd century (Dom Ruynard). – St. Meinrad, delivered from demons by an angel, 9th century (Bollandists). – In Picardy, St. Maccalin, abbot of Saint-Michel-en-Thiérache (Martyrology). – In Camaldoli, in Tuscany, Venerable Michael of the Camaldolese Order (Martyrology).
22	– St. Vincent, martyr. The angels encouraged him in his martyrdom and took care of his body after his death, 4th century (Bollandists). – St. Dominic, abbot of Sora, conversed with an angel at the time of his death, 11th century (Bollandists).
23	– Marriage of the Blessed Virgin. An angel appeared to St. Joseph to prompt him to espouse Mary. – St. Clement of Ancyra, visited in prison by the angels, 4th century (Bollandists).
25	– Conversion of St. Paul. – St. Apollo, fed in the desert, along with his disciples, by the angels, 4th century (Bollandists). – Blessed Henry Suso. The angels eased the difficulties of his illness with ravishing singing, 14th century (Bollandists).
26	– St. Polycarp, bishop of Smyrna, preserved by an angel from a fall from a building, 2nd century (Bollandists).

27	– At the prayer of St. John Chrysostom, the angels preserved Constantinople when it was attacked by the Goths in the fourth century (Socrates of Constantinople). – In Lower Normandy, St. Sulpice of Bayeux, a solitary whose body is honored at Saint-Ghislain, in Hainaut, where the abbot Simon brought it upon returning from a pilgrimage he had made to Mont Saint-Michel (Martyrology). – At the abbey of St-Michel in Tonnerre, St. Theodoric, bishop of Orléans (Martyrology).
28	– St. Thyrsus, martyr in Caesarea, wondrously bore all kinds of tortures through the help of an angel, 3rd century (Bollandists). – St. Charlemagne, Emperor of the West, very devoted to St. Michael (see p. 188).
29	– St. Constantius, bishop of Perugia. His angel exhorted him to courageously bear martyrdom and took care of his body after his death, 4th century (Bollandists). – At the convent of San Miguel de Treviño in the Diocese of Burgos, in Castile, Blessed Radegund, virgin and nun of the Premonstratensian Order (Martyrology). – At Mont Saint-Michel, the healing of a girl from Cancale possessed by the devil, in 1598. – St. Francis de Sales (see pp. 45, 187).
30	– St. Aldegundis, visited and instructed by the angels, 7th century (Bollandists). – St. Bathilde, Queen of France. An angel made known to her the distress of Fontenelle Abbey, 7th century.
31	– St. Peter Nolasco. His angel appeared to him frequently (Roman Breviary).

February

1	– St. Ignatius of Antioch heard the angels singing antiphons on the top of a mountain. From this came the custom of singing antiphons (*Historia Tripartita*). – St. Ephrem, deacon of the church of Edessa, very devoted to St. Michael.

2	– Purification of the Queen of the Angels.
4	– St. Joseph of Leonissa, miraculously delivered by an angel from the torture through which the inhabitants of Constantinople wanted to kill him, 16th century (Roman Breviary).
5	– St. Agatha Hildegard, wife of the Count of Carinthia, unjustly accused before her husband, justified by the angels, [11th][2] century (Bollandists). – St. Francis of St. Michael, lay brother and martyr. – St. Michael Kozaki, one of the twenty-six Japanese martyrs.
7	– St. Lawrence, bishop of Siponto (see p. 183). – St. Romuald, founder of the Camaldolese Order (see pp. 185, 193-94).
8	– St. John of Matha. An angel appeared to him when he was celebrating Holy Mass and made known to him that he was to found the Trinitarian Order for the ransom of captives (Roman Breviary). – St. Stephen, founder of the Order of Grandmont, taken to heaven by the angels, 12th century (Bollandists).
10	– St. William, founder of the monastery of Sainte-Marie-d'Olive in Belgium, converted by an angel, 13th century (Bollandists).[3]
13	– St. Catherine of Ricci, favored multiple times with angelic visions (Roman Breviary).
14	– Apparition of St. Michael at Monte Faito (see p. 230-31).
15	– St. Faustinus and St. Jovita, thrown into the sea with their hands and feet tied, delivered by angels (Roman Breviary).
20	– Our Lady of Boulogne-sur-Mer, brought on a boat through the ministry of angels, in 633. – St. Angela of Foligno saw the Thrones around the Blessed Sacrament (Fr. Faber).
22	– St. Margaret of Cortona, from the time of her conversion, received angelic visits daily, 13th century (Bollandists).
23	– St. Peter Damian (see p. 185).
28	– St. Oswald, bishop of York, served by the angels during Mass (Fr. Faber).

March

1	– Apparition of St. Michael to St. Eudocia (see pp. 163-64).
3	– St. Arthelais, daughter of Constantinople proconsul Lucius, protected by an angel from those seeking to despoil her honor, 6th century (Bollandists).
6	– St. Colette, protected from demons by the angels, 15th century (Bollandists).
7	– St. Paul the Simple one day saw the guardian angel of a bad monk following very sadly this sinner who had lost grace, 4th century (Bollandists). – St. Thomas Aquinas, called the Angelic Doctor. The angels, during his sleep, girded him with a belt to preserve him from impure temptations, 13th century (Roman Breviary).
8	– St. John of God. St. Raphael one day revealed to him that God had tasked him with sharing his ministry to the sick, 16th century (Bollandists).
9	– St. Frances of Rome, widow, frequently conversed with an angel who gave her help in difficulties (Roman Breviary, prayer).
10	– St. Michael appeared to the forty martyrs of Sebaste, who were plunged into an icy lake, [4th][4] century (St. Ephrem).
12	– St. Gregory the Great. An angel, in the form of an old man, asked him one day for charity, and revealed to him on another day that he would be Sovereign Pontiff, 6th century (Bollandists). – St. Paul Aurelian, led by his angel to the region he was to evangelize, and warned by this same angel of the time of his death, 6th century (Bollandists). – St. Theophanes of Constantinople. An angel revealed to him which place he was to holily spend his days after having given his goods to the poor, 9th century (Bollandists).
14	– Blessed Peter of Treja, of the Franciscan Order. This holy man received the most signal graces from St. Michael (Franciscan Roman Breviary).
17	– St. Patrick was led to Ireland by his angel, 4th [to 5th] century (Bollandists).
18	– St. Gabriel the Archangel.

19	– St. Joseph, husband of Mary, often had angelic visions.
20	– St. Cuthbert, often visited by angels who brought him a mysterious heavenly food which nourished his soul even more than his body, 7th century (Bollandists).
21	– St. Benedict, father of Western monasticism, very devoted to St. Michael, 6th century (see p. 191).
22	– Blessed Nicholas of Flüe, famous in Switzerland, gave alms to an angel who appeared in the form of an old man. The angel then favored him with a wonderful vision, [15th][5] century (Bollandists).
25	– Incarnation of the Word, announced by St. Gabriel.
26	– St. Michael of Hietingen, child martyr. – Hubert Salonik, treasurer to the king of Poland, converted by the angels, 17th century (Bollandists).[6]
27	– St. John of Egypt, fed in the desert for ten years by an angel, 4th century (Bollandists).
28	– Venerable Marie de Maillac welcomed to her table an angel in the guise of a poor man, 15th century (Bollandists).
29	– St. Bonitus, bishop of Clermont, celebrated Mass with a chasuble the angels had brought him ([Alexis] Paulin Paris).
30	– St. John of Cybistra, fed for ten years through the solicitude of an angel, 3rd century (Bollandists).
31	– St. Secundus of Asti, soldier and martyr; his life from his conversion until his death was but one continuous interaction with the angels. – St. Guy of Pomposa, abbot, heard the voice of an angel who came to warn one of his monks of the time of his death, 11th century (Bollandists).

April

2	– St. Francis of Paola (see p. 187).
3	– St. Richard of Chichester, professor at Oxford, preserved from death by an angel, 13th century (Bollandists).
4	– St. Plato, abbot of St. Michael's in Constantinople (Martyrology).

5	– St. Vincent Ferrer, devoted to St. Michael. – St. Angelus, Carmelite.
7	– St. Elizabeth, of the monastery in Hoven. An angel announced her death to her, 13th century (Bollandists).
9	– St. Mary of Cleophas saw the angels at the Savior's tomb (see p. 57).
10	– Blessed Mechtild, virgin and abbess, known for her devotion to the nine choirs of angels, 14th century.
11	– St. Leo the Great (see p. 182). He recommended devotion to the angels. "Make friends with the angels," he said.
12	– Blessed Angelo of Chivasso, Franciscan, 15th century (Godescard).
13	– St. Hermengild, Visigoth prince. On the night following his martyrdom, the angels were heard singing divine psalmody around his body, 6th century (Roman Breviary). – St. Justin Martyr, instructed by an angel who appeared in the form of an old man, 2nd century (*Dialogue with Trypho*). – [Blessed][7] Ida of Louvain, received communion from an angel, 13th century (Bollandists).
14	– St. Lidwina, frequently visited by her angel, who appeared to her in a visible form, 15th century (Bollandists).
15	– St. Paternus, bishop of Avranches. A chapel was dedicated to him in the basilica of Mont Saint-Michel, as well as to St. Scubilion, who is remembered on the same day.
16	– St. Magnus, bishop and martyr. His relics are kept in Rome in the church Charlemagne had built in honor of him and St. Michael.
20	– St. Hildegund, of Cologne, protected by her angel, escaped many dangers, and learned the time of her death, 12th century (Bollandists). – St. Agnes of Montepulciano, in Tuscany; she once received communion from the hand of an angel, who brought her, in another circumstance, two clumps of dry earth from Bethlehem and Calvary, as she had desired, 14th century (Bollandists).
21	– St. Anselm of Canterbury, devoted to St. Michael (see pp. 184-185).

25	– St. Mark, evangelist. – Apparition of St. Michael to St. Gregory the Great, above Hadrian's mole (see p. 153).
29	– St. Hugh, abbot of Cluny, preserved several times from death during his sleep by his guardian angel, who appeared to him in human form, 12th century (Bollandists). – St. Robert of Molesme, initially abbot of St-Michel in Tonnerre, then founder of Cîteaux, 12th century.
30	– St. Catherine of Siena, virgin. "She almost always saw angels holding a veil of gold... and in the midst a Host with the semblance of an Infant. Sometimes she saw the angels and saints adoring Our Lord on the altar" (Fr. Faber).[8]

May

1	– St. Arigius, bishop of Gap. Crossing the Durance River one day, the boat crashed against a rock, and his angel preserved his life, 7th century (Bollandists).
2	– Our Lady of the Hermits [Einsiedeln Abbey's church], in Switzerland, consecrated by the angels, 10th century (Bollandists).
3	– Finding of the Holy Cross.
4	– St. Monica, told by an angel of the future conversion of St. Augustine.
5	– St. Pius V, pope. He had received the name Michael at baptism, died in 1572.
6	– St. John, before the Latin Gate, protected by the angels.
7	– St. Stanislaus, bishop of Krakow, martyred in a St. Michael chapel (see p. 149 and corresponding note). – St. John of Beverley, bishop of York, had a cell built near a chapel of St. Michael, to whom he was very devoted. – St. Serenicus, confirmed by an angel in his resolution to withdraw into solitude, 7th century.
8	– Apparition of St. Michael at Mount Gargano (see pp. 226-28).
9	– St. Hermas (see p. 159).[9]

11	– St. Majolus of Cluny, taken by the Saracens, twice saw his chains broken by the angels, 10th century (Bollandists). – St. Anthimus, taken out of the Tiber by an angel.
14	– St. Boniface of Tarsus. Through the help of an angel, Aglaida found this martyr's body (Roman Breviary).
15	– St. Hilary of Galeata. An angel defended him from the evil designs of King Theodoric, who wanted to capture him, 6th century (Bollandists). – St. Isidore the Farmer, helped in his work by the angels, 12th century (Bollandists).
16	– St. Brendan, abbot in Ireland, sent St. Bridget a chalice filled with the Blood of Our Lord on Easter night.
17	– St. Michael appeared to the English who were attacking Orléans, defended by Joan of Arc, [1429].[10]
18	– St. Venantius, martyr, miraculously delivered multiple times by an angel (Roman Breviary).
19	– St. Dunstan, archbishop of Canterbury, visited multiple times by the angels, who were heard singing with him, and who came to announce to him his death, 10th century (Bollandists). – St. Ives, archdeacon of Tréguier, several times gave alms to angels who presented themselves as poor persons, [14th][11] century (Bollandists).
20	– [Blessed][12] Columba of Rieti. The angels celebrated her birth and gave her communion multiple times during her life, 16th century (Bollandists).
21	– St. Felix of Cantalice, Capuchin. Multiple times, an angel watched over the flocks to which he was obliged to tend (Bollandists).
22	– St. Humility, of the Vallumbrosan Order, led by angels multiple times in her journeys, 14th century (Bollandists).
23	– St. Michael, bishop of Synnada, in Phrygia.
24	– St. Simeon Stylites the Younger. Our Lord appeared to him with St. Michael at His right side and St. Gabriel at His left, 6th century (Bollandists). – Venerable Mary of Agreda. St. Michael taught her many things regarding Our Lord and the Blessed Virgin.

25	– St. Aldhelm, founder of Malmesbury, then bishop of Sherborne, very devoted to St. Michael. – St. Gregory VII, pope, very devoted to St. Michael.
26	– St. Philip of Neri, preserved from death by his angel, who often visited him during his life, 16th century (Bollandists).
27	– St. Restituta of Sora, Roman virgin, helped at the time of her martyrdom by an angel whom she had requested from God, 3rd century (Bollandists). – St. Mary Magdalene de' Pazzi (see pp. 98-99).
28	– St. Andrew Salus, of Scythian origin, a soldier favored by the angels, whereas he received only ill treatment from men, 10th century (Bollandists).
29	– [Blessed][13] Bona of Pisa. By her prayers, an angel served as a boatman for two religious who had come to visit her, 13th century (Bollandists).
30	– St. Madelgisilus, disciple of St. Fursey. Left the monastery of Centula at an angel's order and had a cell and oratory built in a place the angel indicated to him, 7th century (Bollandists). – [St.][14] Ferdinand, king of León and Castile, defeated the Moors with the help of St. Michael. – Martyrdom of Joan of Arc, [1431].[15]
31	– St. Mechtildis of Edelstetten obtained from her father a tithe of all the property he owned around the monastery in which she lived. Barely had he made this donation when angels were heard chanting, "Amen." 12th century (Bollandists).

June

1	– St. Caprasius, abbot of Lérins, taken to heaven by St. Michael, 5th century (see p. 166). – John Pelingotto.[16] An angel came to him to usher his soul into heaven, 14th century (Bollandists).
2	– St. Erasmus (see p. 135). – St. Peter, exorcist, freed from prison by an angel.

3	– St. Dorotheus recounted to his monks that an angel one day came into a monastery to bless the monks attentive in praying the office, 5th century (Bollandists). – St. Boniface, apostle to Germany, founder of the monasteries in Amöneburg and Ohrdruf dedicated to St. Michael.
6	– St. Philip, one of the first seven deacons, transported by an angel. – St. Euphemia of Ethiopia, very devoted to St. Michael. – St. Norbert, founder of the Premonstratensian Order, very devoted to St. Michael (see p. 193).
9	– St. Primus and St. Felician, brothers and martyrs, freed from prison by an angel (Roman Breviary). – St. Columba, abbot in the [British Isles],[17] favored with familiarity with the angels, [6th][18] century (Bollandists).
11	– St. Barnabas, apostle.
12	– St. Onuphrius, hermit in the Thebaid, received communion from an angel.
13	– St. Anthony of Padua. An angel brought one of his letters to the general of the congregation, 13th century (Bollandists).
14	– St. Basil the Great, doctor, founder of an order having St. Michael as its patron (see pp. 190-91).
15	– St. Vitus, martyr, visited in his prison by an angel (Roman Breviary).
18	– [Blessed][19] Osanna of Mantua, instructed by an angel on the love of heavenly things, [16th][20] century – In 1009, the translation of the body of St. Aubert, founder of Mont Saint-Michel.
19	– Blessed Michelina, widow, patroness of Pesaro, in the Papal States – St. Juliana Falconieri, visited by the angels during her final hour.
20	– St. John of Matera, founder of the Order of St. Michael of Pulsano, worked miracles through the intercession of St. Michael the Archangel.
21	– St. Aloysius Gonzaga. At his prayer, an angel brought to the procurator of the house where he was doing his novitiate the money needed to cover expenses, 16th century (Bollandists).

23	– St. Marie of Oignies often saw Our Lord surrounded by angels at the elevation at Mass (Fr. Faber).
24	– Birth of St. John the Baptist.
25	– St. William of Vercelli, founder of the monastery of Monte Vergine, favored with seeing angels, 12th century (Bollandists).
29	– St. Peter and St. Paul.
30	– Commemoration of St. Paul. – St. Martial of Limoges. Twelve angels assisted him with his apostolic duties (Fr. Henri-Marie Boudon).

July

2	– Visitation of the Blessed Virgin Mary.
4	– St. Ulrich, bishop of Augsburg, assisted by two angels in celebrating Holy Mass prior to his death, 10th century (Bollandists).
5	– St. Michael of the Saints, Discalced Trinitarian.
6	– St. Sisoës. The monks surrounding him at his deathbed heard him conversing with someone they could not see. "They are the angels," he said, "who have come to take me to heaven, and I am asking them to leave me a little longer so that I can do penance." 5th century (Bollandists).
8	– Image of St. Michael miraculously engraved on the right side of the cross commemorating the one which had appeared to St. Procopius of Scythopolis, martyred in [303].[21]
10	– St. Rufina and St. Secunda, martyrs, thrown into the Tiber with a stone fastened to their necks and delivered by an angel.
12	– St. Paternian, bishop of Fano, fed by the angels in a forest to which they had led him to escape persecution by Diocletian, 4th century (Bollandists). – St. John Gualbert, visited by his guardian angel when on his deathbed, 11th century (Bollandists).
13	– St. Stephen the Sabaite. Angels came to visit him and to announce to him his death, 8th century (Bollandists).

14	– St. Henry (see pp. 187-88). – St. Bonaventure, received communion in his youth through an angel, [13th][22] century (Bollandists).
16	– Our Lady of Mount Carmel (Roman martyrology).
17	– St. Leo IV. This pope built a temple to St. Michael at the Vatican to commemorate a victory over the Saracens.
18	– St. Camillus de Lellis, helped by the angels multiple times during his journeys (Roman martyrology).
20	– St. Elijah, prophet, taken up to heaven by the angels on a chariot of fire (Roman martyrology).
21	– St. Victor, martyred in Marseille, delivered from his prison during the night so he could visit and console the sick. – St. Arbogast, eighteenth bishop of Strasbourg. A chapel to St. Michael was built over his burial place (Godescard). – St. Mary Magdalene. The angels announced to her the resurrection of the Savior. – St. Wandrille, abbot. An angel ordered him to leave the mountains of the Vosges.
22	– St. Meneleus. An angel ordered him to restore the monastery of Menat, 8th century (Bollandists). – The Blessed Virgin sent St. Norbert the white habit of his order through the ministry of an angel.
24	– St. Christina, virgin and martyr, thrown into a [lake][23] by her father and saved by St. Michael (James of Voragine). – Blessed Cunegunda, Poor Clare nun, helped in an illness by an angel, 13th century (Bollandists).
25	– St. James the Greater, apostle.
26	– St. Anne, mother of the Blessed Virgin. An angel announced to her that she would give birth to Mary.
28	– St. Samson, bishop of Dol, went to Brittany at the command of an angel, 6th century (Vincent of Beauvais, *Speculum historiale*).
29	– St. Martha, sister of Lazarus.
31	– St. Ignatius, founder of the Jesuits. It was through the help of the angels that he won St. Francis Xavier over to Jesus Christ (Boudon).

August

1	– St. Peter in Chains, freed by an angel (see p. 25).
	– Establishment of the Order of St. Michael by Louis XI, 1469.
	– St. Peregrinus, hermit, told by an angel to expel demons inhabiting a forest in the outskirts of Ancona.
2	– Our Lady of the Angels (or of Portiuncula).
4	– St. Dominic, founder of the Order of Preachers, helped multiple times by the angels (Boudon).
	– St. Santera, virgin and martyr, had built the chapel of Our Lady of Dordrecht, in the Netherlands, at the spot designated to her by an angel.
5	– Consecration of the church of St. Mary of the Angels in Rome by [Pius IV],[24] in the presence of the sacred college and the entire Roman court (see pp. 18-19).
6	– Transfiguration of Our Lord.
8	– Our Lady of Schiedam, in the Netherlands. St. Lidwina often spent entire nights there in prayer, and, according to her biography, had been led there by her good angel.
9	– Blessed John of La Verna, of the [Franciscan][25] Order, instructed by St. Michael.
10	– St. Lawrence, deacon and martyr. The Church puts these words on his lips: "The Lord hath sent His Angel, and hath delivered me out of the midst of the fire, so that I am not scorched."[26]
	– In Cotignac, in Provence, Our Lady of Grace. The Blessed Virgin, accompanied by St. Michael, showed herself to the eyes of a city inhabitant. A temple was built to commemorate this apparition.
12	– St. Porcarius, abbot of Lérins, warned by an angel of the arrival of the Saracens, 8th century (Bollandists).
13	– St. Hippolytus, martyr. Mont Saint-Michel possesses some fragments of his relics.
	– St. Wigbert, abbot of the monastery of St. Michael, near Erfurt, Germany.
14	– Vigil of the Assumption. On this day, the angels were heard near the city of Soissons, chanting, "For thou art happy, O holy

	Virgin Mary, and most worthy of all praise, because from thee arose the sun of justice, Christ our God."
15	– Assumption of the Queen of the Angels. – St. Michael ushers into heaven the soul of St. Arnulf, bishop of Soissons, 1087 (see p. 166).
18	– St. Helena, empress. She had a temple built in honor of the heavenly spirits at the place where it is believed St. Michael appeared to the shepherds.
19	– St. Joachim, father of the Blessed Virgin.
20	– St. Bernard, abbot, doctor of the Church. He taught how to honor the holy guardian angels. He also received angelic revelations multiple times.
21	– St. Humbeline, sister of St. Bernard, foundress of the Bernardines, an order devoted to St. Michael.
22	– St. Symphorian, martyr. A chapel at Mont Saint-Michel was dedicated to him.
23	– St. Philip Benizi, fed by the angels, 13th century (Bollandists).
24	– St. Bartholomew. Pope Constantine sent relics of this apostle to Mont Saint-Michel. – St. Owen, bishop of Rouen; according to legend, an angel brought him "a prayer to say against storms and lightning."
25	– St. Louis, king of France, very devoted to St. Michael (see pp. 187-88).
27	– Our Lady of Beauvoir in Moustiers-Sainte-Marie, eight to ten leagues from Sisteron. This chapel was built by a lord of the region, freed by an angel from infidel captivity. – St. Joseph Calasanz. This saint received visits from angels multiple times.
28	– St. Augustine, bishop of Hippo. He wrote much about the angels.
29	– Beheading of St. John the Baptist.
30	– St. Rose of Lima. Her guardian angel appeared to her frequently.
31	– St. Raymond Nonnatus. At his death, he received communion from the hand of an angel who appeared in the form of a religious of his order.

September

1	– In Germany, on the first Sunday in September, feast of the holy guardian angels, with an octave.
3	– St. Remaclus, bishop of [Maastricht],[27] warned by an angel, instructed St. Trudo on what he should do to arrive at the priesthood, 7th century (Bollandists).
4	– St. Rosalia of Palermo, often visited by the angels.
5	– St. Lawrence Justinian. This holy bishop recommended devotion to St. Michael (see p. 170). – St. Genebald, bishop of Laon. James of Voragine recounts that an angel came to him to inform him that God had pardoned him of a great sin for which he had done penance.
6	– St. Michael appeared to a man of Laodicea and healed his mute daughter. The Eastern Church celebrates this with a great feast day (see pp. 222-23).
7	– St. Regina, virgin and martyr, in the region of Auxois. According to the legend, "the angels, in the presence of everyone, carried the soul of the saint to heaven as they sang God's glory." Between the 3rd and 5th centuries.
8	– Birth of the Queen of the Angels.
9	– Our Lady of Le Puy-en-Velay. The church was consecrated by the angels, according to a revelation made to St. Evodius, of this city.
10	– Death of St. Aubert, founder of Mont Saint-Michel, in 725. – St. Nicholas of Tolentino. Six months prior to his death, this illustrious bishop was hearing angelic concerts every night. His birth was announced by an angel, 13th century (Bollandists).
14	– Exaltation of the Holy Cross.
16	– Martyrdom of Blessed Michael Fimonaya and two companions, [1628].[28] – Healing at Mont Saint-Michel of a man from Quintin who could neither speak nor walk, 1589.
17	– St. Michael appeared to St. Francis of Assisi on Mount Alverna and imprinted him with the stigmata (see pp. 185-87). – St. Helena told by the angels to seek the true Cross.

20	– Beginning of the preparatory novena for the feast of St. Michael. – St. Eustace, martyr. A chapel to him was built near Rome on a high mountain dominating the Sabina region, which is today a St. Michael pilgrimage spot—likely in commemoration of the archangel's apparition to this illustrious martyr. Mont Saint-Michel possessed some fragments of his relics.
21	– St. Matthew, evangelist. Mont Saint-Michel had a tooth of this apostle in its possession.
22	– Giving of the name Mary to Our Lady, by her mother St. Anne, following the revelation of an angel.
24	– St. Gabriel announces the birth of St. John the Baptist.
26	– St. Nilus the Younger. This holy abbot from Calabria established his dwelling in a hermitage adjoining a small chapel to St. Michael. A flourishing community soon grew there.
27	– St. Cosmas and St. Damian. Put on a rack, they were protected by an angel and felt no pain, despite the efforts of the executioners (James of Voragine). – St. Elzear, Count of Ariano and Lord of Puimichel,[29] and [Blessed][30] Delphina, his wife, 14th century.
28	– Vigil of St. Michael.
29	– Dedication of St. Michael the Archangel. – Martyrdom of Michael de Aozaraza

October

1	– St. Remigius of Reims. An angel announced his birth to a hermit (James of Voragine). – On the first Sunday of October, the feast of the Holy Rosary. The Rosary Chapel at Mont Saint-Michael was within the church ambulatory.
2	– The Holy Guardian Angels. How one should celebrate the feast of the holy angels (see p. 88).
4	– St. Francis of Assisi, often visited by the angels and by St. Michael.
5	– St. Galla, Roman widow, favored with angelic visions.

6	– Octave of the Dedication of St. Michael. – St. Bruno, obtained through his prayers that an angel come to the aid of Roger, Count of Calabria and Sicily, 11th century (Bollandists).
8	– St. Bridget, widow, visited by the angels and devoted to St. Michael. – Reform of the Trinitarians implemented by two hermits of St. Michael near Pontoise, 1580.
9	– St. Denis, martyr.[31]
11	– St. Michael Aragave, one of nine principal propagators of the faith in Ethiopia.
12	– St. Michael took to heaven the soul of St. Wilfrid, bishop of York, 709 (see pp. 166-67).
14	– St. Angadresma, virgin and patroness of Beauvais. Her relics repose in the church of St. Michael.
15	– St. Teresa of Avila. She said, "It sometimes pleased Our Lord to favor me with the vision of an angel of wondrous beauty." This was a seraphim who so lovingly wounded her heart. – Death of St. Norgod, bishop of Avranches, who became a monk at Mont Saint-Michel, 1036.
16	– Apparition of St. Michael to St. Aubert. Dedication of the church of Mont Saint-Michel, 709. – St. Anastasius of Cluny, monk of Mont Saint-Michel, later a hermit.
18	– St. Luke, evangelist. Mont Saint-Michel possesses some of his relics.
20	– Death of Countess Ludovica Torelli of Guastalla, foundress of the Angelic Sisters. These religious have a special devotion to St. Michael.
21	– St. Ursula and her companions. An angel made known to her that she would suffer martyrdom with her companions.
22	– St. Melanius, archbishop of Rouen. The angels had him raised to the episcopacy.
23	– St. Ignatius, patriarch of Constantinople. His relics were placed in the church he had had built near the Bosporus in honor of St. Michael, 9th century. – St. Raphael the Archangel.

26	– Apparition of St. Michael to Constantine. – St. Magloire, bishop of Dol, told by an angel to retire into the wilderness.
27	– St. Michael made victorious the arms of Constantine, who entered Rome as conqueror, 312.
28	– St. Simon and St. Jude, apostles.
30	– Blessed Nanterius, abbot of St. Michael's in Lorraine.

November

1	– All Saints' Day. St. Michael ushered them into heaven (see p. 165).
2	– All Souls' Day. St. Michael is the consoler of souls in purgatory (see pp. 168, 173-74).
3	– St. Hubert, of Liège. An angel gave him a stole which drove away demons and healed the possessed. – Our Lady of Port Louis, in Milan. According to tradition, this image one day received the homage of two angels, whom several persons saw bending the knee before it.
4	– St. Vitalis, martyr. An angel showed him the crown he would wear in heaven.
8	– St. Godfrey, bishop of Amiens, founder of St. Michael's Abbey of Doullens.[32]
10	– St. Miles, bishop of Susa, in Persia. By order of this holy bishop, the angel of the Lord struck with paralysis the schismatic Papa, bishop of Ctesiphon. – St. Andrew Avellino conversed with the angels multiple times.
11	– St. Martin, bishop of Tours, visited by the angels multiple times. "He saw angels," says St. Bernard.
13	– St. Stanislaus Kostka. An angel gave him communion shortly before his death. – In 1496, the Order of St. Michael, instituted by King Louis XI, was confirmed by a bull of Pope Alexander VI.
16	– St. Eucherius, bishop of Lyon. An angel made known the place of his retreat in order for him to be elevated to the episcopal see.

19	– St. Elizabeth of Hungary. Shortly before her death, she sang very harmoniously with her guardian angel, who came to announce her eternal joy.
20	– St. Felix of Valois. An angel told him to found the Trinitarian Order. – St. Bernward, bishop of Hildesheim, in Lower Saxony. He was buried in the church of the monastery he had founded in honor of St. Michael, to which he gave all his possessions and where he took the religious habit.
21	– Presentation of the Blessed Virgin Mary. – St. Gelasius I. It was he who instituted in Rome the feast of St. Michael, on the occasion of the Mount Gargano apparition.
22	– St. Cecilia, protected by her angel.
23	– St. Amphilochius of Iconium, was consecrated a bishop by an angel.[33]
25	– St. Catherine, virgin. The angels broke the wheel on which she had been fastened, and transported her body to Mount Sinai (James of Voragine).
28	– The venerable Simeon Metaphrastes. This historian wrote of the numerous miracles worked in Constantinople through the intercession of St. Michael.
30	– St. Andrew, apostle.

December

1	– St. Eligius, bishop of Noyon. Mont Saint-Michel possessed his stole and maniple.
3	– St. Francis Xavier, apostle to the Indies. St. Michael gave him visible marks of protection (see p. 135).
4	– St. Anno, archbishop of Cologne, founder of Michaelsberg Abbey in Siegburg. – St. Barbara, virgin and martyr. Her relics repose in the church of St. Michael's Monastery in Kyiv, she was helped by an angel during her martyrdom (James of Voragine).
6	– St. Nicholas, bishop of Myra. At the time of his death, he saw the angels come to meet him (James of Voragine).

7	– St. Ambrose, doctor of the Church, very devoted to St. Michael. – St. Eutropius, hermit. St. Michael appeared to him (see p. 127).
8	– Immaculate Conception of the Queen of the Angels. An angel had Abbot Helsin, ambassador of William the Conqueror, work to establish this feast (James of Voragine).
10	– The angels transported the holy house of Loretto.
11	– St. Daniel the Stylite, very devoted to St. Michael. His pillar[34] was located near a church of the holy archangel in Constantinople. – Our Lady of the Angels, in the forest of Livry, four leagues from Paris. In 1212, three merchants from Anjou maltreated by thieves invoked the Blessed Virgin, who sent them three angels.
13	– St. Lucy, virgin and martyr. – St. Odilia, abbess in Alsace, devoted to St. Michael.
15	– Octave of the Immaculate Conception.
17	– St. Begga, widow and abbess, foundress of the monastery of Andenne, near Namur. Among the seven churches she had built to commemorate the seven principal churches in Rome, she dedicated one to St. Michael.
21	– St. Thomas, apostle.
25	– Birth of Our Lord Jesus Christ. St. Michael announced Him to the shepherds and to the souls in limbo (see p. 123).
26	– St. Stephen. This illustrious martyr recalled to the Jews the glorious archangel's signs of protection.
27	– St. John the Evangelist. St. Michael appeared to him on the island of Patmos. A chapel was dedicated to him at Mont Saint-Michel.
28	– The Holy Innocents.
29	– St. Thomas Becket, archbishop of Canterbury. According to James of Voragine, the angels interrupted the priests who, at the death of this martyr, were singing the Mass of the Dead, and intoned instead the *Laetabitur justus* from the Mass of a Martyr.

APPENDIX 2:
LIST OF THE MOST ILLUSTRIOUS PILGRIMS WHO HAVE VISITED MONT SAINT-MICHEL.

This list is very far from comprehensive; it can, however, give an idea of what in times past was the great pilgrimage site of Mont Saint-Michel.

Saints

—Around 800, St. Charlemagne, Emperor of the West. (He is given the title of saint in some churches.)
—Between 1040 and 1060, Blessed Lanfranc, founder of the school of Avranches, then monk at Bec Abbey, and finally Archbishop of Canterbury, in England.
—Between 1060 and 1070, St. Anselm, who also spends some time at the school of Avranches, and who dies as Archbishop of Canterbury.
—In 1048, St. Edward, King of England, makes large donations to the Mount, which he visits.
—In 1256, St. Louis, King of France.
—Between 1417 and 1419, St. Vincent Ferrer, who comes at this time to evangelize Brittany.

Bishops

—In 1004, Roland, Archbishop of Dol, earlier a monk of Mont Saint-Michel, receives burial there.
—Between 1023 and 1027, an archbishop of Rouen comes with Richard II, Duke of Normandy.
—In 1030, Jungoneus, Archbishop of Dol, brother of Alan III, Duke of Brittany.

—In 1030, Robert, Archbishop of Rouen.

—In 1156, Hugh, Archbishop of Rouen, accompanied by the bishops Robert of Évreux, Herbert of Avranches, and Richard de Bohun of Coutances, spends four days at the Mount.

—On November 23, 1158, Cardinal Roland, Chancellor of the Roman Church, who on September 7, 1159, will don the papal tiara under the name of Alexander III, and Cardinal Octavian, who will become Antipope Victor IV.

—In 1172, the bishops of England, Normandy, and Brittany come to the Mount following the Council of Avranches, which had been convened by two cardinal legates, Theodinus, the titular cardinal of St. Vitalis, and Albert, cardinal priest of St. Lawrence in Lucina, on the occasion of St. Thomas Becket's murder. Stephen, Abbot of Cluny, and Benedict, Abbot of Sacra di San Michele, accompany them and form a close friendship with the famous Robert de Torigni.

—In 1223, Theobald, Archbishop of Rouen.

—In 1251, Eudes Rigaud, one of the most renowned archbishops of Rouen.

New Era of Pilgrimages

—1865: Mgr. Bravard, Bishop of Coutances, inaugurates a new era of pilgrimages.

—August 1, 1866: Mgr. Bravard, accompanied by Mgr. Lyonnet, Archbishop of Albi, Mgr. de Charbonnel, a Capuchin bishop and former bishop of Toronto, Canada, Mgr. Nogret, Bishop of Saint-Claude, and the abbot of the Trappist monastery in Briquebec come amidst a gathering of over two thousand pilgrims.

—August 1867: Mgr. Bravard and Mgr. Guilbert, Bishop-Elect of Gap, come to officially present the relics sent by His Holiness Pius IX.

—October 16, 1867: The archangel's basilica hosts one of the most illustrious assemblies of prelates to have ever gathered there. His Eminence Cardinal de Bonnechose delivers an eloquent discourse retracing the past of the illustrious abbey. Also present are Mgr.

Dupanloup, Bishop of Orléans, Mgr. Devoucoux, Bishop of Évreux, Mgr. Hugonin, Bishop of Bayeux, Mgr. Bravard, Bishop of Coutances, Mgr. Guilbert, Bishop-Elect of Gap, the abbot of Briquebec, more than three hundred priests, and more than two thousand pilgrims.

—September 29, 1869: Mgr. Delaplace, [Titular] Bishop of Hadrianopolis and Apostolic Vicar to China, comes to offer thanksgiving to the archangel and to ask him for many favors.

Kings of France

—In 711, three years after the founding, Childebert III inaugurates the era of pilgrimages, and paves the way for his successors and all his subjects.

—In 800, Charlemagne, at the height of his power and glory, comes as a humble pilgrim to Mont Saint-Michel to pay homage to the great archangel and to acknowledge him as the special protector of the French people. He has St. Michael's image depicted on his standards.

—November 23, 1158: Louis VII comes with a numerous retinue of prelates, among whom are two cardinals, one archbishop, one bishop, and five abbots.

—1236 and 1256: St. Louis.

—1271: Philip the Bold comes to thank God for having saved him from the pestilence during the siege of Tunis, and for having been able to bring back the holy remains of his father.

—1311: Philip the Fair brings rich offerings of relics and silver. He places twelve hundred ducats on the altar, set aside for making a gold leaf statue of St. Michael.

—1393: Charles VI comes with his entire court.

—1424: Charles VII brings a stone from La Rochelle which had fallen on his head without doing him any harm,[1] something he attributed to "the favor of St. Michael, to whom he was strongly devoted."[2]

—1447: Queen Marie, wife of Charles VII.

—1462: First pilgrimage of Louis XI; he presents a gold St. Michael statue.

—1469: Second pilgrimage of Louis XI; he institutes the knightly Order of St. Michael.

—August 7, 1472: A vow brings Louis XI back for a third time.

—October 25, 1487: Charles VIII arrives at Mont Saint-Michel, "where he [is] a pilgrim and sojourn[s] for three days, making devotions and offerings, and thanking Monseigneur St. Michael, the leader of his Order, for the happy victory that he obtained against his enemies"[3] in Brittany.

—1518: Francis I is magnificently received by Jean de Lamps, the [thirty]-sixth[4] abbot.

—1561: Charles IX, whose reign begins under the most threatening auspices, and his brother Henry, who will bear the crown under the name of Henry III.

—1777: The Count of Artois, later King Charles X, and the Duke of Orléans, later King Louis-Philippe, with his brother and sister.

Kings of England

—Ethelred, between 1017 and 1023 [sic].[5]

—St. Edward, 1048.

—William the Conqueror, recognizing that his greatest victory had taken place on St. Michael's day, makes large donations to the abbey; he makes multiple pilgrimages there, 1085.

—Henry, son of William, pursued by his brothers, takes refuge at the Mount in [1091],[6] withstands a siege there, and leaves surrendering honorably. Becoming king, he returns in 1102 and rewards the protection he had received with magnificent donations.

—Henry II comes a first time, in 1158, with the Bishop of Avranches, and a second time, with the King of France, Louis VII.

—1659: Charles II comes incognito with some lords and knights.

Dukes of Normandy

—Rollo, first Christian duke, 912.

—William Longsword, son of Rollo, makes numerous donations.

—Richard I, tries to make the canons resume their obligations. Seeing that he cannot succeed, and supported by the counsel of the Archbishop of Rouen and the Bishop of Bayeux, he obtains the authorization of the Sovereign Pontiff to replace them with Benedictine monks in [966].[7]

—Geoffrey,[8] son of Richard I, comes in 993 to commend his father's memory to the monks.

—Richard II, the Good, between 1017 and 1023, celebrates at the Mount his marriage to Judith, a princess of Brittany. Having noticed the church's small size, he has work begun on another church, enlarges the Mount's summit, builds the great pillars, and begins the nave, which could not be completed before his death.

—Richard III, 1028 [sic].[9]

—Robert the Magnificent, in 1030, makes peace at Mont Saint-Michel with Alan III, the Duke of Brittany.

—Robert Curthose, Duke of Normandy and son of William the Conqueror, comes with his new wife, Sybil, upon his return from the First Crusade, to thank St. Michael for the protection he received on the battlefields of Palestine, where he was covered in glory.

Dukes of Brittany

—Conan I chooses Mont Saint-Michel as his burial place and is interred in St. Martin's Chapel (March 12, 1004).

—Alan III, in 1030, accompanied by his mother and his brother, the Archbishop of Dol, as well as a numerous retinue, comes on pilgrimage for the first time; he comes a second time to make peace with the Duke of Normandy.

—1450: Francis I, upon his return from capturing Avranches, comes to have a solemn service celebrated for the soul of his brother Gilles, whom he had murdered. As he is leaving, a monk summons him to appear within forty days before the tribunal of God, "which he did not fail to do," the chronicle says, "for, at the end of this time, he died."

***

One also saw a great number of personages, illustrious by virtue of their name or position, including:

—In 1363, the holy prince Charles of Blois comes barefoot from Rennes to bring precious relics.
—In 1624, Charles Gonzaga, Duke of Nevers and of Mantua, promises a painting "in which the devil's fall would be depicted."[10]
—On September 25, 1665, the Duke of Mazarin, Grand Master of Artillery and the king's lieutenant general in Brittany.
—On November 9, 1665, the Duke of Montausier, Governor of Normandy.
—In 1586, the Mount is also visited by the famous historian [Jacques-Auguste] de Thou, who has left us interesting details.
—In 1661, Madame de Sévigné comes with her daughter. "I fondly remember this trip," she wrote thirty years later.

***

We have made known some of the saints who accomplished this St. Michael pilgrimage in past centuries.

It would not be less glorious, for our celebrated mount, to mention the names of those who have sought to sanctify themselves there.

We shall name some of them:
—St. Aubert, Bishop of Avranches and founder of the first religious establishment.
—Blessed Norgod, also Bishop of Avranches, and subsequently a monk of Mont Saint-Michel.
—St. Anastasius, of Cluny:

> This saint was born in Venice at the beginning of the eleventh century. He was schooled in the sciences, in which he made great

progress. Serious reflections on the vanity of the world inspired in him the resolve to pursue perfection. He left his homeland, came to France, and took the habit in the monastery of Mont Saint-Michel. He gained such a reputation for virtue that St. Anselm, the abbot of Bec, wanted to get to know him. Soon his abbot, probably Suppon, was convicted of simony, and Anastasius withdrew to a small neighboring island, Tombelaine, in order to live an eremitical life. Sometime afterward, he yielded to the pleas of Hugh, the abbot of Cluny, who urged him to enter his monastery. Pope Gregory VII then chose him to go preach the faith to certain Muslims in Spain. He later obtained permission to go live in the wilderness and withdrew into the Pyrenees. Three years later, recalled by Cluny's abbot, he left his solitude, but died on the way, in Doydes, in the Diocese of Rieux, around the year 1085. He has been honored in this diocese.

We have a letter from him on the Eucharist, in which he sets forth the dogma on the Real Presence.[11]

—At the same time as Anastasius, there lived at the mount a monk well-known for his virtues, Robert, to whom St. Anselm wrote a beautiful letter asking his friendship:

Valiant and very dear soldier of God, when I consider the progress of your zeal and the sterility of my laziness, I can hardly dare to remind your holiness of our common friendship. And since there is nothing in all the actions of my such tepid life that might amount to the benefit of your friendship, I blush to call myself your friend; but when I see others running with ease to the homeland above, whilst I can barely move on this road, weighed down as I am by my tepidity and sins, I am compelled out of necessity to cry out to those ahead of me, not so that they slow down, but so that through them my slowness might be incited to greater speed. That is why, as my prayers are such that they serve me little or nothing, I dare not tell you of them; but I ask you to please animate them with your own, so that they are of benefit to both you and me. Such is, before God, the prayer that comes from my lips. May all that is useful to me, be so for you as well. Yes, noble and venerable friend... Take care to perfect in me this charity that will be your own...

—Blessed Serlo, first a canon at Avranches, was later a monk at Mont Saint-Michel.

> His fervent piety earned him the position of abbot in Gloucester, England. William of Malmesbury affirms that he was second to no one in integrity of morals and in the prudent direction of souls. Hugh Menard gives him the title of "Blessed" in his Benedictine martyrology.

—Bernard the Venerable, the thirteenth abbot of Mont Saint-Michel (1131-1149).
—Blessed Robert de Torigni, also called Robert du Mont. Dom Huynes writes of him:

> Heaven destined this abbot to shine on this mount, like a sun after so much darkness, like a propitious star after such furious storms, to be the restorer of this abbey, the mirror of prelates, and the ornament of his order, of whose praises the most learned writers of his time took pleasure in writing, especially Stephen, Bishop of Rennes, his great friend and confrere in monastic profession... He was esteemed by popes, cherished by kings, revered by queens, and generally loved by all (1154-1186).

SOME MIRACLES WORKED AT MONT SAINT-MICHEL, ATTESTED TO BY PUBLIC AUTHORITY.

On Saturday, May 4, 1560, a young girl named Thomasse George was brought to this place from the parish of Saint-Sylvain in the Caux region, taken by her relatives Nicolas Barbé and Pierre Mathieuse. She had been vexed multiple times, night and day, by an invisible spirit, which appeared to her on the fourteenth day of April, telling her, "I am the spirit of your father who commands you to make a trip to Mont Saint-Michel, something I had promised to do but did not accomplish. As an assurance, I am closing your hand and fingers, which you will be able to open only after having completed the trip. The wise girl promptly made known what had happened and asked advice from the vicar of the aforementioned parish, the venerable priest master Nicolas le Gros, who was of the opinion that she should devoutly accomplish this trip, and gave her a testimonial letter as a warrant for both the route and Mont Saint-Michel itself. Arriving at Mont Saint-Michel with her hand tightly closed, she recounted all that had happened. As she was having the Mass said and the priest made the final elevation of the Body of Our Lord, her hand opened as easily as if it had never been closed.

Signed,
Provost

***

Another Miracle

On September 16, 1589, Jean Cario of the city of Quintin in Brittany, having a son named Jacques who was struck with such an illness that he could in no way speak or walk, made a vow to bring him to this place; having done so, through the power of God and the intercession of the holy archangel, he returned from here perfectly healed, as prior to the illness.

Signed,
Payen

***

Another Miracle

On January 29, 1595, Guillemette, wife of Jean Le Redde of the parish of Cancale in the Duchy of Brittany, who had been possessed by the devil for an entire year, was brought to this place. After having been confessed, absolved, and exorcised by Master Jacques Payen, Promoter of the Abbey, she was perfectly healed and delivered, as if she had never been possessed.

Signed,
Payen

***

Another Miracle

On July 14, 1594, Jean Tollevast, son of Jacques, of the parish of Saint-Malo de Carneville, in the Diocese of Coutances, was brought by his mother, his brother, and a cousin of his to this place, bound and handcuffed, and horribly tormented by an evil spirit for a period of six weeks. Being well confessed and exorcised by the Promoter, he was fully delivered, leaving his handcuffs tied in front of the image of St. Michael. Everything was done in the presence of honorable and religious persons: Brother Jean Grimoville, Claustral Prior; Brother Gilles Deverdun, Cantor; Brother Olivier de Bardouil, Prior of Saint-Brolade; Brother Charles de St-Pair, Subcantor; and Rolland Léger,

Prior of Chausey, all monks and priests of the aforementioned abbey and mountain.

Additionally, Master Pierre Souflel, Priest; Pierre Herpin, Subdeacon.

Signed,
Payen

APPENDIX 4:
ST. MICHAEL, ANGEL OF BATTLES.

In the fifth part of his *Histoire du Mont-St-Michel*, Fr. Joseph Deschamps recounts an incident appropriate for inclusion in our book. He says:

We read in an article by Monsieur Raudot, published in *Le Correspondant*, that after the death of Henry III, the city of Avallon, in Burgundy, had embraced the side of the Catholic League. On the night of September 28-29, 1591, the city's besiegers, eluding the vigilance of the sentries, placed an explosive charge of more than three hundred pounds of powder in a sewer beneath the main gate, and rushed through the breach created by the explosion. They believed the city captured; but the mayor and the syndic ran to the forefront of the inhabitants. They fought fiercely. The mayor and the syndic were wounded, three inhabitants were killed before their eyes, and the assailants were driven back, leaving two captains dead and two others prisoners. After this setback, Marshal d'Aumont lifted the siege.

One year later, the mayor and aldermen appeared before the canons of the collegiate church of St. Lazarus, and drew up an act in which, after having recalled their victory on St. Michael's feast day of the preceding year, they added:

"Closely considering this entire miraculous affair proceeding from the hand of God alone, all of this city's inhabitants of both sexes thus stand redeemed and freed from the efforts of Satan and his minions, and not desiring to be degraded or reputed ungrateful for this great benefit and new redemption from a shameful and ignominious death which was prepared against the most conspicuous, even everyone, and from the violent taking of women and girls whose dishonor God did not desire; also having firm faith and assurance that, just as long ago when at the siege of those ancient enemies of France, the English—whilst they were positioned before the city of Orléans at the time of Joan the Maiden—the Holy Archangel Monsieur St. Michael, by divine permission, had appeared on that city's bridge and made himself an obstacle to those enemies, likewise did he appear in this city's breach and make himself the bulwark and defender for all this city's leaders and people against the said heretics and their minions; and joining with the intercession and prayers of Monsieur St. Lazarus, patron of this city, these inhabitants have vowed to God that they and their posterity yet to be born shall consecrate this day to God's service, abstaining from all temporal affairs."

The chapter and the city's leaders decided that each year, on St. Michael's feast day, they would have a solemn procession, in which would participate the city's inhabitants, "down to the schoolchildren, two by two, suitably dressed, each having a lit candle, accompanied and led by the head of the college and his subalterns."

NOTES

Translator's Preface

1. Entry no. 4 of "Catalogue des saintes reliques qui se voyent dans le trésor du Mont-Saint-Michel," found on folio 201 of *Travaux de dom Jean HUYNES et pièces diverses sur l'abbaye du Mont-Saint-Michel, 1601-1700* (Bibliothèque nationale de France, Département des Manuscrits, manuscript identification no. "Français 18947," digitally accessed in October 2021 from gallica.bnf.fr).—Trans.
2. Soyer was born on July 1, 1840, in Saint-James, in France's Manche department. This is according to N.-N. Oursel, *Nouvelle biographie normande* (Paris: Alphonse Picard, 1886), 1:491.—Trans.
3. Letter of Bishop Bravard, included in the front matter of this book.—Trans.

Letter of Bishop Jean-Pierre Bravard

1. Mont Saint-Michel and its abbey had only recently reopened to the public. It functioned as a prison from 1793 to 1863.—Trans.

Author's Preface

1. Turning tables move to the right or to the left, spin, stand on command on one or two feet, knock the number of times requested, etc. Talking boards [also known as Ouija boards—Trans.] point to letters of the alphabet and thereby give answers to questions asked them. Medium writers are persons writing involuntarily under the impulsion of the spirits whose instruments they are. Medium conjurers obtain from the spirits more surprising phenomena: ghostly apparitions, articulate sounds, spontaneous writings, stiffness and insensitivity of all body parts, etc. The phenomenon of medium healers is one of a thousand means that increasingly hastens the triumph of spiritualism, for there is no one who does not value their health. The demons, Tertullian says, give illnesses in order to heal them later.
2. *Letter 102*, para.19. English translation by J. G. Cunningham, as found in *Letters of Saint Augustine, Bishop of Hippo,* ed. Philip Schaff (Buffalo, NY: The Christian Literature Co., 1886), 1:419.—Trans.
3. *Growth in Holiness, or The Progress of the Spiritual Life* (London: Thomas Richardson and Son, 1860), 189n.—Trans.
4. See Translator's Preface remarks concerning Pseudo-Dionysius the Areopagite.—Trans.
5. It is a "guide" in the sense that it informs the reader of the glorious history of the site as a whole, not a detailed map like one might pick up at a museum entrance.—Trans.

Part 1, Chapter 1

1. See Rom 1:20.—Trans.
2. Pseudo-Dionysius the Areopagite, *Celestial Hierarchy*, ch. 4.—Trans.

3. Joseph Addison writes, "Several of the French, Italian and English poets have given a loose to their imaginations in the description of angels: But I do not remember to have met with any so finely drawn, and so conformable to the notions which are given of them in Scripture, as this in Milton" (*The Spectator*, March 15, 1712). Let us cite two examples from John Milton's *Paradise Lost*:

> *"...[H]e soon*
> *Saw within ken a glorious Angel stand,*
> *The same whom John saw also in the sun:*
> *His back was turned, but not his brightness hid;*
> *Of beaming sunny rays a golden tiar*
> *Circled his head, nor less his locks behind*
> *Illustrious on his shoulders fledge with wings...*
> *And now a stripling Cherub he appears,*
> *Not of the prime, yet such as in his face*
> *Youth smiled celestial, and to every limb*
> *Suitable grace diffused, so well he feigned:*
> *Under a coronet his flowing hair*
> *In curls on either cheek played; wings he wore*
> *Of many a coloured plume, sprinkled with gold;*
> *His habit fit for speed succinct, and held*
> *Before his decent steps a silver wand."*

Elsewhere, the poet depicts Raphael as a seraphim:

> *"Six wings he wore, to shade*
> *His lineaments divine; the pair that clad*
> *Each shoulder broad, came mantling o'er his breast*
> *With regal ornament; the middle pair*
> *Girt like a starry zone his waist, and round*
> *Skirted his loins and thighs with downy gold*
> *And colours dipt in Heaven; the third his feet*
> *Shadowed from either heel with feathered mail,*
> *Sky-tinctured grain. Like Maia's son he stood,*
> *And shook his plumes, that heavenly fragrance filled*
> *The circuit wide.*

4. "Sermon pour la profession de quelques religieuses de la Visitation," *Œuvres complètes de Saint François de Sales, évêque et prince de Genève*, 5th ed. (Paris, Louis Vivès, 1872), 5:439-40.—Trans.

5. *Summa Theologica,* trans. Fathers of the English Dominican Province (London: Burns Oates & Washbourne, 1922), II-II, q. 180, a. 6, ad. 2.—Trans.

6. See *Summa Theologica,* I, q. 50, a. 1, ad. 2.—Trans.

7. See *Summa Theologica,* I, q. 55, a. 1.—Trans.

8. *Summa Theologica,* trans. Fathers of the English Dominican Province (London: Burns Oates & Washbourne, 1922), I, q. 58, a. 5.—Trans.

9. René François Rohrbacher, *Histoire universelle de l'Église catholique*, 3rd ed. (Paris: Gaume Frères, 1857), 5:50. This passage is derived from Pseudo-Dionysius the Areopagite's *Ecclesiastical Hierarchy*, ch. 1.—Trans.

10. English translation of the original Latin by M. R., as found in *St. Anselm's Book of Meditations and Prayers* (London: Burns & Oates, 1872), 169.—Trans.

Part 1, Chapter 3

1. *Summa Theologica*, I, q. 108, a. 1.—Trans.
2. *Summa Theologica*, trans. Fathers of the English Dominican Province (London: Burns Oates & Washbourne, 1922), I, q. 108, a. 1.—Trans.
3. Aquinas addresses the differences in Gregory's and Dionysius's ordering of the Principalities and Virtues in *Summa Theologica*, I, q. 108, a. 6.—Trans.

Part 1, Chapter 5

1. Jean-Joseph Gaume, *Traité du Saint-Esprit* (Paris: Gaume Frères et J. Duprey, 1864), 1:171.—Trans.
2. Only three of these names are recognized by the Church: St. Michael ("Who is like God?"), St. Gabriel ("strength of God"), and St. Raphael ("medicine of God"). St. Michael is portrayed trampling Lucifer underfoot; in his left hand, he holds a green palm, and in his right, a lance at the end of which is a flag white as snow, with an incarnadine cross in the middle. St. Gabriel carries a torch in his right hand; in his left hand, he displays a green jasper mirror with various color markings. St. Raphael presents a fish in his left hand and, with his right, leads the young Tobias. St. Boniface says the names of the other four angels were not publicly recognized by the Church in the council held in Rome under Pope Zachary. However, they are named according to certain traditions and private revelations. Uriel ("fire or torch of God") is mentioned in the third and fourth books of Esdras; Christian art represents him holding a drawn sword in his right hand, with his left hand surrounded by flames. Sealtiel ("prayer of God") is depicted with his face and eyes modestly lowered, his hands joined and pressed against his chest in the attitude of a suppliant. Jehudiel ("sting of God") appears in pictures holding a gold crown in his right hand and a whip of three black cords in his left. Finally, Barachiel ("blessing of God") is represented with a cloak strewn with white roses.
3. Frederick William Faber, *The Blessed Sacrament, or The Works and Ways of God* (London: Richardson and Son, 1855), 512.—Trans.
4. Jean-Joseph Gaume, *Traité du Saint-Esprit* (Paris: Gaume Frères et J. Duprey, 1864), 1:173-74.—Trans.
5. Found in Jacques-Bénigne Bossuet, *Élévations sur les mystères* [*Elevations on the Mysteries*], week 23, elevation 5. The book in turn cites the following biblical verses for this passage: Ps 102:20-21 [103:20-21], Dn 3:58-61, Ps 148:2, and Jb 9:13.—Trans.
6. No further source information identified.—Trans.

Part 1, Chapter 6

1. *De diversis quaestionibus LXXXIII*, q. 79.—Trans.
2. Jean-Joseph Gaume, *Traité du Saint-Esprit* (Paris: Gaume Frères et J. Duprey, 1864), 1:40. Gaume cites St. Thomas's *Summa Theologica*, I, q. 110, aa. 1-3. Both St. Augustine's and St. Gregory's quotes within this passage are collocated in St.

Thomas's *Summa Theologica*, I, q. 110, a. 1, and ultimately come from their *De Trinitate* iii, 4 and *Dialogues* iv, 6, respectively. The English translations for Augustine's and Gregory's words are those of the Fathers of the English Dominican Province, as found in the 1922 edition of the *Summa Theologica* published in London by Burns Oates & Washbourne.—Trans.

3. English translation from the original Greek by Frederick Crombie, as found in Alexander Roberts and James Donaldson, eds., *The Ante-Nicene Fathers: Translations of the Writings of the Fathers down to A.D. 325* (New York: Charles Scribner's Sons, 1905), 4:650-51.—Trans.

4. Also of this opinion are St. Justin, Athenagoras, Theodoret, Clement of Alexandria, St. Gregory Nazianzen, Eusebius of Caesarea, St. Jerome, St. Hilary, St. Ambrose, St. John Chrysostom, St. Cyril, St. Gregory, and St. John Damascene.

5. *De diversis quaestionibus LXXXIII*, q. 79.—Trans.

6. English translation of the original Latin by Arthur West Haddan from *On the Trinity*, bk. III, ch. IX, as found in Philip Schaff, ed., *A Select Library of the Nicene and Post-Nicene Fathers of the Christian Church, First Series* (Buffalo, NY: Christian Literature Publishing Co., 1887), 3:63.—Trans.

Part 1, Chapter 7

1. English translation of the original Spanish by Fiscar Marison, as found in Mary of Agreda, *City of God* (Chicago: The Theopolitan, 1914), 4:396.—Trans.

2. Ibid., 4:488.—Trans.

3. Jacques-Bénigne Bossuet, *Explication de l'Apocalypse*, preface, sec. 37.—Trans.

4. Origen cites *The Shepherd of Hermas* as a divinely inspired book, and Rufinus expressly calls it a book of the New Testament. Clement of Alexandria was of the same sentiment. St. Irenaeus, when citing *The Shepherd*, calls it "Scripture;" thus, some have concluded he truly considered it canonical. Lardner has proved that St. Irenaeus used the word "scripture" here in the sense of "writing" or "book."

5. This quoted phrase is an English translation from the Greek by Charles H. Hoole, as found in Hermas, *The Shepherd of Hermas* (London: Rivingtons, 1870), 17.—Trans.

6. The number of saints protected and visited by the angels is incalculable. The *Calendar of St. Michael and the Holy Angels* placed at the end of this book [in Appendix 1] makes known some of them.

Part 1, Chapter 8

1. This English translation is derived from the Septuagint rather than the normally cited Douay-Rheims Bible. See also note 3 below.—Trans.

2. [John Brande Morris, *An Essay Towards the Conversion of Learned and Philosophical Hindus* (London: J. G. F. & J. Rivington, 1843), 82-83.—Trans.] It is worth noting that among the Persians there were officers called the king's "eyes." It was probably only a pagan mimicry based on some tradition. We see that there were seven principal counselors from the time of Ezra.

3. This English translation of Dt 32:8 is derived from the Septuagint and is that found in the 1907 edition of *The Catholic Encyclopedia*, s.v. "angel." The normally cited

Douay-Rheims Bible reads instead, "When the Most High divided the nations, when he separated the sons of Adam: he appointed the bounds of people according to the number of the children of Israel."—Trans.

4. No further source information identified.—Trans.

5. English translation of the Greek by A. E. Taylor, as found in Plato, *The Laws of Plato* (London: J. M. Dent & Sons Ltd., 1934), 97.—Trans.

6. John Brande Morris. *An Essay Towards the Conversion of Learned and Philosophical Hindus* (London: J. G. F. & J. Rivington, 1843), 22.—Trans.

7. English translation is a relay of the French translation of the Greek used by Soyer. Though the specific work is not cited in the French edition, it is evidently from Eusebius's *The Proof of the Gospel*, bk. 4, ch. 8.—Trans.

Part 1, Chapter 9

1. Found in Émile Bougaud, *Histoire de Sainte Chantal et des origines de la Visitation*, 2nd ed., (Paris: Madame Veuve Poussielgue-Rusand, 1863), 1:308-09.—Trans.

2. The rite of *Asperges* occurs before the principal Sunday Mass in the traditional Roman rite.—Trans.

3. St. Francis de Sales, *An Introduction to the Devout Life*, part 2, ch. 16.—Trans.

Part 1, Chapter 10

1. There are Church Fathers who claimed the guardian angels were sent to the faithful only.

2. No further source information identified.—Trans.

3. St. Jerome, *Commentary on Matthew*, verse 18:10. This is the direct English translation of the Latin as quoted in St. Thomas Aquinas, *Summa Theologica*, trans. Fathers of the English Dominican Province (London: Burns Oates & Washbourne, 1922), I, q. 113, a. 2, s.c.; exclamation point is Soyer's.—Trans.

4. No further source information identified.—Trans.

5. Ditto.—Trans.

6. Soyer does not identify the specific text of St. Jerome. The analogy of a mother bearing a child to a tree bearing fruit to argue for the appointment of a guardian angel at birth is also used by Aquinas in *Summa Theologica*, I, q. 113, a. 5, ad. 3.—Trans.

7. No further source information identified.—Trans.

8. Found in "Sermon pour la fête des saints anges gardiens," in *Œuvres complètes de Bossuet* (Besançon: Outhenin-Chalandre Fils, 1836), 2:355.—Trans.

9. Henri-Marie Boudon, *La dévotion aux neuf chœurs des saints anges*, treatise 1, motive 9.—Trans.

10. Here is what Boudon writes on this subject in his book *La dévotion aux neuf chœurs des saints anges* [in treatise 2, practice 10]: "Fr. de Coret of the Society of Jesus... recounts two very remarkable stories. He says that a soul, suffering in purgatory, learned from its good angel that a child had been born who would one day be a priest and get it out of this place of pain, through the first sacrifice of the mass he would offer to God. He added... that in the year 1634, in the city of Vienna, Austria, three other souls appeared to a Jesuit, telling him that their good

angels had brought to them, in the flames of purgatory, the news of the day of his birth, assuring them that someday he would be their liberator. St. Teresa [of Avila] wrote that she had had a revelation that the soul of one of her benefactors would be released from purgatory on the day that the first mass would be said in one of her houses, which greatly hurried her to work for the completion of this house, knowing that this soul would still burn there until the holy sacrifice of the mass could be celebrated in it. I leave you to reflect on what these revelations might give you, if you have a little light; there are a number of things of great benefit to notice in them."

11. St. Augustine, in his writing *On Care to Be Had for the Dead*, mentions apparitions of dead persons left without burial who come to make known to the living the places where their bodies lie, telling them to take care to give them the burial of which they were deprived. This doctor says he is inclined to attribute these apparitions to "angelic operations." If the dead know something happening here below, if the martyrs or the saints come to help us, it is, St. Augustine thinks, through the mediation of angels.

12. Jacques-Bénigne Bossuet, *Sermon pour la fête des saints anges gardiens*. [Found in *Œuvres complètes de Bossuet* (Besançon: Outhenin-Chalandre Fils, 1836), 2:356-57.—Trans.]

Part 1, Chapter 11

1. This passage is evidence of Jewish belief in guardian angels.

Part 1, Chapter 12

1. Found in Jacques-Bénigne Bossuet, "Sermon pour la fête des saints anges gardiens," in *Œuvres de Bossuet* (Versailles: J. A. Lebel, 1816), 16:397.—Trans.

2. The law, he says, was given by the angels (Gal 3:19). St. Augustine says about this passage: "The Apostle distinguishes the promulgation of the New Law from the promulgation of the Old Law..., he explicitly states that the prodigies and voices of Sinai were the work of angels."

3. The same doctor says elsewhere that the glorious privilege of representing God has been reserved to the Seraphim.

4. From bk. 3, ch. 11; relay translation of the French.—Trans.

5. Pseudo-Dionysius the Areopagite, *Celestial Hierarchy*, ch. 4; relay translation of the French.—Trans.

6. Ibid.—Trans.

7. Why a cherubim and not another angel? Watching and seeing from afar are the two qualities of a sentinel. The cherubim possess these two qualities to a supereminent degree.

8. These quotation marks have been carried over from the original French version, but the text between them appears in part to be a juxtaposition of 1 Thessalonians 4:15 and Matthew 16:17 rather than a direct quote from St. Paul.—Trans.

9. These quotation marks have been carried over from the original French version. The passage is evidently quoting non-sequentially from Matthew 13:41-42, 49-50.—Trans.

Part 1, Chapter 13

1. The Prophet calls them the *gods of the nations*; the Son of God says *the prince of this world*; and St. Paul, in another place, says *the ruler of darkness.* [2 Corinthians 4:4 speaks of "the god of this world" in the singular rather than plural, and Ephesians 6:12 says "the rulers of the world of this darkness."—Trans.]

2. English translation of the Latin by William Reeve as found in *The Apology of Tertullian and The Meditations of the Emperor Marcus Aurelius Antoninus* (London: Griffith Farran Okeden & Welsh, 1889), 69-70.—Trans.

3. See 1 Pt 5:8.—Trans.

4. Found in "L'Esprit de Nicole sur les vérités de la religion," in *Démonstrations évangéliques*, ed. J.-P. Migne (Paris: J.-P. Migne, 1843), 3:1052-53.—Trans.

5. Milton portrayed Satan in this form [in *Paradise Lost*]:

    "*Thus Satan, talking to his nearest mate,*
    With head uplift above the wave, and eyes
    That sparkling blazed; his other parts besides
    Prone on the flood, extended long and large,
    Lay floating many a rood, in bulk as huge
    As whom the fables name of monstrous size,
    Titanian or Earth-born, that warred on Jove,
    Briareos or Typhon, whom the den
    By ancient Tarsus held, or that sea-beast
    Leviathan, which God of all his works
    Created hugest that swim th' ocean-stream.
    Him, haply slumbering on the Norway foam,
    The pilot of some small night-foundered skiff,
    Deeming some island, oft, as seamen tell,
    With fixed anchor in his scaly rind,
    Moors by his side under the lee, while night
    Invests the sea, and wished morn delays.
    So stretched out huge in length the Arch-fiend lay,
    Chained on the burning lake; nor ever thence
    Had risen, or heaved his head, but that the will
    And high permission of all-ruling Heaven
    Left him at large to his own dark designs,
    That with reiterated crimes he might
    Heap on himself damnation, while he sought
    Evil to others, and enraged might see
    How all his malice served but to bring forth
    Infinite goodness, grace, and mercy, shewn
    On Man by him seduced, but on himself
    Treble confusion, wrath, and vengeance poured.
    Forthwith upright he rears from off the pool
    His mighty stature; on each hand the flames
    Driven backward slope their pointing spires, and rolled
    In billows, leave i' th' midst a horrid vale.
    Then with expanded wings he steers his flight

Aloft, incumbent on the dusky air,
That felt unusual weight;"

— [Jean-Joseph] Gaume states, "How many holy founders of churches do we not see obligated to begin, upon arrival at their mission, by fighting a dragon; but a dragon of flesh and bones! In Brittany, it is St. Armel, St. Tudwal, St. Efflam, St. Brieuc, and St. Paul Aurelian. Rome, Paris, Tarascon, Avignon, Périgueux, Le Mans, and I do not know how many places in Scotland and elsewhere were witnesses to the same combat. Still today, is it not against the worshipped dragon or serpent that our missionaries in Africa must fight?" [Quote found in *Traité du Saint-Esprit* (Paris: Gaume Frères et J. Duprey, 1864), 1:186-87.—Trans.]

6. The Persians, Medes, Babylonians, Phoenicians, and Egyptians worshipped a serpent [called] *great God, supreme God, father of laws,* and *oracle of wisdom.* One finds the solemn worship of the serpent in Greece: in Athens, Epirus, Delos, and Delphi. Italy, as well as northern peoples, also gave it worship. Today still, in India, there are temples erected in its honor. As beneath the burning sun of Africa, serpent worship exists in our day in the snows of Manchuria.

7. Soyer is possibly referring obliquely to verses such as Matthew 13:4, 19 and Revelation 18:2.—Trans.

8. [In *Paradise Lost*,] Milton admirably depicts this:
"About them [Adam and Eve] round
A lion now he stalks with fiery glare;
Then as a tiger, who by chance hath spied
In some purlieu two gentle fawns at play,
Straight couches close, then, rising, changes oft
His couchant watch, as one who chose his ground,
Whence rushing, he might surest seize them both,
Griped in each paw."

9. Satan is also called in Scripture Belial, Mammon, Moloch, and Beelzebub. The English poet [John Milton, in his *Paradise Lost*,] portrayed him under each of these names:
A. Belial: *"Belial came last; than whom a Spirit more lewd*
Fell not from Heaven, or more gross to love
Vice for itself. To him no temple stood
Or altar smoked; yet who more oft than he
In temples and at altars, when the priest
Turns atheist, as did Eli's sons, who filled
With lust and violence the house of God?
In courts and palaces he also reigns,
And in luxurious cities, where the noise
Of riot ascends above their loftiest towers,
And injury and outrage; and, when night
Darkens the streets, then wander forth the sons
Of Belial, flown with insolence and wine...
A fairer person lost not Heaven; he seemed
For dignity composed, and high exploit.
But all was false and hollow; though his tongue

Dropped manna, and could make the worse appear
The better reason, to perplex and dash
Maturest counsels: for his thoughts were low—
To vice industrious, but to nobler deeds
Timorous and slothful."

B. Mammon: *"Mammon led them on—*
Mammon, the least erected Spirit that fell
From Heaven; for even in Heaven his looks and thoughts
Were always downward bent, admiring more
The riches of heaven's pavement, trodden gold,
Than aught divine or holy else enjoyed
In vision beatific. By him first
Men also, and by his suggestion taught,
Ransacked the centre, and with impious hands
Rifled the bowels of their mother Earth
For treasures better hid."

C. Moloch: *"First, Moloch, horrid king, besmeared with blood*
Of human sacrifice, and parents' tears;
Though, for the noise of drums and timbrels loud,
Their children's cries unheard that passed through fire
To his grim idol. Him the Ammonite
Worshiped in Rabba and her watery plain,
In Argob and in Basan, to the stream
Of utmost Arnon. Nor content with such
Audacious neighbourhood, the wisest heart
Of Solomon he led by fraud to build
His temple right against the temple of God
On that opprobrious hill...
Moloch, sceptred king,
Stood up—the strongest and the fiercest Spirit
That fought in Heaven, now fiercer by despair.
His trust was with th' Eternal to be deemed
Equal in strength."

D. Beelzebub: *"[W]ith grave*
Aspect he [Beelzebub] rose, and in his rising seemed
A pillar of state. Deep on his front engraven
Deliberation sat, and public care;
And princely counsel in his face yet shone,
Majestic, though in ruin...
War hath determined us and foiled with loss
Irreparable; terms of peace yet none
Vouchsafed or sought; for what peace will be given
To us enslaved, but custody severe,
And stripes and arbitrary punishment
Inflicted? and what peace can we return,
But, to our power, hostility and hate,

Untamed reluctance, and revenge, though slow,
Yet ever plotting how the Conqueror least
May reap his conquest, and may least rejoice
In doing what we most in suffering feel?...
Thither [the world of man] let us bend all our thoughts, to learn
What creatures there inhabit, of what mould
Or substance, how endued, and what their power
And where their weakness: how attempted best,
By force of subtlety. Though Heaven be shut,
And Heaven's high Arbitrator sit secure
In his own strength, this place may lie exposed,
The utmost border of his kingdom, left
To their defence who hold it: here, perhaps,
Some advantageous act may be achieved
By sudden onset—either with Hell-fire
To waste his whole creation, or possess
All as our own, and drive, as we were driven,
The puny habitants; or, if not drive,
Seduce them to our party, that their God
May prove their foe, and with repenting hand
Abolish his own works. This would surpass
Common revenge, and interrupt his joy
In our confusion, and our joy upraise
In his disturbance..."
Milton adds: *"[F]or whence,*
But from the author of all ill, could spring
So deep a malice, to confound the race
Of mankind in one root, and Earth with Hell
To mingle and involve, done all to spite
The great Creator?"

What a picture! It is indeed the spirit of darkness, such as he appears to us in Scripture and in history!

10. Soyer does not identify the theologian he is quoting here; however, Mgr. Jean-Joseph Gaume also quotes this entire passage in his *Traité du Saint-Esprit* (Paris: Gaume Frères et J. Duprey, 1864), 1:59-60, and attributes it to the "great Spanish theologian Viguiero." Regarding the biblical passage at the end of the quote from Isaiah 14:13-14, Soyer omitted verse 14 from his quotation of Viguiero in the original French version of this book, but it has been included here.—Trans.

11. *Summa Theologica*, trans. Fathers of the English Dominican Province (London: Burns Oates & Washbourne, 1922), I, q. 64, a. 4.—Trans.

Part 1, Chapter 14
1. See *Summa Theologica,* I, q. 109, a. 1.—Trans.
2. *Summa Theologica,* trans. Fathers of the English Dominican Province (London: Burns Oates & Washbourne, 1922), I, q. 109, a. 2, ad. 3.—Trans.
3. *Conference 8*, ch. 12. [This is a relay translation from the French.—Trans.]

4. Jacques-Bénigne Bossuet, "Sur les démons," in *Œuvres de Bossuet* (Paris: Firmin Didot Frères, 1847), 2:345.—Trans.
5. *Summa Theologica,* trans. Fathers of the English Dominican Province (London: Burns Oates & Washbourne, 1922), I, q. 109, a. 4, ad. 1.
6. Jean-Joseph Gaume, *Traité du Saint-Esprit* (Paris: Gaume Frères et J. Duprey, 1864), 1:215.—Trans.
7. Relay translation from the French. Jean-Joseph Gaume, who also quotes this passage in his *Traité du Saint-Esprit*, cites these words of Porphyry from Eusebius of Caesarea's *Praeparatio evangelica*, bk. 4, ch. 22.—Trans.

Part 1, Chapter 15
1. The following nine verses have a correlation (some more directly than others) to the nine kinds of spirits listed, respectively: Lv 20:27, Nm 5:14, 1 Sm 16:14, 1 Kgs 22:23, Ps 10:7 [11:6], Sir 39:33, Rv 18:13, Mk 5:13, and Lk 13:11. Perhaps these are among the verses Soyer has in mind.—Trans.
2. See Is 13:21-22 and 34:11-15. The Douay-Rheims translation instead has "hairy ones" and "ericius" for "satyrs" and "hedgehog," respectively.—Trans.
3. See Ps 90:13 [91:13].—Trans.
4. *De baptismo*, ch. 5.—Trans.
5. Eusebius of Caesarea, *Praeparatio evangelica*, bk. 4, ch. 23.—Trans.
6. The unnamed writer is Mgr. Jean-Joseph Gaume. This remark of his is found in his *Traité du Saint-Esprit* (Paris: Gaume Frères & J. Duprey, 1864), 1:219.—Trans.
7. From St. Augustine's *De civitate Dei,* bk. 21, ch. 6, as quoted by St. Thomas Aquinas and found in *Summa Theologica*, trans. Fathers of the English Dominican Province (London: Burns Oates & Washbourne, 1922), I, q. 115, a. 5, ad. 3.—Trans.
8. See *Summa Theologica*, I, q. 117, a. 4, ad. 2 and I, q. 89, a. 8, ad. 2.—Trans.
9. See for instance *Summa Theologica*, II-II, q. 165, a. 2, ad. 3.—Trans.
10. See Tertullian's *Apologeticus*, ch. 23.—Trans.
11. Found in "L'Esprit de Nicole sur les vérités de la religion," in *Démonstrations évangéliques*, ed. J.-P. Migne (Paris: J.-P. Migne, 1843), 3:1052.—Trans.
12. St. Gregory says: "You see that one and the same spirit is both called the Lord's spirit and an evil spirit; the Lord's, that is, by the concession of just power, but evil, by the desire of an unjust will." [The English translation of this quote is that found in St. Gregory the Great, *Morals on the Book of Job*, trans. Members of the English Church (Oxford: John Henry Parker, 1844), 1:80.—Trans.]

Part 1, Chapter 16
1. *De patientia*.—Trans.
2. Inspired by a passage from St. Athanasius's *Life of St. Anthony*, the quoted words are actually Mgr. Jean-Joseph Gaume's and found in his *Traité du Saint-Esprit* (Paris: Gaume Frères et J. Duprey, 1864), 1:258.—Trans.
3. See Jude 1:9.—Trans.
4. Source not identified.—Trans.
5. Ditto.—Trans.

6. Ditto.—Trans.
7. St. Jerome expresses the same opinion.
8. May God deign to impress these reflections deep in the hearts of spouses, fathers, and mothers!
9. Christian mothers will gladly read this passage filled with consoling truths.
10. English translation of the original Spanish by Fiscar Marison, as found in Mary of Agreda, *City of God* (Chicago: The Theopolitan, 1914), 4:266-73.—Trans.
11. Ibid., 4:275-77.—Trans.
12. The author of *The Spiritual Combat* [Dom Lorenzo Scupoli.—Trans.].
13. Anonymous English translation of the Italian as found in Laurence Scupoli, *The Spiritual Combat, Together With The Supplement and The Path of Paradise* (London: Rivingtons, 1890), 51-52.—Trans.

Part 1, Chapter 17
1. *Of the High Veneration Man's Intellect Owes to God.*
2. Jacques-Bénigne Bossuet, *Élévations sur les mystères* [*Elevations on the Mysteries*], week 4, elevation 1.
3. *Treatise on the Love of God*, bk. 2, ch. 7.
4. Frederick William Faber, *The Blessed Sacrament, or The Works and Ways of God* (London: Richardson and Son, 1855), 436-37.—Trans.
5. Soyer does not identify the work from which this quote comes, but it is presumably from *On the Cosmos*, whose authorship by Apuleius is disputed. The English version provided here is a relay translation from the French version quoted by Soyer. For a direct Greek to English translation, which varies substantially from the French text and is less explicit in making Soyer's point, see Aristotle, *On Sophistical Refutations. On Coming-to-be and Passing Away. On the Cosmos.*, trans. E. S. Forster and D. J. Furley (Cambridge, MA: Harvard University Press, 1955), 387-97.—Trans.
6. M. le Vicomte de Chateaubriand, *Génie du christianisme, ou Beautés de la religion chrétienne*, 7th ed. (Paris: Le Normant, 1822), 2:278-80; italics in the original.—Trans.

Part 1, Chapter 18
1. No further source information identified.—Trans.
2. English translation of the original Spanish by Fiscar Marison, as found in Mary of Agreda, *City of God* (Chicago: The Theopolitan, 1914), 4:582-83.—Trans.
3. Found in Jacques-Bénigne Bossuet, "Troisième sermon pour la fête de la Conception de la Sainte Vierge," in *Œuvres de Bossuet* (Versailles: J. A. Lebel, 1816), 15:73.—Trans.
4. No further source information identified.—Trans.
5. This is the English version found in *The New Roman Missal* (New York: Benziger Brothers, 1942). The italics is Soyer's emphasis.—Trans.
6. This is the direct English translation of the Classical Armenian, as found in *The Armenian Liturgy Translated into English* (Venice: Armenian Monastery of St. Lazarus, 1867), 18.—Trans.
7. Ibid., 23.—Trans.

8. Ibid., 28, hymn for Palm Sunday.—Trans.
9. Ibid., 29, hymn for the Ascension.—Trans.
10. Corrected to "priest" from the French edition's "deacon" to reflect the instructions found in *The Divine Liturgies of Our Fathers among the Saints John Chrysostom and Basil the Great with That of the Presanctified Preceded by the Hesperinos and the Orthros*, ed. by J. N. W. B. Robertson (London: David Nutt, 1894), 253—Trans.
11. This is the direct English translation of the Greek, as found in *The Divine Liturgies of Our Fathers among the Saints John Chrysostom and Basil the Great with That of the Presanctified Preceded by the Hesperinos and the Orthros*, ed. by J. N. W. B. Robertson (London: David Nutt, 1894), 253.—Trans.
12. This quote is a relay translation from the original French edition of this book. The corresponding text does not appear in the elsewhere cited *The Armenian Liturgy Translated into English.*—Trans.
13. This is the direct English translation of the Classical Armenian, as found in *The Armenian Liturgy Translated into English* (Venice: Armenian Monastery of St. Lazarus, 1867), 36-37.—Trans.
14. Ibid., 37-38.—Trans.
15. [Ibid., 48.—Trans.] Hagiology for Christmas Day, the Annunciation, and the Assumption.
16. [Ibid., 48.—Trans.] Hagiology for Maundy Thursday.
17. [Ibid., 56.—Trans.] Hymn deacon in Armenian Church sings [on certain feast days] prior to the Sanctus.
18. Ibid., 53-56.—Trans.
19. This is the direct English translation of the Greek, as found in *The Divine Liturgies of Our Fathers among the Saints John Chrysostom and Basil the Great with That of the Presanctified Preceded by the Hesperinos and the Orthros*, ed. by J. N. W. B. Robertson (London: David Nutt, 1894), 355.—Trans.
20. Ibid., 313.—Trans.
21. Guillaume Durand, *Rationale divinorum officiorum*. [English is relay translation of Charles Barthélemy's Latin to French translation in *Rational, ou Manuel des divins offices* (Paris: Louis Vivès, 1854), 3:61.—Trans.]
22. Gilbert Grimaud, *La liturgie sacrée.*

Part 1, Chapter 19
1. The Latin Vulgate and its Douay-Rheims English translation mention this angel in Judith 13:20.—Trans.
2. *Introduction to the Devout Life*, part 2, ch. 16.
3. Jacques-Bénigne Bossuet, *Explication de la Messe*, ch. 38.—Trans.
4. From the Roman Breviary's prayers for a journey.
5. This is the English version found in *The New Roman Missal* (New York: Benziger Brothers, 1942).—Trans.
6. Ibid.—Trans.
7. Ibid.—Trans.

8. Prayer for the feast of St. Michael. [This is the English version found in *The New Roman Missal* (New York: Benziger Brothers, 1942).—Trans.]

Part 1, Conclusion
1. A footnote here in the original French simply states, "Imitated from Boudon." A very similar series of exhortations to love the angels is indeed found in the introduction of the seventeenth-century work *La dévotion aux neuf chœurs des saints anges* [*Devotion to the Nine Choirs of Holy Angels*] by Henri-Marie Boudon.—Trans.

Part 2, Book 1, Chapter 1
1. Jean-Joseph Gaume, *Traité du Saint-Esprit* (Paris: Gaume Frères et J. Duprey, 1864), 1:45.—Trans.
2. English translation of the original Spanish by Fiscar Marison, as found in Mary of Agreda, *City of God* (Chicago: The Theopolitan, 1914), 1:104-06.
3. Dr. Neale's English translation of the hymn as found in *The Roman Breviary*, trans. John, Marquess of Bute (London: William Blackwood and Sons, 1908), 4:592.—Trans.
4. In the original French version, Soyer has a footnote here with two quotes he attributes to Fr. Frederick William Faber's *The Creator and the Creature, or the Wonders of Divine Love*. However, the French translations of the two sentences he cites, while exclusively emphasizing the dazzling radiance of St. Michael, are incomplete and displace the emphasis in the original English. The English counterparts, as found in the 1857 edition published in Baltimore by Murphy and Company are: "Though the blaze of St. Michael's beauty and power were able to put us to death, if we saw it in the flesh, we could never feel ourselves in his hands as we are in the hands of God" (84); and "Thus though St. Michael's brightness dazzles us, while we look at it, until we gaze upon it through the many-colored veil of a creature's necessary imperfections, we can see even in him no right or title to the Creator's love, except the gifts which that love placed there first of all" (160-61).—Trans.
5. This is the original English as found in Frederick William Faber, *The Creator and the Creature, or The Wonders of Divine Love* (Baltimore: Murphy & Co., 1857), 147.—Trans.
6. See 1 Thes 4:15 and Jude 1:9.—Trans.
7. The original French incorrectly lists St. Lawrence Justinian as a doctor of the Church, so his name has been removed from this sentence. The English also corrects the placement of St. Thomas from the second set of names for mere theologians to the first set of names for doctors of the Church. Since Soyer's writing, Robert Bellarmine, the last figure listed, has been declared both a saint (in 1930) and a doctor of the Church (in 1931).—Trans.

Part 2, Book 1, Chapter 2
1. St. Ambrose, Rupert [of Deutz], Cornelius a Lapide, etc.
2. Cornelius a Lapide.

3. St. Augustine and Cornelius a Lapide wonder in what manner the *angel* of God had man leave paradise. They say he either led him like Raphael led Tobias or he took him away like the angel took Habakkuk to transport him from Judea to Babylon.

4. Blessed James of Voragine cites legends attributing to St. Michael the mission of expelling Adam from paradise and guarding its entrance. It is certainly from one of these legends that the poet Milton borrows the idea in his account of the expulsion of our first parents. A sixteenth-century bas-relief embedded in the wall of a side chapel in the basilica of Mont Saint-Michel reproduces the same idea.

5. See Genesis 6:2. It is worth noting the Douay-Rheims Bible's commentary on this verse: "The descendants of Seth and Enos are here called sons of God from their religion and piety: whereas the ungodly race of Cain, who by their carnal affections lay grovelling upon the earth, are called the children of men. The unhappy consequence of the former marrying with the latter, ought to be a warning to Christians to be very circumspect in their marriages; and not to suffer themselves to be determined in their choice by their carnal passion, to the prejudice of virtue and religion."—Trans.

6. Cornelius a Lapide says, "The Church alludes to this promise when, in the offertory in the Mass for the dead, it sings, 'Let Michael, the holy standard-bearer, bring them into the holy light which Thou once didst promise to Abraham and his seed.'"

7. The Hebrews in fact give the name of Michael to the one of the three young men who appeared the most eminent. They say the two others were called Gabriel and Raphael, both of whom St. Michael sent to overthrow Sodom and save Lot. The renowned commentators [Nicholas of] Lyra, [Alonso] Tostado, and Cornelius a Lapide admit this sentiment.

8. It is good to note that the angel of God declares himself the God of Bethel.

9. This is the sentiment of Diodorus, bishop of Tarsus and teacher of St. John Chrysostom; it is also the sentiment of St. Basil and St. Athanasius.

Part 2, Book 1, Chapter 3

1. See Acts 7:30, 35, 38, 53.—Trans.

2. Cornelius a Lapide and [Giovanni Stefano] Menochio.

3. "Michael," [Guillaume] Durand states in his *Rationale divinorum officiorum*, "is the angel who was sent to Egypt, worked those famous plagues, parted the Red Sea, guided the people across the desert, and led them into the promised land."

4. [That it is the angel of God] is the sentiment of [Thomas] Cajetan and [Benedict] Pereira.

5. Immediately following this paragraph in the original French is the following two-sentence paragraph which has purposely been omitted due to its incorrect statement about the Koran's title for St. Michael: "The role St. Michael exercises on Sinai merits him a kind of veneration even among the Turks. This is why Muhammad, in his Koran, calls the archangel the 'secretary of the divinity.'"—Trans.

6. Theodoret teaches that this angel was St. Michael.

7. See Jude 1:9.—Trans.
8. The Church Father is Pope St. Gregory the Great. The version of the quote provided is the direct Latin to English translation as found in St. Gregory the Great, *Morals on the Book of Job*, trans. John Henry Parker (London, F. and J. Rivington, 1847), 3-1:182 (in part 5, bk. 26).—Trans.
9. See Ex 32:9; 33:3, 5; 34:9; Dt 9:6, 13; Sir 16:11, and Acts 7:51.—Trans.

Part 2, Book 1, Chapter 4

1. English translation of the original Spanish by Fiscar Marison, as found in Mary of Agreda, *City of God* (Chicago: The Theopolitan, 1914), 1:10.—Trans.
2. Ibid., 1:171.—Trans.
3. Ibid., 2:387.—Trans.
4. Ibid., 2:402-03.—Trans.
5. Ibid., 2:411.—Trans.
6. One account written in the Middle Ages and very widespread then, titled *Life of Our Lady*, confides to St. Michael this glorious message: "Then God the Father said to St. Michael, 'Go into Bethlehem to the shepherds guarding the flock, and tell them that My blessed Son, the Savior of the whole world, is born today, and that they should rejoice greatly in His divinity.' St. Michael descended from heaven to earth and went to the shepherds; and, when he was before them, he cast such a great light that they were all terrified. The angel then said to the shepherds, 'Do not be afraid, for be certain that I am the angel of God who is sent to you. I announce to you that today is born the Savior of all the world, and this is the sign: You will find the child wrapped in swaddling clothes in the manger of the ox and the ass.' And when he had said this, a great company of angels began singing, 'Glory to God in the highest.'"
7. English translation of the original Spanish by Fiscar Marison, as found in Mary of Agreda, *City of God* (Chicago: The Theopolitan, 1914), 2:439-40.—Trans.
8. A scene sculpted on one of the sides of a chapiter in the church in St-Benoît-sur-Loire depicts the flight into Egypt. In the middle is the Holy Virgin seated on an ass with the Christ Child. St. Joseph is walking in front of the ass, which he is leading with a bridle. Behind, on the right side of the chapiter, a dragon is struck down and pierced with a lance by a maimed personage, "in whom," says [historian and archaeologist Arcisse] de Caumont, "I recognize St. Michael."
9. English translation of the original Spanish by Fiscar Marison, as found in Mary of Agreda, *City of God* (Chicago: The Theopolitan, 1914), 3:483-84.—Trans.
10. Ibid., 3:721.—Trans.
11. From the proper offertory prayer for the Mass for the Dead.—Trans.
12. "And Jesus Christ came with a great company of angels, among whom was St. Michael; and when the Holy Virgin saw Him, she said, 'Blessed be Jesus Christ, for He has not forgotten me.' When she had said this, she surrendered her spirit, which St. Michael took. Soon thereafter, the Savior came again with a great company of angels, and told St. Michael and St. Gabriel to take the body of His mother" (the same *Life of Our Lady* cited previously [in note 6 above]). Blessed James of Voragine, who in his *The Golden Legend* compiled the main legendary

features pertaining to the Assumption of the Blessed Virgin, also attributes this glorious mission to St. Michael.

13. A tympanum of the Church of Our Lady in Trier depicts the coronation of Mary. Christ, assisted by an angel (St. Michael), places the crown on the head of His mother.

Part 2, Book 1, Chapter 5

1. *Sermones centum*, 86. [Found in Hugonis de S. Victore, *Opera omnia* (Paris: Garnier Fratres, 1879), 3:1173.—Trans.]

2. This is the English translation of the first antiphon of the first nocturn for Matins on Michaelmas Day, as found in *The Roman Breviary*, trans. John, Marquess of Bute (London: William Blackwood and Sons, 1908), 4:593.—Trans.

3. *Sermones centum*, 86. With the exception of the one sentence referred to in note 2 above, the English is a relay of the Latin to French translation quoted by Soyer.—Trans.

4. Jacques-Bénigne Bossuet, *Explication de l'Apocalypse*, preface. [Found in *Œuvres complètes de Bossuet*, 2nd ed. (Paris: Berche et Tralin, 1885), 1:285-86.—Trans.]

5. According to Sozomen, the fifth-century Church historian. — The church in Bourbon-l'Archambault, France, has old-style stained-glass windows of admirable beauty. The emperor Constantine is depicted at the moment he is deliberating whether to go into battle; an angel promises him victory and shows him the cross with these words: "In this sign, you shall conquer."

6. Found in Jacques-Bénigne Bossuet, "Explication de l'Apocalypse," in *Œuvres complètes de Bossuet*, 2nd ed. (Paris: Berche et Tralin, 1885), 1:325.—Trans.

7. Castel Sant'Angelo, or "Castle of the Holy Angel," was used multiple times as a refuge by the Sovereign Pontiffs. It was here that took refuge, among others, Clement VII, when fleeing the fury of the Spanish after the conquest of his capital in 1527, an event in which Benvenuto Cellini played a singular role he recalls so extensively in his vain memoirs.

8. The original French version identifies the city as "Formana."—Trans.

9. Found in Dominique Bouhours, *Vie de Saint François Xavier* (Brussels: L. de Wageneer, 1852), 154.—Trans.

Part 2, Book 1, Chapter 6

1. These bracketed words are the translator's correction of Soyer's words "At the siege of." Accounts of this incident describe it as an accident. On October 11, 1422, just ten days prior to his father's death and the beginning of his reign, Charles VII was in a meeting hall on the second level of a building in La Rochelle when the floor collapsed and plunged all the attendees down to the ground level. The dauphin, with only some minor bruises, was nearly the only one who came out of the accident essentially unscathed, most being injured and some of them dying. See Siméon Luce, *Jeanne d'Arc à Domremy* (Paris: H. Champion, 1886), xcvii-xcviii.—Trans.

2. The source of this quote is likely Dom Jean Huynes. See part 2, bk. 3, ch. 5, note 3.—Trans.

3. The word *foire* ["fair"] comes from *feria, férie, fête* ["holiday," "feast day," etc.], and this is so fitting since all the old fairs are named after special feast days, patronal feast days for example, celebrated in the regions where they take place. There is hardly a province without fairs on the occasion of St. Michael's feast day. In his history of Mont Saint-Michel, Fr. Deschamps says, "It is to the Church that we owe the first public markets. These gatherings during which religious duties were accomplished at the same time that one tended to commercial or civil business came into being amidst the faithful converging towards this or that famous pilgrimage site. One can say that the cradles of our townships were our churches' courtyards, where they were baptized in the faith. The present liberalism therefore testifies to as much ignorance as ingratitude when it rebels against the Church, the veritable Mother of our nationhood."

4. See Appendix 2 for the list of kings who made this pilgrimage.

5. If one were to believe a tradition preserved in our country, a monk allegedly predicted, more than a century in advance, the dispersion, by the French Revolution, of the monks of Mont Saint-Michel; he even allegedly specified the new use for the old abbey [as a prison—Trans.], for a fixed time. Then, this prediction alleges, religion will retake possession of this monument, and that the time this occurs will be for the Church the signal of a radiant prosperity. And on the day that the statue of the archangel shines again atop the shrine, France and the Church will cast over the world the brightest radiance. God grant that these predictions are founded on His designs!

6. The original French edition of this book was published in 1870, the same year that the forces of Victor Emmanuel II conquered Rome and put a definitive end to the Papal States.—Trans.

Part 2, Book 1, Chapter 7

1. *Les soirées de Saint-Pétersbourg* [*St. Petersburg Dialogues*], vol. 2.

2. Theodoret teaches that the angel who said this to Joshua was St. Michael.

3. A fresco found in the second hall of the Vatican painting gallery and which is due to Raphael's brushwork, recalls this victory. Leo IV is in prayer, the only defense allowed him, but his petitions are graciously answered. Vessels, occupying the horizon, announce a naval battle, as well as the longboat approaching the shore, loaded with prisoners; other enemies, already defeated and led to the feet of the Pontiff, implore his clemency.

4. St. Michael is the patron of the Papal Army, and Church flags have, on top of the pole, the statuette of the archangel, with his wings spread and his hand armed with the blazing sword that strikes down the dragon.

5. The Crusader army was commanded by Louis VII, who had taken up arms at the word of St. Bernard.

6. *Gesta Dei per Francos.*

7. "At the same time" appears in the original French.—Trans.

8. "King" appears in the original French.—Trans.

9. Boleslaus II, nicknamed *the Cruel*, having made himself odious to his subjects through the infamous debauchery to which he immodestly delivered himself, even in public, was excommunicated by St. Stanislaus. Boleslaus had only contempt

for the anathema struck against him; he continued in his disorders, and even attended public prayers. The Bishop of Krakow ordered that the divine office be stopped as soon as the excommunicated prince entered the church. He then withdrew to a chapel of St. Michael located outside the city. The king followed him there with his guards, whom he commanded to slaughter Stanislaus. When the guards entered the chapel, they were so struck with respect at the sight of the holy bishop, that they did not have the courage to execute the order they had received. The same thing happened to a second and third troop of soldiers. Filled with rage, the king lunged at Stanislaus and killed him with his own hand. The emboldened soldiers cut his body into pieces, which they spread here and there, so that they would be eaten by the beasts and birds of prey. However, God preserved the scattered members of His servant. The canons gathered them and buried them in front of the door to the chapel of St. Michael. The death of this glorious martyr occurred on May 8, the feast day of St. Michael['s apparition on Mount Gargano].

Part 2, Book 1, Chapter 8

1. Antiphon from the Divine Office for the feast of St. Michael.—Trans.
2. This is the English version of the prayer as found in *The New Roman Missal* (New York: Benziger Brothers, 1942). The capitalization and italics are added by Soyer for emphasis.—Trans.
3. Jacques-Bénigne Bossuet, *Explication de la Messe*, ch. 38.—Trans.
4. *Homily 14 on Numbers*; italics is Soyer's.—Trans.
5. *Liber responsalis sive antiphonarius*, second nocturn for the feast of St. Michael; italics is Soyer's.—Trans.
6. Jacques-Bénigne Bossuet, *Explication de la Messe*, ch. 38; italics is Soyer's.—Trans.
7. From the *Te igitur* of the canon of the Mass.—Trans.
8. Ibid.—Trans.
9. Ibid.—Trans.
10. Ibid.—Trans.
11. Durand explains this passage in the same way: "*Per manus sancti Angeli tui*, that is to say, through the ministry of angels, spirits who are the ministers of God and present our petitions before the Lord, according to these words of the angel Raphael to Tobit: 'When thou didst pray with tears… I offered thy prayer to the Lord' [(Tb 12:12)]. By this, it is evident that one must believe that the angel assists at the holy mysteries, not to consecrate, because he cannot do so, but to offer to God the prayers of the priest and of the people, according to these words from Revelation [8:4]: 'The smoke of the incense of the prayers of the saints ascended up before God from the hand of the angel.'" [Found in Guillaume Durand, *Rational ou Manuel des divins offices* [*Rationale divinorum officiorum*], trans. from Latin to French by Charles Barthélemy (Paris: Louis Vivès, 1854), 2:321-22 (in bk. 4, ch. 44, paras. 7-8).—Trans.]
12. The Confiteor of the traditional Roman rite.—Trans.
13. No further source information identified.—Trans.

14. From Rev. W. J. Copeland's English translation of the hymn for Lauds on the feast of the Apparition of St. Michael, as found in *The Roman Breviary*, trans. John, Marquess of Bute (London: William Blackwood and Sons, 1908), 2:872. Soyer adds italics for emphasis and identifies the French counterpart to this stanza as from the hymn for Vespers on the feast of St. Gabriel.—Trans.

Part 2, Book 1, Chapter 9

1. The Sister of the Nativity [Jeanne le Royer] also speaks about the end times in her revelations. This is what she says about the role of St. Michael: "God will raise up new prophets whom He will send to console His Church, announcing to her the favors He has reserved for her. The true faithful will have frequent apparitions of their good angels and other spiritual powers designated to protect and console them, particularly St. Michael the Archangel, the most ardent defender of the Church militant, who will be with her always to lead her up to the end. He will even appear visibly in different encounters..." [Found in *Vie et révélations de la Sœur de la Nativité*, 3rd ed. (Paris: Perisse Frères, 1849), 1:321.—Trans.]

2. English translation of the original Spanish by Fiscar Marison, as found in Mary of Agreda, *City of God* (Chicago: The Theopolitan, 1914), 1:218-19.—Trans.

3. Ibid., 4:454-55.—Trans.

4. We shall cite among the Fathers St. Jerome, Theodoret, and St. Thomas Aquinas, and among the commentators Cornelius a Lapide, Nicholas of Lyra, Giovanni Stefano Menochio, Jacques Tyrin, and Willem Hessels van Est.

5. This is the opinion of the author of a writing on the Antichrist which is cited in the works of St. Augustine. St. Peter Damian, Heimon, Peter Lombard, Willem Hessels van Est, John of Gorkum, and Bernadine a Piconio are also of this sentiment. We read the following in the revelations of the Sister of the Nativity [Jeanne le Royer]: "When the Antichrist, triumphant from his victories in the war that he will declare against the Church, will arm himself to crush and abolish her, so he will think, God will send the great archangel St. Michael to the head of His Church, with troops of angels who will surround her.... God made known to me the haughty and diabolic intentions of Satan and his satellites. They will rise towards heaven with great joy and great triumph, with the intention of making war on the Eternal Being, of raising their thrones above His, and of annihilating Him, if they could, aspiring to a glory like that of Lucifer. It is at that moment that God will send the great archangel St. Michael, clothed with the power and justice of God, who will come from the height of heaven before them in a threatening manner, and who will bring terror among the infernal spirits. Our Lord will make His voice heard by the breath of St. Michael the Archangel, and will say: 'Begone, accursed ones, go down into the deepest recesses of hell.' At that instant, the earth will open up and reveal a frightful abyss of fire and flames, into which this steadfast cohort will fall helter-skelter... and all will go to the bottom of the pit of hell" [*Vie et révélations de la Sœur de la Nativité*, 2nd ed. (Paris: Beaucé, 1819), 4:452-55.—Trans.].

6. *Homily 8 on First Thessalonians.*—Trans.

7. *Then, the trumpet's shrill refrain, / Piercing tombs by hill and plain / Souls to judgment shall arraign* (from the *Dies iræ*). [This English version is taken from *The New Roman Missal* (New York: Benziger Brothers, 1942).—Trans.]

Part 2, Book 1, Chapter 10

1. This quote is from book 3. The English version used here is William Wake's translation, as found in *The Shepherd of Hermas, and The Martyrdoms of St. Ignatius and St. Polycarp*, 1st American from the 3rd London ed. (New York: Southwick and Pelsue, 1810), 355.—Trans.
2. *The Shepherd of Hermas*, bk. 3, similitude 8, as found in *The Genuine Epistles of the Apostolical Fathers*, translated by William [Wake], Lord Archbishop of Canterbury (New York: Southwick and Pelsue, 1810), 352-55. The capitalization of all letters in the name Michael and the italicization of the text immediately following it are Soyer's emphases.—Trans.
3. This quotation is a translation of the French used by Soyer. The English translation by William Wake, previously quoted, expresses this sentiment, but not so succinctly. The French is evidently a paraphrase or derived from a variant manuscript.—Trans.

Part 2, Book 1, Chapter 11

1. From the second antiphon of the second nocturn of Matins on Michaelmas Day.—Trans.
2. English translation of the third antiphon of Lauds on Michaelmas Day, as found in *The Roman Breviary*, trans. John, Marquess of Bute (London: William Blackwood and Sons, 1908), 4:598.—Trans.
3. [This is the Alleluia verse for the masses of St. Michael's apparition and dedication.—Trans.] Several times we have witnessed, on the top of a small mountain from where Mont Saint-Michel can be seen, persons kneeling, facing the shrine, and imploring the archangel on behalf of a dying person.
4. This is evidently mild paraphrasing of a passage from Eadmer's *Vita Wilfridi episcopi*, ch. 49.—Trans.
5. The oldest, most original, and most moving French poem, *The Song of Roland*, shows us St. Michael taking the famous hero to heaven: *God sent him down His angel cherubin, / And Saint Michael, we worship in peril; And by their side Saint Gabriel alit; So the count's soul they bare to Paradis.* [This English version is from the translation of C. K. Scott Moncrieff.—Trans.]
6. St. Michael ordinarily exercises the principal role in *psychostasia*, or the weighing of souls after death, a subject often depicted in the ornamentation of ancient churches. We see this in the churches of Montivilliers, Sainte-Croix-de-Saint-Lô, Bourges, Amiens, Saint-Trophime in Arles, Notre-Dame in Paris, etc., in the miniatures of various manuscripts and in stained-glass windows. — In Autun, the large bas-relief at the entrance [of the church] depicts the same concept. There is a balance supported by a hand surrounded by clouds. St. Michael the Archangel and the prince of the demons respectively place on one pan a small handsome man, an emblem of virtue, and on the other pan a monster, an emblem of evil. While the defendant, whose fate is debated at this solemn moment, tries to draw

nearer the archangel, Satan exerts all his efforts to make the balance tilt to his side, and one of his fiends brings a lizard, another symbol of evil, to further load the pan where the sins are weighed; however, the archangel is the winner, his powerful hand imparts a movement to the scale's beam, assuring the totality of good works has the advantage. The sculptor also expressed the elegant concept of two resuscitated men seeking refuge in the undulating folds of the archangel's robe. — In the Napoleon III Museum [section of the Louvre], one can also see a magnificent panel painted by Francesco Signorelli around 1550, depicting St. Michael with a balance in his hand judging the merit of souls. — In the towers of the Beauvais cathedral, they have just installed a clock which is considered a marvel. Among the different scenes depicted by means of an admirable mechanism, one can see the judgment. The Blessed Virgin and St. Joseph, positioned to the right and left of the Redeemer, intercede while St. Michael holds the balance of judgment. This balance oscillates several times; it ultimately tilts to the good side, and the fortunate soul is led by an angel to the gate of heaven, as one hears the sweet harmony of a heavenly chorus. But soon, thunder roars in the distance, and a reprobate soul, preceded by a frightful demon, comes to appear before the supreme Judge. The saints redouble their supplications, but St. Michael's balance leans to the bad side, and, amidst the noise of thunder, the unfortunate soul, who shamefully covers his face, is taken to hell. One experiences at that moment an impression of indefinable terror.

7. All the commentators say God makes use of the ministry of an angel here, whose name they never identify. We believe this angel is Michael, first on account of these words: "Thou art weighed in the balance, and art found wanting;" secondly, because this pertains to avenging the profanation of the vessels of the temple in Jerusalem and the oppression of the people whose protector he was, and this mission belonged to him; and thirdly, because he was ordinarily tasked with representing God when He wanted to manifest Himself to men.

8. From the offertory of the Mass for the Dead.—Trans.

Part 2, Book 2, Chapter 1

1. No further source information identified.—Trans.

2. May 8 and September 29, both universally commemorated in the traditional Roman calendar, celebrate the Mount Gargano apparition and St. Michael's primary feast day, respectively. October 16 is a non-universal commemoration of both St. Michael's apparition to St. Aubert and the dedication of the basilica of Mont Saint-Michel. For more details on the October 16 feast day, see "Pourquoi la Fête du 16 octobre ?" *Annales du Mont-Saint-Michel* 33, no. 7 (October 1906): 150-51.—Trans.

3. This speech is evidently very loose and elaborate paraphrasing on Soyer's part rather than a direct quotation of Scripture. Ezekiel 22:30 is perhaps the one verse that best correlates to his main point. It reads: "And I sought among them for a man that might set up a hedge and stand in the gap before me in favour of the land, that I might not destroy it: and I found none."—Trans.

4. Sequence for the feast of St. Michael.

5. The Confiteor of the traditional Roman rite.—Trans.

6. Soyer does not identify where specifically author Dom Lorenzo Scupoli says this. When Scupoli speaks of honoring and praying to various saints in his *The Spiritual Combat*, the nearest thing he says is the following in chapter 50: "But omit not on any day the Blessed Virgin, Queen of all Saints; your guardian Angel; St. Michael, the Archangel; and all your patrons" (1875 English translation published in London by Rivingtons, pp. 160-61).—Trans.

7. Auguste Nicolas, *La Vierge Marie et le plan divin* [7th ed. (Paris: Vaton Frères, 1869), 3:93.—Trans.].

8. Although modified by Soyer, this is essentially taken from the offertory of the Mass for the Dead.—Trans.

9. *Treatise on the Love of God,* bk. 10, ch. 7.

10. In March 1869, the newspaper *L'Opinion nationale* triumphally announced the results of this diabolical association. It said: "What was only at first a small group of citizens... has become an immense chorus of friends... We count seven or eight civil burials per week. The time has finally come when the honest citizen [!!] understands that it is not enough to devise pretty theories, but that action is better still." [Bracketed exclamation points are Soyer's insertion.—Trans.]

Part 2, Book 2, Chapter 2

1. Henri-Dominique Lacordaire, *Vie de Saint Dominique*, ch. 6.—Trans.

2. Theodoret, *Interpretatio epistolae ad Colossenses*, 2:18 (PG 82:613).—Trans.

3. Found in Jacques-Bénigne Bossuet, "Du culte dû à Dieu," in *Œuvres complètes de Bossuet* (Besançon: Outhenin-Chalandre Fils, 1836), 8:650. Bossuet himself identifies his source for Alexis Aristenus's quote as a recent edition of "the Synodicon of the Greeks" published in England, likely a reference to William Beveridge's *Synodikon sive Pandectae canonum SS. Apostolorum et conciliorum ab Ecclesia graeca receptorum* (Oxford: E Theatro Sheldoniano, 1672). Aristenus's cited commentary is found there in both Greek and Latin in vol. 1, p. 469, under canon 35 of the Council of Laodicea.—Trans.

4. Ibid.—Trans.

5. Eight emperors of Constantinople bore the name Michael.

6. One counts in Rome five churches dedicated to the prince of the angels.

7. There is a hospice in Rome named after St. Michael, where they teach the practical arts to children from poor families.

8. Two feasts are obligatory for the entire Church: those of May 8 and September 29.

9. According to recent scholarship, Drepanius Florus was a name invented by an early editor which conflates the identities of the ninth-century Florus of Lyon and the fourth-century Latinius Pacatus Drepanius—see Roger Green, "Latinius Drepanius Pacatus: The Full Story," review of *Un poète latin chrétien redécouvert: Latinius Pacatus Drepanius, panégyriste de Théodose*, by Anne-Marie Turcan-Verkerk, *The Classical Review* 55, no. 2 (October 2005), 560-61. Soyer renders the name here as "Florus Drepani" and subsequently in bk. 3, ch. 1, as "Florus Drepanius." In the latter instance, Soyer identifies the figure as having lived in the ninth century, which contrasts with this instance, where he is "the most ancient" of Christian poets.—Trans.

10. Multiple provincial councils numbered the September 29 feast day among the great solemnities.

11. Among the chapels built in honor of St. Michael, there was one in the courtyard of the Sainte-Chapelle called St-Michel-de-la-Place. Philip Augustus was baptized there in 1165. It was demolished in 1782. — A street that was called Rue d'Enfer [or "Hell Street"] because, according to popular tradition, there had been on this street a mansion inhabited by ghosts and demons, was renamed Rue St Michel. — When Charles VI, in memory of his pilgrimage to Mont Saint-Michel had given the gate called Porte Gibard the new name Porte St Michel, the associated street took on the name Rue du Faubourg St Michel. [Pierre-Daniel] Huet, bishop of Avranches, claimed that this street had previously been a place of disorder, debauchery, and theft.

12. This is the English translation of the Latin as found in John Baron, ed., *A Collection of the Laws and Canons of the Church of England*, trans. John Johnson (Oxford: John Henry Parker, 1850), 1:496; brackets in the original.—Trans.

13. On August 1, 1869, Manchester opened a Catholic church dedicated to St. Michael.

14. Changed from "Emperor of Germany" in the original French.—Trans.

15. The original French identifies him as "Emperor of Austria, Francis II."—Trans.

16. The name Michael is very common in Japan. One of the twenty-six canonized martyrs bore this name: St. Michael Kozaki. So did another martyr belonging to the Confraternity of the Rosary: Blessed Michael Takeshita.

17. The czars chose for their burial place in Moscow the church of St. Michael [the Cathedral of the Archangel] in the Kremlin. The tomb of one St. Alexis was displayed there. Peter II was the last to have been buried there.

18. Soyer refers to this book as *Doctrine de Mahomet*, without providing any further details.

19. A considerable number of towns and cities have been named after St. Michael. Among them, we shall mention Arkhangelsk, or Archangel, in Russia. This city was built in 1584; it originally only had a monastery dedicated to the holy archangel. There is also San Miguel el Grande [now San Miguel de Allende], in Mexico, known for its industry and commerce; San Miguel, Guatemala, where there is a beautiful church; and San Miguel de Tucumán, the capital of Tucumán Province, Argentina. — The largest island in the Azores is named after St. Michael [São Miguel Island]. This island is remarkable for its fertility. [The geographer Conrad] Malte-Brun says, "The vegetation shines with the most beautiful radiance, and numerous groves diversify the landscape; without much difficulty, the fields produce excellent wheat, corn, a little barley, fava beans, and rice in abundance. In the gardens, they cultivate oranges of excellent quality and many other fruits. The vineyards, established mainly over volcanic soil, yield 5,000 pipes of wine annually. The pastures are good and abundant. The valley of Furnas provides delicious honey; on the coastline, sponges are neglected; and especially in the sea, there are sardines which feed the common people" [found in *Précis de la géographie universelle,* 4th ed. (Paris: Aimé André, 1836), 7:552-53.—Trans.].

Part 2, Book 2, Chapter 3

1. Pius IX was the reigning pope at the time this book's original French edition was published.—Trans.
2. A pious belief, Fr. Frederick William Faber says, designates St. Michael as a guardian angel for all the reigning popes throughout history.
3. This is at least what certain traditions say.
4. A historian said of St. Gelasius, "The mores of this pontiff honored his knowledge and his talents. He was of a rare piety, given to prayer or to holy conversation with the most worthy servants of God during any time left to him outside his sublime duties…. He fed all the poor he could find, lived as a poor man himself, and in the practice of the most rigorous austerities." [In the original French, Soyer states only that this quotation is "cited by Feller." These are the words of historian Mathieu-Richard-Auguste Henrion as found in *Histoire générale de l'Église*, 4th ed., (Paris: Gaume Frères, 1841), 2:538.—Trans.]
5. Voltaire said of this pope: "He was born a Roman. The courage of the first ages of the Republic came back to life in him, in an age of cowardice and corruption— like a beautiful monument of ancient Rome one sometimes finds in the ruins of the new one" (*Essai sur les mœurs et l'esprit des nations*).
6. The Normans led by Robert Guiscard.
7. *Vie de St Autbert.*
8. This is E. Gurney Salter's direct English translation of the Latin as found in St. Bonaventure, *The Life of Saint Francis* (London: J. M. Dent & Co., 1904), 138-40.
9. We saw in the preceding chapter how much these two nations, Germany and England, were devoted to St. Michael when they were Catholic.
10. See p. 135.
11. The church is also known today as the Church of Saints Michael and Magnus. The original French text here says the qualification *in Sassia* ("in Saxony") is due to a nearby *rue des Saxons* or "Saxons Street." The English translation intentionally omits this claim since the historical Saxon presence in this section of Rome is ultimately a more plausible reason for the qualification.—Trans.
12. In the calendar in Appendix 1, see the names of some of the saints particularly devoted to St. Michael.

Part 2, Book 2, Chapter 4

1. These are some of the monasteries and abbeys: Saint-Michel-de-Cuxa, in the diocese of Perpignan, founded around the year 878. This monastery contained the tomb of St. Peter Orseolo, the Doge of Venice, who after living as a penitent in this abbey, died a holy death here. — Saint Michel in Dijon, established at the time of King Robert, at the end of the tenth century. — Saint Michel in Senlis, founded around the year 1094. — Saint Michel de Tonnerre, on Mont Volute. This abbey became so famous in the fifteenth century that Cardinal Alain, the legate of Pope Callixtus II, counted it as one of the twelve most illustrious in Gaul. The relics of St. Thierry, bishop of Orléans, were venerated here. — Saint-Michel-en-l'Herm, in the diocese of Luçon. Through a bull of Clement X, the abbey's revenue went to the Collège Mazarin in Paris, in 1671. — Saint-Michel-en-

Thiérache in the [former] diocese of Laon, founded by Blessed Maccalin. — The Benedictines built other monasteries under the patronage of St. Michael such as: Gaillac, on the Tarn River (this monastery being the origin of the city of Gaillac); Honcourt Abbey, in the valley of Villé, in the Strasbourg diocese (Frederick I, Emperor of Germany, took this monastery under his protection); Honau Abbey, in the same diocese, founded by Adalbert, the brother of St. Odilia; Malmesbury in Wiltshire, England (St. Aldhelm was its abbot for thirty years, and William of Malmesbury, the twelfth-century historian, was one of its most illustrious figures); Mondsee in Bavaria [now in Upper Austria]; Metten in the diocese of Passau in Bavaria, founded by Charlemagne; Ohrdruf, founded by St. Boniface, close to the city of Erfurt (St. Wilbert was its first abbot); Pessan, not far from the city of Auch [in France]; Schuttern Abbey, in the diocese of Strasbourg [now within the archdiocese of Freiburg, Germany], founded by an Englishman of royal blood named Offo [who is identified as Irish in other sources]; Siegburg, in the diocese of Cologne (the archbishop St. Anno began its construction and dedicated the church to St. Michael); Tréport, in the diocese of Rouen, founded by Robert, the Count of Eu, one of the valiant companions of William the Conqueror (the former abbey's church now serves as a parish church); and Saint-Mihiel, in the diocese of Verdun, an abbey founded the same year as the apparition of St. Michael on Mount Tombe. — Among the abbeys for Benedictine nuns, there are: Saint-Michel de Doullens in the diocese of Amiens, founded by St. Godfrey, bishop of Amiens (it is said the keys to the city were each day confided to the abbess); San Miguel de Pedroso, Spain [in present-day Burgos Province]; and Michelfel, near Basel, Switzerland, founded by Berthold, bishop of Basel.

2. Multiple abbeys and monasteries which were daughter houses of Cîteaux were named after St. Michael and placed under his patronage, including: San Michele in the diocese of Siena; St. Michael on Blessed Virgin Island near Buda, Hungary [possibly present-day Margaret Island within the city of Budapest]; Michaelstein in the former diocese of Halberstadt [in present-day Saxony-Anhalt, Germany], which was a daughter house of Kamp Abbey; San Bernardo near Valencia, Spain (Pope Paul III changed its name to San Miguel in memory of the chivalric order founded by King Ferdinand I of Naples); Ebrach, in the diocese of Würzburg, in Bavaria, a very beautiful and very rich abbey, a daughter house of Morimond Abbey. Located there is the burial place of Empress Gertrude, the wife of Emperor Conrad III. This latter abbey had the privilege of receiving, in the choir of its church, the hearts of all the bishops of Würzburg, which were transported there with great pomp on a carriage drawn by four horses.

3. Bolland's successors wanted to leave posterity the memory of the greatness and magnificence of St. Michael's Abbey in Antwerp by providing the plan of this illustrious abbey in their *Acta Sanctorum*, under June 6.

4. This virgin is called *Virgo ad sanctum Michaelem*.

5. St. Michael's in Treviño, Spain, also belonged to this order.

6. St. Michael's in Tarascon.

7. One counted thirty-five monasteries in this order, among others those of Classe, near Ravenna, St. Mary of the Angels in Florence, Holy Cross in Fonte Avellana, St. Gregory in Rome, etc.

8. The Monastery of the Immaculate Conception in Agreda, Spain.
9. These words are part of a declaration written by Mary of Agreda entrusting her monastery and all its nuns to the special patronage and protection of the Virgin Mary, St. Michael, and St. Francis of Assisi. This English version is a relay translation of the French found in Marie de Jésus d'Agréda, *La cité mystique de Dieu,* 2nd ed. (Paris: Madame Veuve Poussielgue-Rusand, 1862), 6:565-66.— Trans.
10. There exists in Paris a society called the Dames of St. Michael, also known as the White Ladies. They devote themselves to the education of youth and take in young girls who are former prostitutes or in detention due to police measures or paternal correction. In 1790, they occupied a St. Michael Convent on Rue Saint-Jacques, built in 1623 for the religious of the Visitation Order.

Part 2, Book 2, Chapter 5
1. The name of St. Michael has also been given to forts which defend cities: in Rome, Malta, etc. The latter fort [in Senglea, Malta] is famous for the attacks it withstood.
2. Other histories put this date at 1147. This and certain other details in Soyer's account differ from the prevailing narrative found in sundry online sources. Accounts like Soyer's can be found in Pierre Hélyot, *Dictionnaire des ordres religieux,* s.v. "Aile de Saint-Michel (Chevaliers de l')" (Paris: J.-P. Migne, 1847), 1:177-79, and Genaro del Valle, *Historia de las instituciones monásticas* (Madrid: Imp. Ce. Angosta de S. Bernardo, 1842), 1:222-24.—Trans.
3. Pierre Hélyot, *Dictionnaire des ordres religieux* [s.v. "Michel (Des Chevaliers de l'Ordre de Saint-) en France" (Paris: J.-P. Migne, 1863), 2:957-68—Trans.].
4. Pierre Hélyot, *Dictionnaire des ordres religieux* [s.v. "Michel (Chevalerie de Saint-) en Bavière" (Paris: J.-P. Migne, 1859), 4:840-41—Trans.].
5. Pierre Hélyot, *Dictionnaire des ordres religieux* [s.v. "Conception de la Bienheureuse Vierge Immaculée (Chevaliers de l'Ordre de la)" (Paris: J.-P. Migne, 1847), 1:1082-83—Trans.].
6. The Knights of the White Eagle to which Soyer is referring is probably the Polish order.—Trans.

Part 2, Book 2, Chapter 6
1. *Letter 102*, para.19. English translation by J. G. Cunningham, as found in *Letters of Saint Augustine, Bishop of Hippo,* ed. Philip Schaff (Buffalo: The Christian Literature Co., 1886), 1:419.—Trans.
2. Saint-Similien is a church in Nantes.—Trans.
3. An *oublie* is a small cake made of light batter and cooked between two irons. There were three kinds of *oublies:* 1) the *large* or *flat oublies;* 2) the *supplication oublies,* later called *waffles;* and 3) the *oublies* called initially *oublies d'étriers* and subsequently *petits métiers.*

Part 2, Book 2, Chapter 7
1. In his poem *Les Éleuthéromanes,* Denis Diderot writes of how the liberated man, "for lack of a rope, would weave priest entrails in order to strangle kings." Soyer's rewording of Diderot, as well as his general line of thought in this immediate

portion of the manuscript, is clearly taken from Mgr. Jean-Joseph Gaume, as found in page 463 and surrounding pages of the first volume of *Traité du Saint-Esprit* (Paris: Gaume Frères et J. Duprey, 1864).—Trans.

2. Sermon for the feast of St. Augustine.

3. Jean de La Fontaine.—Trans.

4. The *Solidaires* are committed to dying in hatred for God and the Church. This association, as we see it, is under the leadership of Satan. Would it not then be time, once again, to form associations to combat it?

Part 2, Book 2, Chapter 8

1. Found in Théophile Lavallée, *Histoire des Français depuis le temps des Gaulois jusqu'en 1830*, 4th ed. (Paris: J. Hetzel, 1844), 1:285.—Trans.

2. Found in *Dictionnaire géographique, historique, descriptif, archéologique des pèlerinages anciens et modernes et des lieux de dévotion les plus célèbres de l'univers*, s.v. "Saint-Michel de Cuxa" (Paris: J.-P. Migne, 1859).—Trans.

3. This marvel of Le Puy-en-Velay is well-known in Velay and Auvergne. It has been celebrated by poets of the region.

4. Found in Prosper Mérimée, *Notes d'un voyage en Auvergne* (Paris: H. Fournier, 1838), 235-39. Mérimée also regretfully reports that, at the time of his writing, the frescoes had very recently been vandalized, and one found nothing more than a "horrible whitewash."—Trans.

5. *Dictionnaire des abbayes et des monastères*, s.v. "Michel de l'Aiguille (Saint-)" (Paris: J.-P. Migne, 1856).—Trans.

6. A charming little oratory was built a few years ago on the mountain overlooking the city of Mortain, and which is more than 800 French feet [over 850 feet] above sea level.

7. Its tower rises 402 French feet [about 430 feet] from its base.

8. The monastery of St. Michael is one of the most beautiful buildings in the city. The tombs of several dukes of Lüneburg are located there.

9. The church of St. Michael the Archangel at the Kremlin was used as a burial place for the czar (according to Conrad Malte-Brun).

10. The cathedral of St. Michael, which dates back to the twelfth century, is regarded as one of the most famous works of architecture in Europe (Conrad Malte-Brun).

11. We made some of these sculptures known in the eleventh chapter of the first book. On one of the ancient gates of the city of Cambrai, the Selles gate, a meter high bas-relief deserves particular attention. It depicts St. Michael trampling underfoot a winged dragon, which raises its head and tail and grabs the archangel's shield with its mouth and claws. The saint brandishes a short sword in his right hand; he is dressed like a sixteenth-century soldier.

12. Found in *Abécédaire ou rudiment d'archéologie*, 3rd ed. (Paris: Derache, 1854), 354; text in brackets is Soyer's insertion.—Trans.

13. The Marquise de Créquy speaks of this statue in her *Souvenirs*: "The pinnacle of the edifice is of a work so rich, yet so light, that we have not seen anything similar, unless it is in those English prints one could call *belles infidèles* [beautiful but unfaithful to the original], as are the translations of [Nicolas] Perrot d'Ablancourt. We saw gleaming atop that pinnacle a large, gilded statue, which represents St.

Michael the Archangel, and which turns on a pivot according to the direction of the winds. We were told that the wind and movement of this image, whose raised, blazing sword defies and dismisses lightning, was something incredible to behold during the storms in these tempestuous regions."

14. A statue was indeed placed back atop the spire after the original French version of this book was written.—Trans.

15. Rev. [Émile-Auber] Pigeon.

16. Dom [Jean] Huynes.

17. *Souvenirs de la marquise de Créquy* (Paris: Librairie de Fournier Jeune, 1836), 1:89.—Trans.

18. Maurice Cousin de Courchamps is generally believed to be the true principal author of the Marquise de Créquy's *Souvenirs.*—Trans.

19. *Souvenirs de la marquise de Créquy* (Paris: Librairie de Fournier Jeune, 1836), 1:89.—Trans.

20. This remarkable fresco is by Eugène Delacroix.

21. Edgar Quinet, *Du génie des religions* [(Paris: Charpentier, 1842), 125].

22. In this chapter, we have spoken of anything in a temple that might call attention to the glory of St. Michael. To be complete, we could have also spoken of bells and clocks. — A venerable Franciscan writes to us that, in Canada, he attended the blessing of a bell by Bishop Bourget which was dedicated to St. Michael. — We have spoken elsewhere of the admirable clock in Beauvais.

Part 2, Book 3, Chapter 1

1. Blessed James of Voragine says of this church in his *Golden Legend*, for the September 29 entry on St. Michael, that it was built in a place where the goddess Hesta was previously worshipped.—Trans.

2. This is an excerpt of Chester D. Hartranft's Greek to English translation of Sozomen's *Ecclesiastical History*, bk. 2, ch. 3, as found in Henry Wace & Philip Schaff, eds., *Nicene and Post-Nicene Fathers of the Christian Church, Second Series* (New York: Christian Literature, 1891), 2:260-61.—Trans.

3. This city was reestablished and entirely rebuilt by our conquerors from Normandy, who left from the area surrounding Coutances, Hauteville in particular.

4. Derived from James of Voragine's *The Golden Legend*, s.v. "Feast of St. Michael"; English is relay translation of French version used by Soyer.—Trans.

5. From *Gesta Roberti Wiscardi.*—Trans.

6. This is the beginning of the hymn:
    Clarent angelici sublimia festa diei
     Allatura piae dona beata animae.
    Hunc etenim Michael, aulae caelestis alumnus,
     Conspicuo nobis consecrat ore diem,
    Dignatus Petri Paulique invisere sedem
     Imperiumque fovens, inclita Roma, tuum.
    [The hymn can be found in *Analecta hymnica medii aevi*, ed. Guido Maria Dreves (Leipzig: O. R. Reisland, 1907), 2:210, where the author is identified as Florus of Lyon. See also part 2, bk. 2, ch. 2, note 9.—Trans.]

Part 2, Book 3, Chapter 2

1. Henri-Marie Boudon, *La dévotion aux neuf chœurs des saints anges*, treatise 2, practice 8.—Trans.
2. The French title is *Notre Dame de Bonne Délivrance*. In addition to "Happy Deliverance," one will find *Bonne Délivrance* rendered in English as "Good Deliverance," "Good Delivery," and "Happy Delivery."—Trans.
3. This sentence's translation purposely omits the original French's problematic and undocumented claim that William, Count of Mortain, built this church during the reign of William the Conqueror. For more information on St. Michael's Mount, see Charles Henderson's brief history in *The Cornish Church Guide* (Truro: Oscar Blackford, 1925), 160-62. Henderson mentions, among other details, that there was "doubtless" a monastery there in the centuries preceding the Norman Conquest, and that a Norman abbot affiliated with Mont Saint-Michel subsequently had a church built there in 1135. Henderson also alludes to the legend of an ancient St. Michael apparition at the location.—Trans.
4. Hangzhou is a city of 700,000 inhabitants. Shanghai and Ningbo count no less than 300,000 souls each.
5. Bishop Delaplace could not be present in Dinghai this year for the St. Michael celebration, but he did make the pilgrimage to St. Michael of Mount Tombe, where he sang Mass on September 29, 1869. His Excellency said he had much for which to thank the archangel, and many favors to ask him. He noticed the sculpted wooden candelabras and their arrangement, which reminded him of that of St. Michael's in Dinghai. The large candelabras in the Chinese church are also made of wood, but they exhibit that finish and exquisite delicacy that the Chinese know how to give to a work of art. The altar is a little bit like Mont Saint-Michel's, but much better executed and with precious, fragrant wood. The tabernacle represents a dome. Bishop Delaplace is to exchange and replace it with a tabernacle similar to the one at Mont Saint-Michel, from which he carries away a sweet and precious memory.
6. Bishop Delaplace, having recently showed us a sketch of the island of Zhoushan, which he very much wanted to outline for us, told us, "If I were to fall onto the island today, no matter where, I would not be ten minutes away from several Christian homes."

Part 2, Book 3, Chapter 3

1. Austériac allegedly corresponds to present-day Beauvoir. See Mgr. Joseph Deschamps du Manoir, *Histoire du Mont Saint-Michel au péril de la mer et du Mont Tombelaine avec un guide-livret du visiteur*, 4th ed. (Paris: Jules Gervais, 1880), 25, 31.—Trans.
2. Cf. 1 Cor 14:32.—Trans.
3. Of what did this severity of the archangel consist? The canon of St. Aubert does not say, but Fr. Feuardent makes it known to us: "The true and discreet pastor, wanting to test whether this vision and revelation was from God, delayed again until the third apparition, in which the angel, reprimanding him for his slowness to believe and obey, touched his head as with a finger and made a hole in his head, which still appears today, as a perpetual and assured testimony to the truth. This

is not harder to believe than that the angels expelled Adam and Eve from the earthly paradise, that [an angel] spared Isaac from the sword of his father; that God, through angels, delivered Lot from Sodom while blinding the infidels, that [angels] saved Daniel and his companions from the flames and from the lions, assisted Moses when Pharaoh threatened to cut to pieces all the children of Israel, preserved Jerusalem from the plague, delivered St. Peter and St. John from Jewish prisons, and finally, performed an infinite number of other miracles to the glory of God and in favor of His servants."

Monsieur Houssard, a medical doctor in Avranches, carefully examined the head of St. Aubert. The following is his report: "This head, this relic preserved until 1791 in the abbey of Mont Saint-Michel, from where it was brought to Avranches, rescued by pious hands from profanation, was consigned to the church of St. Gervais in Avranches, and is still there today, enclosed in a reliquary. It was there, more than fifty years ago, that we saw it for the first time, and that recently, we scrupulously examined it with the greatest care.

"The bones of the skull and face are all connected to each other. Only the mandible and teeth from the upper jaw are missing.

"Upon first inspection, one notices, towards the middle or center of the right parietal bone, an oblong opening from back to front, large enough to insert one's thumb. The edges of this opening are somewhat thin and smooth on the outside as on the inside. Nothing on the opening's circumference or in any area of the bone where it is noticed could make one assume that it is due to any traumatic cause, the action of any instrument, or any caustic or corrosive application. Everything is smooth as if this opening had been made without violence and occurred long enough before the death of the subject. One cannot further assume that this opening results from the application of a trephine, whose form is not at all present.

"To resolve this question, we devoted ourselves very specifically to the observation and examination of this opening, which, as we already stated, has no traces of a surgical operation or a chemical application.

"We then did the most minute and exact bibliographic and historical research, and we arrived at the certainty that it was in no way the result of the application of a trephine or of a similar operation."

Sending this report to the bishop, Dr. Houssard said that, as far as he was concerned, he did not hesitate to believe that the opening one sees in St. Aubert's head is in fact the effect of a miracle such as recounted in the legend, that he seemed to see the effect of the fingerprint of the archangel, who on God's behalf threateningly gave His orders to His servant, and was making known to him as well that God wanted to be adored in this place.

Bishop Bravard, who provided us these details, authorized and even ordered their insertion. In a letter that he addressed the doctor, His Excellency said to him, "I thank you with all my heart for your letter and for your study on the head of St. Aubert. I will preciously keep your writing; it is of great weight. The testimony of a man so renowned as you in the field of medical science weighs considerably on the balance. It is impossible to believe in a trephine or other natural cause, when you see no way of explaining by this the singularity of the hole made in the head of Mont Saint-Michel's great creator."

4. "Did the Son of God not promise that those who believed in Him would work miracles such as He did, and even greater ones, and that if they say to a mountain, 'Be thou removed and be cast into the sea,' that it would be done? Was this not highlighted by St. Gregory of Neocaesarea?" (Feuardent).

5. This miracle recalls the snow that, in the month of August, outlined the perimeter of the Basilica of St. Mary Major in Rome.

6. This account from which Soyer is quoting, originally written in Latin, is known as the *Revelatio ecclesiae sancti Michaelis.*—Trans.

Part 2, Book 3, Chapter 4

1. These relics were placed in the treasury of Mont Saint-Michel. Pierre Toustain, a monk of this monastery and prior of Villamère, had a gilded angel made in 1449, which held the piece of marble brought from Mount Gargano. — The piece of vermilion cloth or cape was encased in a gilded silver heart in the year 1413 by Nicolas Guernon, a monk and claustral prior of this abbey.

2. Regarding these miracles, Fr. Feuardent, addressing the incredulous, tells them: "Have miracles not been equally easy for God to do through His archangel as through the staff or rod of Moses, which worked so many marvels in Egypt, taking them across the deserts of Arabia; through the ark of the covenant into Jericho; to the Jordan between the Philistines and the Bethsamites; through the mantle of Elijah on the river; through the bones of Elisha bringing a dead man back to life; through the pool with the porticoes healing all kinds of illnesses; through washing in the pool of Siloam giving sight to a man blind from birth; through St. Peter's shadow healing all illnesses; through St. Paul's chains expelling evil spirits from human bodies; through the relics of St. Stephen and the flowers that had merely touched them working such illustrious miracles, as the blessed St. Augustine recounts."

3. [This passage is a continuation of the *Revelatio ecclesiae sancti Michaelis* cited in the previous chapter.—Trans.] Fr. Feuardent states further regarding this miracle: "Incredulous atheists, enemies of miracles, and deniers of God's infinite power mock this; on the other hand, all good and faithful Christians, honoring God and admiring Him in His works, will believe it as easily as God making a woman from the side of man, changing water into wine and wine into blood, a staff into a serpent and a serpent into a staff, and making living waters flow from solid rock."

4. Did this dragon really exist? Should it not be understood as a fantastic manifestation of the demon as an animal, which holy church founders were obliged to fight upon arrival in their mission? In Brittany, it was St. Armel, St. Tudwal, St. Brieuc, and St. Paul Aurelian. Rome, Paris, Tarascon, Avignon, and a great number of other places were witnesses to the same combat. Here, it is a matter of a dragon of flesh and bone! The dragon, in fact, is too often named in Holy Scripture and even in ancient tongues to be nothing but a fantastic animal. Moreover, recent geological discoveries have come to furnish proof of biblical claims and of the ancient belief of peoples.

5. This English version of the account is a relay of the French translation done by historian Fr. Émile-Auber Pigeon and provided by Soyer in the book's original French edition.—Trans.

Part 2, Book 3, Chapter 5

1. Henri-Marie Boudon, *La dévotion aux neuf chœurs des saints anges*, treatise 2, practice 7.—Trans.
2. Presently called Saint-Sylvain.—Trans.
3. Soyer does not identify the source of this quotation, but all but the last six words of it are found and attributed to Benedictine chronicler Dom Jean Huynes in Édouard Le Héricher's *Itinéraire descriptif et historique du voyageur dans le Mont-Saint-Michel* (Avranches: Librairie d'Auguste Anfray, 1857), 51.—Trans.
4. Presumably an allusion to 1 Kings 19:19-21, when Elisha left everything to follow Elijah.—Trans.
5. See Ps 103:4 [104:4].—Trans.
6. The year is instead identified as 1045 in Dom Jean Huynes' *Histoire générale de l'abbaye du Mont-St-Michel* (Rouen: A. Le Brument, 1872), 1:89 (in treatise 2, ch. 10).—Trans.
7. An invisible hand severely struck Drogon in front of the altar, after which he became ill and was sent to spend his remaining days on one of the Chausey islands. For further details, see Dom Jean Huynes, *Histoire générale de l'abbaye du Mont-St-Michel* (Rouen: A. Le Brument, 1872), 1:89-92 (treatise 2, ch. 10).—Trans.
8. The *Promptuarium exemplorum*, a collection of wonderful stories much enjoyed in the Middle Ages, provides us an account whose primitive simplicity we must leave untouched: "A peasant was taking his cow and calf to Mont Saint-Michel. Fearing death at the sight of the flood tide that was sweeping through the route, he let out a cry, saying, 'St. Michael, come to my aid and deliver me, and I will give you the cow and the calf.' But seeing himself delivered from danger, he said, 'St. Michael was quite foolish to believe that I would give him my cow and my calf.' But the flood tide swept in again, and he let out a new cry, saying, 'O good Michael, help me and deliver me, and I will give you the cow and the calf.' Delivered a second time, he said, 'O St. Michael, you will have neither the cow nor the calf.' Then the flood tide enveloped him a third time, drowning him and the cow and calf with him."

Part 2, Book 3, Chapter 6

1. Pastoral letter on Mont Saint-Michel.
2. "The Mont Saint-Michel pilgrimage," says one author cited by [Joseph] Deschamps, "was so much a necessity, and almost a duty, from the eighth through the fifteenth centuries, that the fiction writers and poets of the time never neglected the opportunity to speak of it." In one twelfth-century poem, on the conquest of Brittany, the author has King Charlemagne go there on pilgrimage. And Ludovico Ariosto, in his poem *Orlando furioso*, believes he must have his hero go there.

3. Fr. [Gervais] de La Rue says that before the Revolution, one still saw the bourgeois of our beautiful province's cities form associations to go on pilgrimage to Mont Saint-Michel, leaving with a flag, beating drums, and a pilgrim's staff in hand. The one who was the first to catch sight of the mount was declared king of the association. They returned the same way, their cloaks decorated with shells; the king wore a crown, and they ended up forming St. Michael confraternities in the parishes from which they came.

4. Fr. Deschamps says everyone knows that the pilgrims of times past wore the seashells over the article of their clothing which, as a result, was called a *pèlerine* [a cape whose name is derived from the French word for pilgrim—Trans.]; what everyone does not know is that this custom owes its origin to the pilgrimages to Mont Saint-Michel, whose bay provides very pretty shells and abundant fishing, "like the manna in the desert," providing the inhabitants of these regions an excellent food. From Mont Saint-Michel, this custom was passed on to the pilgrimage place of Santiago de Compostela, and successively to all those whose memory has spanned the ages.

5. Taken from Fr. Deschamps' *Histoire du Mont-Saint-Michel*.

Part 2, Book 3, Chapter 7

1. English translation of the original Spanish by Fiscar Marison, as found in Mary of Agreda, *City of God* (Chicago: The Theopolitan, 1914), 1:170-71.—Trans.

2. Found in Auguste Nicolas, *La Vierge Marie et le plan divin*, 7th ed. (Paris: Vaton Frères, 1869), 3:189.—Trans.

3. English translation of the original Spanish by Fiscar Marison, as found in Mary of Agreda, *City of God* (Chicago: The Theopolitan, 1914), 4:33-34.—Trans.

4. One tradition recounts that it was St. Michael the Archangel, when he appeared atop Hadrian's mole, who first intoned this antiphon: *Regina caeli, laetare, alleluia; Quia quem meruisti portare, alleluia; Resurrexit, sicut dixit, alleluia.* [Queen of Heaven, rejoice, alleluia; For He Whom you did merit to bear, alleluia; Has risen as He said, alleluia.] The Church added the rest.

5. Found in Bernard of Clairvaux, *Opera omnia*, ed. Jean Mabillon (Paris: J.-P. Migne, 1860), 4:1740.—Trans.

6. Henri-Marie Boudon, *La dévotion aux neuf chœurs des saints anges*, treatise 1, motive 11.—Trans.

7. Bishop Louis-Édouard-François-Désiré Pie, discourse given at the celebration of the reinstallment of the statue of the Blessed Virgin in the crypt of Chartres Cathedral, September 15, 1857.

Appendix 1

1. The dates for feast days listed in this calendar are transcribed exactly as found in the original nineteenth-century French edition of this book, regardless of occasional discrepancies with the universal Roman calendar.—Trans.

2. The original French says 12th rather than 11th century.—Trans.

3. The 1907 *Catholic Encyclopedia* states that the Bollandists' account of St. William of Maleval, who died on February 10, 1157, is unreliable due to interpolations with at least two other Williams.—Trans.

4. The original French says 3rd rather than 4th century.—Trans.
5. The original French says 14th rather than 15th century.—Trans.
6. The Bollandists' details for Hubert are found in their *Acta Sanctorum* March 26 entry for St. Gabriel the Archangel.—Trans.
7. The original French calls Ida "venerable," but she has been considered a blessed since prior to the book's 1870 publication.—Trans.
8. Found in Frederick William Faber, *The Blessed Sacrament, or The Works and Ways of God* (London: Thomas Richardson & Son, 1856), 535.—Trans.
9. It is disputed whether the St. Hermas celebrated on this day is the same Hermas who wrote *The Shepherd.*—Trans.
10. The original French has 1425 instead of 1429.—Trans.
11. The original French has 16th rather than 14th century.—Trans.
12. The original French has Saint rather than Blessed.—Trans.
13. The original French has Saint rather than Blessed although Bona had not been canonized at the time the French was published.—Trans.
14. The original French has Blessed rather than Saint although Ferdinand had been canonized well before its publication.—Trans.
15. The original French has 1429 rather than 1431.—Trans.
16. The original 1870 French edition titles him a saint, but he was not even beatified at the time.—Trans.
17. Columba was associated with Ireland and Scotland. The original French says England rather than the British Isles.—Trans.
18. The original French says 13th rather than 6th century.—Trans.
19. The original French says Saint rather than Blessed.—Trans.
20. The original French says 12th century, but Osanna lived in the 15th to early 16th century.
21. The original French says 308 instead of 303.—Trans.
22. The original French says 14th instead of 13th century.—Trans.
23. The original French says sea instead of lake.—Trans.
24. The original French says Paul V instead of Pius IV.—Trans.
25. The original French says Order of Canons Regular instead of Franciscan Order.—Trans.
26. These words appear in the fourth antiphon for the office of Lauds on St. Lawrence's feast day.—Trans.
27. The original French says Tongeren instead of Maastricht.—Trans.
28. The original French says 1629 instead of 1628.—Trans.
29. Literally "Michael's hill."—Trans.
30. The original French says Saint rather than Blessed.—Trans.
31. The following sentences appearing in the original French are intentionally removed from this entry: "He wrote a wonderful treatise on the holy angels. He took the name Philangelus, which means 'friend of the angels.'" Soyer is evidently conflating the martyr St. Denis of Paris, whose feast is October 9, with Pseudo-Dionysius the Areopagite. See also remarks in Translator's Preface concerning the conflation of these persons' identities.—Trans.
32. The original French identifies the founding year of the abbey as 1138, which is intentionally omitted in the translation. According to the National Library of

France's online record at https://data.bnf.fr/fr/13748270/abbaye_saint-michel_doullens__somme/ (accessed in October 2021), the abbey was "perhaps" founded in 1104 although its name is not recorded for the first time until 1138. Since biographies date St. Godfrey's death sometime in the second decade of the twelfth century, the 1138 founding date is not possible if he indeed was a founder. St. Godfrey is mentioned as but one of the possible founders in *Dictionnaire des Abbayes et Monastères*, s.v. "Michel de Doullens (Saint-)" (Paris: J.-P. Migne, 1856).—Trans.

33. Fr. Joseph Pohle rightly points out that this claim of St. Amphilochius's angelic consecration, alleged by Nicephorus Callistus in his *Historia Ecclesiastica* (bk. 11, ch. 20), "is open to serious objections" and that "such extraordinary reports must be established by incontrovertible evidence, lest the certainty of the sacramental economy be exposed to grave danger"—see Pohle's *The Sacraments: A Dogmatic Treatise* (St. Louis: B. Herder, 1915), 1:164. For St. Thomas Aquinas's position on whether angels can administer the sacraments, see also *Summa Theologica*, III, q. 64, a. 7.—Trans.

34. Stylites, by definition, live atop pillars as a form of ascesis.—Trans.

Appendix 2

1. The original French again states here that this incident happened within the context of a siege. For why this detail is intentionally omitted from the translation, see part 2, bk. 1, ch. 6, note 1.—Trans.

2. The source of this quote is likely Dom Jean Huynes. See part 2, bk. 3, ch. 5, note 3.—Trans.

3. Guillaume de Jaligny, *Histoire de Charles VIII* (Paris: Abraham Pacard, 1617), 71.—Trans.

4. The original French incorrectly numbers Jean de Lamps as the twenty-sixth rather than thirty-sixth abbot. For a list of Mont Saint-Michel's abbots up to the eighteenth century, see chapter 6 of Fulgence Girard's *Histoire géologique, archéologique et pittoresque du Mont Saint-Michel au péril de la mer* (Avranches: E. Tostain, 1843).—Trans.

5. King Ethelred the Unready died in 1016.—Trans.

6. The original French says 1084 instead of 1091. The well-documented research of historian C. Warren Hollister supports the latter as the year of the siege. See Hollister's book *Henry I*, edited and completed by Amanda Clark Frost (New Haven: Yale University Press, 2008), 80.—Trans.

7. The original French gives 996 instead of 966 for the year of the Benedictines' arrival. Sources supporting the year 966 include *Dictionnaire des Abbayes et Monastères*, s.v. "Mont-Saint-Michel, près Tombelaine" (Paris: J.-P. Migne, 1856) and Joseph Deschamps du Manoir, *Histoire du Mont Saint-Michel au péril de la mer et du Mont Tombelaine avec un guide-livret du visiteur*, 4th ed. (Paris: Jules Gervais, 1880), 41.—Trans.

8. Geoffrey himself did not inherit the title Duke of Normandy. It went to his eldest brother, Richard II.—Trans.

9. Richard III died in 1027.—Trans.

10. Soyer does not identify the source of this quote, but Joseph Deschamps du Manoir attributes it to the monk Dom Louis de Camps when he quotes this same phrase in his *Histoire du Mont Saint-Michel au péril de la mer et du Mont Tombelaine avec un guide-livret du visiteur* (Paris: Jules Gervais, 1880), 216.—Trans.
11. Derived from Fr. Alban Butler's account via Jean-François Godescard's French adaptation.

OTHER TRANSLATIONS
BY RYAN P. PLUMMER

CATEGORY: FAITH

Mystic of the Holy Wounds: The Life and Revelations of Sister Mary Martha Chambon, by the Visitation Sisters of Chambéry (St. Louis: Lambfount, 2019). *Definitive biography of Sr. Mary Martha Chambon (1841-1907), the humble French nun who received visions and messages from Jesus Christ encouraging devotion to His Sacred Wounds.*

CATEGORY: FICTION

The Avengers of the King, by Jean Drault (St. Louis: Lambfount, 2022). *At the height of the Reign of Terror, the cunning Baron Jean de Batz and his network of men and women royalist conspirators must defy all odds to inflict on Robespierre and other French Revolution leaders the lethal justice they deserve. Epic novel inspired by real persons and events.*

CATEGORY: POLITICS

The End of Democracy, by Christophe Buffin de Chosal (Arcadia, CA: Tumblar House, 2017). *Eye-opening critique of the democratic system, exposing democracy's true nature and the real interests it serves.*